J·O·H·N S·O·A·N·E

J·O·H·N S·O·A·N·E

THE MAKING OF AN ARCHITECT

Pierre de la Ruffinière du Prey

THE UNIVERSITY OF CHICAGO PRESS · CHICAGO AND LONDON

PIERRE DE LA RUFFINIÈRE DU PREY, associate professor of art history at Queen's University, has prepared a catalogue raisonné of Soane's architectural drawings in the Victoria and Albert Museum, London.

CREDITS FOR ILLUSTRATIONS

Chapman (Plymouth), Fig. 6.2; Cheshire County Museum Services, Fig. 9.8; City of Birmingham Art Gallery, Fig. 6.7; Corporation of London, Fig. 11.6; Country Life, Figs. 2.8, 14.8; Courtauld Institute of Art, Figs. 3.2, 3.3, 3.14; Fotomas Index, Figs. 3.1, 3.4, 3.12; National Monuments Record, Figs. 2.6, 6.8, 12.11, 12.12, 12.17, 13.19, 13.21; Museum of London, Fig. 10.10; Paul Mellon Center for Studies in British Art (London), Figs. 6.4, 6.5; Secrétariat régional de l'inventaire de l'Ile de France, Fig. 9.18; Foto Tosi (Parma), Figs. 9.17, 9.19; Franklin Toker, Fig. 5.19; Ulster Museum, Fig. 6.1. The line drawings, Figs. 3.9, 4.4, 13.4–13.8, 13.13–13.15, 14.3, were specially prepared for this book by Alexander Wilson, AADIPL.

The University of Chicago Press, Chicago 60637
The University of Chicago Press, Ltd.,
London

5 4 3 2 1   82 83 84 85 86 87 88

Library of Congress Cataloging in Publication Data

Du Prey, Pierre de la Ruffinière.
  John Soane, the making of an architect.

  Bibliography: p.
  Includes index.
  1. Soane, John, Sir, 1753–1837. 2. Architects
—England—Biography. 3. Neoclassicism (Architecture)—England. I. Title.
  NA997.S7D85   720′.92′4 [B]   81-16453
  ISBN 0-226-17298-8   AACR2

Contents

Illustrations

Unless otherwise stated, the artist or designer of every work illustrated was John Soane. Dates are provided only when inscribed on the work, except for portraits, where a date is always supplied.

Acknowledgments

WRITING ABOUT AN ARCHITECT who never forgot a kindness has been a constant reminder to me of the pleasant duty I can now perform by thanking in print all those who helped me. I would like to begin by acknowledging the indispensable financial assistance I received from my alma maters, Princeton and the University of Pennsylvania, from the Samuel H. Kress Foundation, and from my staunchly supportive colleagues on the Advisory Research Committee of Queen's University. I owe a special debt of gratitude to Phyllis Lambert for generously making possible the color plates in this book. Without the assistance of all these individuals and institutions my work could not have gone forward.

In remembering the various collections which made drawings and manuscripts accessible to me, I naturally want to mention first of all Sir John Soane's Museum. I gratefully acknowledge the Trustees' permission to reproduce and quote from material in their care, and I thank the staff who, for more than a decade, opened for me the innumerable doors, drawers, and cabinets in that labyrinthine building. I am similarly obliged to the archives of the Harrowby Manuscript Trust; the Royal Academy of Arts; St. Luke's Hospital, Woodside; the Society of Dilettanti; Trinity College, Dublin; Coutts and Company; Barclay's Bank, Gosling's Branch; and the Royal Bank of Scotland, Drummonds Branch. The resources of the National Monuments Record and National Register of Archives in London saved me much time and duplication of effort.

The drawing collections of the Victoria and Albert Museum and the Royal Institute of British Architects were frequently put at my disposal under most advantageous conditions for which I have to thank the kindness of their curators, Michael Kauffmann and John Harris, respectively. In Italy I was courteously received at the state archives in Florence, Mantua, Milan, Parma, and Venice, as well as at the Museo Correr and Biblioteca Querini-Stampalia, Venice, the Istituto Paolo Toschi, Parma, and the Archivio Vicariato at the Lateran. The American

TO
Beatrice, Nicolas, and Julie
"my pretty chickens
and their dam"

xvii

Academy in Rome greatly facilitated my researches in that city of cities.

I would like to pay a well-earned collective tribute to the many county archivists of Great Britain who cheerfully answered my letters and initiated me into the mysteries of their record offices. Although not archivists in the strict sense, I include in this category the parish priests who expertly searched their parochial records on my behalf, or permitted me access to them. I also want to mention the kind cooperation of the Public Record Offices in London, Belfast, and Edinburgh, and those of the Greater London Council and Corporation of London.

Librarians everywhere greeted me with a knowledgeable enthusiasm which increased the effectiveness with which I could consult their rare book or manuscript collections. Foremost among the institutions I would like to thank are the British Museum, the Royal Institute of British Architects, and the Avery Architectural Library, Columbia University. I am also grateful to the Accademia di belli arti, Florence; to such civic libraries as those in Bath, Sheffield, and Reading, England; Geneva, Switzerland; Bergamo, Venice, and Verona, Italy; not to forget the Guildhall, Hammersmith, Marylebone, Newington District, and Westminster libraries, in London. University libraries all over North America granted me readership privileges, as did the Library of Congress Periodicals Division, and the Henry E. Huntington Library, San Marino. Finally, I salute my friends in the Queen's University Library system, and by extension the many other collections that made items available to me through the interlibrary loan service.

I take special pleasure in remembering the kindness of individual owners who have permitted me to consult and reproduce works in their possession, who have corresponded with me, and have so often welcomed me into their homes, Soane-designed homes among them. These people include: Lady Mary Clive, Lady Crista Hervey-Bruce, Lady Naomi Mitchison, Elizabeth Eglington, Frances Jackson, Nora Sclater-Booth, the Misses P. and C. E. Patteson, Lord Aldenham, Anthony Bosanquet, Avery Colebrook, Maldrin Drummond, John G. Dunbar, J. D. G. Fortescue, the Earl of Bradford, the Earl of Wharncliffe, the Earl of Harrowby, Major N. Chamberlayne-Macdonald, Major J. W. Meade, Father Thomas Nicolson, Sir Aubrey St. Clair-Ford, Bart., and Sir Joshua Rowley, Bart., the Administrations of the Prince de Ligne and the Principe Torlonia, J. P. Spang, Ben Weinreb, and last but not least Mr. and Mrs. Robin Carver. Institutions I would like to mention and thank are the Trustees of the British Museum, the National Gallery and National Library of Ireland; Cheshire County Council Museum Services; Claremont and Solihull schools; the National Trust; Norfolk County

Council, Burnham Westgate Hall; Norwich Union Insurance Company; the Museum of London; St. Joseph's Mission, Burn Hall; Towneley Hall Art Gallery and Museums, Burnley Borough Council; London Borough of Waltham Forest Museum of Local History.

I would also like to record the names of the professional photographers I have worked together with in friendly collaboration: Michael Brandon-Jones, John Brebner, Emil Erkan, B. S. Evans, Fillinghams of Durham, John Freeman, Angelo Hornak, Gerry Locklin, Godfrey New, Douglas Smith, and last but not least Jeremy Sundgaard.

Chief among those I would like to thank for discussing aspects of Soane with me is Sir John Summerson. From the first day I visited the Soane Museum in a state of breathless excitement, he did everything he could to help in his capacity as curator. Above all, he shared with me his deep understanding of Soane and his times, from which I have learned more than I can say. I also want to acknowledge my mentors, David R. Coffin and the late Donald D. Egbert, who taught me so much about the craft of scholarly research and writing. Others who generously shared with me their time, their ideas, and their knowledge include the following: Susan Agate, Elena Bassi, Marcus Binney, Joseph Burke, Renato Cevese, Christopher Chalklin, Howard Colvin, Jeffrey Cook, Kerry Downes, the late Raymond Erith and his partner Quinlan Terry, Desmond FitzGerald the Knight of Glin, John Fleming, Brinsley Ford, the Honorable Desmond Guinness, Sabine Hojer, Ian R. Hooper, Peter Howell, Gervase Jackson-Stops, Thomas J. McCormick, Edward McParland, Robin Middleton, Sandra Blutman Millikin, Susan Moore, Humphrey C. Morgan, Werner Oechslin, John Riely, John Robinson, Edward Teitelman, Franklin Toker, Russell Vincent of Fielden and Mawson, Clive Wainwright, Peter Willis, and John Wilton-Ely.

A confraternity of colleagues, many of them here in Canada, allowed me to presume upon our friendship by showing them my manuscript in progress. The final version would have been more flawed had it not been for the suggestions of Marianna Woods, Michael Fox, Alexander Hawthorne, James Inglis, Stephen Johnson, Harold D. Kalman, George Laverty, Rolf Loeber, Robert Malcolmson, Michael McCarthy, Douglas Richardson who also contributed in other important ways, my editorial "oracle" Charles Beer, and my "severest" but dearest critics, my parents. Special thanks are in order to my tolerant, painstaking readers, John Newman, and Damie Stillman. Enid Scott and Mabel Burns performed the near-miracle of turning my not very legible handwritten text into typescript.

Ending on a personal note, my family joins me in recalling the hospitality extended to us by our dear friends Anne and Charles, Feli and

Donald, Iris and Pauli, Lorraine and Eric, Liz and Sandy, Toos and Antony, Lorna, Winifred, Edmond of Eel Bay, and most especially Anne of Orchard House. But the greatest debt of recognition I have saved until last, and that is the one I owe to my wife. By turns she has acted as my scribe, research assistant, chauffeur, typist, editor, and indexer. Her talents, moral support, and ability to see things in their true light have contributed inestimably to bringing my work to completion.

Eel Bay, Ontario
6 June 1981

Introduction

Sir John Soane's Museum without Walls

THE EIGHTY-THREE-YEAR-OLD British architect Sir John Soane, last of the Georgian Neoclassicists, died at his home in 1837, the year of Victoria's ascent to the throne. Soane willed that his London townhouse with all its contents become a public museum after his death. This unusual bequest to the nation ensured a lasting record of his important contribution. In his lifetime he had significantly changed the face of the capital city and the provinces as well as the whole British architectural profession. And although many of his buildings have since been altered or demolished, his museum lives on, functioning at the same time as the most complete artistic archive of the period. Letters, notebooks, accounts, architectural drawings numbering in the thousands, models, plaster casts, and an intact office library form just part of Soane's legacy. Priceless though these documents are in reconstructing his life and work, they are enhanced by the Soane building that contains them. Beginning in 1812, Soane transformed his private dwelling at 13 Lincoln's Inn Fields into the future receptacle for his artistic last will and testament. Its Portland stone facade, deliberately quasi-public in appearance, projects in front of the adjacent brick row houses. Its Athenian caryatids and Gothic corbels, mounted on the smooth surface like prize butterflies on a pin board, proclaim the architectural nature of the collection within. It stands out today as it always has. Soane saw to that in the carefully worded Act of Parliament he obtained to safeguard his gift in perpetuity.

I saw that strangely compelling exterior for the first time one autumn day in 1965. As I entered, the interior immediately intrigued me with its orderly clutter, its diminutive rooms and courtyards expanded by means of dramatic spatial vistas or lighting effects. I had recently come from studies of Central European architecture, and I thought I detected a kinship between Soane's approach to space and that of certain Baroque masters. I remember an excited telephone call to a friend to come and

I had again and again contemplated that person's dwelling place, a very odd shell,— denoting the abode of a very "odd fish." The most unobservant passenger could not traverse the north side of Lincoln's Inn Fields without having his attention positively "arrested" by the strange facade of the house occupying about the center of the range.

George Wightwick
"The Life of an Architect"

see what I had "discovered." There and then, in the enthusiasm of the moment, I determined to learn more about the Soane Museum's architect-creator. My intuitive first reaction set in motion useful researches into the origin of Soane's style. But it was also a salutary warning against preconceived notions, because I subsequently found that any connection between Soane and the Baroque was generic in nature.

During a year spent at the Courtauld Institute of Art, I grew to understand better the complexities of the Soane Museum and its collection. Its intensely personal aspect emerged from beneath the institutional guise. Almost nowhere is the man who built it out of sight. His bust scans the visitor, his portrait gazes on, reflected countless times in a looking glass. Truly here was a mirror of one artistic personality if only it could be fathomed. Uncanny mementos of Soane thrust themselves forward from even the most unexpected corners. With almost masochistic thoroughness he laid bare his professional frustrations and personal tragedies as *he* saw them. The museum owes its existence at least as much to selfish spite as to selfless generosity. Soane's growing disappointment with his two sons led to a bitter impasse. Neither wanted the architectural career their father had selected for them. One of the sons rebelled violently against his parents. It was said he brought on the death of Mrs. Soane from chagrin. The architect spent his last twenty-two years alone, brooding upon the ruins of his dynastic hopes and sensing his alienation, with no one left to carry on the style he had developed. The Soane endowment effectively kept his fortune from the hands of ungrateful relatives. It preserved undisturbed a magpie's nest, the fruit of decades of hoarding. It established a potential breeding ground for generations of architects to come. It also created an ideal place to study Soane. He had seen to that, too, by neatly circumscribing the field for research within four walls. As a good propagandist, he did all he could to promote and perpetuate a history of himself. Obviously this "official" version had pitfalls for the future biographer who got too close to the material.

To a large extent the state of the literature on Soane determined my point of departure; the period before he established a flourishing practice had been least written about. To begin at the beginning, so to speak, would lessen my reliance on secondary source material. And unlike others, Soane had enshrined his juvenilia, not discarded it. For an architect who compulsively returned to his early experiences, which he liked to call "the gay morning of youth," those extensively documented student years between his birth and his return in 1780 from studies abroad were bound to be important. That was the basic premise upon which I began my work.

Upon further reflection, however, it seemed reasonable that a reader would wish to see the architect apply in practice some of the skills he had learned as a student. The question then arose of where to stop; Soane himself provided the answer. In the spring of 1784 he had married, signifying that he felt secure enough to start a family. At about the same time he took on his first articled pupil; an architectural office, with its implicit division of labor, came into being. Until then Soane carried out the work entirely singlehanded. With the establishment of an office, other, thornier questions arose to do with assistants' intervention in the drafting or designing process. Besides, after 1784 a lengthy hiatus occurs in preserved Soane notebooks, correspondence, and bank accounts. making that year a natural place to end. These reinforcing historiographical considerations seem borne out by Soane's own development. By 1785 he had already in place the capacity for design, the business acumen, and the network of clients which led to his first famous works. I have occasionally stepped outside these chronological limits, however, to bridge the gap between early works and later ones which grow out of them.

From the period 1753–85 I have selected for discussion a dozen thematic topics related to Soane and to his profession at large. This organization provided me with a flexible, shifting viewpoint. It allowed me to emphasize traits and trends that might otherwise have become dispersed among the documentation. In the natural course of events many fascinating byways of Soane's early development have had to be omitted. But for those who wish to explore further, extensive notes supply sufficient guideposts. And despite the thematic treatment, a more or less chronological sequence has been maintained to avoid confusion. The exception is the first chapter, which deliberately plunges into the midst of Soane's day-by-day routine. Subsequent chapters return to pick up the thread of his life in such a way as to explain where and how he acquired the abilities he demonstrated as a young practicing architect.

Right from the moment of his first successes, Soane was surrounded by critical controversy. I have tried to avoid these vilifications and vindications of his character as an artist and as a man. This has not prevented me, however, from endeavoring to make what I consider necessary critical interpretations of his works and his personality. I have analyzed the draftsmanship of his drawings. I have discussed his design theory in terms of its intellectual content. And I have measured his behavior by the ethical standards of his time. From this necessarily follows the socioeconomic and interdisciplinary criteria I have used. It also follows that my researches would develop along comparative lines.

Much of my work on Soane has led me simultaneously in two directions. Centripetally I spiralled inward through layers of data to arrive at a chronicle of Soane's activities together with a catalogue raisonné of all he produced. Centrifugally my study moved outward to compare the life and works of Soane's peers, friends, and rivals with his own. Seen from this double vantage point, Soane lost none of his individuality. But by being placed alongside his contemporaries in their proper milieu, his achievements were thrown into bolder relief and a more objective assessment of them became possible. Paradoxically perhaps, the more I went in search of Soane beyond the confines of his museum, the more I sensed his strengths and failings in a new perspective.

Inevitably, *John Soane: The Making of an Architect* will erode some of Soane's self-generated myth of predestined greatness. The title itself shifts Soane slightly from his accustomed position in center stage by emphasizing the sense in which he is typical of others. In the process I may have disturbed a cornerstone of Soane's monument to himself on Lincoln's Inn Fields. In its place stands a Soane museum without the walls that immured him for so long. His genius emerges from enforced seclusion brightly to illuminate the artist himself, his contemporaries at home and abroad, and the whole complex business of launching a successful architectural career.

P·A·R·T O·N·E

TRAINING AND EDUCATION

·1·

Three Episodes from the Notebooks of the Architect

AMONG THE LEGACIES left by the architect John Soane, none is potentially more precious than the stack of his well-worn, pocket-sized notebooks. Beginning in June 1780, at the time he returned to London from studies abroad, Soane recorded his daily activities. These notebooks—continuous except for one gap (1785–88)—constitute an extraordinarily complete chronicle of an architect's business career. Yet they remain virtually unconsulted in the same bundles they have been in since Soane's death in 1837. The reason for this anomaly lies in the nature of the entries themselves. Only rarely do the columns of expense-related figures or the dry lists of comings and goings allow any insight into the artist's emotional or intellectual life. Until his death, Soane maintained this strict distinction between professional and private aspects of his artistic personality. The title of his privately printed autobiographical *Memoirs of the Professional Life of an Architect* underscores the aspect of impersonality. Bearing in mind this consistent policy of Soane's, it is not surprising that his notebooks, singularly devoid of anecdote or humor, have gathered dust.

As with so much of the vast archive housed in Soane's museum, the notebooks have a curiously self-conscious tone. They seem prepared and carefully scrutinized with some future biographer in mind, one who would have little choice but to sing Soane's praises. Only on occasion did the architect inadvertently drop his guard and reveal his thoughts or feelings. More often than not the Soane notebooks make colorless reading, except for what can be extracted from them by implied association. In so full an account, any silence becomes pregnant with meaning, omissions take on significance, and code words betray the architect's secretiveness on certain subjects. Taken as a whole, the day-to-day information makes possible some broad observations about typical architectural practice of the period. From the many-sided though tinted mirror of Soane's life and practice, three facets are selected for discussion

To a mind naturally active no torture is like the pain of idleness.

John Soane to Timothy Tyrrell
27 February 1808

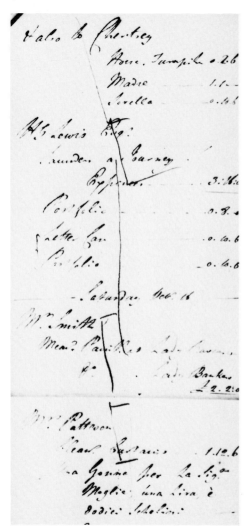

Fig. 1.1. Two notebook pages, 1784
(SM, Soane Notebooks, 13, p. 44).

here. One reflects Soane's genius for organization. A second divulges some of his concerns as an artist. A third provides unexpected clues to his humble family background. All three help to dispel the mythic success story generated by Soane himself and the invidious rumors circulated by those who wished to defame his character. Despite their limitations, the notebooks reward patient examination because they reveal their author in his true colors to a greater extent than he might have imagined.

The Family Circle (15–16 October 1784)

A striking passage from the early Soane notebooks illustrates how the architect guarded his privacy, while still keeping track of his own movements. He used the device of writing in Italian or in an abbreviated code language to preserve the details of his personal life from prying eyes (fig. 1.1).[1] According to this naive shorthand system, the word "Chertsey" signified one of his return visits to his former boyhood home in Surrey, and the words "madre" and "sorella" referred to his mother and sister, who still resided there. The architect's mother, née Martha Marcy, is recorded in the family Bible to have married John Soan on 4 July 1738. The name, spelled alternately Soan, Soane, or Soanes, occurred fairly frequently in the Thames valley region until the nineteenth century. The origins must stretch back to Anglo-Saxon times. A manor of "Soanesfelt" appeared in the Domesday Book. Renamed Swallowfield, it continued to house Soanes for centuries. One branch split off and settled in the Thameside village of Whitchurch. Another branch boasted the builder and carver Joseph Soanes, who flourished from 1761 to 1776.[2] Finally, there was Francis Soan, who established a branch at Goring-on-Thames, where he was innkeeper of the Swan. His occupation caused early lexicographers to conflate Swan and Soan.

Although John Soane knew something about his lower middle-class background, he never mentioned it.[3] In 1783 he decided to add a final *e* to his name and went to the lengths of "correcting" all his earlier signatures. The new, more aristocratic spelling is symptomatic of Soane's class consciousness. His aspirations to gentility were crowned with success when he adopted a coat-of-arms (fig. 1.2) and had a knighthood conferred upon him in 1831.[4]

Martha Soan lies buried at Chertsey, where she died on 4 February 1800.[5] Two years earlier the artist, John Downman, had drawn her portrait (fig. 1.3). At age eighty-four she was still a handsome woman. Her son John resembled his mother to a remarkable degree. In the earliest known representation of him (fig. 1.4), an undated miniature of about

1770, the youth is seen to have inherited the large, wide-spaced eyes, heavy lids, and high, arched brows continuing downward to form a prominent nose. He was the youngest of the five children who survived infancy. Among them were two daughters, Susannah and Martha, either one of whom might have been the "sorella" to whom John distributed money. The girls were baptized at Goring, Oxfordshire, as their father had been before them in 1714. John Soan, the head of the household, earned his living as a bricklayer, or so the Goring burial notice described his occupation in 1768. The eldest son, William, followed in the paternal trade. William's departure to set up an independent practice as a builder at Chertsey would explain how the widowed Mrs. Soan, at least one of her daughters, and the youngest of the family, John, turned up in Surrey sometime around 1768. William never left Chertsey and died there near-blind at the age of eighty-five. An anecdote records that the young John assisted his brother by carrying hods of mortar to the bricklayers.[6] Clearly the Soans came from strong stock. John, like his mother and brother, lived to be an octogenarian.

John Soane spent a relatively short part of his boyhood at Chertsey. Strangely enough, despite an otherwise complete pedigree (see Appendix 1), his own place and date of birth remain undocumented—the first of many questions perhaps deliberately left unanswered. But the architect's notebooks and the Royal Academy Student Register both corroborate his birthday, 10 September 1753, and this is traditionally accepted. Soane's obituary writers, along with his early memorialists, concur on the location as having been at, or very near, Reading in Berkshire.[7] Other evidence also points to Reading. One early source claims Soane attended a private school there run by William Baker. A fragmentary document links the Soane family with the rental of a house in Reading as early as 1761. This rental brings to light a long-standing connection between the Soans and their landlord, Timothy Tyrrell. The younger generation maintained the tie. Timothy Tyrrell, Jr., born at Reading in the same year as Soane, became the architect's oldest friend, trusted lawyer, and confidential correspondent.[8] When both men went to London to seek their fortunes, they often met for business or pleasure. Before he owned a horse of his own, the architect borrowed Tyrrell's mare for trips out of town. Tyrrell also gave some tuition to Soane's first apprentice, Jack Sanders.[9] On 15 October 1784, the name Sanders appears alongside those of Soane's nearest of kin (fig. 1.1). This is appropriate because Sanders became almost a member of the family. His coming made a full-fledged architectural office out of what had been a one-man operation. In July of the next year the architect paid the carpenter Alexander

Fig. 1.2. Soane Coat of Arms (SM, bookplate).

Fig. 1.3. Portrait of Mrs. Soane (the architect's mother), in pastel, by John Downman, 1798 (SM, Mrs. Soane's Morning Room).

Fig. 1.4. Anonymous miniaturist, John Soane, ca. 1770 (SM, Strong Room).

Copland for enlarging the drafting room in which Soane and Sanders worked side-by-side.[10] For these reasons, among others, the end of the year 1784 marks a turning point in Soane's career—a logical termination for this study devoted to his establishment of a firm.

At the opposite end of the same chronological framework stands another important nonfamily member: the man whom Soane, in a rare autobiographical note, called "Mr. Peacock of Chertsey." James Peacock, the individual who snatched young Soane from obscurity, rounds out the circle of those most intimately bound up with the architect's early life. The story, as told by Soane, has a familiar ring to readers of the lives of artists: "at the age of fifteen . . . through the kindness of a near relative [William Soan], I was introduced to Mr. Peacock, an eminent surveyor, and from the friendship of that gentleman, in 1768 I became a pupil of Mr. Dance."[11] Goring or Reading, or some community in between, may have been Soane's birthplace, but Chertsey was undeniably the cradle of his career, and Peacock acted as nursemaid.

In gradual stages, then, the Soans migrated downstream from Goring, to Reading, to Chertsey, and finally to London. The family's slow drift from rural backwaters to the metropolis culminated in John Soane's rise to fame and advantageous marriage. On 16 October 1784, the day after Soane's return from Chertsey, he noted—again in Italian—a present of money to his recent bride (fig. 1.1). The couple had been married two months before at Christ Church, Blackfriars Road, Southwark.[12] The wedding, which took place on 21 August, ushered in a new era for the architect. At the age of thirty-one he felt confident enough in his position to start both a family and an office. He had come a long way from a provincial boy with poor prospects to a young man marrying above his station.

On 4 March 1783, Soane's notebooks for the first time carry references to business dealings with George Wyatt, a well-to-do London builder and real estate speculator. Precisely a year later, Soane was on good enough terms to entertain Wyatt, his wife, and their niece Elizabeth Smith, who was twenty-two or twenty-three years old at the time. After that, Soane's courtship of the eligible young Elizabeth proceeded in a rapid whirl of social activities: trips to the theater, excursions, dinners, and gifts, all minutely accounted for in the notebooks. The engagement must have been announced that May, when Soane began referring to "Eliza" and had her portrayed by one of the gifted Dance brothers.[13] The future Mrs. Soane was something of an heiress. Following the death of her childless uncle in 1790, Soane wrote: "my income was so much increased as to render me independent of professional emoluments."[14] In the meantime sons had been born to carry on the Soane name: John, Jr., in 1786, and George, named, perhaps, after the family's Wyatt benefactor, in 1788.

Mrs. Soane completes the picture of the architect's private world, which he kept so separate from his professional one. This protectiveness of his personal life was motivated by an extreme persecution complex that overshadowed even his happiest days. Some of the mental strain that gave rise to it was perhaps alluded to by Soane's biographer, T. L. Donaldson, when he wrote: "The humble sphere of Sir John Soane's early life . . . but proves the strength of character, which enabled him to raise himself by his own exertions and abilities to so distinguished a rank."[15] Soane's strenuous road to success seems to have marked him as a touchy, fearful man, especially vulnerable to insinuations about the "humble sphere" of his origins. Late in life he complained that: "a *corps collectif* . . . has pursued me incessantly, on every opportunity . . . to the present moment." As early as 1780, clients had recognized Soane's paranoic "fancies" as being "constitutional therefore not to be helped."[16]

The Exhibition of 1784 (5–7 April 1784)

On Wednesday, 7 April 1784, Soane recorded in his notebook the visit he made to his former employer, George Dance, in order "to hear a discourse respect[in]g [the] Exhibi[tion]."[17] Earlier that year, Dance, a founder of the Royal Academy, had been elected to the all-important hanging committee for the forthcoming sixteenth spring exhibition (fig. 1.5).[18] Even in the Academy's enlarged new quarters at Somerset House, a perennial sore point among exhibiting artists remained whether their works hung above or below "the line," that is, the picture rail that formed a division one-third of the way up the wall. They felt discriminated against if the committee placed them too high, too low, or in a bad light. Architects had an even more legitimate complaint because they were relegated to a side chamber. No doubt Soane's visit to Dance had something to do with a proposed reorganization of the shows on a more equitable basis. Whatever the two men's discussion, the notebook passage illustrates how a veteran member and a recent graduate of the Academy both considered it their professional club. To a large extent their intellectual lives revolved around its lectures, exhibitions, and the debate of its internal politics. Progressively with the years, Soane gravitated closer and closer to the Academy orbit. From his first places of business in rented West End accommodations,[19] he eventually moved in 1792 to a freehold house at 12 Lincoln's Inn Fields, ten minutes' walk from the Academy's headquarters on the Strand. As early as 1780

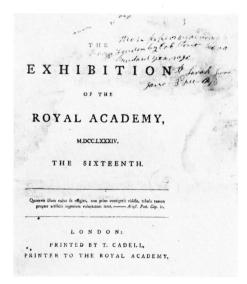

Fig. 1.5. Cover of the 1784 Royal Academy exhibition catalogue (Queen's University, Kingston, Ontario).

8

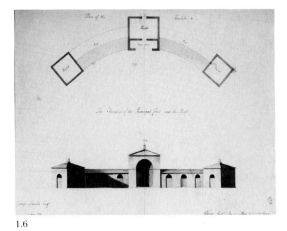

1.6

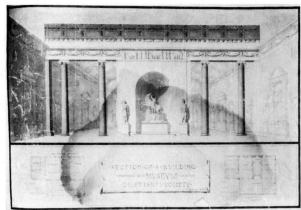

1.9

1.7

1.10

1.8

1.11

Soane's name had been put up for associate membership.[20] His election as A.R.A. finally came in 1795; promotion to full R.A. followed in 1802.

With few exceptions, Soane stalwartly contributed year after year to the Academy's annual shows, until he totaled 168 entries in all between 1772 and 1836 (see Appendix 2). The exhibition of 1784 illustrates how seriously Soane took the whole matter. According to his notebook, he set aside two days before his visit to Dance for preparing his six entries. This was a lot of time to take out of an extremely busy schedule. Obviously, Soane valued the exhibition as a showcase for his work. The survival of the drawings he exhibited—or ones very similar to them—permits an assessment of their appealing draftsmanship and careful selection. They range from the utilitarian to the visionary and from town to country, as if to make up an ideal architectural pattern book with examples for all tastes and purses.

Rearranged as they might have appeared, hanging pell-mell on the walls of Somerset House (figs. 1.6–1.12), the drawings illustrate the whole gamut of building types from the simple to the grand. At the lower end of the social scale stands the entry entitled "Offices at Burnhall" in the 1784 catalogue of the show. It represents a cow barn in remote County Durham and might appear an odd choice for a man trying to impress the public. It was the first such farm structure to be

1.12

Fig. 1.6. Burn Hall cow barn, plan and elevation, 1783 (SM, Drawer 64, Set 3, Item 100).

Fig. 1.7. Mausoleum design, elevation (SM, AL, Cupboard 22, Folio 1, Item 34).

Fig. 1.8. Malvern Hall, north elevation (SM, Drawer 5, Set 3, Item 13).

Fig. 1.9. Museum design for the Society of Dilettanti, London, plans and section, 1784 (SM, Drawer 13, Set 4, Item 7).

Fig. 1.10. Blackfriars Bridge, Norwich, plan and east elevation, 1783 (SM, Portfolio 3, Item 9).

Fig. 1.11. Brancepeth Castle, gate and lodges, elevation (SM, Drawer 62, Set 8, Item 44).

Fig. 1.12. Great Room, Somerset House, London, during the Royal Academy 1784 exhibition, by John Henry Ramberg (BM, Prints and Drawings, 1904. 1.1.3).

included in the sixteen years since the Royal Academy exhibitions had begun.[21] Yet Soane took an obstinate pride in this building, to the extent of including it in his book of 1788. The drawing's neat execution in pen and wash, with ruled border, careful lettering, and convincing illusionism lived up to the high standards of presentation set by the Academy (fig. 1.6). The rendered cast shadows emphasize the imaginativeness of the semielliptical form, used elsewhere by Soane as a favorite aesthetic device. He thereby transformed what might otherwise have been a banal, rectangular design—young Soane had a horror of being banal. In the detailed provisions of the plan, Soane tried to demonstrate his grasp of the design on the practical side. (In execution, the owner, George Smith, had to compensate for the dangerous oversight of under-ventilated haylofts.) With rustic connotations in mind, Soane kept his cow barn utterly simple, though pleasingly balanced in proportions. The model cow barn was therefore in step with the latest wave of severe Neoclassical taste, and the most progressive trends in agricultural building. It illustrated the maxim that not even a manger was too lowly for a talented architect eager for work.[22]

Soane's entry of a mausoleum design in the 1784 exhibition contrasted with the cow barn. Mausolea were among the most fashionable subjects submitted to the Royal Academy shows. Prior to 1784 no less than eighteen had appeared, two of them by Soane himself. He expended special care on this, his third mausoleum project. He began work on it in January 1783, according to his current notebook, but then laid it aside until the following year.[23] Although the nomenclature remains vague, the mausoleum in question here can be related to a later copy of a lost Soane original (fig. 1.7). It takes as its starting point an earlier design published by him (fig. 5.12). But the upper story is radically reworked in line with Soane's archaeological investigations in Italy. The courtyard of the gladiators at Pompeii provided him with the precedent for the stopped fluted, baseless Doric order (fig. 7.7), which he introduced into the monopteral temple atop his mausoleum. Such a direct reference would have flattered the antiquarianism of well-traveled exhibition-goers. They might also detect in Soane's eclectic inclusion of the grim reaper's skeletal statue an allusion to the Baroque cult of the dead.[24] If the cow barn appealed to the practical-minded, then the mausoleum addressed itself to more romantic souls.

Country houses were the bread and butter of the contemporary architectural trade and uppermost in the minds of prospective clients scouting the Academy shows for young talent. The elevation of Malvern Hall, Warwickshire (fig. 1.8), may be close in appearance to the one exhibited by Soane as entry 523 in 1784. It exemplified the most lucrative side of his early practice: the building or altering of private residences in the provinces. The impressively large extent of the drawing somewhat glorified the true state of affairs at Malvern Hall. Here, as at a number of other locations, Soane simply added wings to an existing structure.[25]

The Malvern design, as such, will be dealt with in the context of Soane's relationship to the patron, Henry Greswolde Lewis (see chap. 6). The drawing itself, however, is of interest because it is not by Soane. The unsure and somewhat mechanical treatment of such elements as the curving porch and the decorative urns on the parapet point to the intervention of an office assistant. Soane only had young Sanders to help him, so presumably he is the one responsible for the north elevation. Moreover, he is known to have been closely associated with the Malvern project.[26] Soane's recourse to Sanders for his draftsman is understandable in view of the amount of work passing through the office in 1784. In fact, as the years went by, the drawings on display in the Royal Academy were to an increasing degree executed by others to *designs* by Soane. The Malvern elevation, probably for the first time in Soane's career, raises the issue of office collaboration in the drafting process. Because of the special status of architects, works not entirely original in the manual sense would go on show, whereas they would never have been condoned from a painter or sculptor. In terms of Soane's graphic oeuvre, therefore, the exhibition of 1784 marks a transitional phase after which the problematic question of hands will become a factor to contend with in a study of the architect's artistic output.

One of the drawings certainly executed in the days before Soane's visit to George Dance is the one dated April 1784, representing a proposed museum for the Society of Dilettanti. Battered and stained, the sheet still reveals its Royal Academy connection in the studied *trompe l'oeil* effect of an inscribed tablet at the bottom (fig. 1.9). To either side are ground plans of a pair of existing London townhouses off Grosvenor Square. Soane proposed to convert these two dwellings into one large repository for the treasures of the Society. Quite apart from its great interest as a building type (see chap. 11), it represents Soane's first serious essay in townhouse design—and his last for a good many years. Significantly, the appearance of the interior takes precedence over the conventional facade treatment. It was behind the elevation of such a row house that a designer might make his mark. Soane had a problem with the existing stairwell that subdivided his floors down the middle. Disguising the central feature as a giant niche, he opened the upper storey into three interconnecting, barrel-vaulted rooms. In this sequence of visually linked spaces, screened from one another by columns, Soane displayed the type of ingenuity seen much later in the conversion of his own premises at 12–14 Lincoln's Inn Fields into a museum. The intended structure for the Society of Dilettanti anticipates, in every way, Soane's unique personal contribution to the domain of museum architecture.

The public sector of architecture always appealed most to Soane because it offered the broadest scope, biggest challenges, and greatest monetary and artistic rewards. Bridges in particular held a fascination for him from the 1770s onwards, to the extent that he may have considered a specialized career in civil engineering. As it happened, he had occasion to build only two bridges during his long lifetime. In each case he made a point of exhibiting the design at the Royal Academy. The first such instance was in 1784 when Blackfriars Bridge, in Norwich, was already nearing completion. The contract drawing illustrated here (fig. 1.10) is unlikely to have been the one selected for display. With the various signatures scrawled upon it, it shows the bridge as executed rather than as Soane ideally visualized it. At first he had hoped for a gently curving flight of steps on either side to complement the delicate rise of the arch. It probably entered the 1784 exhibition in this perfectly equilibrated form, although by then it had become clear that a public house impinging on the right-hand side of the site made steps there impossible.[27] The quest for an acceptable aesthetic expression forced Soane to endow his bridge with a fictitious symmetry it could never in fact enjoy. In the context of a Royal Academy display, this was a case of putting one's best foot forward. The notable technical achievements of Blackfriars Bridge (see chap. 11) could not, in the eyes of exhibition-goers, compensate for a faux pas like asymmetry. All this points to a grave flaw in the academic tendency to value appearance above content. Soane, among others, felt the necessity to revise and improve upon his designs for the benefit of the viewing public. Strictly speaking, the motive was not to mislead, but the net result was a fantasy world of beautifully rendered drawings that had little real bearing outside the walls of Somerset House. Soane's Royal Academy entries drifted more and more into this realm of the unreal that sometimes bordered on artistic deception.[28]

Though Soane craved public works and public recognition, private commissions dominated the bulk of his early output. His sixth and final entry in the 1784 Royal Academy exhibition is of a forbidding gateway to Brancepeth Castle in County Durham (fig. 1.11). To harmonize with the medieval stronghold, seen in the left background, Soane designed one of his few early attempts at a Gothic Revival style. Only in later years did Soane come to feel any affinity for the nonclassical world. This lack of sympathy shows up in the rigid symmetry of the two lodge buildings and their pasteboard flimsiness reminiscent of a child's toy fort. The drawing illustrated here, although undated and unidentified, is in all likelihood the one exhibited at the Royal Academy. Its composition agrees generally with Soane's rough sketch for Brancepeth (fig. 1.13). Furthermore, an exact but dry copy of it exists in Soane's *liber veritatis* entitled Precedents in Architecture 1784. Finally, the watercolor style recurs in several other Soane presentation drawings produced in the early 1780s (see figs. 5.17, 13.3). All of them have the same wet, rather diffused brushwork in the landscape elements framing the architecture. Soane had admired such naturalistic settings in the exhibition drawings of John Yenn (fig. 5.4), and he realized their power to bring to life a flat elevation. One can see how these appealingly puffy trees and clouds might have attracted the acclaim he received. Momentarily breaking with the matter-of-fact tone of his notebooks, Soane interjected the favorable critique of the *Morning Chronicle* newspaper, which read: "S[oane] is an architect improved & improving, we recommend the Brancepeth Castle Gateway . . . not to be overlooked."[29] Critical applause was always music to Soane's ears. In 1784, as a further mark of artistic coming of age, he received this fleeting piece of publicity. At last he had gained recognition alongside his peers in the prestigious forum of the Royal Academy.

The Architect on the Road (4–17 August 1784)

Frequent business trips formed an extremely time-consuming part of an eighteenth-century architect's profession. Soane turned this rigorous round of tours of inspection and visits to clients into a cornerstone on which to build his future success. His notebooks reveal with exhaustive thoroughness the complex logistics involved in such trips: the careful planning laid in advance, the arduous journey itself, and the unexpected contingencies that had to be met with en route. Soane certainly earned his enviable reputation for exacting standards, close work schedules, and tight adherence to budgets. The notebook entries covering a two-week period in August 1784 portray a typically hard-driving Soane itinerary, characteristic of his stamina and determination.

On 3 August Soane had just returned to London from a protracted stay supervising the construction work at Malvern Hall. Immediately the next day he again set off, this time in the direction of East Anglia. Traveling via Ipswich, he reached Earsham Hall, on the border between Norfolk and Suffolk, at 3:00 on the afternoon of Thursday, 5 August.

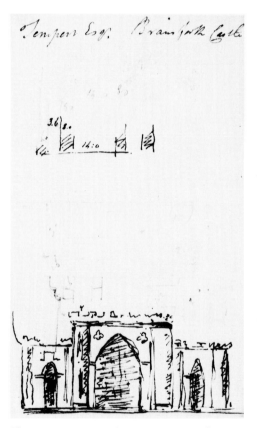

Fig. 1.13. Brancepeth Castle, gate and lodges, sketch (SM, Soane Notebooks, 8, p. 26).

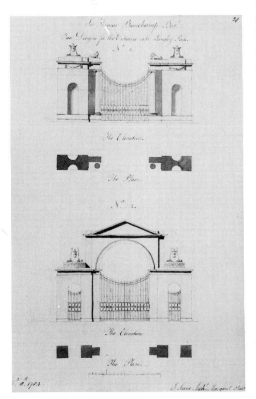

Fig. 1.14. Langley Park, two designs for a gate, plans and elevations, 1784 (SM, Precedents in Architecture 1784, fol. 29 recto).

The following morning at 10:00, he left for Norwich, some 14 miles away, arriving for lunch. He remained there until 8 August, using the Surrey Street residence of his friend, John Patteson, as his temporary headquarters. Sunday evening found Soane at Taverham Hall, outside Norwich, where he stayed until Thursday, 11 August. He then journeyed the 13 miles to Letton Hall, near Shipham. Very late on Thursday he returned to Norwich, but the next morning took a hired horse to Saxlingham. That same afternoon he went to Earsham and reassessed the work in progress. He rose early on Saturday, 14 August, in order to have breakfast with a prospective client at Costessey. He then continued another 2 miles to revisit Taverham. That Sunday he spent again in Norwich, holding business meetings. Monday he set out at 5:00 A.M., arrived at Letton by 9:00, pushed on to examine some construction at Cockley Cley, and finally reached Thetford, where he boarded a London-bound coach at 11:00 P.M. He returned home on 17 August after a fortnight on the road. Four days later Soane married Elizabeth Smith. Their honeymoon is an undocumented interlude in the notebooks which resume the record of the architect's hectic routine as if nothing had intervened.

In the course of Soane's August trip to Norfolk, he came into contact with at least ten current or prospective clients. He saw nine of his projects going on simultaneously in various stages of completion. He visited some of the sites more than once. At a conservative estimate, he covered some 300 miles over highways and along rutted back roads. His out-of-pocket traveling expenses, including gratuities, totalled £7.4.0. If the pace seems breakneck, it is really not at all unusual.[30] From the early spring until the late autumn, and sometimes in the depths of winter too, Soane made his rounds of inspection. In a much more fragmentarily documented way we know that the same applied as well to fellow architects. Sir Robert Taylor, for one, used to sleep in his carriage between appointments. James Wyatt charged a fixed amount for each mile traveled, and was actually killed in a coaching accident while returning from a project. William Blackburn died en route to a job.[31]

Soane's mid-August Norfolk trip is more than a representative travel document. It provides a cross section of the multifarious activities carried out by the architect because it cuts through the complex layered structure of Soane's practice at a given moment. Individual building histories, of course, extend in a "horizontal" way, with their own built-in sequence. The notebooks, however, make possible the examination of the overlapping of these works, one with another, in terms of depth as well as length. As a result of studying one two-week-long slice, so to speak, various coexisting strata emerge that show the steps taken by an eighteenth-century architect from the inception of a commission to its completion.

At the very beginning of the building process stands the introduction of architect to client. This can be accomplished in a variety of ways. Soane relied upon word-of-mouth as the surest method of getting known. An example of this grapevine principle in operation occurred on the evening of 9 August, when Soane attended a dinner party at Taverham Hall given by the owner, his client Miles Sotherton Branthwayte. Soane recorded having met, among the guests, Sir Thomas and Lady Beauchamp-Proctor, of nearby Langley Park. Out of force of habit, Soane noted down Sir Thomas's address.[32] What had started as dinner table conversation ended up five days later in a firm request for Soane to prepare designs for an entrance gate to the park at Langley. Certainly Branthwayte may have aided the process by putting in a good word for Soane. It is also likely that Soane made a favorable impression by producing a quick sketch on the spot, as he had done in July of the previous year while on a social visit to the Tempests at Brancepeth Castle (fig. 1.13, and compare fig. 1.11). As with Brancepeth, the hasty sketch would then develop into more carefully planned proposals as the next step in the procedure of gaining a commission.

When Soane returned to Norfolk in September 1784, he left three alternative designs with the Beauchamp-Proctors. Other instances of Soane presenting "multiple choices" are known, although the drawings rarely survive intact as in the case of Langley (figs. 1.14, 1.15). Cunningly diverse, each design is a variation upon the same standard width of swing gate stipulated by Soane at the outset.[33] The intention was to whet the appetite of Sir Thomas, and it worked. Eventually he proceeded to build not one but two sets of gates at Langley, neither of which resembles the original proposals exactly. The multiple-choice procedure allowed the architect to put to the test the patron's inclinations and seriousness.

Once letters or verbal agreements had been exchanged, designs sent, and negotiations entered into, Soane would examine the proposed site. When it was a question of a new building, this simply meant selecting the best location in consultation with the owner. "Settled situation of stables," Soane wrote on the morning of 14 August, after he had breakfasted at Costessey Park with his prospective client, Sir William Jerningham.[34] When an existing building was concerned, a more complex procedure ensued. Soane would make a survey of the structure. A case in point was the greenhouse at Earsham Park drawn in plan on the afternoon of 5 August (fig. 1.16). Sometimes these measured drawings

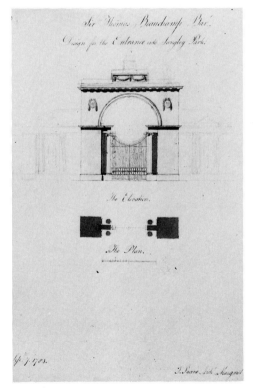

Fig. 1.15. Langley Park, design for a gate and lodges, plan and elevation, 1784 (SM, Precedents in Architecture 1784, fol. 29 verso).

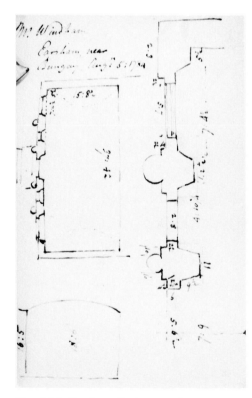

Fig. 1.16. Earsham Park, greenhouse, measured sketch plan, 1784 (SM, Soane Notebooks, 12, p. 32).

are difficult to distinguish from the rough form of an autograph design, except that the actual dimensions come out in odd fractions of inches. If Soane himself made a proposal, he would simplify the measurements and schematize the outline, as when he suggested turning the same greenhouse into a music pavilion for William Windham (figs. 1.17, 1.18). At Earsham he sketched on a notebook page how the rectangular plan could be altered internally to accommodate the new apsidal-ended room, executed later that summer. The cross section, with its sketchy urn and ornamental coffering, evokes the classic little setting which Soane created and which still stands. He slipped a new kernel so deftly into an old shell that the entire building was considered to be his.[35]

On the basis of measured surveys, sketches or preliminary designs, a final set of "fair" drawings would arrive for the client's approval. Those for Sir William Jerningham's stables did not come until January 1785. (Soane, in turn, had to wait until 22 August 1792 for his fee!) With the final designs went the various estimates. Soane's reputation for reliability rested to a large extent upon these, so they received special care. While at Letton Hall on 11 August Soane prepared such an estimate. He calculated the cost of the shell of the house at £2,837. His client, Mr. Dillingham, ordered Soane to proceed to the next step, that of contracting with workmen for the prices estimated. That same day an agreement was reached with the bricklayer, Philip Barnes, to carry out the work at Letton.

Establishing a climate of mutual trust stood at the heart of Soane's success in any project. As an indication of how highly he valued good relations with craftsmen, no less than seven are mentioned in the notebook pages covering the period 4–17 August. The names Dove, Wilkins, de Carle, Barnes, Fox, Dobson, and Ewen occur and recur. As an example, Mr. Ewen accompanied Soane on his return to Letton on 16 August when a schematic floor plan of the house was perhaps drawn for his benefit (fig. 1.19). Ewen probably assumed the important post of clerk of works, for which Soane had budgeted £50 in his Letton estimate. The clerk would look after the day-to-day operation of the building site during the architect's long absences elsewhere.

The preliminaries of choosing a location, submitting designs, and accepting estimates were now superseded by the commencement of the construction. The first step was groundbreaking or demolition, which Soane usually tried to supervise; he did so at Saxlingham Rectory on 13 August in the company of the contractor, Thomas Dove. Next would come the laying of the foundation; Soane saw to this at both Taverham and Letton during his mid-August trip to Norfolk. From this point on

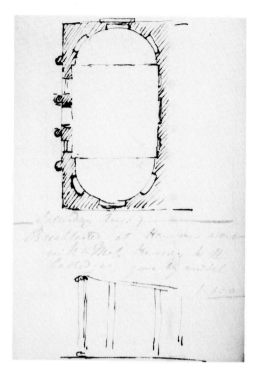

Fig. 1.17. Earsham Park, design to convert the greenhouse into a music pavilion, sketch plan (SM, Soane Notebooks, 12, p. 33).

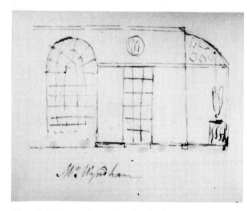

Fig. 1.18. Earsham Park, design to convert the greenhouse into a music pavilion, sketch section on the long axis (SM, Soane Notebooks, 12, p. 36).

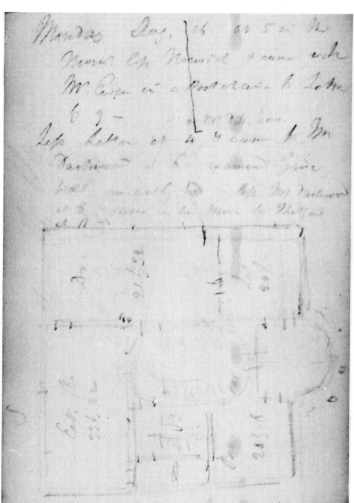

Fig. 1.19. Letton Hall, sketch plan (SM, Soane Notebooks, 12, p. 53).

Soane would follow the progress of work and check the craftsmen's accounts tallied with what had been carried out. On Friday, 13 August, for instance, Soane returned to Earsham, having agreed on 6 August to undertake the alterations there. In the meantime he had signed on Dove to handle the greenhouse conversion, and Dove's men had swiftly descended on the Monday. Four days later, when Soane and Dove arrived, they "surveyed," that is mensurated, the amount accomplished in the interim. Even for the efficient Soane this kind of tight schedule sets a speed record. Soane's close supervision repaid him once more during his mid-August trip; he returned to Taverham to correct errors that had brought the masons to a standstill.

In between Soane's on-site consultations, problems were bound to arise over the interpretation by Norfolk carftsmen of a London-based architect's instructions. At Taverham Soane found unexpected trouble from faulty guttering, and he promised to send working drawings of the cornice to scale. On the basis of these, a full-size template could be made to avoid further difficulties. As a result of these experiences, Soane became a confirmed believer in the virtues of wooden scale models. One was prepared for Taverham, another for Letton, Saxlingham Rectory, and Blackfriars Bridge. None survive, though the names of their makers and costs do. With respect to models, Soane practiced the teachings of his friend James Peacock, who was unusual for stressing in his publications the importance of models as a visual aid to workmen and owners alike.[36]

With work fully underway and going well, there still remained a plethora of small details of a structural or decorative nature to be dealt with by Soane. On 15 August he noted that John de Carle, the contractor for Blackfriars Bridge in Norwich, had ordered a lamp standard as a crowning feature for the guard rails. De Carle acted in fulfillment of Soane's wishes and the detailed sketches that had been provided on a previous visit to Norwich (fig. 1.20). On 3 May, Soane had already received his fee of £63. Even so, the commission dragged on. As late as July 1791 Soane paid the ironsmiths, Russel and Co., either for the same lamp or a replacement.[37]

Blackfriars Bridge is an exception to the rule among Soane's early works. Few of them have so clearly defined or tidy an ending. In fact, Soane made it his business to keep in touch with his former clients and might even find the excuse to pay them a social visit from time to time.[38] The client, having been satisfied with the architect, would keep him in mind for further commissions. Thus, in a rare surviving letter from Soane to a patron, we read how the architect had managed to reduce the "extremely unreasonable" bill of Theodore de Bruyn, the Swiss painter who had just finished some decorating at Earsham. Soane diplomatically concluded his message with the words, "I hope you will never find me wanting in attention, but studious to have the good opinion of my Employers." Perhaps not coincidentally, Soane drew on the back of the same letter his proposals for additional alterations at Earsham.[39]

Soane's notebook entries, accounts, letters, and drawings, taken all together, depict the practice of architecture as an unfolding continuum. The origins of one work are seen to overlap with another, and even the idea of the definitive completion of any one thing seems to lose precise meaning. Sharp, distinct divisions, whether chronological or stylistic, blur into one relatively indistinguishable whole. The separateness of commissions, and their dates of execution expressed in round figures, are primarily created by, and for the aid of, the historian.

To judge from the material preserved by Soane, a fair picture of the mind of an architect would be a seething mass of creative impulses, calculations, deadlines, and petty details. Projects, large and small, all jostled for his immediate attention, popping up when the moment was ripe, then subsiding for months or years at a time, rarely disappearing forever. Obviously it was impossible to maintain for long these incessant physical and creative demands. For Soane the answer to increased popularity was the establishment of an architectural office late in 1784.

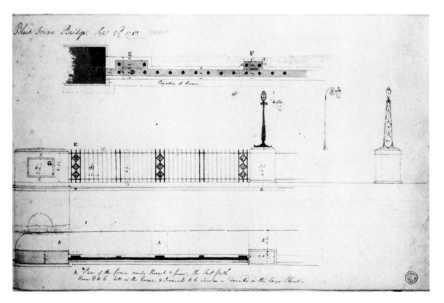

Fig. 1.20. Blackfriars Bridge, Norwich, plans and elevation of guard rails, 1783 (SM, Portfolio 3, Item 6).

With a sense of relief—but also perhaps with some reluctance too—he relinquished his total control over the complex artistic process.

The events leading up to the transferral of responsibility from one creative individual to an office staff, are the subject of this book. Its chapters each in turn investigate aspects of architectural education and early professional practice that taught the techniques and gave the inspiration necessary to success. At no point is it argued that Soane's actions are unprecedented or even that his youthful talents are especially unusual. On the contrary, one justification for this study of Soane is precisely that, to an extent never realized, an eighteenth-century architect's formative period can be shown to conform closely with patterns still current today.

·2·
New Ethics and New Planning

THE SCREEN OF TREES on Ealing Green still preserves the leafy character that once gave Pitzhanger Manor its attractive suburban charm, a bracing seven-mile walk from the center of London. More clearly than any other place, Pitzhanger (pl. 1) evokes the stages of John Soane's architectural career. In it is locked the secret of his earliest training. It owes its present form to the period of his most prolific activity. Its sale in 1810 marked his dashed hopes that his sons would succeed him.

The story of Pitzhanger begins with the traditional date of 1768–70 given for George Dance the Younger's alterations to the house for his future father-in-law, Thomas Gurnell.[1] In 1800 the Gurnell heirs disposed of the property to John Soane, by then a man of private means. The reason for Soane's attachment to the house stemmed from the fact that, as he recalled, it was "the first whose progress and construction I had attended at the commencement of my architectural studies."[2] With a characteristic sense of history, the mature Soane returned to the scene of his architectural infancy. Out of fondness for the old building he altered it in such a way as to retain the side wing with which he had principally assisted. To this he added a new centerpiece that paid tribute to some of the influences that had shaped him as an artist.

As was later the case with his London townhouse, Soane saw the facade of his suburban retreat "as a picture, a sort of portrait."[3] The Pitzhanger "portrait," of course, depicts the artist-owner himself. In it he alluded to his debt to Antiquity, the Renaissance, the work of Robert Adam, and especially the work of Dance. The spread eagles beneath the windows referred to the ancient bas relief at SS. Apostoli in Rome, and the freestanding columnar treatment, with its adjacent roundels showing the chariots of Sun and Moon, recalled the Arch of Constantine in the same city. Adam had used a highly reminiscent tetrastyle device on the garden front of Kedleston Hall, Derbyshire, which Soane admired. Moreover, the whole conglomerate nature of the composition at Ealing

If you are a young man . . . seek the acquaintance of such as are your superiors, men of undoubted sense and abilities; and be swift to hear everything that may tend to give you the least instruction; always taking care to behave with the greatest respect to them.

Essay on the Duties and Qualifications of an Architect

21

was, according to Soane, in "imitation of an Italian Villa...[where] we see an immense quantity of ancient remains of sculpture and arch[itectural] fragments." He must have had in mind the Roman Renaissance because when he dropped the Constantinian roundels from the final Pitzhanger design, he replaced them with copies of lion statues he knew from the Villa Medici on the Pincian Hill.[4] Finally, Soane remembered Dance's use of identical roundels on the facade of Cranbury Park, Hampshire, where Dance employed him as he had done twelve years earlier at Pitzhanger.[5] This last connection served to reinforce for Soane the meaning he attached to Pitzhanger as, above all, a monument commemorating his allegiance to Dance. Historically and stylistically it testifies to the undying esteem of a pupil for his revered first master. It expressed for Soane an affection so deep-seated that it withstood the vile backbiting when, as a Royal Academician, he found himself in a different camp from Dance.[6] Even so, right at Pitzhanger, there were signs of the two men's ultimate rift over the question of professionalism. A fragmentary early letter concerning Pitzhanger draws attention to Dance's neglect at keeping deadlines.[7] Whereas Dance could afford to be casual in such matters, Soane could not.

According to Soane's account of the crucial events leading up to his arrival in London, he left Chertsey in 1768. Thanks to James Peacock, he found employment with George Dance, the recently appointed Clerk of the City Works. Beyond any doubt the youngster had established himself by March 1769 on Chiswell Street, Moorfields, where the Dance family home was located.[8] Although only a dozen years in age separated Soane from Dance, a gulf existed between the social backgrounds of the two. Dance had enjoyed the royal road to the architectural profession. His father had financed a liberal education and extensive travel abroad and had even provided an official position to succeed to. Soane had no such patrimony presented to him, nor could he purchase the privilege of an apprenticeship in London.[9] So he began by working for Dance, probably in some menial capacity such as office boy, and from there gradually he climbed his way up in the office hierarchy. In later years malicious rumors about Soane's early servility were spread by the Dances themselves, so there must be an element of truth to the stories.[10] But this gossip does not answer the key question about the exact nature of Soane's duties and training.

Little information exists about the running of the Dance office during the critical period after 1768. At the time, designs were being prepared for such important buildings as Newgate Prison and the Old Bailey Sessions House. More experienced hands than Soane's would have been

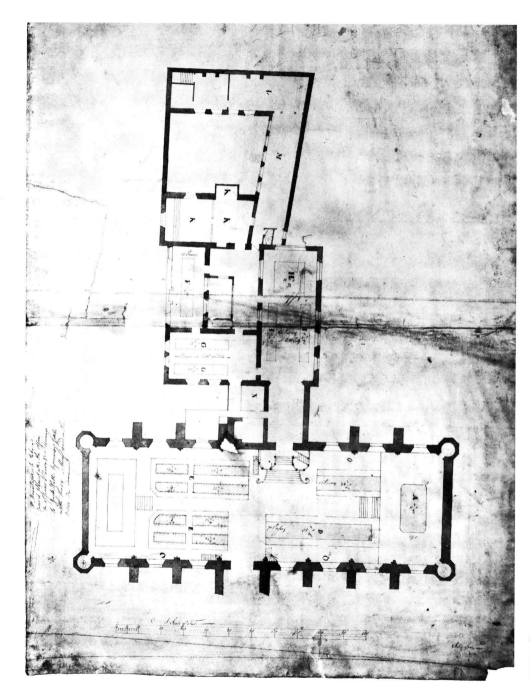

Fig. 2.1. Guildhall, London, seating plan for the Lord Mayor's banquet (CLRO, Surveyor's City Lands Buildings, Item 4).

entrusted with these large tasks. To him fell the routine job of copying out the seating plan for the annual Lord Mayor's Dinner held in the London Guildhall (fig. 2.1). With some pride the draftsman signed his name "John Soan" in the lower right-hand corner. The signature in bold round characters looks fully mature, but the clumsy handling of the clustered piers along the walls points to Soane's lack of familiarity with drafting techniques. In order to cope with the trickiest part, the intricate staircase, he resorted to the expedient of transferring the plan by pin pricks from an earlier drawing.[11] If, for the sake of argument, this plan is said to represent Soane's level of competence by 1770, then he obviously had a lot to learn over his remaining two years with Dance.

The strong ties between former employer and employee persisted after their separation in 1772. A pencil portrait of Soane, dated 1774 on the contemporary frame (fig. 2.2) is attributed to Nathaniel Dance, George's elder brother, another talented member of this artistic family. The relaxed informality of the portrait reflects the affable comradeship and filial regard that Soane must have enjoyed in the Dance office. The intimate picture of Soane, in the absence of other evidence, still suggests that he had been virtually adopted into the bosom of the Dance household. This in itself was perhaps reason enough for the young man's veneration of the kindly Dance.

Soane praised in glowing terms Dance's "perfect knowledge of the ancient works of the Greeks and Romans" and his "correct taste." These words referred specifically to the single accomplishment by the master that had left the deepest impression on his pupil. Soane, it seems, could vividly recall Dance's showing his drawings of a *magnifica galleria* (fig. 2.3) and boasting that they had won him first prize out of a field of twenty-nine competitors at the Academy in Parma, Italy.[12] To the young Soane, the *magnifica galleria* of 1763 summed up Dance's gifts. It evoked golden visions of years spent abroad in the pursuit of one's art. Indeed, the *magnifica galleria* is a brilliantly evocative and typically Italianate piece of design. A solemn, monumental facade precedes a sequence of sumptuous, top-lighted art galleries echoing to the splash of water from fountains. Artistically speaking, Soane was reared among the strong chiaroscuro effects and sober classicism of these marbled halls. Here he imbibed the desire to emulate the sweeping bravura of the design, and Dance's rousing competition motto: *Mihi turpe relinqui est* ("It is a shame for me to be left behind").[13] From Dance he contracted the incurable love of great public buildings with unlimited budgets that people the fantasies of many architects. And when George Dance's sons offered his drawings for sale, Soane acquired the *magnifica galleria* along with the

Fig. 2.2. Portrait of John Soane, by Nathaniel Dance, ca. 1774 (SM, Mrs. Soane's Morning Room).

others, numbering some 1,300 in all. As previously with Pitzhanger, he preserved and enshrined the memory of his association with Dance in order to cement his claim as self-appointed heir.

Although much had been written about the stylistic reliance of Soane on Dance, the young man's early works do not show this to the same degree as some of his later executed buildings like Pitzhanger.[14] At the beginning of Soane's career, Dance's influence was of such a general kind that it cannot be traced to specific motifs from the master. Rather,

Fig. 2.3. George Dance II, *magnifica galleria* design, elevation and section (SM, Dance Cabinet, Slider 4, Set 11, Item 2).

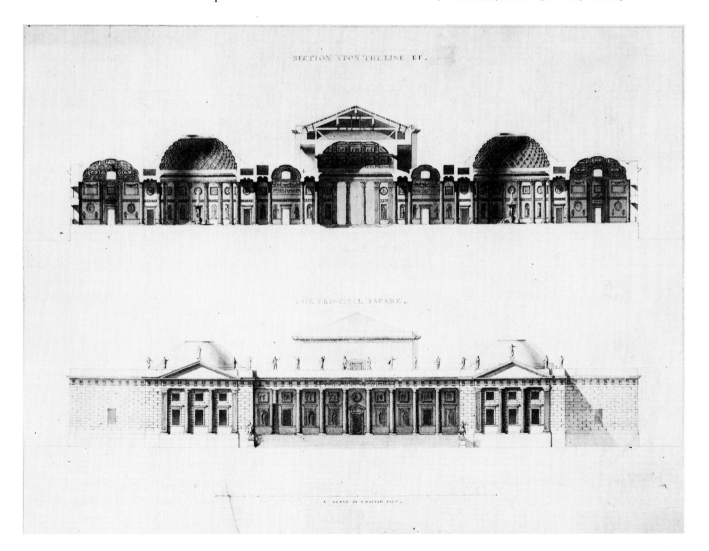

Dance inspired Soane by exposing him to the joys of artistic creativity, especially in the grand manner of *magnifica galleria*. But his buildings, large or small, civic or domestic, were all so individual and different that they taught by their example a flexible approach to each design problem. Dance himself, in a rare theoretical pronouncement, cautioned against "rigid adherence to a certain style."[15] This quality of freedom to exercise judicious choice was the one that Dance's contemporaries and architectural brethren most often remarked upon in his work. The jurors at Parma academy commented about the *magnifica galleria* that "Everything . . . appears suited to its place . . . and suited to its subject." Young Soane came to be impressed with Dance's "propriety of application" in eliminating unnecessary drip mouldings from the interior of All Hallows Church, London Wall. And Samuel Pepys Cockerell summed up current opinion when he told Joseph Farington that each of Dance's designs above all "explained the purpose for which the building was intended."[16] Dance's wide-ranging eclecticism, always kept in check by rational considerations of usage, constituted a genial style all its own—consistent, if one may say so, by very virtue of its extreme diversity.

In emphasizing the instrumental role of Dance upon the young Soane's education, it has become a corollary to play down or totally ignore James Peacock, who introduced the two. With respect to his influence on Soane, Peacock was far more than the mere "hodman" he liked to call himself.[17] Sometime soon after Dance's return from Italy in 1764, Peacock met him in his capacity as surveyor to a builder.[18] In their own best interests these two men of different talents formed an architects' cooperative that lasted a lifetime. The accommodating Peacock contented himself with playing second fiddle to Dance. Although Peacock preferred to keep in the background as Dance's assistant, he spoke out often enough under the guise of anonymity, or thinly veiled pseudonym. Paradoxically, the self-effacing Peacock had quite a prolific output as theorist on architecture, as inventor, and crusading social reformer. By contrast, Dance hardly published a word. It is as if, by tacit agreement, Dance made the official appearances for the team, while Peacock acted behind the scenes as the spokesman.

James Peacock deserves to be better known as a writer. His little octavo *Oikidia, or Nutshells* strikes a refreshing note of frankness among the often pompous architectural publications of the period. The text that accompanies the plans and estimates for "small villas" is original in its common sense approach and in its jocular tone. Peacock lightheartedly debunked clients and fellow architectural writers when he introduced his work with the mock apology:

the reader . . . is not to expect, in these little plans, any of that extra-ordinary latitude very commonly taken . . . . Men who are determined to keep their arms akimbo, and would sooner lose the point of an elbow, than abate half a hair's breath of their accustomed strut, should look into folio volumes.[19]

Rejection of rigid rules of proportion, a reliance on scale models, emphasis on workable plans in preference to overdecorated facades, and hints for do-it-yourself estimates contribute to the remarkable character of this book.

Oikidia, which appeared in 1785, was by no means Peacock's first publication. He had brought out a pamphlet on economics by the year 1778, though he did not take the credit for writing it until later. A curious fact about Peacock was the repeated way he avoided using his own name, as when he signed *Oikidia* with the tongue-in-cheek anagram, José Mac-Packe. The recourse to anonymity in itself speaks loudly in favor of Peacock's authorship of *An Essay on the Qualifications and Duties of an Architect.* This anonymous pamphlet, published in 1773, also shares enough stylistic similarities with *Oikidia* to link them both to the same writer.[20] In view of its early date and probable author, the *Essay* has a direct bearing on the training of Soane within the circle of Dance and Peacock.

The purpose of the *Essay,* first and foremost, was to exonerate George Dance from the charge that inferior materials had been substituted for use at Newgate Prison.[21] This connection with Dance has led some to suppose that he addressed the public in his own defense—surely an unwise move for a City official, and quite out of keeping with his reluctance to appear in print.[22] The more pugnacious Peacock could take up the cudgel on Dance's behalf. The writer of the text made a point of disclaiming much acquaintance with Dance—a sure sign he knew him well, but wanted to mislead his readers. At the same time, the author gave a rather long-winded defense of Dance's Clerk of Works, who, though he is not named, was none other than Peacock himself. What is more, the pamphleteer could not forbear slipping in a pun at the architect's expense when he quoted the adage "if the foundation *dance* it will mar all the mirth of the house."[23] And since Soane was there in the Dance office when the theories were current that were later put forward in the *Essay,* that document is of the utmost importance in establishing the sort of architectural training he would have received.

Broadly speaking, the *Essay* falls into three parts, the first two of which have the least bearing on Soane. One part is an apology for the action—or rather inaction—of the Newgate architect, alluded to as "Mr. D." in the text. The appearance of the *Essay* some months after Dance's temporary resignation, and Peacock's overhasty application for the post, may have been intended to smooth ruffled feelings between the two men.[24] The second part of the *Essay* defines the terms "architect" and "surveyor." The difference of terminology was relatively slight according to the essayist. It turned upon the question of having a gift for design—Dance had it; Peacock did not, as the absence of elevations in *Oikidia* and the rather mechanical quality of the plans prove. The third part of the *Essay* was addressed to young prospective architects or surveyors and has the most relevance to Soane's situation.

For the outline of an ideal architectural training, the essayist admitted to relying on the time-honored theories of Vitruvius and Alberti concerning the architect as universal man.[25] In practical particulars, however, he relied much more on his personal experience *and* the example of Dance. Reminiscent of Dance was the emphasis on having a good liberal education, traveling abroad, and learning foreign languages, especially French. Soane, in turn, came to be influenced by these precepts. Though to him the Grand Tour must have seemed unobtainably far off, he studied French seriously. He could read it, and write it reasonably well as a young man.[26]

If these down-to-earth prescriptions sound hackneyed, it was not the case when they went into print. Rarely, if ever, had such ideas been written in so straightforward a fashion. For instance, the essayist stressed his belief that the architect's duty in life was to serve as a model to society. He should avoid swearing, drunkenness, whoring, and avarice. He should be "careful to gain the goodwill of the workmen under [him] . . . civil and complaisant to tradesmen." All these qualities recall the Christian virtues listed on Peacock's tombstone epitaph.[27] His puritanical code of behavior, combined with the Protestant work ethic underlying it, had a profound influence on Soane's attitude to business conduct. But the two virtues of humility and forgiveness that Peacock found so easy to espouse in his career of cozy subservience were more difficult for Soane to adopt. Dance and Peacock together handed down to their pupil the highest artistic ideals and the best moral principles. Yet Soane found something lacking for one with his ambitions.

As characterized by Soane, the collaboration of Dance and Peacock fell into the pattern familiar from architectural firms of more recent times. According to Soane's analysis, Dance was the design partner with no head for hard figures, Peacock made up in accountancy skills for what he lacked in originality.[28] A Peacock project (fig. 2.4) strengthens the impression that he had limited abilities. The drawing, copied by Soane into an early sketchbook, shows a feeble and cluttered scheme for a three-

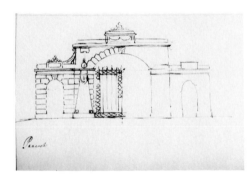

Fig. 2.4. Gateway design, after James Peacock (SM, Miscellaneous Sketches 1780–82, p. 14).

part ornamental gateway enclosing the parade grounds adjacent to Finsbury Square, on which Peacock lived, and in whose development he had a hand. Peacock's suggestion of flaming grenades atop his obelisks was actually included by Dance in the executed version of 1793.[29] The grenades, and the heaps of cannon balls above, bring to mind Peacock's contemporary statements in *Oikidia* relating to what he called "characteristic beauty."[30] According to this principle, displays of weaponry would be suitable to the function of the Honorable Artillery Company for which the gate was intended. In the realm of decoration, therefore, Peacock and Dance were thinking along the same lines. Their joint influence on Soane in this regard will be discussed later. What Dance and Peacock possessed least was the determination to succeed that fired Soane's imagination from the start. As time went on, the two older men developed a tendency to become easily sidetracked. Dance whiled away his later years in dream designs, whimsical cartoons, and Sunday sketching sessions. Peacock became preoccupied with his theoretical publications and his water filtration system. Perhaps Soane's original contention that the pair lacked "practical knowledge" when they first met, continued to hold true for their knowledge of the ways of the world. Dance was aware that further association might prove detrimental to his disciple's development.[31] He suggested that Soane enter the employ of another architect. That, at least, is Soane's account. Other, less flattering versions of the story exist. One anecdote implies that the joking among Soane and his fellow assistants may have had a cruel side to it, and that Soane, no longer able to stand the taunts about his humble beginnings as a "hack," had left for that reason.[32] Whatever the real truth, by the spring of 1772, Soane used Henry Holland's office address as his own when he exhibited his first design at the Royal Academy of Arts.

From 1772 until March 1778, John Soane remained attached in one way or another to the Henry Holland and Lancelot "Capability" Brown partnership. Payments to Soane from the account of Henry Holland & Son at Gosling's Bank begin in 1773 and continue sporadically until they total well over £3,100. These sums of money, often as large as £100, add up to far more than Soane's due as "a clerk at an annual salary of sixty pounds."[33] In his first year he handled some £936. Compared with the £25 and £15 sums paid around the same time to another Holland employee, Christopher Ebdon, one can gather the magnitude of Soane's new responsibilities. Almost immediately, Soane came to hold a position of considerable trust in a flourishing organization. Sadly, though, when once the information buried in bank vaults is dug out, it remains relatively mute evidence. In accord with general banking practice of the day, only the date, check number, and amount appear next to the payee's name in the debit columns. The scribes of the ledgers never specify the nature of the payments. Only in one case can a payment be connected with a particular event. Before Soane left for Italy in 1778—on the eve of his departure to be exact—Henry Holland, Jr., drew him a check for £30 from his personal account. This may have been a final reckoning, but more likely it represents a farewell gift from a satisfied employer. When Soane returned to London in 1780, Holland welcomed him back with the offer of a temporary address.[34] In view of these lucrative and apparently amicable arrangements, it is strange that Soane made so little reference to his days with Brown and Holland.

Soane's incumbency as clerk for the Holland and Brown partnership coincided with a boom period for the office. A catalogue of major works begun or completed during his term there is impressive in itself: Claremont, Surrey, 1771–74; Benham, Berkshire, 1773–75; Cadland, Hampshire, 1775–78; Brooks's Clubhouse, London, 1776–78; a dairy for Hill Park, Kent, 1777; and housing speculation at Knightsbridge, London, from 1777 onward.[35] Exclusive of small jobs, the list amounts to an impressive total of undertakings in the domestic sphere. When one compares Dance's tiny output of public buildings over the same six years, one sees that Soane had jumped from the somewhat sleepy atmosphere of the Dance office in the City to the bustling activity of the one on Half Moon Street in the West End.

The informal partnership of Henry Holland, Jr., and Lancelot Brown went back to 1771, although the two families knew each other before that, and eventually became linked by marriage.[36] Brown, already well established as a successful landscape garden designer, took on a younger partner because of the important commission from Lord Clive of India to build a new mansion at Claremont. Brown had his architectural limitations. His contract elevations of 1771 for Claremont show competence; an interior, such as the gallery at Corsham Court of the decade before, displays a more heavy-handed approach. Often in the past, Brown had farmed out the interior work to others, as at Croome Court, Worcestershire, where Robert Adam was employed. At Claremont, however, Brown kept the business for himself by enlisting the younger Holland. As time went on, Holland took on more of the architectural and decorative work while Brown restricted himself to the landscaping. At this point in the Claremont proceedings Soane entered the scene. Holland was in need of an assistant and Dance was willing to let Soane go. The transfer occurred to the mutual satisfaction of all parties. Holland, it is known, "was accustomed to speak of Dances integrity and abilities in the highest terms."[37]

Largely because of Soane's presence, Claremont is one of the best documented houses by the Brown and Holland partnership. As a new man on the job, Soane approached his duties with special thoroughness. He also manifested, for the first time, his habit of preserving any and all documents that came into his hands. What Pitzhanger stands for in his relations with Dance, Claremont represents with respect to his new employers. Claremont conveys the clearest notion of Soane's activities as Brown and Holland's clerk and also his farsighted endeavors on behalf of his own improvement.

At an early date, in a slim volume misleadingly entitled "Copies of Bills 1785," John Soane began copying out the estimates for the shell and interior finishing of Claremont. He followed this with later bills submitted by the joiners John Hobcraft, L. Lambourn, and R. Wilson.[38] In the process he comandeered two small price books that apparently had belonged to contemporaries or predecessors of his at Claremont. One of these books contains, among other things, plasterers' bills from William Pearce of 1772–73, an estimate of carvers' work dated 22 June 1771, and an account of joiners' work dated May 1773. The other book may have belonged to Henry Wood, the carver whose bills of 1771–72 for Claremont figure in it. Large sections of this second book were copied into a third one commenced in Soane's own handwriting on 9 March 1772, presumably the date on which he began work for Holland and Brown.[39] The fortuitous survival of so many originals and copies tells what Soane was about. In order to get practice at costing craftsmen's work, drawing up estimates, or submitting accounts in the customary format, Soane set himself the task of copying and recopying out-of-date material. The lessons so painstakingly learned were not soon forgotten. In 1781, when setting up his own practice, he returned to his old Claremont price book to record the account of one of his first personal clients, Wilbraham Tollemache.[40] Only the longhand has matured; the billing techniques pick up exactly where they left off nearly a decade before.

Soane's education by rote had another advantage. It familiarized him with the craftsmen in the building trades. He knew their names and could begin to relate to them once he understood their problems. The *Essay* had emphasized the value of this kind of contact for a young man entering the profession. Soane, as Holland's clerk, put into practice what the *Essay* had preached. Significantly, Soane's two earliest surviving letters were written in a friendly tone to Henry Wood, the carver whom he had met in connection with Claremont.[41]

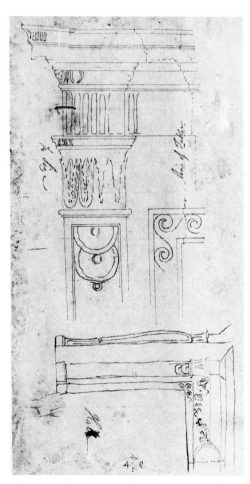

Fig. 2.5. Claremont Park, tracings of design for the entrance hall chimneypiece after Henry Holland (SM, OSMAS, Item 16).

When Soane commenced working for Holland in 1772, Brown's four brick walls at Claremont would have been under way for well over a year. The inside, to Holland's design, remained to be done, and, according to Soane's copies of estimates, the cost amounted to as much again as the shell.[42] The splendid suite of rooms at Claremont initiated Soane into the mysteries of fashionable interior design. As with the lessons to be learned in accounting, Soane coveted some permanent record of Holland's gifts as a decorator. Into an early scrapbook album the young man pasted half a dozen small slips of tracing paper onto which he had copied drawings by his employer for decorative details at Claremont (fig. 2.5). Soane thus went about assembling an archive of ornaments for his future use. One of the tracings is of special interest because it relates to a room for which Soane claimed some personal credit. Long after either Holland or Brown could dispute him, he wrote that the Claremont entrance hall "had been finished from drawings made by me."[43] He could not, of course, be referring to the overall dimensions; those had been set at 26 by 34 feet in the original plans of 1771. He must, therefore, have intended to indicate his participation in the arrangement and decoration of this handsome space.

Elaborately paved in black and white marble, its oval plaster ceiling designed to match, the Claremont entrance hall (fig. 2.6) blends sumptuousness with the chilly restraint typical of such rooms in earlier English country houses. The martial air of the enriched Doric frieze echoes the rectangular bas relief panels, one of which represents a victor's magnanimity to the vanquished. Trophies of arms over four side doors and in the centers of the end walls have a justification in this house for a soldier of fortune such as Lord Clive. Despite the special circumstances, none of these elements is without a precedent. In particular, the reddish engaged columns, in the kind of imitation marble called *scagliola*, point to a specific source. Similar Doric columns stand around the entrance hall of nearly identical size at Harewood House, Robert Adam's early masterpiece in Yorkshire. Recently the bases, shafts, and capitals at Harewood have been repainted to the porphyry red indicated in Adam's drawings of 1765. A date of two years later appears inscribed in the plasterwork as executed. Apart from the use of the same color and order—thought "proper" by Adam for use in a number of his halls—the trophies of arms are nearly identical at Harewood and Claremont. The trophies, modified and elongated, recur in the entrance hall of Newby, another Yorkshire house by Adam. In that case the more up-to-date plasterwork is dated 1771.[44] Moreover, the paving at Newby distinctly recalls the general scheme at Claremont. By 1772–73 it is not surprising to find

Adamesque imitations of the exceedingly popular style initiated the decade before. But the references at Claremont seem unusually direct and specific, especially so since Adam's *Works* did not start to appear in print until 1773. Unless the busy Soane or Holland had undertaken a pilgrimage to Adam's Yorkshire houses, how could they have known such interiors in so much detail? Even the one original departure at Claremont, the tympanum of the central overdoor, went back to a source sanctioned by Adam, the *Ruins of Palmyra* by Wood and Dawkins.[45]

Fig. 2.6. Claremont Park, entrance hall.

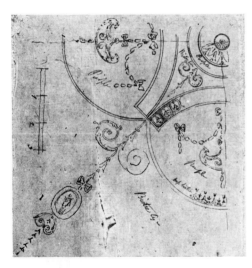

Fig. 2.7. Ashburnham House, Dover Street, London, tracing of anteroom ceiling design after Robert Adam (SM, OSMAS, Item 151).

A reason for the Adam derivation of Claremont is bound up with the centralization of the arts in one place. Though houses sprang up in the remote provinces, the most specialized craftsmen always operated from London. All the major architectural firms were also based in the capital. This explains a degree of familiarity with the latest ideas through an unofficial brotherly network. William Pearce, the plasterer for Claremont, could have consulted with the Rose family, who had worked on Harewood and Newby. The same fraternization could have accounted for some direct involvement of Adam at Claremont. Robert Adam had provided the interiors for Brown's design at Croome Court, which suggests a degree of collaboration between the two architects. In the case of Claremont, one of the Adam brothers—presumably Robert—passed judgment on the house during an undated tour of inspection. Fortunately Soane recorded from memory a dialogue according to which "Mr. Adam's objected to the State bedchamber at Claremont, as the Bed can't face the light, in Mr. H[olland's] opinion it should not as when it is so most people complain of not being able to sleep so well."[46] Soane's anecdote could document his own first meeting with Robert Adam, whom he certainly knew and personally liked. With an autobiographical ring to his voice, Soane used to praise Adam to his students, and elsewhere he called him a "friend to artists of every description."[47] It is as if Soane were remembering the open reception he had received as a nervous beginner presenting himself at Adam's door.

Interspersed among the Soane tracings after Holland are a number of others, apparently unrelated to work for the Brown and Holland partnership. Several can be directly connected with Robert Adam. One in particular (fig. 2.7) is a copy of an Adam ceiling design for Lord Ashburnham's London townhouse. The copy and the Adam originals, dated in the spring of 1773, are back together again in what is yet another astonishing outcome of Soane's obsessive quest for memorabilia about his youth. Gratitude for past kindnesses in the Adam office prompted Soane in 1833 to take the extraordinary step of saving the complete Adam drawings from dispersal by housing them under his own roof.[48]

Robert Adam's reactions to the Claremont entrance hall have not been recorded. He surely would have felt at home in an environment that owed so much to his ideas on orchestrating color and form. The volumetric, as well as decorative, aspect would not have escaped the man who set about describing "movement" in architecture in terms of "diversity of form," "convexity and concavity," "novelty and variety."[49] At Claremont "movement" took the shape of columns placed in a ring that made an interesting oval space within a more conventional rectangular one. The idea of breaking up a monotonous boxlike room went back to the earliest stages in the planning of Claremont's interior. A preparatory scheme for the hall is pasted in the so-called Clive Album and is inscribed by the otherwise unknown draftsman, John Ashby (fig. 2.8).[50] It is not known whether he preceded Soane or worked at the same time with him, and, if so, whether in a design capacity. Even if Soane did not "invent" the remarkable columnar treatment at Claremont, he certainly learned from it and pressed it into service on his own account. The same chain of

Fig. 2.8. Claremont Park, entrance hall, preliminary plan and elevation by John Ashby (George Clive Collection).

influences repeated itself with the "tribune" room-type. Once again Adam had been the first in England to propose such a top-lighted cylindrical chamber and to call it by its rightful name. Holland carried one out at Benham, when Soane was working for him.[51] Then Soane went on to perfect the feature to such an extent that it is most commonly associated with him. In matters of interior design, Soane was more of a skillful follower than an innovative leader.

Of course neither Adam, Holland, nor Soane could copyright motifs like the "tribune" or the columnar ring. The whole repertory of forms belonged in the public domain. From around the middle of the century a movement toward greater internal variety had gained steadily in momentum. It included the scenographic stairhalls of James Paine the Elder, and those of Sir Robert Taylor. It characterized the diversely shaped spaces of Adam and such early followers of his as James Wyatt and Thomas Leverton. As will be seen, it manifested itself externally in the rooms that project from facades designed by William Chambers, John Carr, or Isaac Ware. It liberated the confines set by the single- or double-cube room of Palladian derivation. Yet strong elements of neo-Palladianism remained in the work of all these architects. The Neoclassical revolution in taste, for which Adam boasted responsibility, did not happen overnight. But it was certainly well advanced by the time Soane reached Claremont.

From the vantage point of Claremont, it is possible to summarize Soane's development in terms of the formative influences that were brought to bear upon him. He had closely heeded the *Essay*'s admonition to "seek the acquaintance of . . . men of undoubted sense and abilities."[52] By chance as much as by design, he had found himself in the best artistic circles, and he profited from the experience. He had acquired a grandeur of vision from the innovative Dance. Peacock had inculcated the soundest business ethics and had contributed also to Soane's formulation of a narrative architecture, suited to all occasions. With the Brown and Holland partnership, Soane gained practical training in the intricacies of running an efficient, successful architectural operation. Holland, moreover, passed along planning principles, as well as notions of decoration in an Adamesque vein. Adam, perhaps the most gifted of the group, unofficially tutored Soane in various ways. In exchange Soane offered his teachers a doglike fidelity that outlived them and extended to the preservation of their office papers. Doggedly, too, he set about assimilating their ideas until they had become an integral part of his makeup.

Soane instilled in his employers a sense of confidence, and they responded with almost paternal solicitude toward him, since none of them had sons to carry on in their footsteps. Nevertheless, Soane's humble background precluded him from their dynastic system of advancement by birthright. He must have realized that, unless he asserted himself, he would always remain a trusted amanuensis, or habitual odd man out. To satisfy his personal ambition he would have to sacrifice past relationships by striking out on his own. There are distinct signs of restlessness on his part toward the end of his time with Holland and Brown. Encouraged by his successes in the Royal Academy Schools, Soane made the daring move of going into practice for himself in 1777. Almost inevitably, his dramatic and hitherto unknown debut at the St. Luke's competition brought him into conflict of interest with Dance.

·3·

Architecture for Madness:
The St. Luke's Competition

IN 1750 ST. LUKE'S HOSPITAL FOR POOR LUNATICS was founded by a group of philanthropic Londoners, among them the architect George Dance the Elder. As his personal contribution, he had donated his services for the design of the original St. Luke's premises in Moorfields (fig. 3.1).[1] His son and namesake lived around the corner on Chiswell Street, as did the young Soane when he came to work in the Dance household around 1768. Master and pupil must, therefore, have known St. Luke's well from a safe distance. Already by this time the asylum had become overcrowded, so great was the demand for the free care offered by the charitable institution. There was talk of expanding the old facilities, but the City overruled the idea. The suburbs had spread too far in the direction of Moorfields. A new location, more remote from the center, was chosen.[2]

The position of the City authorities and the subsequent actions of the governors of the hospital illustrate a distinct split in society's feelings on the subject of madness that still pertains today. For centuries its inexplicable causes, the suddenness or violence of its symptoms, the unpredictability of its cures had baffled those who witnessed it. Even, or perhaps especially, in the Age of Reason people found cause to be troubled by what one recent writer has called "le péril souterrain de la déraison, cet espace menaçant d'une liberté absolue."[3] As before, the natural reaction was to incarcerate those no longer in their right mind. Eighteenth-century humanitarianism, however, argued that this incarceration ought to promote well-being, if not necessarily the restoration of inmates to their senses. The floating *Narrenschiff* of the later Middle Ages and the subterranean oubliette of the Renaissance developed into the asylum of the Enlightenment, with its connotations of safety and freedom from persecution. A typical asylum like St. Luke's, though it was banished out of town, also embodied the interrelated principles of classification, segregation, hygiene, diet, regular exercise, and therapy that have governed most psychiatric institutions ever since.

The curiously shaped piece of land allotted to the new St. Luke's had a 550-foot frontage along Old Street, which ran between the villages of Clerkenwell and Shoreditch. It then stretched backward to form a rectangle with a narrow dogleg section that extended the property to a total depth of around 350 feet. On this challenging site the governors of St. Luke's decided to construct afresh, and proceeded to the selection of an architect. A St. Luke's building subcommittee, composed entirely of businessmen untrained in architecture, was formed on 4 December 1776. It made its first brief report the following 5 February. Exactly a year later, in their second report, the eleven members announced that they had selected George Dance the Younger to be their architect. It was a reasonable choice: Dance already acted as the surveyor of the hospital, he was the son of the first builder, and he, too, might be expected to donate his services. After some delay, and the submission of several further estimates, each more drastically cut than the last, a ceremonial laying of the foundation stone took place on 30 July 1782. The patients, numbering 129, moved in on New Year's Day, 1787. Those are the bare facts as related in the official records of St. Luke's.[4] A great deal more had gone on than ever got into the minutes, however. The overlooked proceedings were precisely the ones that influenced the destinies of Dance, Soane, and a number of their architect contemporaries. The issue is also raised of the open competition, a widespread custom that easily fell subject to misuse.

In the twelve-month interval between the first and second building subcommittee reports, St. Luke's had launched a momentous open competition along the lines of the one for Blackfriars Bridge, London. Staged as recently as 1759, the Blackfriars contest had drawn 69 entries.

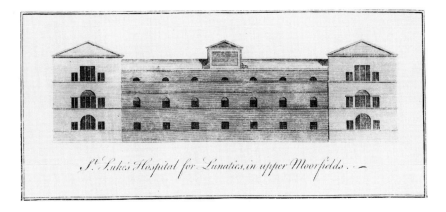

Fig. 3.1. George Dance I, old St. Luke's Hospital, London, engraved elevation.

A decade later Dublin held a similar one for a new Royal Exchange, and it attracted only a slightly smaller number.[5] Eight years after that it was St. Luke's turn to initiate a competition, the existence of which has escaped scholarly notice, although it is not for want of having been plainly advertised. Beginning in late April 1777, London newspapers carried the following announcement on the front page.[6]

St. Luke's Hospital for Lunaticks.

THE Committee for building St. Luke's Hospital being defirous to avail themfelves of the Ideas of various Artifts, in order to enable them to fix upon the beft Defign of an Hofpital for Lunaticks, fuch Perfons as may be inclinable to produce Drawings of their own Invention for that Purpofe may call at St. Luke's Hofpital, in Moorfields, where a Plan of the Ground is left, and where further Information may be had relative to the Number of Patients, any Day, except Mondays or Fridays. Each Defign is to confift of two Plans at leaft, a Section of the moft material Part, and an Elevation of the principal Front, the Whole to be drawn to a Scale of 14 Feet in an Inch. That Defign which fhall be moft approved by the Committee will entitle the Author thereof to 100l. and that which fhall be deemed to rank in the fecond Place in Point of Merit will entitle the Author to 50l. All the Reft of the Drawings will be returned to their refpective Authors, who are not to receive any Premium or Reward whatever. Each of the faid Defigns is to be delivered fealed up, and marked with fome diftinguifhing Character or Motto, to the Secretary, Mr. Webfter, in Queen-Street, Cheapfide, on or before the 31ft inft.

Like most competitions, the St. Luke's one used the popular press to lay down its rules and regulations. It specified the size, number, and scale of drawings. It provided for the anonymity of contestants by means of mottos. In the case of St. Luke's, a detailed architectural program was available for architects to consult; although lost, many of its major points can be deduced from surviving entries to the competition. Finally, alluring cash prizes were to be awarded to the winners of the first and second places. Most important of all, a final date for submission of drawings was set at the end of May, a mere five weeks away. There is strong evidence that news of the competition had leaked out before the official announcement.[7] But the time restriction still appears unrealistically short, even by eighteenth-century standards. Compared with the five months allowed the competitors for the Dublin Royal Exchange, the shorter space of time assigned for a structure at least as complex was a piece of insanity. Yet at least eight entries were received, despite the further fact that no written guarantee had been given that the winner's designs would be the ones executed. As it happens, the only additional documentary evidence concerns the unreasonable deadline; one poor candidate "with a French motto" missed it by three days.[8]

The guarantee of anonymity, along with the subcommittee's failure publicly to announce the winner and runner-up, helps to make the mystery of the St. Luke's competition singularly difficult to solve. Fortunately, the contemporary memoirs of the architect James Gandon make it clear that he took first prize. He mentioned winning the sum of £100—precisely the amount awarded by St. Luke's—and he variously described his designs as for "the new Bethlehem Hospital," or the "New Lunatic Asylum, London."[9] The drawings have disappeared, but they were intended for a plot of 540 feet by 350 feet, whch roughly corresponds to the Old Street site designated for St. Luke's. Gandon said he had devised the scheme in frequent consultation with the philanthropist John Howard, the greatest living authority on contemporary prison and asylum structures. The strain of having to prepare a design under such pressure of time brought Gandon to the point of a nervous breakdown. He recovered only to see all his efforts "handed over to another person, some man of mere lath and plaster."[10]

How did George Dance manage to walk away with the commission despite an arduous open competition? Demonstrably Dance had not won the prize. He probably never contemplated competing at all; in his official position as surveyor to St. Luke's it would have been improper for him to do so. But he *could* enter into a gentleman's agreement with the sub-committee. Their hands were in no way tied once they gave out the prize money. The best designs became their legal property to do with as they pleased. A similar sequence of events occurred in 1810 when James Lewis, the surveyor for Bethlehem Hospital, received instructions to amalgamate into a design of his own the best features of winning competition drawings.[11] In this instance Lewis benefited from the same iniquitous system under which he had suffered as an unsuccessful St. Luke's competitor.

Faced with a bewildering array of drawings, the St. Luke's sub-committee designated the work of each entrant by a number. One such set thus bears the number *2* inscribed in the top right-hand corner of each of the two sheets preserved (figs. 3.2, 3.3). Their versos have as an identifying symbol a star hexagon between laurel sprigs. Because of the fact that these drawings turned up among Dance's papers, they have never been doubted to be his work.[12] Now, however, in the light of our knowledge of an open competition that Dance could not have entered in good faith, the authorship of the drawings must be reassessed.

In overall massing, scheme 2 bears a remarkable similarity to St. Luke's sister mental institution, Bethlehem Hospital, commonly known as Bedlam (fig. 3.4).[13] The central and end pavilions of the St. Luke's scheme omit the outmoded seventeenth-century rooflines of Robert

Fig. 3.2. Anonymous, design for St. Luke's Hospital, London, elevation (SM, Dance Cabinet, Slider 4, Set 1, Item 3).

Fig. 3.3. Anonymous, design for St. Luke's Hospital, London, section (SM, Dance Cabinet, Slider 4, Set 1, Item 4).

Fig. 3.4. Robert Hooke, Bethlehem Hospital, London, engraving of the facade.

Hooke's Bedlam. But the long connecting wings that link the extremities with the middle are virtually identical. At St. Luke's the designer simply substituted an Italian vocabulary of articulation for the French one of Bedlam. A labored neo-Palladian language accounts for the appearance of rustication and Serlian windows, tightly squeezed into three-storey-high relieving arches. These differences of expression apart, the St. Luke's proposal is a thoroughly traditional one, well calculated to please a building subcommittee composed of conservative city fathers.

Who was responsible for scheme 2? Certainly it was not Dance. On grounds of style, the extreme derivativeness of the proposal, and the uncertain handling of motifs, such as the cluttered end pavilions, militate against connecting the work with Dance's distinguished oeuvre. Once having removed it from Dance, to whom, in turn, may it be assigned? The answer to this question is far from easy, given the secrecy that shrouds the entire St. Luke's competition. Perhaps the drawings are Gandon's, although the same weaknesses that removed the attribution from Dance should also argue against his accomplished younger colleague. Perhaps the nameless second-prize winner is the designer. Or it could be the work of another competitor altogether, who never claimed his drawings when invited to learn the results on 27 June 1777.[14] One way or another, the drawings could easily have passed into Dance's possession when the subcommittee handed over to him the job of building the new hospital.

In its own right, scheme 2 is not without interest in that it begins to reveal aspects of the architectural program laid down for the St. Luke's competition. The sectional drawings show another side of the hospital—that lurking behind the grandiose facade (fig. 3.3). To either side of the central administrative block, with its columnar stairhall, stretch long barren galleries giving access to the cells for the inmates. Doors off the gallery open into individual gloomy rooms, lighted by only one unglazed window set high up on the wall and barred on the outside for safety's sake. Some sunshine and air could filter downward, but, located where it was, the opening made escape impossible. Similar lunettes had been used before at old St. Luke's (fig. 3.1), and would become a distinctive feature of Dance's replacement. The window-type obviously formed part of the now-lost program for the new hospital and reflected St. Luke's relatively enlightened attitudes to mental illness. Significantly, St. Luke's in this respect later served as a model for the most advanced psychiatric institution of the century: William Tuke's Retreat, near York. Tuke's architect, John Bevans, studied St. Luke's in 1794, in preparation for designing the Retreat.[15] The St. Luke's lunette intrigued Bevans in particular. From it he developed the so-called moral treatment window-type whose name alludes to the advanced techniques practiced by Tuke. Just as at St. Luke's, the windows of the Retreat opened to view the heart and soul of the institution. Patients in the Retreat had the illusion of freedom—as opposed to the reality of "immoral" incarceration—because the iron bars that protected them from themselves imitated the normal glazing bars in a sash.

Among the hitherto unidentified drawings of William Newton, Soane's senior by a generation, is one (fig. 3.5) that can now be definitely connected with St. Luke's.[16] It bears the numeral *8* in the same place as on the previous proposal discussed. This means that at least eight entries were submitted, Newton's being the highest number discovered so far. His longitudinal section of the hospital, taken roughly in the middle of the complex, shows two open courtyards with galleries ranged around them. These galleries service the standard sort of cells, entered by a heavy door and lighted by the typical St. Luke's lunette. The courtyards function as exercise yards in keeping with the prevalent medical theories about mental illness. One of the most respected authorities of the day spoke out against the insane being "shut up in loathsome prisons as criminals."[17] He, moreover, had a direct connection with the treatment offered at St. Luke's, having been its first physician. The doctor, who rejoiced in the name of Battie, wrote his important *Treatise on Madness* in 1758, which put the diagnosis and treatment of the disease on a scientific

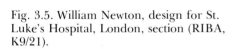

Fig. 3.5. William Newton, design for St. Luke's Hospital, London, section (RIBA, K9/21).

Fig. 3.6. James Lewis, design for St. Luke's Hospital, London, elevation, *Original Designs in Architecture.*

footing. Battie released the mad from their chains as Philippe Pinel was also to do later that century in France. Dr. Battie advocated what he called "management" in preference to the harsh repressive measures meted out by others. His prescription for dealing with madness consisted of cleanliness, dry air, a balanced diet, and recreation such as could be enjoyed in the controlled environment of courtyards like those provided by William Newton.

Prominently placed in the center of Newton's courtyards are single-storey structures combining the functions of privy, bath house, and heating plant. This was in line with Battie's pronouncements on cleanliness; remedial measures were also implied. Several years before Battie's book appeared in print, Dr. Charles Lucas had brought out his *Essay on Waters.* Lucas discussed, among other things, the beneficial effects of water on the various forms of madness. His common panacea for hypochondria, hysteria, and manic depressive states was "the judicious application of water" in the form of hot or cold baths.[18] The practice of hydrotherapy, as it is known, has a long history. Dunking, near-drowning, dousing by surprise, and simple cleansing, all came to be widely used, either as shock therapy or for relaxing catatonic seizures. Cold and hot baths existed at Bedlam and old St. Luke's, though Battie himself was ambivalent about hydrotherapy.[19] In comparison to his contemporary, Dr. John Monro of Bedlam, Battie made more subtle distinctions between kinds of insanity (original versus consequential madness), and the sorts of measures appropriate to administer in each instance. He is sometimes credited with a repudiation of the "concussive force of the cold bath," as he described it. Actually he did not rule out such violent physical methods; rather he urged caution in their application.[20] For this reason, baths continued to be a feature of treatment at St. Luke's and were included in the program for the new building, as can be seen in the work of Newton's rival competitors.

By the time of the St. Luke's competition, James Lewis, a slightly younger contemporary of John Soane's, was just establishing an architectural practice for himself in London. As already seen, he eventually specialized in hospital design. He made his unsuccessful debut in this branch of the profession at the St. Luke's competition. Although the proceedings had taken place in secret, he broadcast his involvement by publicly exhibiting his drawings "of an intended new hospital for lunatics to have been built in Old Street Road."[21] Still not satisfied, in 1796 he published engravings of the plans and elevation at the end of his book *Original Designs in Architecture* (fig. 3.6).[22] Like the facade of scheme 2 (fig. 3.2), Lewis's facade for St. Luke's relies on the same syntax of

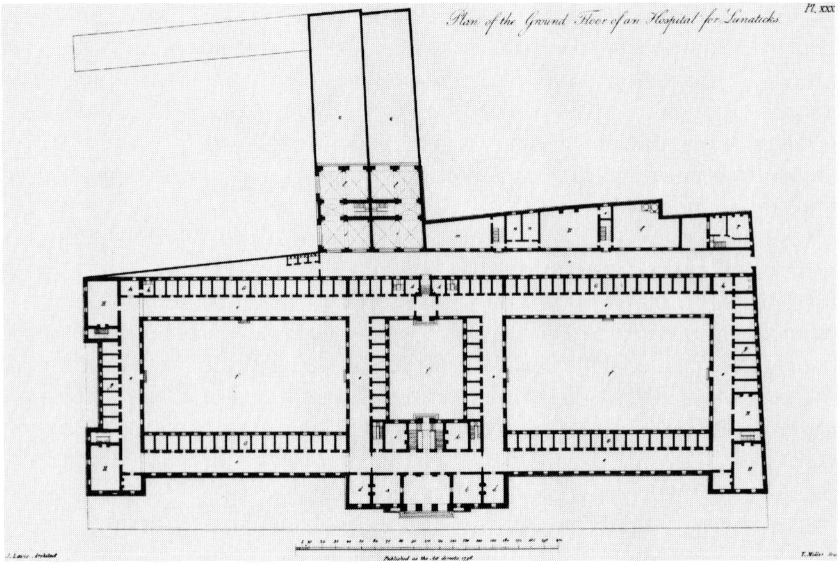

Fig. 3.7. James Lewis, design for St. Luke's Hospital, London, plan, *Original Designs in Architecture*.

choppy projections and recessions typical of English neo-Palladianism. A marked similarity also exists in the use of a central cupola which, together with the statues beside the entrance, returns to the common source of Bedlam (fig. 3.4). Only the broad Doric pediment indicates any willingness to experiment. In planning, too, he showed little imagination (fig. 3.7). He organized his structure around two conventional courtyards as William Newton had done. Lewis made the best of a lopsided plot, by locating his infirmary wing in the separate dogleg section that extended to the north. In this way the infirmary, another requirement of the St. Luke's program, stood apart in order to reduce the danger of communicable diseases. Lewis furthermore provided for servants' quarters in the attics, and baths in the basement, along with the coal and beer cellars.[23] So-called small beer was served as a daily beverage in the hospital, a liberal custom being reintroduced to the geriatric wards of the present day. Dr. Battie went so far as to recommend wine for inebriating patients in special cases.[24]

On grounds of completeness, none of the three entries discussed so far can compare with John Soane's. He preserved his drawings for St. Luke's in their entirety. More astonishing still, he produced not one but two separate sets. Reading the competition announcement with care, he determined that nothing precluded him from competing more than once. With a true gambler's instinct, he increased his chances by entering two competing proposals. The first, numbered *3* in the usual spot, carries the motto *Mihi turpe relinqui est*—that resounding Dance battlecry (figs. 3.8, 3.9 and see fig. 2.3). The second set, numbered *7*, has the motto: "To Your Decree I Bend" (figs. 3.10, 3.11).[25] Both accommodate roughly the same 250 occupants, with a slightly higher preponderance of females to males. Both also depart quite radically from the other schemes by placing the exercise yards at the front of the site instead of toward the rear. And both testify to Soane's enormous energy and courage in raising his own personal stakes so high.

In Soane's proposal 3, two wings curve outward from a central administration block to enclose wedge-shaped exercise yards strictly segregated from each other and from the pavement of Old Street.

Fig. 3.8. St. Luke's Hospital, London, first design, elevation and section (SM, Drawer 13, Set 1, Item 4).

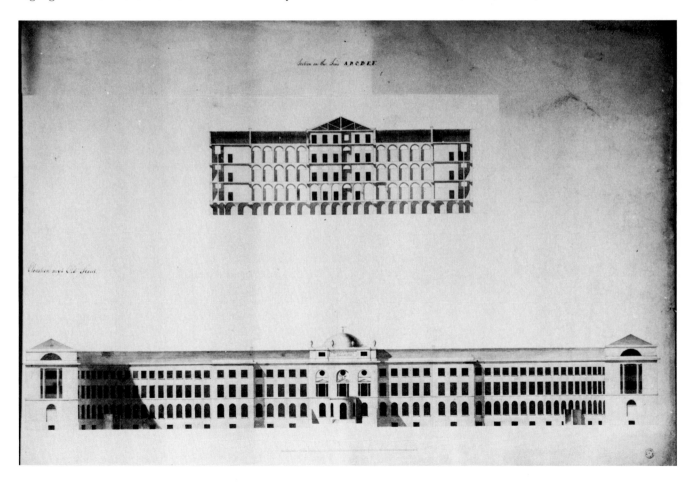

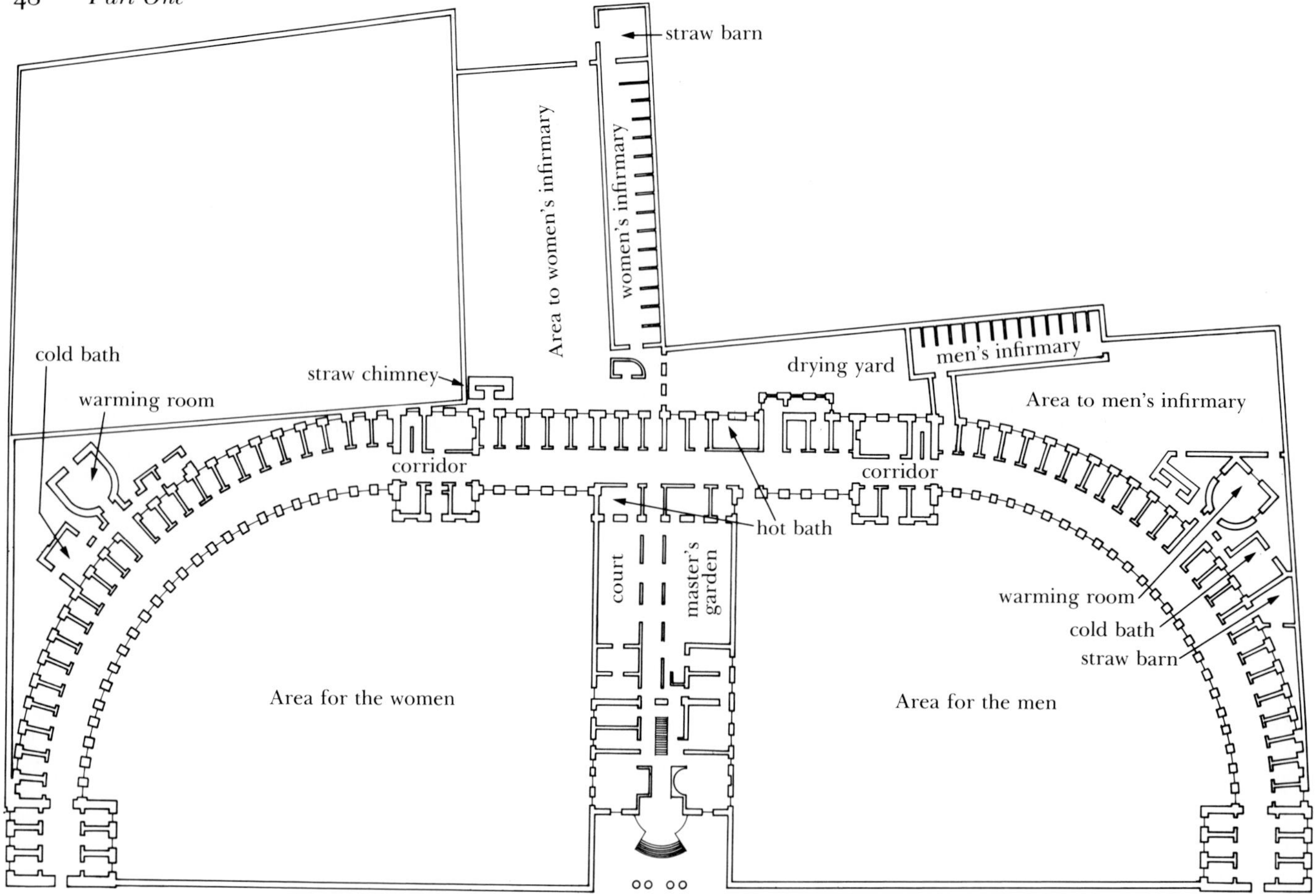

straw barn

women's infirmary

Area to women's infirmary

cold bath

warming room

straw chimney

men's infirmary

drying yard

Area to men's infirmary

corridor

hot bath

corridor

court

master's garden

warming room

cold bath

straw barn

Area for the women

Area for the men

Fig. 3.9. St. Luke's Hospital, London, first design, plan (after SM, Drawer 13, Set 1, Item 5).

Elaborate provisions on the plan make clear that males and females were separated at all times—a feature probably common to the other schemes. Two grilles, or barriers of iron, reinforced this separation, and also kept away outsiders. In the eighteenth century there was some question as to who most endangered whom: the raving maniac, or the idly curious member of the general public.

It is not clear whether metal grilles existed at old St. Luke's, but they certainly did at Bedlam as depicted in the artist William Hogarth's satirical portrayal of the madhouse scene from the *Rake's Progress*. Hogarth introduced the central figure of a lady of fashion who bribes her way inside the gates. Tittering to her maid, she amuses herself with observing the deranged behavior of the occupants. This crude voyeurism was so common at Bedlam that the St. Luke's rules of procedure forbade that patients be "exposed to public view." Dr. Battie also railed against the "impertinent curiosity" of those who took pleasure in ridiculing the mad.[26] The gates of Bedlam acted as the turnstile to a common peep show, whereas those designed by Soane for St. Luke's would have been a deterrent to the carnival atmosphere depicted by Hogarth. According to Enlightenment beliefs, even insane persons had a right to their self-respect. Perhaps the architect's humane sentiments were in part in-

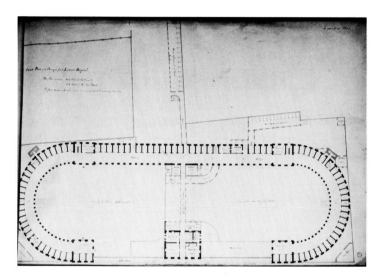

Fig. 3.10. St. Luke's Hospital, London, second design, plan (SM, Drawer 13, Set 1, Item 9).

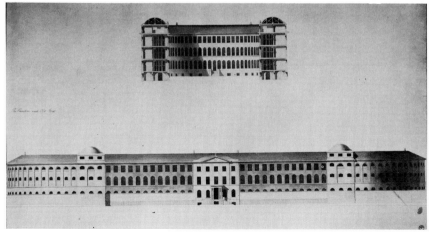

Fig. 3.11. St. Luke's Hospital, London, second design, elevation and section (SM, Drawer 13, Set 1, Item 7).

fluenced by those of the painter. One of Soane's first major art purchases was the entire set of pictures for Hogarth's *Rake's Progress.*[27]

Hogarth showed the cells of incontinent patients to be lined with straw that could be swept out and replaced daily. This practice from Bedlam and old St. Luke's accounts for Soane's inclusion of hay barns on his plan, as well as a furnace in which to burn the soiled sweepings. To avoid fire hazards, the furnace chimneys project out at the back of the cell wing. At this point, Soane hit on the happy expedient of locating the heated common rooms just adjacent to the smoke stack so the patients could enjoy a little warmth. It did not occur to him to take the logical step of also placing the hot baths nearby. He provided them at the opposite extremity of the complex, along with a plethora of other practical amenities: segregated infirmaries; communal privies; a director's suite; a matron's apartment; a physician's waiting room; an apothecary's shop; a drying yard for the linen, and so forth. Without being an inmate himself, how did the architect acquire so detailed a knowledge of a mental institution's inner workings? The study of St. Luke's competition gives a rare insight into methods eighteenth-century architects employed in gathering data for a project.

James Gandon, the winner of the St. Luke's competition, recounted that he had collected information by minutely investigating the old hospital. The traumatic experience led to horrible nightmares of the scenes he had witnessed.[28] Soane, by comparison with Gandon, carried out a more diversified search for potential prototypes. He must have been aware that, in the years immediately preceding the 1770s, London had experienced a virtual explosion in building hospitals.[29] To one degree or another they had a generic kinship to St. Luke's, though none was specifically psychiatric in nature. The most recent of them all, Middlesex Hospital, had only just been completed to the designs of James Paine the Elder, when it attracted Soane's attention as a possible model. Somehow Soane borrowed an original ground plan which he transferred by pin pricks to another sheet. In this mechanical way he obtained a personal copy of the layout. He then proceeded to fill in by hand the dimensions of certain rooms and the names of the functions assigned to them, such as the cold bath or the matron's linen closet.[30] These sorts of facilities had obvious relevance to St. Luke's. Soane simply modified the information from the Middlesex Hospital for inclusion in his scheme. In the process he amplified upon the common program he shared with the rest of the St. Luke's competitors: that is, the standard exercise yards, hydrotherapy baths, and escape-proof lunette windows (fig. 3.8 *top*). Soane surpassed the others in the profusion of his practical provisions.

Quite apart from his great attention to detail, he utilized a far more up-to-date stylistic treatment.

Soane substituted novel features for the traditional ones seen in the facades so far discussed. In place of the time-honored central cupola, a Roman Pantheon-style dome imparts a sleekness that carries over to the rest of the building. In place of neo-Palladian angularity, the curving walls introduce smooth transitions. In place of rustication patterns the end pavilions culminate in giant baseless Doric columns, revived here perhaps for the first time since Antiquity on a monumental scale.[31] Finally, in place of the conventional Serlians, Soane inserted the more fashionable version, called the Wyatt window.[32] Above the central one he placed a pair of reclining statues tearing at their long tresses of hair. Like James Lewis (fig. 3.6), Soane meant these figures to evoke the famous sculptures by Cibber that stood beside the gates to Bedlam for so many years (fig. 3.12). Two statues personifying Dementia and Melancholia provided a somber keynote to the entire function of the asylum.[33]

Soane's elevation number 3, replete with the latest motifs, would have appealed to knowledgeable connoisseurs, whereas his practical plan would have partially counteracted the impression of art at the expense of function. He may have entertained some qualms himself about whether he had placed his emphasis correctly. At any rate, he was motivated to undertake the almost superhuman task of preparing, within the short time allotted, a second entire set. This one, numbered 7, can be placed slightly later than the other in terms of relative chronology (fig. 3.11). Its draftsmanship shows signs of sloppiness, as if executed in a last-minute dash to make a deadline. Also, greater maturity is evident in the planning of the second submission. Its geometry is taut in comparison to the limpness of scheme 3. In the earlier scheme the galleries curve around the exercise yards flaccidly. As a result of further consideration, Soane endowed the enfolding arms of his later cell blocks with the recoil of a steel spring, like a giant lock about to snap shut—a not inappropriate imagery.

The apparent difference in the height of the two elevations (cf. figs. 3.8, 3.11) is purely a question of the vantage point of the drawings. Both asylums shared similar dimensions. The second one appears to be a storey lower because the vaulted basement is concealed by a screen wall running the entire length of the entrance facade. This hides from sight a certain amount of asymmetry at the back of the site, resulting from an honest acceptance of the site's limitations. Given the same dimensions, the second scheme would have been cheaper to build. In Soane's mind economy had replaced considerations of art. Archaeological references,

Fig. 3.12. Robert Hooke, Bethlehem Hospital, London, engraving of statues above the entrance gate.

Fig. 3.13. George Dance II, St. Luke's Hospital, London, aquatint showing the facade facing Old Street (Author's Collection).

Fig. 3.14. George Dance II or assistant, St. Luke's Hospital, London, penultimate elevation design (SM, Dance Cabinet, Slider 4, Set 1, Item 1).

Wyatt windows, and an expressive sculptural program all went by the board. Perhaps, in the interval between the first and second schemes, the architect had reread the stringent St. Luke's regulations concerning plainness in its buildings. A contemporary wit had specifically ridiculed Bedlam as a "costly . . . college for such a crack-brained society."[34] For all the relative simplicity, Soane's second scheme is not inelegant. The centerpiece, though stripped of ornament, retains prominence by projecting as far forward as the light-well on the street would permit. The element of repeated round-headed windows echoes nicely the curved plan. The effect works especially well where the back of the wings wrap around into full view, revealing the distinctive St. Luke's lunette, set within a multistorey arch. George Dance employed exactly this relieving arch motif when he came to build St. Luke's (fig. 3.13).

If, as seems likely, Dance drew upon the best ideas submitted to the St. Luke's competition in his composite design, that would explain how he came to rely on Soane's experiments. Notably, Dance seems to have been impressed with Soane's logic in placing exercise yards at the front, rather than in courtyards at the rear, as the majority of known contenders had done. An exception is the pair of similar unidentified elevations among Dance's drawings relating to St. Luke's (fig. 3.14).[35] The screen wall treatment and fenestration pattern recall closely the version Dance built and that proposed by Soane. The designs, neither of which is finished enough to have been a competition entry, must therefore be preliminary ones prepared for construction. But the ridiculous spiral topknot on the dome and the abundance of swags point to meddling by a lesser light in the Dance circle, possibly Peacock.[36] Dance assimilated useful features like the screen wall and multistorey arch into his final, much scaled-down proposals. St. Luke's, as built to a radically trimmed budget, looks a lot like the simpler of Soane's two designs, only flattened out. Because of budgetary restraints and almost in spite of his art, Dance arrived at a bleak, institutional appearance well suited to an asylum. An eminent physician is supposed to have remarked that St. Luke's "always excited unpleasing sensations in his mind; he often looked at it, but never without horror." To this John Soane added that a greater tribute could hardly have been paid to the evocative "powers of architecture."[37] At St. Luke's, Dance created a suitably depressing air, which is heightened by the mournful screech of the sea birds wheeling overhead (fig. 3.13).

It is not surprising that some of Soane's ideas should be reflected in the St. Luke's as built. In July 1781, Dance hired him for the preparation of the final estimates, and a few scattered references to St. Luke's occur in the Soane notebooks.[38] This was ostensibly Dance's way of helping to ease Soane's financial straits during a lean period in his early career. Surely the master also knew of his former pupil's involvement with the hospital competition. Was there possibly an element of collusion in the behavior of the two? Whatever the circumstances, Soane swallowed his pride and never revealed his drawings. His defeat at the St. Luke's competition remained, until now, one of his best-kept professional secrets. To see the prize go to Gandon but the commission go to Dance also taught Soane a lesson he never forgot. In a plea for "fair and open competition," he later commented upon the system of favoritism that tended to benefit established architects with good connections, rather than younger men in need of work.[39] Other contestants in Soane's predicament would probably have agreed that the hospital committee acted in a duplicitous manner when it took their ideas without compensation.

Notwithstanding the negative outcome from Soane's personal point of view, his unexecuted designs for St. Luke's deserve serious consideration. They hold up extremely well in comparison to those of his peers. Indeed, they rank so high qualitatively as to call for a reappraisal of his youthful work. His supposed derivativeness from Dance[40] is not borne out by the new evidence of the 1777 schemes for St. Luke's. To be sure, the *élan* of Dance's *magnifica galleria* (fig. 2.3) recurs in the sweeping lines of Soane's St. Luke's. And, as if in homage to his teacher, Soane also re-used the Parma competition motto. The dominant compositional theme of curvaceousness, however, allies less with Dance and more with the theory of "movement" expounded by the Adams and incorporated into house plans by Soane's current employer, Holland. By 1777, the young man had fully realized the potential impact of such curved forms; they reappear quite often in his contemporary academic designs, as we will see. At St. Luke's the curves function not as a compositional tool so much as an integral part of the whole. The repetition of curved elements in window frames or multistorey arches creates the feeling of an all-pervasive geometric principle controlling every aspect of the structure.

The practicality of Soane's plans for St. Luke's is as striking as its design logic. Soane's awareness of day-to-day human needs came from his experiences as assistant in the Dance and Holland offices. An indication of the mundane jobs he had to perform is a drawing pasted in a Soane album. Although not in his hand, it was mailed to him in care of Henry Holland's address. It shows the plumbing of a water closet, on which Soane had to pass judgment. Ironically, it was once connected with Soane's provisions for St. Luke's,[41] though, of course, flush toilets were unknown in eighteenth-century madhouses. But the kind of practical problems he had to face taught him how to handle complex structures with interrelating amenities.

Fame eluded Soane in the St. Luke's competition. This, as it turned out, was a blessing in disguise. Coincidentally both Soane and James Gandon, the winner, became eligible that same year to compete for a traveling scholarship to Rome, by virtue of being Royal Academy gold medallists. Gandon unwisely passed up his chance for the Rome prize in part because he hoped to build St. Luke's.[42] Soane no longer entertained any illusions on that score and therefore allowed his name to go forward. As the next chapter reveals, Soane easily won the scholarship which brought special, far more lasting advantages than any transitory ones the quickly forgotten St. Luke's competition might have conferred. Yet the case history of St. Luke's in its own right has a thread of genuine pathos running through it, entwined with grim humor, and hope for the future of mental health.

·4·

Soane at the Royal Academy

A GOOD WAY OF DESCRIBING the period from 1700 to 1800 would be to call it the Century of Academies. Over that hundred years, academies sprang up everywhere in Europe, increasing at the average rate of one per annum.[1] They may have varied in size, scope, and small details of organization, but to a remarkable extent they resembled one another. The basic similarity among them can be attributed to the influence of the academies of art founded by King Louis XIV. By the end of the seventeenth century they began to exert their prestige as models of the successful academic tradition established in the arts. In its simplest form, the academic philosophy proclaimed that art had reached the stage in its development where it could be rationally discussed and propounded. In place of the vagaries of personal inspiration, one *correct* style, based on a single set of principles, would prevail among all accepted academic artists. The whole system connoted an autocratic air of centralized control that suited the French monarchy. Perhaps this accounts for the fact that Great Britain was among the last of the major European powers to institute official academies of the arts. Once having accepted the requirements of academicism, it clung to them. The Royal Academy of Arts, London, founded in 1768, continues functioning to this day. Its archives and library preserve a complete record of its activities, and much that pertains to its student John Soane, who, for his part, retained visual documents which supplement the Academy's information. The two separate pieces, when fitted together, present a fascinatingly detailed mosaic of academic training as practiced in London during the last quarter of the eighteenth century. It is true that the development of the Academy is well enough known from existing literature to make an account of its early history superfluous.[2] It is also true that, by analogy to the workings of sister academies, the institutional organization of such bodies is fairly common knowledge. But Soane's schooling in London's Academy focuses attention on the less widely discussed teaching of ar-

We are very sure that the beauty of form . . . the art of composition, even the power of giving a general air of grandeur to a work, is at present very much under the dominion of rules.

Joshua Reynolds
Sixth Discourse on Art
10 December 1774

chitecture, as opposed to studio art. Besides, Soane's personal progress provides a remarkable perspective on academy life seen from the student viewpoint.

On 25 October 1771, at a Council meeting of the Royal Academy of Arts, nine new students gained admittance to the Academy Schools, including the eighteen-year-old John Soane.[3] At the time he began his sixty-six-year-long association with the Academy, enrollment might have been considered a daring step to take. Though it later became a pillar of artistic orthodoxy, at the outset the Academy had the reputation of a renegade institution. In order to avoid detection by such established groups as the Society of Artists, the Academy had been organized in great secrecy. After no small amount of behind-the-scenes manipulation, it unexpectedly burst upon the London art world on 10 December 1768, complete with a royal charter. The prestige of royal assent was the brain child of Joshua Reynolds, first president of the Academy, and William Chambers, its first treasurer and a confidant of George III. The two principal framers of the charter were themselves trained abroad, and they set out a threefold program for the Royal Academy, modelled on institutions on the Continent. First, they sought to establish a new artistic hierarchy through the formation of an elite of forty like-minded academicians, elected for life. Second, through the staging of annual exhibitions, they sought to maintain financial independence from the state, and improve the taste of the art-loving public.

Fig. 4.1. Old Somerset House, London, new gallery wing, elevation, 1770 (SM, Drawer 74, Set 2, Item 2).

(Opposite page)
Fig. 4.2. Old Somerset House, London, new gallery wing, sketch plan, 1780 (SM, Miscellaneous Sketches 1780–82, p. 3).

Fig. 4.3. Old Somerset House, London, new gallery wing, sections and details (SM, Miscellaneous Sketches 1780–82, p. 4).

And last, they sought to perpetuate their ideals by espousing a pedagogical role, based on the premise that art could be taught according to fixed rules. In all three of these ambitious goals the Academy soon succeeded beyond the most sanguine hopes of its founders. Students flocked to accept the free education provided. Ticket receipts from capacity crowds at the spring exhibitions insured the Academy could sustain itself. And the first body of academicians established the prestige of Academy membership by including eminent representatives from the arts of painting, sculpture, and architecture. Among them, George Dance was the last of the original signers of the Academy's constitution.[4] He became a lifelong supporter of the institution and probably influenced his disciple Soane to join the Schools as soon as he had sufficient preparation.

Before submitting to the Council a portfolio of drawings in order to gain entry into the Schools, Soane had probably been admitted on an early acceptance basis for some time. His case suggests the existence of a probationary period that is otherwise never stated as official Academy admissions policy.[5] Only such an explanation accounts for Soane's ability, a matter of five days after admittance, to enter a drawing from his portfolio into competition for a silver medal (fig. 4.1). The inscription on the drawing, dating it back to 1770, suggests that he had heard of the subject matter for 1771 through the grapevine before it was announced.[6] The choice for the silver medal was a natural one. It commemorated the Academy's true homecoming: in January 1771, Old Somerset House had been turned over to the Academy by its royal patron, George III. It remained the headquarters for many decades to come. Soane's masterful rendering of Old Somerset House singled out the architectural nucleus of the former palace, the famous late seventeenth-century gallery which everyone, including Soane, believed to be a work of Inigo Jones rather than John Webb. Here, within a recognized masterpiece, the Academy appropriately made its home.

Soane had an understandable attachment to Old Somerset House, one of the first monuments he had delineated, and the physical setting of so many of his student trials to follow. Nine years after the silver medal drawing, on the eve of the building's demolition, Soane made a nostalgic pilgrimage to the now empty rooms, once crowded with his schoolmates. He recorded for posterity the exact arrangement of the main rooms as it had been in his day (figs. 4.2, 4.3). His pen sketches agree with the description of a student in 1777 who wrote "There is one large room for the Plaster Academy; one for the Life . . . a large room in which lectures are given every Monday . . . and among many other apartments, there is a choice library."[7] During their first decade, the Schools had no less than

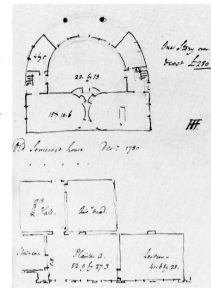

4.2

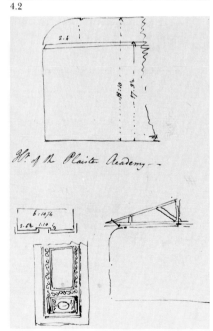

4.3

356 young men enrolled. Even taking into account a rapid rate of attrition, had all of them chosen to assemble there at any one time, the Somerset House quarters—their palatial aspect notwithstanding—would never have contained them. Young Soane, intimately aware of the cramped circumstances, proposed to abolish them. As a student exhibitor in 1776, he prepared an ideal plan for a new Academy building (fig. 4.4) at virtually the same point that William Chambers was being selected the actual designer of the new Somerset House, which opened its doors to students in May 1780.[8] This was not the last time that Soane's student

Fig. 4.4. Academy of arts design, plan (after SM, Drawer 45, Set 1, Item 17).

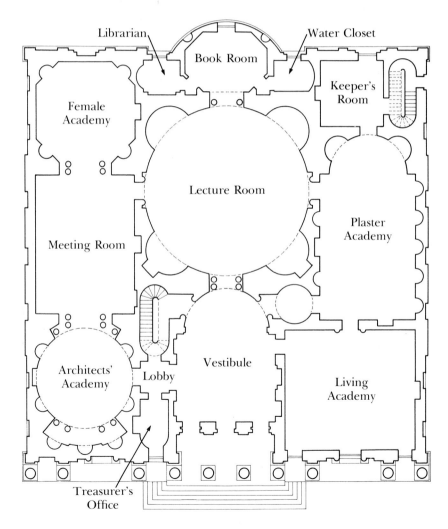

projects showed a prescient awareness of actual projects under discussion (see chap. 9). At the old Royal Academy, it seems, the walls had ears.

In Soane's Academy plan he displayed his ingenuity at creating and manipulating complex interiors. At the same time he demonstrated his acquaintance with the Academy's needs and shortcomings. The suite of three interconnecting rooms along the left-hand side could accommodate the annual exhibition during its six weeks' run, while the rest of the year it reverted to other uses. The most complex of the spaces Soane reserved for the student architects, who apparently had no proper working area in Old Somerset House. The unusual shape of this atelier, Soane must have imagined, would inspire the architects in their studies. He made ample provision for sculptors and painters too—a large studio area occupied each of the other three corners of the building. The lecture theater, no less vital in the Academy's teaching program, dominated the center with a span of 48 feet. When not in use for evening classes, it doubled as a reading room for the library beyond. The remaining space in the middle of the left-hand facade held the business meetings of the Council and the sessions of the General Assembly when it convened to judge students' work. Soane's plan, therefore, reads like the four-part syllabus of the Schools with its emphasis on the library, the lectures, the studio, and the juries of student work.

The Library

The training of architects presented a problem to academies in general because of the space requirements of architects' drafting tables.[9] Architects needed room to spread out in. Instead of drawing from the nude or a plaster cast in a studio, their place was out-of-doors, measuring a monument, on a building site, or in the stone cutter's yard. At an early meeting, the Council of the Royal Academy got around some of these difficulties by specifying a somewhat unusual curriculum for the architects. It was more flexible in that it took account of the student's need to avail himself of the facilities of an architect's office. As for the academic duties, it spelled out that "In regard to the Students in Architecture it is expected from them only that they attend the Library and Lectures more particularly those on Architecture and Perspective."[10] The student's daily office work would count in lieu of the studio hours put in by aspiring painters and sculptors. Of an evening—just as if he were enrolled in a night school—the young architect would work in the library or attend the lectures.

Reynolds, the Academy president, boasted as early as March 1769 that "we have already expended some hundred pounds in purchasing books relating to . . . Art." During a visit to Paris in 1774, his colleague, William Chambers, bought two further consignments of books, mainly architectural ones.[11] Some of the titles acquired then are known. A few special presentation copies are inscribed or were entered into the Academy's book of donations. All these and many more appear in Thomas Stothard's manuscript 1815 shelf list, and almost all of them can still be found in the Royal Academy library. When these statistics are evaluated in the light of the static acquisitions policy of the library between 1780 and 1815, the architectural holdings in Soane's time must have amounted to at least 170 volumes; the real total may have been as high as 200. Intact and still in use, the library is one of a number of such legacies handed down from eighteenth-century academies to the present.

Free from any obligation to buy, the architectural students of the Academy could draw inspiration from the rarest of treatises, could indulge in the most revolutionary theoretical works, and pore over the most lavish modern folios, even if only once a week.[12] In one and the same place they received an influx of foreign ideas to put to the test against the writings of the recognized masters, the publications of the English neo-Palladians, and archaeological accounts of travelers to ancient remains in Dalmatia or the Levant. All the bookish elements of a new synthesis were assembled in the library of Old Somerset House. It remained for young intellects avidly to put the pieces together as we know they did. One amusing anecdote relates the conversation between Richard Wilson, the second Academy librarian, and a hapless pair of students whom he caught copying from books:

> Wilson hobbling around the library table, and suddenly stopping said "What are you about, what are you doing? I am sketching, Sir. Sketching! take your hand off the book, boy. And what are you about," he said addressing another youth. "Drawing from this print. Drawing! Don't paw the leaves, sirrah! You'll spoil the book!"[13]

Wilson's familiar form of curatorial intimidation earned him the students' nickname of "Old Cerberus." With his vigilance he unknowingly impeded the expressed purpose of the library. The Royal Academy operated on a principle of selective eclecticism. The books, especially the illustrated ones, were meant to be plundered for ideas, as a means of formulating and improving taste. On several occasions, Soane's student career gives proof of the more or less successfully disguised acts of plagiary he was encouraged to carry out.

Soane did not need to enter the Academy Schools to become addicted to the printed page. His love of books is one of his earliest known and most persistent traits. In 1837, the year of his death, he left a personal library of some eight thousand volumes, divided almost equally between art books and general literature.[14] This inveterate collector became a bibliophile at a tender age, as numerous inscribed volumes attest. As might be expected, most of Soane's earliest surviving books—in all about a dozen octavos—deal with applied mathematics so necessary in the building trade his family practiced. For example, John Robertson's *A Complete Treatise of Mensuration* first belonged to Soane's brother, William, before being handed down in 1765. John Everard's *Stereometry* passed to Soane in 1767, John Ward's *Young Mathematicians Guide* came in 1769, and so forth.[15] In his copy of Seller's *Practical Navigation*, Soane used a blank fly leaf to practice penmanship. The tail of the second *J* down the page he turned into a comic face, and after 1783 he went back carefully to add the final *e* to his name. The precise dating of such volumes, their self-conscious updating and meticulous preservation, convey—across the centuries—a feeling that young Soane had an uncanny sixth sense for history, and deliberately made tracks that future biographers could follow.

Soane bought widely in the areas of general fiction, poetry, drama, and travel literature.[16] By comparison his architectural purchases were slow to start. The oldest inscription dates only from 1771 (fig. 4.5). The historically important inscribed copy of Fréart's *Parallel* is perhaps the only signed book to have gotten outside Soane's library. After a nine-year gap, Soane inaugurated his career as serious collector of architectural books with a purchase of Marie-Joseph Peyre's *Oeuvres d'architecture*.[17] This did not mean that Soane never consulted architectural sources during the formative decade of the 1770s. As will be seen, Soane was already well acquainted with Peyre's book when he finally bought it. But such architectural texts were even then quite expensive, and beyond the grasp of an architect until he entered practice. Soane's copy of Ward's mathematics primer cost only two shillings in 1769, whereas two years later he spent almost nine times as much on the *Parallel*, though both were already second-hand at the time of purchase.

Instead of buying expensive architectural books, Soane transcribed from copies available to him. His manuscript notebook entitled "Extracts from various Authors on Architecture J. Soane abt. 1776" runs to fifty pages of quotations or paraphrases taken from the sources he most admired: Robert Morris's *Lectures on Architecture,* William Chambers's *Treatise on Civil Architecture,* Stephen Riou's *Grecian Orders of Architecture,* and finally the first volume of Stuart and Revett's *Antiquities of Athens.*[18] Of the notes, those from Morris look the oldest on the basis of hand-

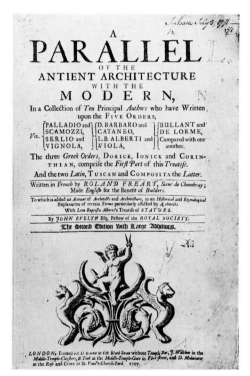

Fig. 4.5. Title page of Soane's inscribed copy of Roland Fréart de Chambray's *Parallel of the Ancient Architecture with the Modern* (RIBA, Library).

writing, those from Chambers are the most copious. None of them, however, reveal Soane as a budding architectural thinker. He skipped over Chambers's refutation of Abbé Marc-Antoine Laugier's controversial theories. Riou's dramatic acceptance of the baselessness of Greek Doric columns drew no comment from Soane. Neither Stuart and Revett's influential plates and text, nor Morris's far-reaching statements about a rationalized role for ornament, seem to have interested him. Soane restricted himself almost entirely to neat rules or facile prescriptions for the most mundane aspects of planning, proportions, and the orders. These notes mirror his taste in general literature too. In other notebooks he illustrated, by his selection of examples, that he preferred pat statements and well-turned aphorisms from as catholic a selection of writers as Shakespeare and Pope Clement XIV (Ganganelli).[19] Soane wanted to lean on accepted precedents in architecture, just as he sought maxims for polite behavior and conversation in society. Though he has often been characterized as a revolutionary figure, his notes prove that he was not so at the outset. In his youth he had no patience for the fine points of theoretical dispute. What seem to us the most prophetic utterances of his favorite authors interested Soane not in the slightest.

The question of where Soane could have studied expensive architectural books poses no problem in the light of Royal Academy bylaws governing regular attendance at the library. In Soane's day, copies of all the books he transcribed from, except Riou, stood on the shelves at Old Somerset House. Other indications also link his notebook entries to the Academy milieu. Soane quoted at least once from the lectures of Thomas Sandby.[20] Perhaps, then, the books that he copied from formed a sort of required reading list for Professor Sandby's course.

The Lecture Room

The Royal Academy regulations regarding architects stipulated student attendance at Samuel Wale's lectures on perspective and those on architecture by Professor Sandby (fig. 4.6). Accordingly, Thomas Sandby set to work writing his six annual lectures in time for the first year's crop of students in the Schools. Two lectures reached near-completion in the autumn of 1769 in order to be commented on by Sandby's more eminent architectural colleague, William Chambers. The Council exerted the ultimate right to censor the texts of lectures, but Sandby's passed muster.[21] Then Sandby suddenly became too ill to continue. It is unlikely that he ever delivered his lectures in person that academic year. Instead, he deputized Chambers to stand in for him. This

Fig. 4.6. Pencil portrait of Thomas Sandby, by George Dance II, 1794 (RA).

would explain the existence of manuscript lectures by Chambers, which were put aside once Sandby took up his regular duties on 8 October 1770.[22] From then onward Sandby repeated his course of lectures year after year until his death in 1798. The bound copy of these lectures, garnished with small addenda and snatches of doggerel verse, seems to confirm what is so often found in classroom practice—the texts remained impervious to major change or improvement over the entire quarter century in which they were delivered. The Academy never made clear whether the student needed to repeat the same lecture course annually. This would have been a tedious business to sit through for all but the newcomers. Sandby tended to drone on without much new material to maintain interest. He took too much to heart the threat of possible censorship. He entirely avoided comment, let alone criticism, of the current architectural scene, out of deference to living or even recently deceased artists. With no topical grist for his mill, Sandby offered his audiences pretty bland fare; neither was he much of an original thinker. Yet, for all its faults, Sandby's course provided his students with the closest thing they ever got to a university education.

Taken as a whole, the Sandby lectures repeatedly embody two distinct and apparently quite contradictory schools of thought: the romantic and the rational. That the two coexisted at all is a reflection on the inconsistency of many an eighteenth-century academic artist like Sandby. Probably the romantic, illogical persuasion more faithfully reflected Sandby's own emotional outlook, as when he exhorted the students by saying:

> As the beauty and perfection of Architecture consists, principally in the great and magnificent, joined with symmetry and proportion; it is above all things necessary that the young Student . . . should as early as possible in life, habituate himself to the study of the sublime and beautiful . . . of the stupendous works of nature.[23]

Surely this was Sandby speaking directly from personal experience as a gifted nature painter and landscape garden designer. Nature for him acted as "the great assistant and guide to Art."[24] The concept was not as simple as it seemed at first. Nature had various connotations for Sandby, one of which he evoked when he spoke of the "sublime . . . stupendous works of nature."

At several points in his lectures, Sandby obliquely acknowledged his debt to a friend of the Royal Academy, the politician and philosopher Edmund Burke.[25] Sandby's use of such terms as "sublime," "stupendous," and "magnificent," derived directly from Burke's potent aesthetic subjectivism, as contained in his *Philosophical Enquiry into the Origins of Our Ideas of the Sublime and Beautiful.* The key to art's successful imitation of nature's awe-inspiring effects lay, for Sandby as for Burke, in translating the sublimity of Nature into "magnificence." Sandby's concept of "magnificence"—synonymous with Burke's idea of "grandeur"—meant, primarily, greatness of size. And Burke's frequent recourse to architectural analogies indicated the special applicability of his ideas to the three-dimensional art of architecture. What exactly Sandby had in mind is illustrated by his original architectural design, which he called the bridge of magnificence. He intended it as the *pièce de resistance* of his sixth and last lecture. It must have stirred his students as nothing else throughout the entire dreary course. Soane himself could recollect from his student days the "powerful impression the sight of that beautiful work produced on myself and on many of the young artists of those days."[26] On the end facade of Sandby's bridge (fig. 4.7) the sheer size, coupled with dramatic effects of light and shade, was intended to overpower the viewer. The central arch alone was 50 feet high, so Sandby informed his audiences. On the side facade, supposed to stretch 1,153 feet, Sandby exploited the shock effect of unfolding a drawing which in itself extended more than half the width of the lecture room at Old Somerset House. Around such superhuman size there hung an aura of

Fig. 4.7. Thomas Sandby, bridge of magnificence design, elevation of the end facade (J. P. Spang Collection).

the mysterious and unbelievable, which led to that *frisson* of "terror" seen by Burke as the prime source of sublime sentiments.[27]

In the subconscious mind of John Soane, Sandby's insistence upon the austere power and majesty of nature struck a responsive, pantheistic chord. Only very occasionally did Soane's nature worship burst forth from beneath the surface, but when this happened the architect had clearly been moved to heights of emotion. It occurred once when Soane committed to paper a rapt account of the Alps, through whose abysses he traveled on his return from Italy to England. Almost literally echoing one of his favorite authors, Jean-Jacques Rousseau, Soane expressed himself spellbound by the scale of mountain chasms or roaring torrents. Another time, in late January 1784, while en route to Burnham, Norfolk, Soane resorted to Burkean terminology to describe a "terrible" blizzard he had to pass through.[28] He thus revealed the literary sources that helped condition his emotional sensibility.

Dramatic, at times violent, acts of nature only partly account for the meaning the term "nature" had for Sandby. The dark, unknowable side of nature had an altogether more rational, benign aspect to which Sandby also appealed in his lectures. This unemotional doctrine held that nature provided the measured and reasonable model which all art should follow. The professor evoked the image of the trees of the forest primeval that had supposedly inspired the orders. Architecture, therefore, had its very roots in nature. If reason could prevail over capricious taste, then everything would revert to the primitive, divine logic embodied in what Sandby called "natural principles."[29] Among these principles, one decreed that a work of architecture should logically appear to tell exactly the function it served. On this point Sandby developed the doctrine of "character," a topic of somewhat more substance than most for the listeners to his lectures. As Sandby himself defined it: "every building ought to have a character, or expression, united to its destination . . . . we cannot call the application of trite or frivolous ornaments the expressive signs of purpose and destination."[30] The eminently reasonable notion of "character," expressed in this simple way, reached an impressionable student audience, probably eager, like Soane, for easy recipes to follow in order to succeed.

The doctrine of "character" was by no means an original invention of Sandby's. In the 1750s Abbé Laugier had written "qu'un édifice . . . convient à sa destination; c'est à dire que la décoration des bâtiments ne doit pas être arbitraire."[31] A copy of Laugier's *Essai* was in the Academy library, and in any case William Chambers knew it well at the time he advised Sandby on his lectures. In fact, when called upon to substitute at short notice, Chambers had made the same point as Sandby but with more verve. "Character," Chambers stated, "is an Essential Quality of Beauty and Grandeur the bulk and dignity of a Matron would be disgusting in a Virgin of fifteen . . . . in like manner the Gloom and Solemnity of a temple . . . would ill suit a Banqueting room." Moreover, Chambers could draw on the lectures he had attended as a pupil at the Parisian Ecole des arts, run by the famous pedagogue Jacques-François Blondel.[32] Blondel can take credit for turning the hints of Laugier and earlier writers like Germain Boffrand into a sort of science. In the published form of his lectures, Blondel professed to be able to earmark every single building type with its suitable nuance of architectural expression. Through the principle of *caractère* he sought completely to rationalize the hitherto whimsical domain of ornament, so that buildings would speak their usage, and become a true *architecture parlante*.[33]

Parallel to this French, academically oriented tradition, there existed one more homespun and native born. The earliest exponent seems to have been Robert Morris. Morris's *Lectures,* purportedly delivered to students in the 1730s, constituted an important English precedent for Sandby. We also know that Soane studied Morris carefully, although he failed to take note of the author's crucial statement, "ornaments certainly give a noble contrast to a design, where they are appropriate to the purpose of the building." Morris may have been recommended to Soane by Peacock, whose autographed copy of the *Lectures* eventually passed into Soane's hands. Peacock himself, in some of his later writings, borrowed heavily from Morris, among other things the concept of "characteristic beauty." Ideas similar to Morris's began to be voiced in the anonymous *Critical Observations on the Buildings and Improvements of London* (1771). Four years earlier the notion had been expressed in the writings of John Gwynn, which Soane probably knew, as will be seen shortly.[34] One further printed source, exactly contemporary with Sandby's oral pronouncements in the Academy, completes this brief survey of the use of "character." In 1770 Thomas Whately published his *Observations on Modern Gardening,* and Soane purchased a copy in 1778. Whately devoted an entire chapter to "character" with respect to gardens. This notion, which had such specific connotations in the context of narrative architecture, became somewhat watered down by Whately. It took on more the aspect of what might be called "mood" or "atmosphere." Still, Whately's influential text demonstrates the extent to which "character" had become an acceptable term in general parlance.[35] Soane may not have been quick to pick up theory at this or at any stage, but here was one design concept it would have been hard to miss.

Fig. 4.8. Academy of arts design, elevation (SM, AL, Cupboard 22, Folio 1, Item 31).

The lessons in characteristic decoration were not lost on Soane. In his ideal Academy design of 1776, the same sort of rather trite symbolic sculptures as used by Sandby reappear in figures of the sister arts on the main facade pediment (fig. 4.8). Such appropriate deities as Venus and Apollo adorn the niches. There is nothing extraordinary about this iconographic program, nor about the fashionable chaste ornateness of the elevation as a whole. Nevertheless, the Academy design takes on meaning when seen against the background of Sandby's lectures, and Soane's obsession with "character" from this date onward. Many years later, Soane found himself in the chair of Professor of Architecture at the Academy. To his audiences he reiterated Sandby's words when he said "character is so important that all its most delicate and refined modifications must be well understood and practiced."[36] Sandby's lectures—which Soane had had copied in their entirety—made a deep impression. Their insistence that art embody the splendid phenomena of brute nature, awakened romantic murmurings in an often suppressed side of Soane's personality. At the same time, the doctrine of "character," typical of such rationalizations of the Age of Reason, caused him mentally to compartmentalize architecture into its different classes of buildings and the expressions compatible with them.[37] The dialectic between rational and romantic attitudes became reflected in much that was produced by Sandby's students, both outside the Academy and while they still worked within its studios.

Life in the Studios

The student painters and sculptors of the Academy spent most of their time drawing from live models or plaster casts, and designing

Fig. 4.9. Edward Francis Burney, Plaster Academy, Old Somerset House, London, 1779 (RA).

original work for the exhibitions or prize competitions. The royal charter laid down rules for the organization of these classes. A full-time instructor, the Keeper, looked after the day-to-day running of the studios. Nine other academicians, called Visitors, volunteered to take turns dropping in during the sessions in order to criticize the students' work. A charming student watercolor of the plaster cast room at Old Somerset House (fig. 4.9) portrays the tutorial system in operation. The young men have positioned themselves on hard boxes around the cluttered room and are busy sketching. Looking over the shoulder of one of them and pointing to his drawing board is the Keeper of the period, George Michael Moser. As has been remarked, the architectural students had a less clear-cut timetable based upon hours spent in the studio. Nevertheless, the aspiring architects profited from the element of camaraderie in the close quarters of Old Somerset House. The academicians foresaw fraternization as a fruitful source of inspiration among the students rubbing elbows with one another daily. But the founders of the Academy were powerless to legislate such a thing as school spirit. It emerged of its own accord as a result of the physical disadvantages the Schools struggled against, and the infectious enthusiasm often associated with a new institution. The students' contribution to the mainstream of Academy life rarely gets a mention in the official records. Were it not for John Soane, this whole side of student affairs might have remained almost unknown.

Fig. 4.10. Portrait of John Soane, by Christopher William Hunneman, ca. 1776 (SM, New Picture Room).

Chief among the benefits to be derived from the Schools was companionship among young artists. Friendships established by Soane included those with at least six of his contemporaries that we know of: Richard Holland, John Hobcraft, Edward Foxhall, Robert Furze Brettingham, John Matthews, and Christopher William Hunneman.[38] All but the last were training to be architects like Soane. Hunneman became a miniaturist of some repute, but while at the Royal Academy he executed one work on a larger scale, an oil portrait (fig. 4.10) of his friend Soane, said to have been painted in 1776.[39] Compared with earlier representations (see figs. 1.4, 2.2) this one seems more earnest. The architect's face looks leaner and perhaps a bit careworn from the intensely competitive period of his life at the Schools. The pressure had differing results depending on the mettle of the individual student. Young Holland (cousin of Soane's employer Henry), along with Hobcraft and Foxhall, all opted for the building trades instead of architecture. In their various capacities these friends aided Soane when he set up professional practice. Robert Furze Brettingham, although he accompanied Soane to Rome, never made much of the Brettingham name that he had adopted from his cousins, the distinguished Norfolk architects. He retired early in comfortable circumstances. As for John Matthews, his pathetic fate may have been typical of the disappointments that led many promising young artists inexplicably to drop from sight. Soane

Fig. 4.11. James King mausoleum design, elevation (SM, AL, Cupboard 22, Folio 1, Item 33).

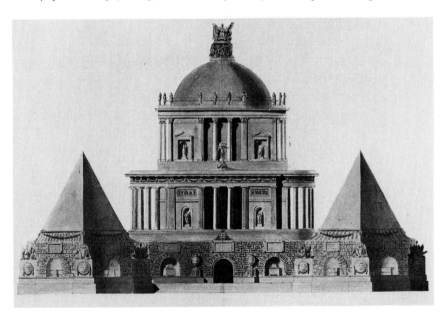

recalled that Matthews had prepared villa designs for the Academy gold medal competition of 1771 but did not win. As a result "This ingenious and indefatigable artist . . . neglected his studies and passion for architecture, became dissolute and sottish, and finally ended his days in prison!"[40] Soane was in a position to sympathize. His own drawing for the silver medal in that year (fig. 4.1) had been submitted a day late and had been disqualified on account of this technicality.[41] But Soane's reaction to this humiliation differed obviously from that of the despondent Matthews. Of all his comrades, only Soane continued to strive for excellence and recognition in his field.

One of Soane's student projects commemorates especially well his years of artistic collaboration and friendship within the studios of the Academy. It is the James King mausoleum, named after one of Soane's young companions who drowned in a boating accident on 9 June 1776. The following year, for the Academy exhibition, Soane produced his mausoleum design of which a later copy exists (fig. 4.11) characterized by the concept of magnificence that had been drummed into him during the Sandby lectures. Other influences are also present in the James King mausoleum.[42] Apart from its eclecticism, however, there is another aspect of Soane's student milieu which this design reflects best. Some of its overblown characteristics gave rise to a sketch by Soane's schoolmate John Flaxman (fig. 4.12). Flaxman facetiously entitled it "For the Exhibition of 1777, A Mausoleum adorn'd with Colossal Sculpture being an attempt at something in a new Style." The dismembered heads and gesticulating hands that project from every surface, parody the idea of *architecture parlante* currently in vogue within the Academy. A naked statue atop the roof irreverently displaying his mammoth posterior overawes the tiny antlike onlookers and makes sport of the tendency to phantasmagoric hugeness. Flaxman spoofed good-naturedly the grandiloquent James King mausoleum that Soane submitted to the real exhibition of 1777. A direct connection between the two drawings—the one in earnest, the other in fun—is suggested by similar Flaxman sketches still pasted on the leaves of a Soane scrapbook album.[43] Moreover, on the verso of Flaxman's sheet of paper is another mausoleum, close in composition to Soane's Moorish dairy (fig. 5.11). Flaxman called his design a "Mausoleum for Ching Chang Chow, Emperor of China." And insofar as phonetic differences between Ching and King are slight, the point made is clear. Flaxman's caricatures cautioned Soane to refrain from grotesque excesses.

The Flaxman sketches tell much about the leavening ingredient of humor among the students in the Schools. Apart from their outlandish

Fig. 4.12. John Flaxman, mausoleum design, 1777 (V&A, 3436.110 recto).

aspect, Flaxman's pencil drawings do contain a serious element. With insight he grasped the ludicrous lengths to which people were willing to go in pursuit of the novelty which he stigmatized as the "new style." After all, the Academicians had hand-picked the ablest talents to inherit their artistic legacy. Tended together in the hothouse atmosphere of Old Somerset House, the students were encouraged to cross-pollinate one another's imaginations. Sometimes the hybrid products got out of control in their search for a place in the sun.

The Prize Competitions

Short of expulsion for misconduct, the Royal Academy failed to set any limit to the length of time a student might remain in the Schools; nor did it specify the rate or even the stages at which advancement should take place. In practice, though, the awarding of Academy prizes provided the necessary hierarchical framework and impetus for students to excel. In this form of artistic olympiad, the first heat took the form of a silver medal awarded for each of the three arts in a competition open to all beginners. Winners of this round could then qualify for the biennial gold medals given, one each, for painting, sculpture, and architecture. The gold medal formed the Academy's equivalent of a diploma with honors; it marked graduation from the Schools. As competition became increasingly fierce there would inevitably be some nonwinners—like Soane's unfortunate friend Matthews—who would simply have to drop out. In this regard Soane's rise in the Schools was nothing short of meteoric.

After his initial failure to win a silver medal in 1771, Soane reacted with vigor when another chance offered itself the next year. The Council announced its call for the best measured drawings of "the Front of the Banqueting House facing the Horse Guards."[44] At his second attempt Soane made sure to meet the early November deadline. On the first of the next month, in accordance with normal Academy practice, the academicians gathered in general assembly to vote on the anonymous entries identified with a letter of the alphabet pasted on each one. As only a pair of candidates had presented themselves for the two silver medals in architecture, they won uncontestedly. Nine days later, on the anniversary of the Academy's foundation, the minutes recorded that the prizes were "adjudged to the Letters Q and R.... The President was then informed by the Keeper, that...the Drawing in Architecture Marked Q was the work of John Rudd and R of John Soan."[45]

Joshua Reynolds, the distinguished president of the Royal Academy, reserved for himself the right to distribute medals personally on Foundation Day and to read one of his famous discourses prepared for the occasion. In the discourse of 1772 he concluded with a warning to the students against a sense of false pride that might infect a young institution in the first flush of popular acclaim and attention.[46] His remarks applied indirectly to Soane, who had just cockily walked off with an easy silver medal victory. It is true, however, that Soane and Rudd had earned their award by the enormous amount of hard work that had gone into measuring such a London landmark as Inigo Jones's 1622 Banqueting House. Rudd's working copy, covered with measurements,[47] shows that he and Soane had clambered all over the facade facing Whitehall. Soane's presentation version (fig. 4.13) is in every respect as detailed, but omits most of the dimensions in favor of an atmospheric rendering. The lines have been carefully inked in over pencil, watercolor wash has been brushed on to give the three-dimensional effect of cast shadows, and in a final flourish swirling copperplate penmanship takes the place of cumulus clouds in the sky. The point of this long-drawn-out exercise was to familiarize students with every inch of a famous monument in order for them to discover the secrets of good design. According to the academic theory, first perfected by Jacques-François Blondel in Paris, approved examples of architecture like Jones's Banqueting House

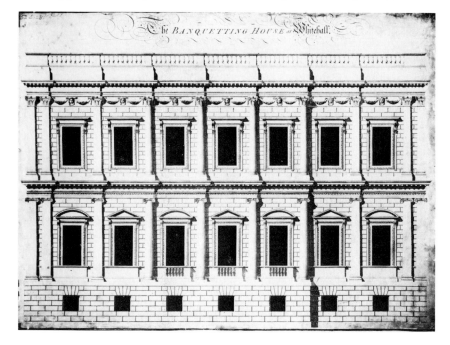

Fig. 4.13. Banqueting House, Whitehall Palace, London, elevation (SM, Drawer 74, Set 2, Item 1).

would help form the student's taste. Such a supreme test of manual dexterity and perseverance as the silver medal represented was not to be confused with the more taxing demands of the gold medal. Soane rose to the new challenge, but no more is heard of Rudd!

The year 1774 marked the time for the next in the biennial gold medal competitions. As no candidates had presented themselves for the previous contest in 1772, the same trial subject of a nobleman's town-house was again assigned.[48] On this occasion, moreover, there was an added incentive for the students to compete. On 21 March 1774, Reynolds informed the Council that the Society of Dilettanti had offered two scholarships to Italy or Greece. It was decided that, after the gold medals had been awarded, the nominees for scholarships would be picked from the three gold medalists.[49] Naturally, candidates turned up in full force, among them Soane. He was not about to pass up the offer of free education abroad that would have fulfilled the dreams he had nurtured since his days in Dance's office.

Unlike the straightforward silver medal competition, more elaborate rules pertained to the gold medal contest. An original design prepared in agreement with a set subject or program was just one of two steps. The bylaws of the Academy further stipulated:

> The candidates for the premium of the gold medals, are to attend upon the fifteenth day of November, in the Royal Academy, in order to give a proof of their abilities, by making a sketch of a given subject in the presence of the Keeper. The subjects for the sketches to be determined by the President and Council . . . shall be sealed up, and drawn for by the senior student, on the morning of the trial. The time allowed for making these sketches to be five hours.[50]

This passage describes the procedure of the time-restricted sketch, *prova,* or *esquisse,* dreaded by eighteenth-century architectural students in European academies. Not only did the victims have a mere five hours to invent and draw a design "from scratch," but, worse still, they had no prior idea of what the required subject might be.

On the appointed day at Old Somerset House, the lot drawn for the 1774 *esquisse* fell to a temple of Mars. Soane's design of it still bears the identifying letter *N* pasted on a corner to differentiate it from others' work (fig. 4.14). For five hours' frantic effort Soane's temple is not bad, even though it derives almost entirely from William Chambers's Temple of Bellona in the grounds of Kew Palace.[51] The young student borrowed from Kew the dome, portico, manly Doric order, and trophies of arms in the metopes, appropriate to a god of war. Soane's temple facade differs

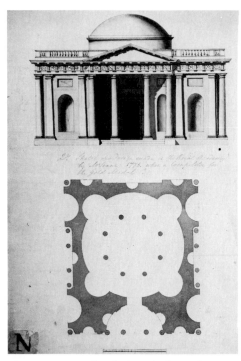

Fig. 4.14. Temple of Mars design, plan and elevation (SM, AL, Cupboard 22, Folio 4, Item 103).

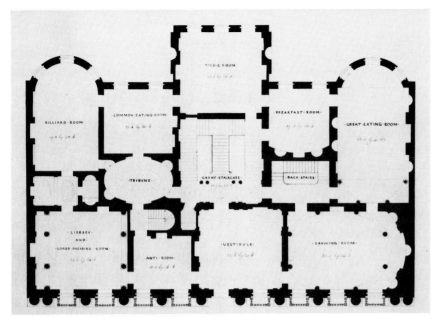

Fig. 4.15. Nobleman's townhouse design, plan (SM, Drawer 45, Set 1, Item 28).

mainly in greater width and a complicated plan inspired by antique mausolea. This deftly executed sleight of hand was the more ingenious because it flattered Chambers, who, Soane knew perfectly well, would sit on the jury when it convened on 1 December to judge the *esquisses* and the townhouse designs accompanying them.

On 10 December 1774, the gold medal contestants and their fellow students gathered in the lecture room to learn the decision of the academicians. The President opened the sealed ballots, ending an agonizing nine days of uncertainty for the contestants. With tension mounting, he announced that the gold medal in architecture had been won by the designs marked with the letter *M*. The author, Chambers's apprentice Thomas Whetten, stepped forward to accept a resounding victory of ten out of seventeen votes. The anonymous competitor *L* had received five votes, and Soane had come in a miserable third. His stratagem of pleasing the jury had gone awry.

The reason for Soane's defeat is clear from the plans he submitted for the townhouse. One of them, that for the main floor (fig. 4.15), shows that, still seeking to curry favor with the judges, Soane had copied the outline of Chambers's bow windowed garden facade at Melbourne House, Piccadilly.[52] On top of that he had tried to cram the interior with every imaginable complex room shape. As at the Claremont entrance

Fig. 4.16. Anonymous, townhouse design, elevation (RIBA, E3/2¹).

hall (see fig. 2.6), the apartment in the bottom right corner has an oval ring of columns. From the repertory of Henry Holland, Soane borrowed the feature of a top-lighted tribune. Even the adjacent double apsidal water closet is a spatial gem. Soane had been misguided by his exuberant overenthusiasm. His townhouse verged unpardonably on the vulgar. He had been too obviously chic for his own good.

The academicians found more to their liking an altogether different solution, the anonymous drawing of a palatial townhouse (fig. 4.16), which happens to be 120 feet in width, and therefore agrees with the program specifications set for 1774. This elevation might be by Whetten or perhaps one of the numerous other apprentices of Chambers in the Schools.[53] It distinctly resembles Chambers's 98-foot-wide Melbourne House entrance facade, enlarged by almost a third. It also bears comparison with Soane's scheme, the elevation of which can be reconstructed from his surviving set of plans. Both schemes called for a nine-bay arrangement. The anonymous one stuck close to the traditional Renaissance palazzo formula that Chambers himself preferred: rusticated basement, and orders restricted to the piano nobile. Just to be unusual, Soane placed nearly freestanding giant columns across the entire front, separated from each other by small balconies precariously overhanging the basement storey light well—a decidedly queer-looking solution from a conservative juror's point of view.

The competitive nature of Royal Academy prizes, and the subjective verdicts of the juries, engendered a whole succession of poor losers. Fortunately, the annual exhibitions provided a ready escape value for such discontent. If unwilling to retire like a good sport, the contestant could seek vindication before the public by displaying the designs he felt had not received their due. Soane did so with his first unsuccessful silver medal drawing in 1773, and again in 1775 when he showed his town-house scheme. Feelings ran high at the Academy. Under these strained circumstances, Soane may have secretly gloated when he learned his rival, Thomas Whetten, had failed to receive the traveling scholarship from the Society of Dilettanti.[54]

History would prove Soane had been justified in his sense of self worth. In essence, Whetten had trounced Soane as much by luck of the draw as by excellence of design. It transpired that the subject chosen for the 1776 gold medal, "A Triumphal Bridge with the Plan Elevation and Section,"[55] suited the flamboyant Soane much better. He immediately set to work on what was to become the great victory of his student career.

With unusual vividness Soane recollected that, while working on the bridge designs after office hours and on Sundays, "I found myself so pressed for time . . . that . . . my being employed on the drawings of the bridge preserved me from a watery grave."[56] He referred, of course, to the boating party he had missed and that had taken the life of his friend James King. But the fateful accident we know occurred in June, five months before the November deadline for the bridge design! The anecdote reveals that Soane began to associate divine providence with the work ethic. He had the feeling that some guardian angel was watching over him as he industriously prepared for his second gold medal competition.

Following normal Academy protocol, Soane would have presented himself for the *esquisse* two weeks after the submission of his gold medal drawings. Minutes of a Council meeting held 25 November reveal that Soane had written a letter explaining why he had been unable to attend on the fifteenth. The Council accepted the apology, and the General Assembly were informed on the day of ballotting "that Mr. Soan . . . was indulged with drawing . . .: The Door of a Church, dedicated to the Evangelists."[57] Soane sat the five-hour examination all alone. At the end he had produced an entire church facade rather than a portal. The four evangelists did not offer enough scope to his imagination, so he included statues of all twelve apostles (fig. 4.17). What is more, on this occasion Soane plagiarized himself rather than anyone else. The church facade is in reality nothing more than a reduced and modified version of one of the end pavilions of his triumphal bridge design (fig. 4.18).

Fig. 4.17. Church portal design, plan and elevation (SM, Drawer 45, Set 1, Item 14).

Fig. 4.18. Triumphal bridge design, elevation of the entrance facade (SM, Drawer 12, Set 5, Item 6).

Once again—and for the last time—Soane went to the Foundation Day prize-giving ceremonies. While the students waited outside the lecture room, Reynolds read out the results of the secret ballot as follows:

The Ballot for determining the Premium of a Gold Medal for the best Design in Architecture being examined the Suffrages were—

Designs Marked	No of Suffrages
I	13
K	1
L	2

The President declared the Premium of a Gold Medal for the best Design in Architecture was adjudged to the Letter I . . . the work of Mr John Soan.[58]

The doors then opened, the students came in and, in the words of an anonymous eyewitness, Soane "stood *first* to receive the gold medal from the hand of the President, who accompanied the honor . . . with such appropriate commendations of his performance, and such prophetic hopes of his perseverance, and consequent success, as were in our opinion, far more valuable than even the medal."[59] Soane had received an overwhelming vote of confidence. This momentous triumph marked, in many ways, his artistic coming of age.

The triumphal bridge theme had an impeccable lineage stretching back to Antiquity. Andrea Palladio, in a design for the Rialto, had been among the first to revive it during the Renaissance. Fischer von Erlach illustrated imaginary Roman bridges in his *Entwurf einer historischen Architektur*. Bernardo Vittone and Piranesi later popularized the type in Italian artistic circles. The young French *pensionnaires* at the Académie de France à Rome expanded upon the idea. A fellow student of theirs, William Chambers, brought a knowledge of these bridge designs back with him to England. The result was his own unsuccessful competition drawing for Blackfriars Bridge, London, done in 1759.[60] John Gwynn, another unlucky contestant on the same occasion, gave vent to his ideas in his unorthodox book *London and Westminster Improved* (1766). He suggested the construction of a new bridge that would embody his favorite concept of "magnificence."[61] Thomas Sandby slightly later took Gwynn's proposal, charged it with Burkean overtones, and produced his own bridge of magnificence (fig. 4.7) for the Academy lectures. Chambers, Gwynn, and Sandby, imitating the visions of their Continental predecessors, dreamed of one day erecting a magnificent bridge over the Thames. As all three were founding members of the Academy, the 1776 triumphal bridge contest was an almost foregone conclusion.

Young Soane cannot have known in detail about the centuries-old tradition behind the triumphal bridge. In fact, contrary to what one might expect, he avoided the obvious sources like Palladio, Piranesi, Sandby, or Robert Mylne's Blackfriars Bridge standing downstream from Old Somerset House. These models would have been far too near at hand. Soane went out of his way to seek inspiration in Marie-Joseph Peyre's elevation design for an academy building (fig. 4.19). Peyre, another of the French *pensionnaires* in Rome from 1753 to 1755, devised his visionary structure in the Roman milieu, and waited for ten years before publishing it in his collected *Oeuvres d'architecture* (1765). By virtue of the printed medium, the group of designs became by far the most influential of the French grand prix type. Somewhere Soane came across a copy.[62] It transformed his outlook; it gave him the courage to release

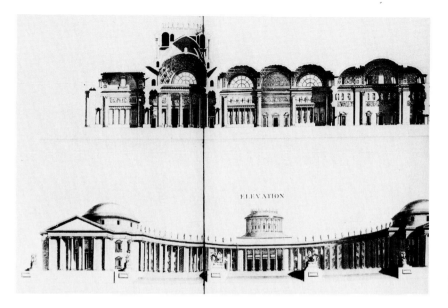

ELEVATION

Fig. 4.19. Marie-Joseph Peyre, academy design, engraved elevation and section, *Oeuvres d'architecture.*

artistic energies hitherto pent up or misdirected.

Soane borrowed shamelessly the Frenchman's curving colonnades, his domed and pedimented end pavilions, and, above all, the hypaethral drum of the centerpiece in the foreground (not to be confused with the shadowy mass of a colossal dome set further back). The Gallic flavor of Peyre's design is disguised by English trimmings. Lions and unicorns and the arms of George III adorn curious capstanlike pedestals set upon the parapet to either side of the entrance arch. Here they fittingly salute the glorious return from battle of some native son of Albion. One of the two sectional drawings (see pl. 2, fig. 4.19) copies closely the intricate lozenge-shaped coffering pattern from the other. It was here, however, that Soane released his boldest flights of imagination.

His vast domed space is subdivided into four smaller alcoves set off by columnar screens that heighten the contrasts between areas of light and shade. Lower down, the heavily rusticated piers and arches of the bridge seem almost to groan under the weight from above. Prowlike cones of stone are extruded from the spandrels as if by the terrific internal pressures. Carrying on this natural metaphor, the lighter superstructure opens at the top into a ring of winged *nikes* wafting some victor's spirit skyward to seek its apotheosis in the billowing storm clouds of Sublime nature. Soane, youthful student of Burke and Sandby that he was, had captured something of their vision of art's ability to match the elements.

Fig. 4.20. Anonymous, triumphal bridge design, section (V&A, 3338).

To descend from the sublime to the ridiculous, it is only necessary to compare Soane's bridge with another one (fig. 4.20) by a contemporary. The anonymous cross section in question, taken through the middle of a bridge, has a central carriageway and footpaths just like Soane's. Obviously once part of a larger set, the sectional nature of the drawing fits the conditions set for the 1776 gold medal contest; the flanking rostral columns moreover proclaim its triumphant "character" beyond a doubt. The handling betrays a Chambers pupil's weak imitation of the master's "watery" brushwork technique and his nostalgic device of introducing a bit of crumbling masonry around the roof line.[63] Pitting this cross section against Soane's would have left the jury of 1776 in little difficulty as to how to select a winner. Granted, Soane's design is not original; it is still vastly superior artistically to what his young contemporaries at the Academy could apparently produce. Soane's stupendous production rises majestically as if pumped up by overheated artistic inspiration. In contrast, the conception of the anonymous competitor looks crestfallen and deflated. The physical length alone of Soane's 4-foot ground plan (fig. 4.21) must have impressed the English judges who, with the exception of the French-trained Chambers,[64] were unaccustomed to seeing things on such a large scale. The dimensions call for a bridge 1,186 feet long. The two extremities, in the shape of grappling irons, anchor the structure to the shore. Vast colonnaded footpaths flank the even vaster carriageway. Along the processional route Soane almost ran out of bellicose deities to whom to dedicate his wayside temples large and small. A generic similarity—but no more—links these

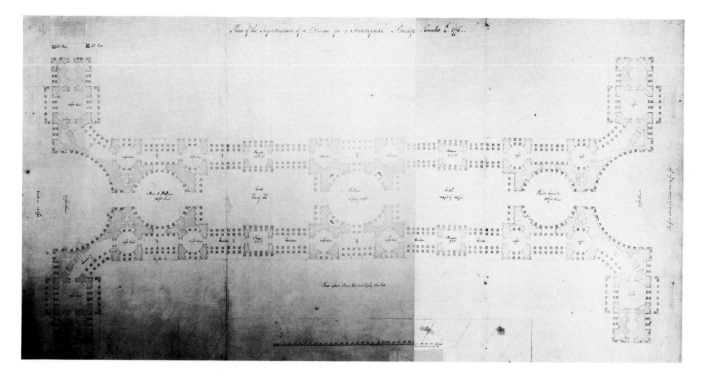

Fig. 4.21. Triumphal bridge design, plan, 1776 (SM, Drawer 12, Set 5, Item 5).

columnar corridors to those of Piranesi and Sandby. Whereas Piranesi's three-part affair never disguised its impassability, and Sandby made the lame provision of housing along the bridge, Soane steered a middle course between the practical and the impractical. An element of feasibility, however remote, always tempered even his wildest schemes on paper.

In an unprecedented fashion, the fame of Soane's triumphal bridge spread beyond the walls of Old Somerset House. According to an eyewitness, "it was much applauded by the most celebrated artists of those times."[65] People agreed that Soane had created an architecture for a British master race, a race of giants and heroes. It answered something in the awakening consciousness of a nation on the threshold of full imperial power; it could not and did not go without recognition. Pressing the advantage of his newfound fame, Soane prepared a side elevation of his triumphal bridge, not called for in the contest program. Even using a small scale, it still stretches almost 9 feet from end-to-end (fig. 4.22). If slowly opened out with a sense of theatrical timing, it could be a staggering experience. Here the full grandeur and magnitude of the

Fig. 4.22. Triumphal bridge design, side elevation (SM, Drawer 12, Set 5, Item 1).

conception unfolds upon the viewer. Soane designed the drawing with this dramatic effect in mind. The audience he had intended it for was none other than George III.

In a conversation years later, the architect revealed his stratagem to the diarist Joseph Farington, who wrote:

> Before he applied to the Academy to be sent to Rome, He waited on Sir Wm. Chambers, who He prevailed upon to show some drawings which He had made to the King, which Sir William told Soane His Majesty approved, and directed that he shd. be sent to Rome by the Academy. Soane considered himself certain of the appointment gave up the situation He was then placed in. When Sir William moved the business in the Academy Sir Joshua Reynolds opposed the appointment of Soane, unless it came *regularly* by *election* of the Academicians.[66]

Chambers, of all the academicians, knew the work of the French *pensionnaires* best and was in a position to appreciate that Soane had carried off a *tour de force* by capturing the spirit of those visionary architects with

such conviction and flair. Chambers altruistically aided Soane even to the detriment of his own pupils. Perhaps, as Farington intimated, he was engaged in games of artistic king-making with Reynolds; if so, the Academy minutes carry no direct evidence of it. In any event, royal approbation and the protection of Chambers did Soane no harm in his last academic ordeal. As he later acknowledged of the outcome: "I can never be sufficiently grateful to the royal patron of my youth."[67]

Beyond the gold medal, the Academy had a further prize for exceptional students in the form of a three-year traveling scholarship to Rome. As luck would have it, one became vacant in 1777, and in the rotation system established among the arts it was destined for a student architect. All former gold medallists were eligible, but only two allowed their designs to be put forward: Soane and his old rival Whetten. On 10 December 1777, after the normal ballotting, the marathon General Assembly session proceeded to another, separate vote.[68] Which of the two candidates should go to Italy? The answer was that Whetten's townhouse simply could not match Soane's triumphal bridge. Soane won an overwhelming victory with twenty out of twenty-four votes; his vindication

Fig. 4.23. Triumphal bridge design, Parma Academy version, side elevation (SM, Drawer 73).

over Whetten was complete. One star had begun to fade, the other rose in the ascendant.

When Soane finally set out for Italy in 1778 with an annual stipend of £60,[69] he owed it to the outstanding triumphal bridge and the academic educational system that had produced it. Between the two they served Soane as talismans in new and unfamiliar surroundings. One of his first recorded acts when he reached the Continent was to call on the famous French civil engineer Jean-Rodolphe Perronet in Paris.[70] In Italy and Switzerland, too, discussions of bridges or viaducts crop up quite frequently in Soane's travel notebooks, indicating that he had not lost interest in the subject. For instance, on the strength of his personal experience with the triumphal bridge, he pronounced the Florentine Ponte S. Trinità "neither handsome or strong and wants character."[71] His studies of Swiss wooden bridges are so extensive as to merit separate consideration in the next chapter. When it came to academies abroad, Soane sought and gained honorary association with those of Florence and Parma. At Parma Academy he had the chance to reunite his triumphal bridge with the correct academic background which had given rise to it in the first place.

Soane's *morceau de réception*, sent to Parma in 1780, consisted of another triumphal bridge modified in the light of his Italian travels. Looking back on the design of 1776, he would have been in agreement with the modern critic Emil Kaufmann, who wrote: "No bridge was ever expected to bear so heavy a load of classical features."[72] Soane proceeded to produce a chastened version. The original drawings in Parma have disappeared. Recently, however, *pensieri* have come to light which Soane claimed were sketched in Italy, and from which "finished drawings of the whole design on a large scale, were made, and presented to the Ducal Academy of Parma."[73] One of these *pensieri* shows the side elevation of the bridge (fig. 4.23). In comparison with the gold medal winning version (fig. 4.22), this new one is denuded of much of its sculptural ornament. The domeless drums at either end are lopped off, reducing considerably the spiky skyline. Most important of all, a severe, baseless Doric order supplants the festive Corinthian one.

In its stripped-down state, Soane's Parmesan bridge design points to the artistic reawakening that forms a subject for later chapters. At the same time, notwithstanding the increased tendency to severity, Soane remained obsessed with the same sort of academic honors associated in his mind with the first bridge. He had a weakness for such distinctions because there was something infectious and lasting about the competitive spirit engendered by the educational process he had undergone in the Schools. That instinct for wanting to win, once ingrained, was not easily shaken off. It colored and even soured his future outlook. The Royal Academy had sharpened the necessary cutting edge to what Soane himself called "the ambition I had cherished from early youth, to be distinguished as an architect."[74]

Publish or Perish

*Proposals for Publishing a Work
in Architecture To consist of designs
for Public and Private Buildings
with their internal
decorations . . . , engraved by the most
eminent Masters and printed on
Royal paper with such letter press as
may be necessary to elucidate the
several designs; the utmost care
and exertion have been employed
in the several compositions
for this Work, the whole being
intended to form a set of designs
to please the different tastes in
Architecture and to render the work
generally useful and immediately
calculated for execution.*

John Soane to Isaac Taylor
March 1777

AT THE ROYAL ACADEMY EXHIBITION in the spring of 1777, John Soane listed a home address as an alternate to Henry Holland's office location. According to custom, this signified the young man's willingness to undertake private commissions on a freelance basis. From the same accommodation located on Hamilton Street, Soane simultaneously launched a proposal for the first of his numerous publishing ventures. By bringing out a book, he was obviously seeking to capitalize upon his reputation as a recent gold medallist. And, as Robert Adam once astutely remarked, such a form of self-advertisement was "conducive to raising all at once ones name and character . . . . with an uncommon splendour."[1]

The recipient of Soane's prospectus was Isaac Taylor, the London bookseller who also ran a specialized architectural press. In view of Soane's relative obscurity, the table of proposed contents that he sent Taylor laid out a book of completely unrealistic proportions. In addition to illustrations of his triumphal bridge, he called for churches, villas, a senate house, residences in town, mausolea, garden buildings, and samples of interior decoration. In all there would have been eighty plates. That was the state which negotiations had reached in March 1777.[2]

By the time the book appeared, over a year later, Taylor had whittled it down from folio to octavo size and had priced the slim volume of thirty-seven engravings at a modest six shillings. Of the grand buildings originally intended, only the James King mausoleum withstood the editorial cuts and occupied a double-page spread. The rest of the plates in the work, which Soane entitled *Designs in Architecture*, illustrate garden structures: seats, temples, a fountain, an obelisk, and various pavilions suitable for ornamenting landscaped grounds.

At one point in his discussions with Taylor, Soane presented an ornamental title page layout, mentioning "Grecian, Gothic, and Moresque styles."[3] The stark letterpress cover of the published version omits any reference to the two Gothic examples, or the single Moorish style building that had survived the weeding-out process. Clearly Soane, in the giddy aftermath of the gold medal victory, had overrated the demand for his ideas, and underestimated the necessity of gradually accumulating a wealth of designs from which to choose. At his age he did not have the backlog of material sufficient for thirty-seven plates, let alone eighty. In addition, Soane labored under enormous pressure of time. The award of the traveling scholarship interrupted him in the middle of his production schedule. From the opening of his negotiations with Taylor, until his precipitous departure for Italy under the gathering clouds of war,[4] barely a year elapsed. Meanwhile, Soane had had to submit two sets of competition drawings for St. Luke's lunatic asylum, had improved upon his portfolio to show to George III, and had continued to work long hours for Henry Holland. Soane was a very busy young architect. He simply overtaxed himself with too many demands. This explains, in part, the uneven quality of his first book.

All Soane's major biographers have found it necessary to apologize for *Designs in Architecture*. For many of them it poses an awkward stumbling block in the path of an otherwise brilliant career. T. L. Donaldson described the contents as "conceived in all the weakness of the style then prevalent." Arthur Bolton wrote of "a youthful indiscretion." More recently John Summerson has called it "a collection of slight and somewhat affected studies." For Johannes Dobai these are "ziemlich unreife Entwürfe." A rumor even circulated in Soane's own day that he "bought up all the Copies that he could and tried to suppress the work."[5] And one can well imagine that Soane, looking back from a position of respectability, might have regretted so blatant and hastily contrived a piece of self-propaganda.

Critical hindsight cannot, however, detract from the value of *Designs in Architecture* as a true reflection upon the sources of its author's early style. Certainly *Designs in Architecture* was concocted in a hurry; it is crude stuff compared with the laborious and carefully guarded distillations of material that Soane had submitted to the Royal Academy. In consequence of the imbalance, however, certain elements of his artistic process appear with far greater clarity. A representative cross section taken from the engravings in the book shows what models impressed him and how he set about changing them to suit his own ends.

A good starting point would be a pavilion that indicates his derivative method (fig. 5.1). The design in question is one of the better ones in the book, because it follows an excellent source as closely as it does. Soane based it on the casino by William Chambers at Marino near Dublin, an

Fig. 5.1. Pavilion design, engraved elevation, 1778, *Designs in Architecture.*

Fig. 5.2. William Chambers, casino at Marino, Dublin, engraved elevation, *Treatice on Civil Architecture.*

engraving of which (fig. 5.2) had been included at the end of Chambers's *Treatise on Civil Architecture.* Soane, who had transcribed long passages from the *Treatise,* must have admired the illustrations also. From the Marino prototype Soane took the tripartite organization culminating in a raised central attic with urn-shaped chimney pot. His admiration for Chambers notwithstanding, he set about simplifying the Marino building by omitting much of its exquisite detailing. The trait of paring down surfaces characterizes most of the book's borrowings. But the lingering Chambers flavor cannot be denied; nor is it surprising. The contact between the two men was demonstrably closest at this point; to some extent Chambers had even taken Soane under his wing by helping him obtain the royal traveling scholarship and by providing him with an ideal educational program for a student abroad (see chap. 7). Moreover, he may well have introduced Soane to his office staff, who worked closely together in the style Soane sought to emulate.

Soane devoted the first five of his plates to garden seats, those glorified park benches once so common to English landscape domains. A representative Soane specimen of this type (fig. 5.3) again suggests the possibility of direct contact with Chambers via a member of his circle, an apprentice named John Yenn. A typically accomplished Yenn drawing in ink, watercolor, and gouache depicts the garden seat shown at the Academy in 1775 (fig. 5.4). Soane might have admired it at the exhibition or seen it in Chambers's office. With almost servile reliance, Yenn fell back on the attic ornament for the Casino at Marino (fig. 5.2) and the identical Greek key motif in the frieze that had also been used by Chambers on occasion.[6] Once more Soane could not resist trying to improve upon his sources, this time with disastrous results. Yenn copied closely his master's consummate skill at combining ornaments in the manner of the Frenchmen Delafosse and Neufforge.[7] Soane, straying from the beaten path, lapsed into incongruous inventions. His piled-up sphinxes, urns, and swags look gauche and slightly wobbly.

Soane's Egyptian temple (fig. 5.5) is another probable instance of close connections with the Chambers circle. Here the smooth pyramidal shape with projecting portico can be traced to an exact prototype in Chambers's Franco-Italian album (fig. 5.6). While he was abroad in the 1750s, Chambers had compiled the scrapbook by pasting into it small drawings of designs he had admired. Later he must have kept the volume in the office for easy reference. There is a documented instance of Yenn's use of it;[8] Soane's case is slightly less clear-cut, but he would have found the sophisticated sequence of antecedents that stood behind his Egyptian temple difficult to assemble entirely on his own. The sources stretch back

5.3

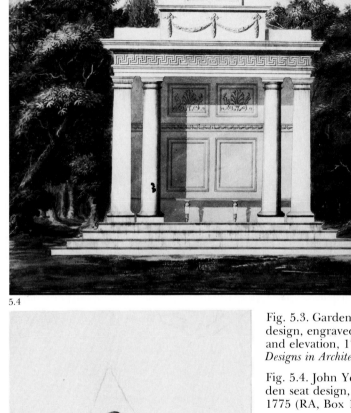

5.4

5.5

5.6

Fig. 5.3. Garden seat design, engraved plan and elevation, 1778, *Designs in Architecture*.

Fig. 5.4. John Yenn, garden seat design, elevation, 1775 (RA, Box 1.C.1).

Fig. 5.5. Pyramidal temple design, engraved elevation, 1778, *Designs in Architecture*.

Fig. 5.6. William Chambers, pyramidal temple design, elevation (V&A, 93.B.21, Item 32).

to the reconstruction of the pyramids in Fischer von Erlach's *Entwurf einer historischen Architektur* and to the visionary pyramidal schemes of the French *pensionnaires* in Rome, like Nicolas-Henri Jardin, whose work Chambers knew.[9] Closer to home, Soane could independently have seen John Carter's Egyptian-style pyramidal dairy in the *Builder's Magazine* for August 1777 (fig. 5.7). Soane owned a copy, and it provided him with a close parallel, even to the extent that it used the same words, "designs in architecture," as part of its subtitle.[10]

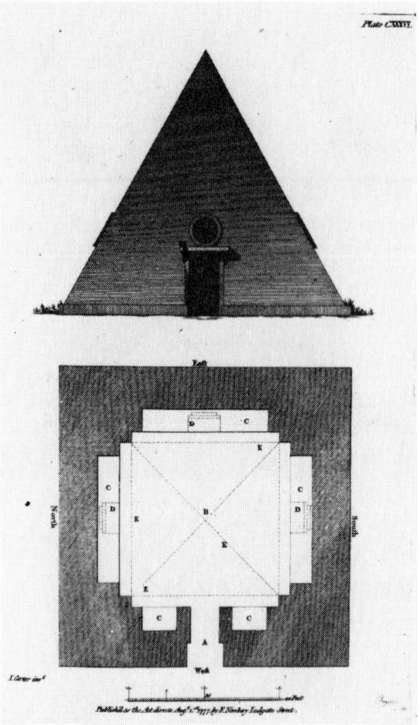

Soane tried to blend the two sorts of architectural literature that constituted a precedent and an inspiration to *Designs in Architecture*. At one end of the scale stood the numerous mid-century pattern books aimed at milking a ready market in the building trades. At the other extreme were lavish productions like Chambers's *Treatise* or his earlier book on the garden buildings at Kew.[11] Soane, like Carter, sought an uneasy middle road. They both combined the high style of Chambers, catering to an aristocratic audience of buyers, with the small size and somewhat inept engraving (figs. 5.5, 5.7) that kept costs down and contributed to a deceptively plebeian appearance. All in all, however, the designs themselves aspired to be as sophisticated in content and as varied in style as anything Chambers had published.

The search for novelty at any price led Soane to bevel the edges of a normal tetrahedron (pl. xxx), indent the corners of a traditional square (pl. xv), flute any otherwise unadorned moulding (pls. i, viii, xiii, xvi), and festoon yards of swag over everything (pls. iv, vi, xxvi, xxviii). He tried his hand at some unconvincing essays in carpenter's Gothic (pls. v, xi). He included two designs on a contorted triangular plan (pls. xii, xix) that look so cramped on the inside, it is hard to imagine anyone would have taken them seriously as habitable architecture. Yet they have gained some unwarranted credence by being often associated with the theoretician Laugier's straight-faced proposal for a triangular church. They seem more akin to the whimsical triangular houses of such architects as Carter, William Halfpenny, or Theodore Jacobsen.[12] One can only conclude that Soane became panicky when faced with having to produce enough "new" designs to fill a book before his impending departure abroad. Few of his attempts could redeem a basic bankruptcy of ideas.

Soane sought for novelty of style as well as novelty of plan and ornament. This is what probably directed him to the obscure William Wrighte, best known for his book on garden buildings entitled *Grotesque Architecture* (1767).[13] Among Wrighte's designs was a series of buildings in the "moresque" style, inspired by Chambers's "mosque" and

Fig. 5.7. John Carter, pyramidal dairy design, engraved plan and elevation, 1777, *Builder's Magazine.*

Fig. 5.8. William Wrighte, Moorish temple design, elevation, *Grotesque Architecture*.

Fig. 5.9. Circular temple design, engraved elevation, 1778, *Designs in Architecture*.

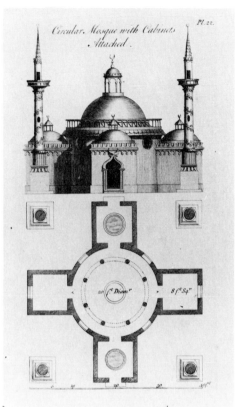

Fig. 5.10. William Wrighte, Moorish mosque design, engraved plan and elevation, *Grotesque Architecture*.

"Alhambra" at Kew Gardens. One of Wrighte's least derivative designs (fig. 5.8) appealed to Soane. He widened it slightly, discarded the pseudo-Islamic decorative elements, and redubbed it a circular temple (fig. 5.9). Essentially he applied to Wrighte the same process of simplification he had used with Chambers. The result demonstrates Soane's ability to grasp the geometry underlying Wrighte's mass of applied ornament. Soane cleaned up the structure he had borrowed and brought out its planar shape. This can be seen particularly in the extraordinary abstract geometric quality of the entrance. In contrast to some of his other designs, Soane chiseled sharp edges onto the circular temple, planed down its surfaces, and cut apertures into them—a technique that lent itself well to the engraver's burin. Whereas Wrighte's design resembles confectionery, Soane's resembles crisply folded card. Aspects such as these reveal Soane's aesthetic sensibility, asserting itself from behind a facade of ornament in Chambers's manner or in the exotic styles of Wrighte.

Among "moresque" buildings as a whole, none had so much influence as the mosque of 1761 at Kew, which Chambers engraved in 1763.

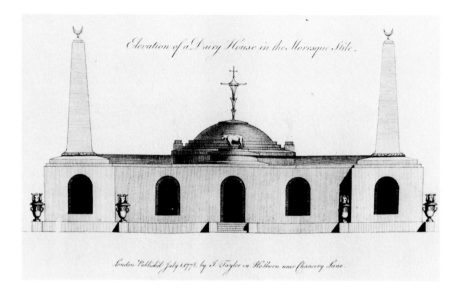

Fig. 5.11. Moorish dairy design, engraved elevation, 1778, *Designs in Architecture.*

François-Joseph Belanger copied it almost exactly in a design of the 1780s for Beloeil in Belgium.[14] Wrighte's *Grotesque Architecture* departed somewhat more from the Chambers original by moving the minarets closer toward the center (fig. 5.10). Remoter from Kew than these attempts at reproduction, Soane's dairy in the "moresque" style (fig. 5.11) used simplification to good effect. Soane achieved a successful massing of plain geometric shapes by stripping away pseudo-Arabic details except for the simple crescent moons, which he left atop the minarets he turned into obelisks. He then endowed the building with cow-headed jugs on the terrace and a bovine statue over the entrance.[15] These were strokes of felicitous invention fully in "character" with the dairy's function. This dairy rises above the juvenile imitations contained in the book. It is the least affected and most prophetic design of them all. Perhaps it might be argued that the prismatic quality of shapes and the sleek wall surfaces are attributable, in part, to the technical limitations of such small-scale engravings. Still, one senses here the architect's unmistakable taste for the simple hard-edged qualities that he imparted to his mature works.

In terms of audacity as opposed to purism, the grand finale of *Designs in Architecture* comes appropriately at the very end of the book. It was a new, simplified James King mausoleum (fig. 5.12). As exhibited at the Royal Academy, its three-decker elevation (fig. 4.11) had all the disproportionate enormity and unwieldy grandeur of a traditional wedding

Fig. 5.12. James King mausoleum design, engraved elevation, 1778, *Designs in Architecture.*

Fig. 5.13. William Chambers, Frederick, Prince of Wales, mausoleum design, elevation (SM, Drawer 17, Set 7, Item 718).

cake. But, as we have seen, Soane's tendency to excess did not escape some gentle mockery from his fellow students in the Royal Academy Schools (fig. 4.12). In response Soane made two modifications. First, he lowered the James King mausoleum by one tier. Second, he changed the finial on the dome, which had consisted of female figures dancing, arms entwined. This feature comes directly from William Chambers's Frederick, Prince of Wales, mausoleum (fig. 5.13), done at Rome in the early 1750s, but probably exhibited later at the Royal Academy, where Soane might have seen it.[16] The engraving of the James King mausoleum (fig. 5.12) substituted for the finial the same capstan motif Soane had used in his triumphal bridge design. Yet for all his dissembling he now came

Fig. 5.14. James King mausoleum design, plans, 1777 (SM, Drawer 45, Set 1, Item 16).

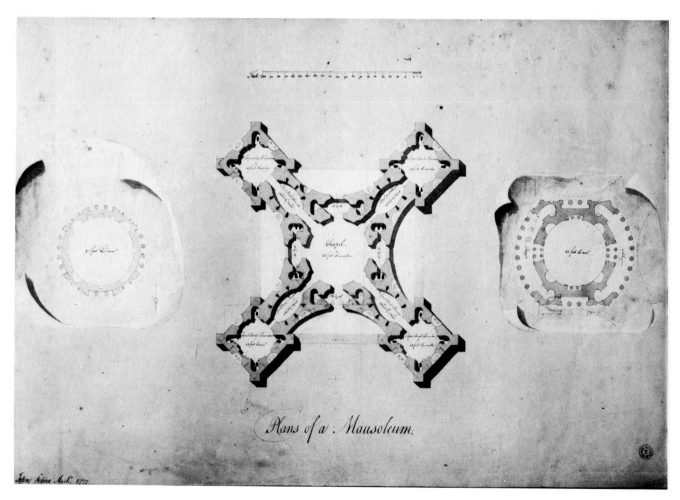

Plans of a Mausoleum.

closer than ever to Chambers's rusticated basement, domed profile, columnar loggias, and above all the compositional device of surrounding the main building with outlying structures. Soane replaced Chambers's obelisks with pyramids, while still remaining within the tradition of Roman academic dream designs. His motive may have been to intensify the funereal "character" he wanted to evoke. Soane stressed narrative decoration by legions of lamenting angels, and enough caskets for a necropolis. In this context the pyramids, with their mortuary connotations, administered the artistic coup de grâce.

As with the triumphal bridge, so too with the James King mausoleum, Soane turned for ideas to the printed source that most readily made

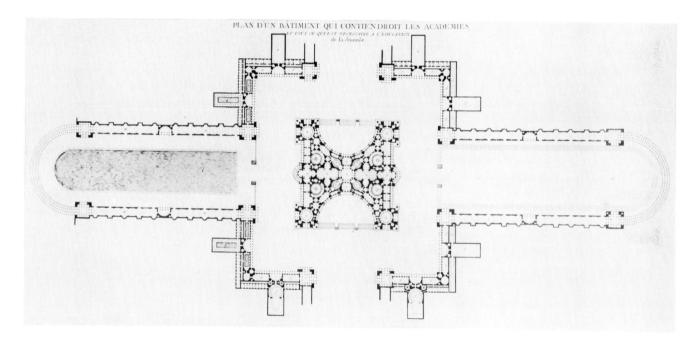

available Continental design theories, Marie-Joseph Peyre's *Oeuvres d'architecture*. Chambers would have approved of such sophisticated eclecticism from a young Academy student. Soane unintentionally heightened the similarity to Peyre when he drew his plans for the 1777 exhibition in such a trompe l'oeil way that they seem to leap up off the page (fig. 5.14). The ground floor level, in the center of the sheet, has the shape of a letter *X*. Surely Soane had Peyre's *académie* complex in mind (fig. 5.15). If the concavities to the front and rear of Peyre's plan are

Fig. 5.15. Marie-Joseph Peyre, academy design, engraved plan, *Oeuvres d'architecture*.

repeated at the sides, one arrives as Soane may have done at a shape close to that of the James King mausoleum.

The triumphal bridge and the James King mausoleum share a common heritage. Both employ Peyre as a start. Both seek eclectically to disguise the fact. Both by their virtuosity convey Soane's ebullient mood as the head of his class at the Royal Academy Schools. Both blend bombastic self-confidence with patriotism; the mausoleum looks like the final resting place of the same British hero who had recently crossed the bridge in glory. Together with the Moorish dairy, but in a different way, the James King mausoleum stands apart from the rest of *Designs in Architecture*. They each show a willingness for daring experimentation. Most important of all, perhaps, they illustrate that Soane could learn from and improve upon past mistakes.

As the critics have rightly remarked, *Designs in Architecture* is bursting with innate contradictions. From one plate to the next the architect's search for a style of his own veers crazily, first one way, then another. It indicates his publish or perish state of mind, in which he lost any instinct to discern that he was not really ready to place himself before the public eye. For all that, and despite the critics, it is clear that *Designs in Architecture* had a respectable commercial success. Running through two additional printings in 1790 and 1797, it achieved a fairly wide circulation. And, despite the defects imputed to the book, it earned its author at least one recorded commission, amounting to 8 guineas.[17] A year after Soane returned from Italy, Lady Elizabeth Craven requested from him several designs for garden structures. She may have known young Soane when he worked on her country house at Benham under Henry Holland's supervision.[18] In any case, *Designs in Architecture* would have brought Soane to her attention as a rising authority on gardens. The Craven commission, small and apparently without concrete outcome, justified Soane's short-term expectation that he would receive needed publicity from the publishing enterprise.

Soane began by sketching several garden seats for Lady Craven (fig. 5.16) on 19 October 1781. The schemes have more than just a generic similarity to the ones he had produced three years earlier for the engraver. At first sight they give little indication of his Italian interlude. No doubt such designs had certain formal limitations and conventions which were hard to break. Nevertheless, the small pen sketches have considerable vigor. One of them was singled out as having enough merit to be worked up to the next stage of realization (fig. 5.17 *bottom half*). Despite misleading inscriptions added later, this presentation drawing and another pasted above it exemplify Soane's best early watercolor tech-

Fig. 5.16. Three garden seat designs, plans and elevations (V&A, 3306.162 recto).

nique. He tried hard to please his client. Amid soft, somewhat wooly landscapes, he set down prismatic little structures gleaming new in the sunshine. The upper building, a pavilion, resembles the Temple of Solitude from the published designs (fig. 5.18) in that they feature the Serlian motif set inside a relieving arch. Both look back for inspiration to Robert Morris's *Rural Architecture*.[19] Sparse though the Soane engraving is, the watercolor carries Morris's "cubistic" neo-Palladianism even further toward the pure forms of square and tetrahedron. The passage of time and exposure to Italy have served to strengthen the plainness in Soane's art.

Quite apart from the Lady Craven commission, critics have overlooked the popularity of *Designs in Architecture* among the lower echelons of Soane's professional colleagues.[20] Two of his architectural contemporaries each appropriated a design, one with proper acknowledgment, one without. The borrowings probably represent more instances, lost or as yet undiscovered.

The more sneaky of the two architects was a twenty-four-year-old Irishman named James Donnell, or O'Donnell.[21] In 1798, long before he embarked on a distinguished career as a church designer in North America, he produced an elevation for a mausoleum (fig. 5.19) derived almost entirely from one published by Soane twenty years earlier (fig. 5.20). The resemblance between the pairs of garlanded shields on the superstructures is so close that O'Donnell must have traced them from *Designs in Architecture*. Once again, the original Soane scheme was not

Fig. 5.17. Pavilion and garden seat designs, plan and elevations (SM, AL, Cupboard 22, Folio 5, Items 77, 78).

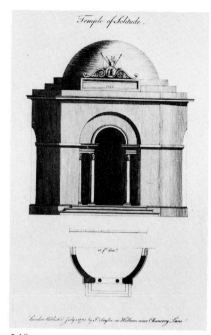

5.18

5.20

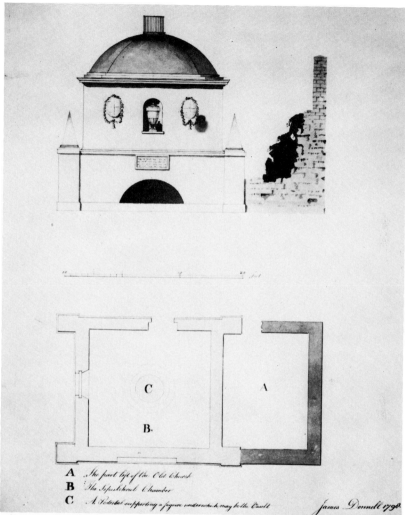

5.19

Fig. 5.18. Temple of Solitude design, engraved plan and elevation, 1778, *Designs in Architecture*.

Fig. 5.19. James Donnell, mausoleum design, plan and elevation, 1798 (National Library of Ireland).

Fig. 5.20. Mausoleum design, engraved plan and elevation, 1778, *Designs in Architecture*.

without its own borrowed precedents. The elliptical arch located in the rusticated podium had distinct associations with sepulchral works by Chambers and his circle.[22] If O'Donnell is any indication to go by, then *Designs in Architecture,* itself the product of dubious artistic license, became, in its turn, a source of material for others to exploit without giving due credit. O'Donnell's position as an untried beginner in a tough profession was exactly analogous to Soane's situation a generation earlier. Under pressure to produce, both men resorted to the same short cuts to inspiration. As if on a merry-go-round, designs circulated from one architect to another, often becoming more debased at each revolution.

Unlike O'Donnell, John Plaw, the second architect, was older than Soane, and he published several pattern books before he emigrated from the British Isles to Canada.[23] Plaw's modestly priced volumes all carry Taylor's imprint and all resemble *Designs in Architecture* in their general content: usually no more than a list of illustrations followed directly by the plates. The first Plaw publication to appear was *Rural Architecture* (1785). In it he admitted that his casino plan "for a connoisseur" (fig. 5.21) came from the "Hunting Casino, designed by Mr. Soane, in a small book published by Mr. Taylor."[24] Plaw also borrowed elements from Soane's elevation (fig. 5.22), though less heavily. Plaw's popular little book went through no fewer than seven reprintings, spreading Soane's name and reputation. Ironically, Soane owned only the first half of the 1785 edition, and thus may never have known directly of Plaw's indebtedness to him.[25] The importance of Soane's ground plan, with the bowed garden facade, will be discussed extensively in a chapter devoted to his development of the "villa" concept from ideas based on Chambers and the French. In the specific context of *Designs in Architecture,* Plaw's borrowing of the plan has significance in that it demonstrates the links between pattern books. The success of one triggered the creation of another. Not only did they relate to the same system of supply and demand, but they fed upon one another for their very meat. Even so, a glut of publications to one's name did not always spell architectural achievement. Plaw's books merely served to eke out his meager practice; Soane went from strength to strength, although after *Designs in Architecture* he never again resorted to publishing as a source of income or to drum up business. His *Plans, Elevations, and Sections* (1788–89) dealt almost exclusively with completed buildings rather than marketable schemes. In the 1777 prospectus he had offered "designs to please the different tastes in architecture . . . useful and immediately calculated for execution." By 1788 his tone had changed noticeably when he ended his introduction to *Plans, Elevations, and Sections* with the

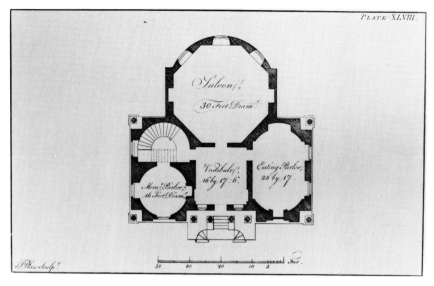

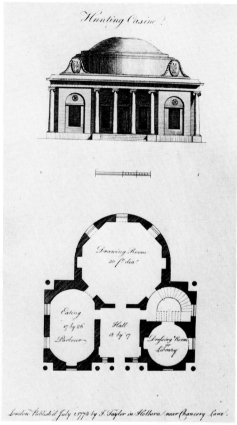

Fig. 5.21. John Plaw, casino design, engraved plan, *Rural Architecture.*

Fig. 5.22. Hunting casino design, engraved plan and elevation, 1778, *Designs in Architecture.*

words: "If the public should judge as favorably of them as the individuals for whom they have been executed, I shall flatter myself that my time has not been misapplied."[26]

In the decade that separates *Designs in Architecture* from *Plans, Elevations, and Sections,* there are many tentative indications that Soane had a book in mind related to his studies abroad (see chap. 8). Although solid proof is lacking, this would have been a natural enough outcome of the Grand Tour. Good precedents existed in the printed works of Robert Adam, Charles Cameron, or Stuart and Revett, to name only a few. Soane's own intentions for a second book that never came about were a matter for conjecture until an obscure engraving of the bridge at Wettingen recently came to light (fig. 5.23). The plate, inscribed with Soane's name, has escaped notice because it served to illustrate the first volume of William Coxe's *Travels in Switzerland.*[27] The original elevation drawing, on which Coxe's engraver based himself, belonged to an extensive group by Soane devoted to the wooden bridges erected by the Swiss master carpenters Hans Ulrich and Johann Grubenmann. The "hanging work" principle on which they were constructed made possible cheap yet long single spans that were easy to cross and no obstruction to water traffic beneath. The Grubenmann's special joinery technique gave the elliptical main arch sufficient strength and springiness to bear the weight of a roadbed, which was slung below and stiffened on the sides by hang posts. These virtues of the Grubenmann system, perfected in the 1750s

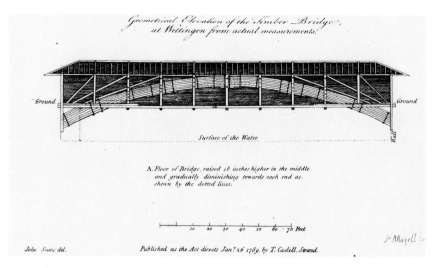

Geometrical Elevation of the Timber Bridge, at Wettingen from actual measurements.

Ground   Ground

Surface of the Water.

A. Floor of Bridge, raised 18 inches higher in the middle and gradually diminishing towards each end as shewn by the dotted lines.

10   20   30   40   50   60   70 Feet

John Soane del.   *Published as the Act directs Jan.ʳ 26 1789, by T. Cadell, Strand.*   J.ᵖ Mazell

Fig. 5.23. Bridge at Wettingen, engraved elevation, 1789, in William Coxe's *Travels in Switzerland.*

and 1760s, intrigued Soane's patron, the Bishop of Derry, who had drawings and engravings made of the bridges in 1770–71. Probably at the Bishop's instigation, the architect stopped long enough on his return journey to England in May 1780 to survey the bridge at Wettingen and two other Grubenmann structures. In the first instance his intention was to ingratiate himself with his patron. It must also be remembered that he had a genuine fascination with bridges going back over the years. But the engraving in Coxe's book makes one suspect all the more strongly that whatever publication Soane was contemplating abroad, it would surely have included the Swiss bridges material.

Travel books like Coxe's enjoyed a popularity with the public never accorded to anything written by Soane. In 1790 the influential *Monthly Review* and *Gentleman's Magazine* carried reviews of *Travels in Switzerland,* but the same periodicals entirely overlooked *Designs in Architecture.* This is not surprising. Critical reviews of art books are the great exception in the eighteenth-century English press. Compared to the spate of informed art criticism in the *Mercure de France,* the British produced a mere trickle. The most luxurious publications received a passing mention and then only occasionally. The emergence of spirited architectural criticism began to take place after 1800. In this connection, it is significant that the earliest known review of *Designs in Architecture* is a very late one, written in 1837. In old age Soane's hypersensitivity about the weaknesses of his own first book had become fairly common knowledge. With malicious glee, therefore, the critic W. H. Leeds, under the appropriate pen name Candidus, touched upon Soane's sore spot when he sarcastically mentioned "that simplicity and chasteness which so conspicuously mark...those unique specimens which he gave to the world in his never-to-be-forgotten Designs for Casinos and Garden Buildings."[28] By this time Soane was at last beyond the sting of the critics' barbs: he had died two months earlier. Ironically a flattering obituary notice of him appeared a few pages further on in the same issue of the *Architectural Magazine*.[29]

P·A·R·T T·W·O

TRAVELS ABROAD

·6·

A Portrait Gallery of Clients

THE ROYAL ACADEMY SCHOLARSHIP to Italy was, as Soane realized, much more than an opportunity to study the architecture of his spiritual homeland. His *Memoirs* clearly articulate the advantages to be gained from meeting one's future clients on neutral Italian soil—advantages of paramount importance to all student artists abroad. Nathaniel Dance, in a letter of 1762, put the matter more candidly than most when he wrote of Grand Tourists: "Their having known you abroad, makes them interest themselves for you more than otherwise they wou'd think of."[1] In the sunny climate and casual atmosphere of Italy, potential clients of wealth and social standing felt in an expansive mood. Away from home, they were temporarily freed from the constraints of the English class system, which so decidedly stratified the position of artist vis-à-vis patron. One such artist spoke of his Italian sojourn as "the only period of my life which I can say I ever pass'd with pleasure in the company of my superiors."[2] What a stinging indictment of the snobbery that kept such men below the salt at home, but elevated them to respectability abroad!

At the Caffé degli Inglesi in Rome, at the Hotel alle Crocelle in Naples, or at similar foreign haunts of the British, artist and client met on almost equal footing. The expatriate artist, because of his longer stay abroad, had at least a smattering of foreign languages. Wealthy tourists on the wing needed interpreters, middlemen, traveling companions, or cicerones.[3] Hence artists hired out their services, or freely gave them in exchange for promises of employment once they had returned home— promises that often seem to have been made in the heated moment of enthusiasm, and as often only followed up halfheartedly. Soane is an example of someone who brought to realization almost none of the projects he initiated for acquaintances on the Grand Tour. Even so, the unexecuted schemes provide fascinating evocations of foreign sights and experiences shared with the patrons. Besides, whatever the fate of individual commissions, a chain of further ones invariably trailed behind. In

I was sent to Italy to pursue my studies . . . . This was the most fortunate event of my life, for it was the means by which I formed those connections to which I owe all the advantages I have since enjoyed.

John Soane
Memoirs of the Professional Life of an Architect

109

6.1

6.2

6.3

Fig. 6.1. Portrait of Frederick Hervey, the Bishop of Derry, by Pompeo Batoni, 1778 (on loan to the National Gallery of Ireland).

Fig. 6.2. Portrait of Thomas Pitt, by Joshua Reynolds, 1764 (J. D. G. Fortescue Collection).

Fig. 6.3. Portrait of Philip Yorke, by George Romney, ca. 1784 (National Trust, Wimpole Hall).

Fig. 6.4. Portrait of Rowland Burdon, by Pompeo Batoni, 1779 (N. Sclater-Booth Collection).

Fig. 6.5. Portrait of John Patteson, by Philip Reinagle, ca. 1781 (P. and C. E. Patteson Collection).

Fig. 6.6. Portrait of John Stuart, by Joshua Reynolds, ca. 1778 (Directors of Coutts and Co.).

Fig. 6.7. Portrait of Henry Greswolde Lewis, by John Constable, 1809 (Earl of Bradford's Collection, Weston Park).

a society where letters of introduction and recommendation by word-of-mouth counted for so much, the grapevine was the principal means of an artist's becoming known in the right quarters.

After a slow start in the late spring and summer of 1778, John Soane made the best "catch" of the season among Grand Tourists in Rome, for he was adopted as the protégé of the aristocratic Frederick Hervey, Bishop of Derry and subsequently Earl of Bristol (fig. 6.1). When and how their first meeting took place is not certain. Despite the voluminous family correspondence of the Bishop,[4] Soane's name is never once mentioned—a tacit indication of the patron's real attitude toward the artist. Because the Bishop caught malarial fever at Castel Gandolfo during the summer of 1778, it is not likely that he could have made contact with artists before he reestablished himself at Rome in September.[5] When the Bishop eventually bestowed his discriminating favor, it meant a great deal. The younger son of a prominent Suffolk family, he had the independent means to pursue his passion for travel, politics, the natural sciences, and the arts. When he picked out Soane, he was on his third lengthy Grand Tour, and the veteran of numerous dealings with artists.[6] The Bishop was an admirer to be prized above others, not so much for his money, or even his acknowledged cultivation as a connoisseur, but because of entree to his circle of friends and acquaintances, which proved to be vast. The designs Soane undertook for the Bishop of Derry represented, therefore, a small fraction of what accrued to him as a result of having joined forces with so well-connected an individual.

It was through the Bishop that Soane made his influential and lasting friendship with a future client, Thomas Pitt (fig. 6.2), nephew of the

6.4   6.5   6.6   6.7

recently deceased Earl of Chatham. The Bishop had ardently admired the Elder Pitt's statesmanship. So when Pitt's look-alike nephew arrived in Rome, early in December 1778, the prelate installed him as the chief ornament of his circle.[7] Thereafter, Soane would have had ample opportunity to meet Pitt, especially when the whole party set off to winter at Naples. There Pitt came down with an illness that confined him to his bed for a number of months. At one point Soane visited him frequently and also wrote him several letters seeking advice and criticism; Pitt had the great merit of being an accomplished amateur architect. This marked the start of a warm, lifelong correspondence between near-equals.[8] Quite apart from Soane's and Pitt's mutual discussions of possible commissions, this contact contributed to Soane's success as an official architect under the administration of Pitt's first cousin, William, who became Prime Minister in 1783.

One of the Bishop's younger acquaintances, Philip Yorke (fig. 6.3), arrived at Rome in mid-October 1778 and soon after received a dinner invitation from the prelate.[9] Again the affiliation was political; Yorke was the grandson of the former Lord Chancellor, the first Earl of Hardwicke. Yorke made the Grand Tour at the expense of his wealthy uncle, the second Earl, to whom he addressed affectionate and lengthy reports. In one of these, recounting a recent trip to Paestum, he wrote in admiration of "An English architect by name Soane [sic] who is an ingenious young man now studying at Rome." In this way, Yorke expressed a budding esteem for Soane that grew with time. The respect was mutual. Soane would have appreciated Yorke's discerning judgments of the monuments they visited—opinions displaying an independence and maturity of mind well beyond his years.[10] Soon afterward Yorke commissioned work from Soane and thereby became one of the architect's earliest and youngest clients; he was not yet twenty-two years old. He remained a steadfast employer over the next two decades, offering work on a multiplicity of projects large and small.[11]

The Bishop of Derry's knowledge of vulcanology attracted to him a fanatical amateur naturalist by the name of Thomas Bowdler, an obscure medical graduate who later gained immortality as the expurgator of Shakespeare's writings. Bowdler was a bit of an obsequious busybody, which caused the Bishop to make cruel innuendoes about his physical deformity (this may explain why there is no known portrait of Bowdler).[12] As the letters of Bowdler attest, he was hardly a great lover of the arts. He had few, if any, direct dealings with Soane in the short run. Subsequently, however, when Bowdler came into a position to help Soane, he exerted what influence he could on behalf of the architect whom he professed to know intimately.[13] Also, Bowdler must have performed the service of introducing the architect to his friend Rowland Burdon (fig. 6.4). Bowdler and Burdon had traveled the Highlands of Scotland before setting off for Europe together.

Rowland Burdon, only son of a "Gentleman of Large Fortune"[14] in County Durham, probably met Soane in Naples early in 1779. They remained close friends and sometime business associates for the next fifty-eight years. Together with Bowdler, Burdon had a hand in organizing a tour of Sicily and Malta in the spring of 1779. They invited Soane to join them and several others. One of the party, in a mocking tone, described Burdon as "quite an Enthusiast after Antiquities."[15] It was this strong love of art that formed the common bond between Soane and Burdon. At the end of the expedition to the islands, Soane and Burdon, by now inseparable, returned to Rome long enough for Burdon to sit for a handsome oval portrait by Pompeo Batoni. Then, with Soane as his companion, Burdon set off to see the cities of central and northern Italy before parting from the architect and heading home in September 1779.[16]

Thomas Bowdler had attended medical school at Edinburgh with Dr. Philip Martineau of Norwich. It is probably through this connection that Bowdler made the acquaintance of John Patteson (fig. 6.5), a young Norfolkman and friend of Martineau's. Bowdler persuaded Patteson to take part in his "Sicilian jaunt." This was a lucky event for posterity. Patteson, destined to head the family wool stapling business,[17] dutifully kept his widowed mother informed of his travels every step of the way. Writing from Rome on 12 April 1779, he revealed that "The Architect whom I mentioned to be of our Sicilian Party, is a young man whose

Abilities twice gained him the Premium of the London Academy and who is now on his Studies here with a Pension from our King."[18] The treasured but unpublished Patteson family letters give a vivid picture of Soane as a companion of well-born Grand Tourists, respected by them for his talents and achievements. Patteson's biographical sketch is far more complete, in fact, than any to be found in the standard published accounts of contemporary Englishmen abroad, which almost never mention Soane.[19] Moreover, thanks to Patteson, Soane's participation in the trip to Sicily and Malta is more than a hazy chapter in the architect's travels. Through Patteson, Soane became acquainted with his friend and fellow Huguenot, Richard Bosanquet. This later provided a connection with Richard's cousin, Samuel Bosanquet, head of a banking firm and an influential future client of Soane's.[20] More than anyone else, Patteson immediately took it upon himself to promote Soane's career through useful introductions to the leading families of Norfolk. Before Soane left Italy, he had met Patteson's countrymen, Charles Collyer and Edward Roger Pratt, who later patronized him. Upon returning to England, Soane proceeded to establish his most lucrative trade in East Anglian country houses.

Bowdler, as self-appointed impresario of the Sicilian expedition, enlisted his Scots friend, John Stuart, heir to the baronetcy of Allanbank (fig. 6.6). Stuart had recently married an heiress to the Coutts banking empire and was honeymooning in Italy. Nevertheless, he consented to leave Naples for a quick visit to the Sicilian geological sights with Bowdler. The three other members of the party split off to make a longer tour with Soane.[21] In early July the two groups of explorers met back at Naples, where Soane renewed contact with Stuart. The following winter in Rome, the architect became a daily visitor to the Stuarts, who must have seemed his likeliest sources of employment before they frittered away the Coutts dowry. But there is evidence that, once back in Britain, Soane presumed too much upon his intimate relations with the family and overstepped the fine line between patron and artist.[22]

The last of the Sicilian Grand Tourist triumvirate was Henry Greswolde Lewis (fig. 6.7). Of all Soane's early clients, he fits least neatly into the interlocking network of family ties and friendships that connect them. No one took much notice of this Warwickshire squire, though his Neapolitan hotel bills, still preserved, single him out as the "Mr. Lewis"[23] mentioned in contemporary letters. He could rightly claim the distinction of having given the architect his largest single commission before he got an entire house to build. Moreover, through Lewis's elder sister, Anna, Soane came to the attention of her husband, Wilbraham Tollemache, whose various commissions did much to bolster business during his early practice.[24]

The eight individuals enumerated thus far by no means cover all of Soane's Grand Tourist contacts, who number at least a dozen more. Only those men who commissioned him on the spot, or exerted their influence on his behalf, will be discussed here. They were the cornerstone of his career, and they fully justified the importance artists attached to cultivating their acquaintance. Free sketches or estimates, shopping errands performed to ingratiate oneself, these were the sorts of services by which an artist insinuated himself into the good graces of prospective clients.[25] The process had reached the level of a high art by Soane's time, as scattered references to his activities indicate. While still in Italy, Patteson reported to his mother about "talking over Plans for you," with the architect, "to give you two rooms in Front 23 or 24 by 18 but in a few posts you shall have the Draughts in small."[26] And in a letter addressed to Rome, Agnes Stuart wrote Soane "My son desired that a Draught of Allanbank house might be sent you . . . which will no doubt Receive much Improvement by Your corrections and amendments."[27] On the strength of such offers of employment, Soane must have believed himself launched as an architect.

The Bishop of Derry realized full well the competitiveness of the expatriate artistic community in Rome and its willingness to supply advice free of charge. Early in 1778, he let it be known that he was looking for the best design he could find for a dining room he intended to add to his house, Downhill, on the Antrim coast of northern Ireland. He laid down some unofficial ground rules in the form of Palladian room dimensions of a cube and a half and then sat back to see what would happen. As he expected, artists came forward of their own accord. By July 1778, a letter sent from Ireland alluded to an "Italian Architect."[28] A Scotsman, John Henderson, apparently delivered the first acceptable proposal. Soane, a relative latecomer on the scene, produced an alternative design that superseded Henderson's in the Bishop's fickle affections. Henderson resented this intrusion on what he considered his territory. A malicious rumor circulated, according to which, Soane said, "it was whispered that my design was a copy of another made by Mr. Henderson . . . before my arrival." To still these accusations of plagiary, Soane insisted on an objective trial of the two designs. Soane and Henderson named as judges their traveling companions, Robert Furze Brettingham and Thomas Hardwick, respectively. The outcome, of course, was a hung jury.[29] Soane, the upstart, retained the Bishop's favor, but in the process lost a valuable working relationship with Hardwick, as will be seen (chap. 8).

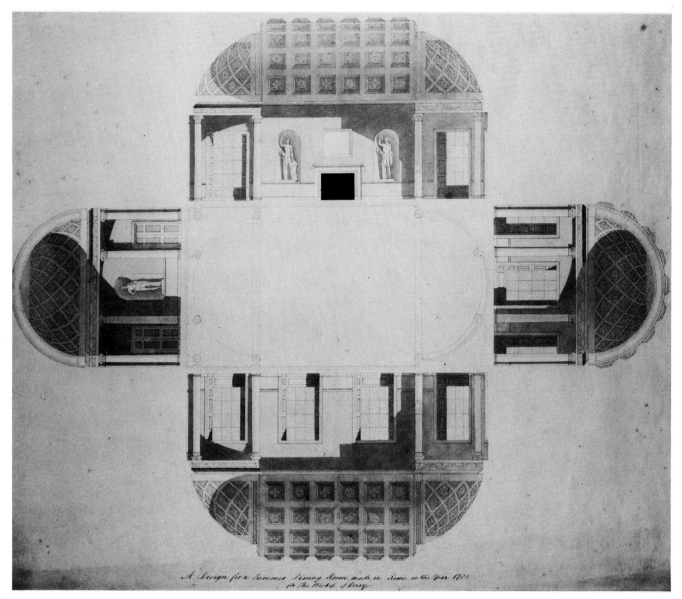

A Design for a Summer Dining Room made in Rome in the year 1780 for The Bishop of Derry.

Fig. 6.8. Summer dining room design for Downhill, plan and elevations, 1780 (SM, Drawer 45, Set 1, Item 33).

As Soane readily admitted,[30] the summer dining room design was a close adaptation of the Claremont entrance hall (figs. 6.8, 2.6). The Bishop somewhat complicated this typical piece of Soanean legerdemain by specifying an off-axis entry into the room from the existing house at Downhill. At first Soane disguised the awkward transition with his familiar oval ring of columns and a bow window at the end of the room furthest from the entrance. Thus the Claremont design began a dramatic transformation reflecting the changes in Soane's style under the heady influence of his exposure to Italy. Then, as the next step in the evolution, he turned the room into a double apsidal-ended affair. The coffered apses and barrel vault increase the sculptural play of light and shade. The use of classical statuary in niches strengthens the plastic effect. The white of the marbles, offset by the apple green shade of the walls, would have created a serene, museumlike setting, ideal for the contemplation of the antiquities the Bishop was collecting for his house.[31] Furthermore, the room's seasonal designation imitates descriptions of similar apartments in Antique villas.

The final stage in the evolution of the summer dining room came as a result of the Bishop and Soane's joint trip to Naples. After departing from Rome on 23 December, they spent Christmas Day en route near Terracina, exploring the ruins of a supposed villa that had belonged to the gastronome Lucullus. Armed with a free interpretation of Plutarch's life of Lucullus, the Bishop searched for and thought he had identified the legendary "Apollo" dining triclinium, which Soane drew and measured (fig. 6.9). Here the ancient Roman was said to have provided a famous banquet for Pompey and Cicero, who had been skeptical of his notorious Epicureanism.[32]

Then in Naples, the Bishop and Soane hit upon the idea of making the Downhill dining room into a replica of the "Apollo" triclinium. Two pages of Soane's current notebook illustrate semicircular, niche-lined schemes on the Roman model (fig. 6.10). Sandwiched between these is a third plan with the word "Lucullus" identifying it.[33] So it is possible, in this case, to see Soane's thoughts drifting back and forth from the real buildings of Lucullus to the proposed copy for his modern counterpart, the Bishop.

In every way, the transition of the summer dining room from Claremont pastiche to Lucullan pseudo-triclinium is remarkable. In the approved Neoclassical manner, Soane, once he had first-hand knowledge of Antiquity, sought to reproduce it—even to the extent of combining excavations with literary sources, and respecting the original form-function relationship of the triclinium as far as possible. The Claremont

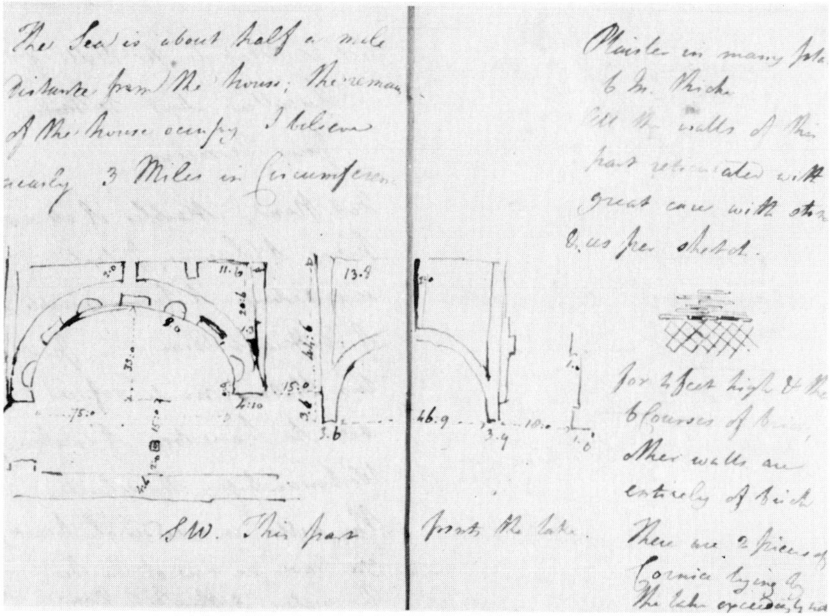

Fig. 6.9. Sketch plan of triclinia at the site of the supposed Villa of Lucullus near Terracina (SM, "Italian Sketches and Mem.," pp. 190–91).

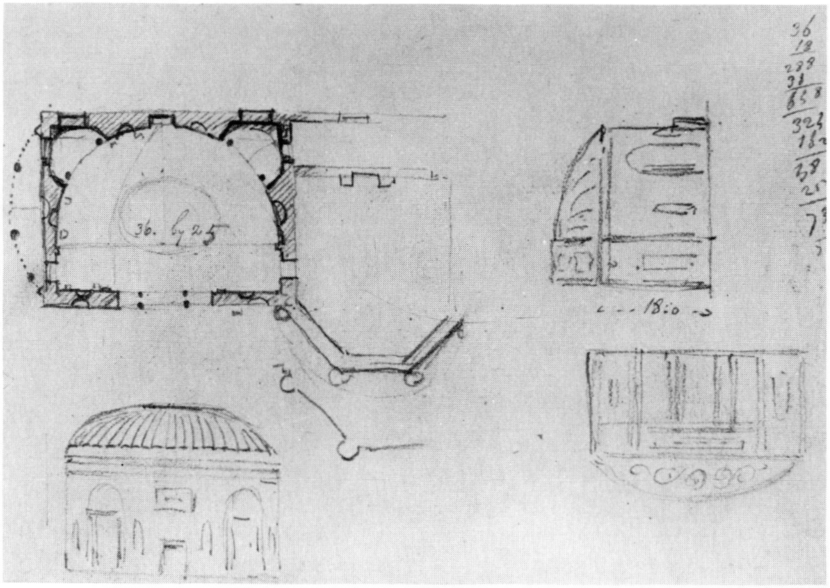

Fig. 6.10. Dining room design for Downhill in the form of a triclinium, sketch plan and sections (SM, "Italian Sketches 1779," p. 172).

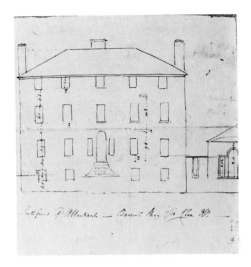

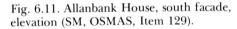

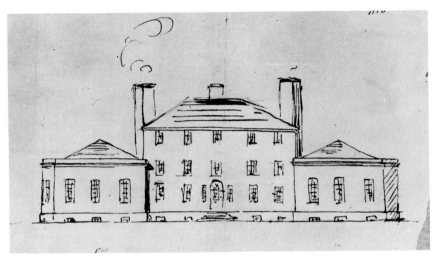

Fig. 6.11. Allanbank House, south facade, elevation (SM, OSMAS, Item 129).

Fig. 6.12. Allanbank House, south facade, sketch elevation showing proposed wings (SM, OSMAS, Item 128).

scheme had no claim to these rich and complex archaeological allusions, for which the Bishop may take partial credit.

The summer dining room proposal began Soane's lengthy and troubled association with the Bishop.[34] The entire episode ended on 2 September 1780, when Soane, who had left Italy prematurely at the Bishop's insistence, departed from Downhill after a thirty-eight-day stay with nothing but £30 to show for his pains. The rest of his bill, amounting to £400, was never paid. Soane bitterly recalled fifty-eight years later: "Experience . . . taught me how much I had overrated the magnificent promises and splendid delusions of the Lord Bishop of Derry."[35] Nor was this the last of Soane's Italian commissions to evaporate into thin air once he returned to the British Isles.

From Downhill Soane made his way across the Irish Sea to Allanbank, near Berwick-on-Tweed. At the Scottish seat of the Stuarts he hoped to profit from the assurances of employment they had proffered in Rome. Soon after his arrival, on 22 September 1780, he measured the ground plan and basement of the existing house.[36] About the same time he drew the back, or south, elevation (fig. 6.11). The survey paved the way for the extensive renovations and alterations to the building that had been discussed in Rome. Another contemporary sketch (fig. 6.12) of the same facade indicates the sophisticated conversions he proposed to carry out. According to this scheme, he intended hiding from view the two front, or northern, service blocks, by extending the south facade in either direction with low, one storey wings. These rough proposals were all that Soane achieved at Allanbank, before leaving hurriedly for Castle

Eden, County Durham. At this point the thread of events is picked up by a rare surviving exchange of letters. They must be characteristic of many others in the deferential tone adopted by the architect and the opinionated one of the client. In the letters, Soane guarded against the appearance of any tendency to extravagance that might put Stuart off. In spite of this, things began to go wrong almost immediately. Soane started the correspondence on 8 November 1780, on a note of optimism and somewhat contrived urgency, that betrays his anxiety lest the Downhill fiasco repeat itself. Although he had not finished the drawings, he told Stuart he had hired a London joiner to begin work on various fittings for the refurbishing of the old house. After vouching for the craftsman's skill, he went on to add:

I once thought of Mahogany doors for the Eating Room, Draw[in]g Room and Library but white doors in the Eating Room, and gilt doors with looking Glass panel in the drawing Room will produce a much better effect—more cheerful indeed I wish to gild a great part of the Mould[in]gs in the drawing Room, there is a grandeur in gilding that carving never produces, add to that it will be much newer.[37]

Soane's vision of lots of gold reflected in mirrors is not typical of the average British interior of the day. Though the Italian allusions may have been clear to Stuart—who approved of them—they call for a few words of explanation.

The decorative use of mirrors was not unheard of in England in Soane's time. They had been installed at Strawberry Hill, Middlesex, and Northumberland House, London, before Soane made such a feature of them in his own townhouse. His source of inspiration both in 1780 and later would appear to relate to a specific travel experience he shared with Stuart. During the early days of the Sicilian tour, in April 1779, the party had visited the Prince of Palagonia's villa at Bagheria near Palermo.[38] The contemporary guidebook they took with them drew attention to the Prince's fetish for lining entire rooms and all their furniture with looking glass. Soane certainly recollected the Villa Palagonia when writing about his own house.[39] It would seem a natural outcome of the Grand Tour that he should do so for Stuart's benefit at Allanbank. The eccentric Sicilian mode, properly modified of course, could be imported to Scotland for an effect of shimmering novelty. Continental reflections of this sort flattered the cosmopolitan outlook of architect and client alike.

Unfortunately, Soane's fears about Stuart's capriciousness were well founded. Stuart's reply of 5 December stopped Soane's attempts to push him into action. "The Men are still continuing to quarry the Stones,"

Stuart nonchalantly wrote; "at the same time, I don't think I shall be able to begin building til the next spring for I find several demands for money I did not think of and it is scarce to beget in these times."[40] Soane responded with feigned ingenuity; "I hope you do not mean the spring of 1782 . . . . I hope and flatter myself I shall not be reduced to the necessity of stopping [work]." But, of course, that was exactly what Stuart did mean! With a few strokes of the pen, he concluded the matter with the words "We shall in the meanwhile be considering about the rest."[41] In short order he had buried the unrealistic dreams born in the carefree atmosphere of Rome.

At Castle Eden, parental home of Rowland Burdon, Soane received a warm welcome such as he had encountered at Allanbank. On 6 October 1780, he measured the existing castle with a view to some minor alterations to the entrance porch.[42] The very next day, however, he presented one of his multiple-choice type of drawings for an entirely new house (fig. 6.13). Thus Soane, by rapid degrees, induced potential patrons to think in grander and grander terms. (Perhaps in the case of Stuart he encouraged him to plan beyond his means.) Several of the alternative designs made at Castle Eden show tripartite little buildings with central porticos, intended as country houses. They unmistakably recall the Palladian-style villas in North Italy, which Burdon and Soane must have admired together on their travels. Soane recorded the appearance of some of them from his carriage window, as he hastened through the Veneto on his way home in May 1780 (fig. 6.14). The

Fig. 6.13. Country house designs, sketch plans and elevations, 1780 (SM, OSMAS, Item 121 recto).

Fig. 6.14. Villas Maldura *(top)* and Molin *(bottom),* near Padua, sketch elevations (SM, "Notes Italy," p. 323).

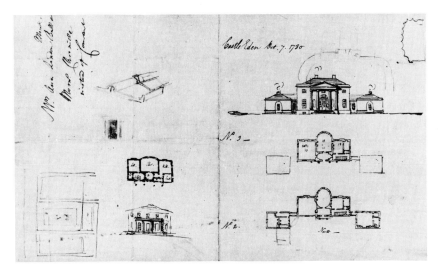

Fig. 6.15. Country house design, plan and elevation (SM, Drawer 5, Set 2, Item 8).

sketches, inaccurate as to detail, nonetheless capture well the blocky angularity of the Villas Maldura and Molin near Padua.

Eventually some member of the Burdon family circle commissioned Soane to carry the October designs to the stage of a finished presentation drawing. The architect produced a plan as well as an elevation in ink and tawny yellow watercolor that, although undated, has all the earmarks of his early draftsmanship and contemporary autograph handwriting (fig. 6.15 and cf. fig. 10.13). Moreover, an aquatint published by Soane in 1793 links the design to one for an unnamed "gentleman in the north of England" and precisely dates it to 1781.[43]

In many ways the Castle Eden country house may be regarded as one of the most significant domestic designs of Soane's early period. The plan is neat and compact—only 60 feet by 25 feet on the main block. It seems designed with a bachelor or a newly wed gentleman farmer in mind. And the vaulted "evidence room" in the right-hand wing suggests a justice of the peace as the destined inhabitant. The gently bowed center of the rear facade became an extremely important feature of Soane's country house planning throughout the 1780s and will be discussed in that context later. As for the elevation, it points to Soane's exploitation of plain surfaces as a replacement for the classical detailing he had seen in the villas of Palladio, Scamozzi, or their imitators. A repetition of subtle horizontal accents forms the binding element for the composition. There are horizontal eaves, unusual horizontal lintels above the door and the end pavilion windows, and horizontals in the module of the bricks themselves. The design avoids the monotony of blank expanses of wall, by introducing shallow relieving arches. In its stark simplicity and grave slow-moving rhythms, it is a far cry from the jerky staccato beat of buildings in the Palladian idiom. At the same time, the overall massing and tightly organized plan form a bridge between the Italian villa tradition Soane and his clients had admired and the type of model smaller house that the architect would develop out of this. In this way the design's seminal importance in Soane's oeuvre was not lost, although the house itself was never built.

In contrast to Soane's disappointments at the hands of the affable but ineffectual Burdons, the vacillating Stuart, or the egocentric Bishop, the architect's dealings with Philip Yorke were blessed from the start by a mutual understanding that went back to 1779. The year before, Yorke had visited the Corsini Chapel in S. Giovanni in Laterano. He praised the Roman building as "one of the most perfect pieces of modern architecture."[44] As a memento of his Grand Tour, he commissioned Soane to make a watercolor drawing of the resplendent marble resting place for

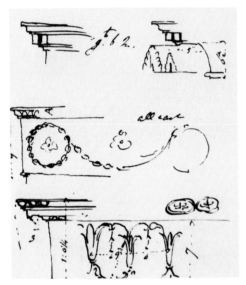

Fig. 6.16. Chimneypiece designs for John Patteson's townhouse, Norwich (SM, Soane Notebooks, 1, p. 59).

the Corsini pope, Clement X (pl. 3). Soane's account book entries refer to sketching and measuring the chapel in Rome and then preparing a presentation drawing back in London.[45] Fortunately Soane made the copy for himself that is dated July 1779. Despite some artistic license, the watercolor, one of Soane's handsomest in its blurry way, faithfully reproduces the rich purples, golds, and porphyry red of the High Baroque interior. Soane, while in Italy, did not restrict his studies to Antiquity. The eclectic design process encouraged scrutiny of the "best" from the Renaissance and Baroque as well. In fact, the domed and cruciform Corsini Chapel may contain the germ of the idea that bore fruit in eleven years' time, when Soane designed the sumptuous yellow drawing room at Wimpole, Yorke's Cambridgeshire seat.

John Patteson, true to his "unfeigned offer of service where and whenever it is in my power,"[46] corresponded with Soane frequently after the architect had settled definitely in London at the end of 1780. The nature of their early transactions involved Soane as an agent for buying trinkets, sheet music, a child's hobbyhorse and so forth.[47] More importantly, Soane passed along orders to his friend, the carver Edward Foxhall. Soane charged no commission, because Patteson had advanced him £50 while he was in Italy. Besides furniture, Foxhall supplied several chimneypieces costing the fairly large sum of £81.5.7.[48] These were all that remained of the ambitious schemes, mooted in Rome, for altering the Pattesons' Norwich townhouse, constructed not so long before by Robert Mylne.[49] Two pages of Soane's notebook sketches relate to the chimneypieces, suggesting that he, rather than Foxhall, was their designer (figs. 6.16, 6.17, and see fig. 6.12). For the sake of economy wood was used with applied ornaments of moulded plaster, as Soane indicated on the drawings—a far cry from the brisk trade in Italian statuary marble chimneypieces carried on by numerous of Soane's confreres.[50] To make matters worse, Soane depicted the floral motifs awkwardly—he had little gift for drawing freehand from nature. The designs also lack personal conviction, especially compared with a scheme as recent as the starkly simple one for the fireplace in the summer dining room (fig. 6.8). What had happened between Italy and England? Plunged into a competitive world of fashionable practitioners, Soane had wavered in his own preference for plainness and had temporarily faltered. He soon regained his footing. Several years later, he evolved a standard personal type of chimneypiece, idiosyncratic in its use of fluting. John Patteson installed a version (fig. 6.18) alongside the earlier ones in Surrey Street. The discrepancy over such a short time indicates the rapidity with which Soane established a decorative style all his own (see chap. 14).

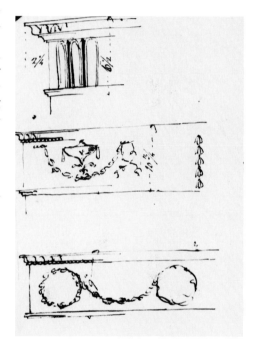

Fig. 6.17. Chimneypiece designs for John Patteson's townhouse, Norwich (SM, Soane Notebooks, 1, p. 60).

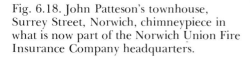

Fig. 6.18. John Patteson's townhouse, Surrey Street, Norwich, chimneypiece in what is now part of the Norwich Union Fire Insurance Company headquarters.

Thomas Pitt used the excuse of poor health to travel abroad in 1778–79,[51] only to catch a fever in Naples, where he lay bedridden for several months—a captive audience for Soane. A letter from the architect to Pitt, mailed to Naples in August 1779, alludes to previous discussions about altering Pitt's London townhouse, a sketch of which had been enclosed.[52] Just at this point Soane produced a remarkable hydrotherapeutic bathhouse design (fig. 6.19). Pitt's grave illness could have inspired it. Moreover, Soane placed his new building at one end of a drab Georgian structure that bears a strong resemblance to Pitt's two-storey residence off Oxford Street, London, known from an old photograph in the National Monuments Record. The proximity of Pitt's large garden to adjacent Hyde Park would account for the trees in the drawing. Finally, the verso of the same piece of paper has a sketch in a hand other than Soane's. As the subject matter relates to the text of Soane's August letter (see chap. 9), there is a good chance the artist was Pitt, working on the back of the bathhouse design sent earlier by Soane.

Bathrooms, whether designed for purposes of health or beauty, gained popularity at a slow rate in eighteenth-century Britain, compared with the vogue they enjoyed in the rest of Europe. Soane had first-hand acquaintance with the Claremont bathroom, one of the rare recent examples to be constructed in England.[53] The architect quickly seized upon the theme as one likely to come into fashion. His *Designs in Architecture* offered to the public a combination garden seat and bathhouse (fig. 6.20), which it is instructive to compare with the design for Pitt. In contrast to the musty underground location of the Claremont room, Soane brought both his structures out into the open. The earlier bathhouse is conspicuously simple in the best manner of Soane's contemporary Moorish dairy (fig. 5.11). The bathhouse for Pitt, like the majority of the commissions from Grand Tourists, goes out of its way to stress its Mediterranean nature. The fastidious little building is decked out with Doric columns, urns in niches, and an Antique-style saucer dome. Sun floods in through an oculus at the top, and an Italianate "loggia" in the front. On the left, at *A*, would have been a skylighted changing room. A hot water boiler in the compartment on the opposite side completes the amenities which, together with the richly articulated interior space, are intended to recall the thermal establishments of the ancient Romans. All in all it reflects the warm Neapolitan environment in which it was bred and died; Soane's working relationship with Pitt, however, long outlived the demise of the bathhouse scheme.

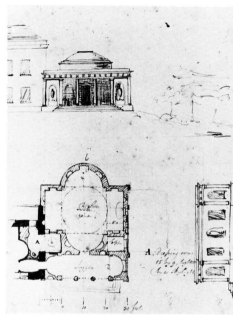

Fig. 6.19. Bathhouse design, sketch plan and elevations (SM, OSMAS, Item 135 recto).

Fig. 6.20. Bathhouse and garden seat design, engraved elevation, 1778, *Designs in Architecture*.

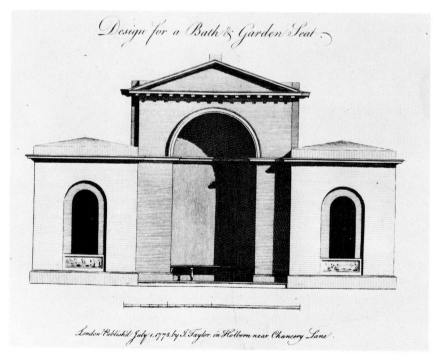

Design for a Bath & Garden Seat

London Publish'd July 1. 1778 by J. Taylor in Holborn near Chancery Lane.

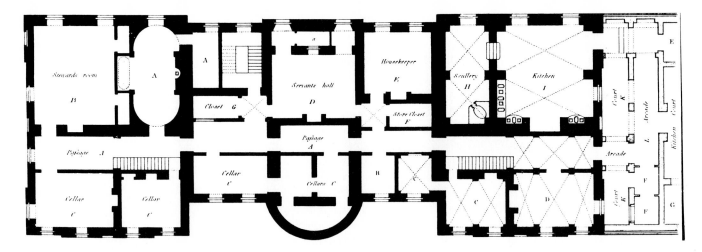

Fig. 6.21. Malvern Hall, engraved
basement plan, 1789, *Plans, Elevations,
and Sections.*

Direct Continental reflections reached a bizarre climax in Soane's work for his least colorful ex-Grand Tourist client, Henry Greswolde Lewis. But Lewis must have been a man of discriminating tastes, for he subsequently also patronized the painter John Constable (fig. 6.7). From Soane he commissioned in 1783 designs for new wings and an entrance porch for Malvern Hall, near Solihull (fig. 1.8). Externally the porch is the outstanding feature. Semicircular, executed in Meriden sandstone, its frieze reproduces the bull's head and garland motif from the celebrated Temple of Vesta at Tivoli. To any well-traveled visitor, the porch announces Lewis's education on the Grand Tour, by referring to a popular monument of the ancient world.

At the time Soane was expanding Malvern, he converted a large part of the existing interior of the main house. As a final touch of modernization, Soane proposed to erect a newfangled bathroom in the old basement (fig. 6.21 at *A*). Were it not for the obvious advantages with drainage, this would seem a dank and inconvenient place. Nevertheless, it was the preferred position, especially among the fashionable Parisian installations which Soane may have had in mind.[54] In all respects other than location, the Malvern arrangement relates closely to the Pitt bathhouse (fig. 6.19). Soane sketched a pencil plan similar to it in the lower right-hand corner of his fascinating drawing for the Malvern bath (fig. 6.22). To compensate for the subterranean situation, Soane ingeniously contrived indirect illumination from a door, a window, and two skylights, while ensuring privacy with frosted glass as in a modern lavatory. He supplemented natural light by the flicker of *torchères* reflected from a looking glass above a couch—reminiscences, perhaps, of the Villa

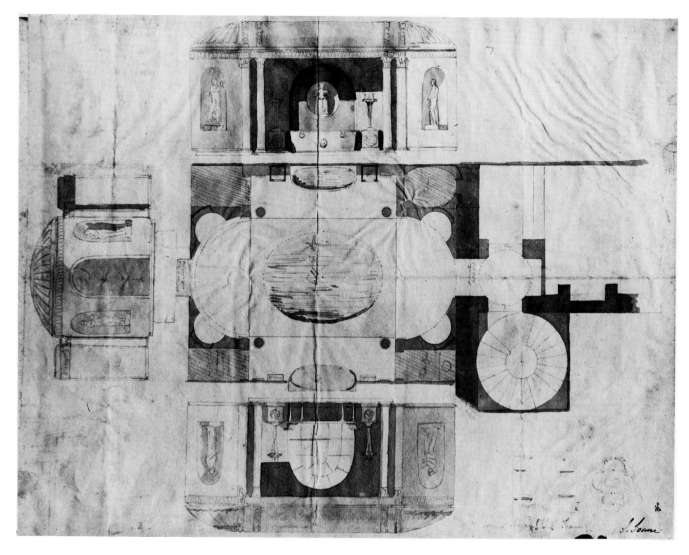

Fig. 6.22. Malvern Hall, bathroom design, plan and elevations (V&A, 3436.188).

Palagonia, and the Apollo triclinium of Lucullus. To mitigate the resemblance of the interior decor to that of his summer dining room (fig. 6.8), Soane installed a plunge bath in place of a dining table, and a sarcophagus-shaped hot tub in lieu of a chimneypiece. Had Lewis not at the last moment eliminated the room,[55] it would have been of almost barbaric splendor, though only 24 feet in length. It evoked the decadence of the late Roman empire, the *frigidarii* and *caldarii* of whose *terme* its plan recalled. It also evoked for Soane and his client their Roman holiday frame of mind. Although the bath was never erected, it was at Malvern that Soane capped the phase in his early style when he relied most on the Continent for inspiration. In 1798 he executed for Lewis what he called a "Barn à la Paestum,"[56] in fond allusion to their joint rambles in Southern Italy many years before.

A list of Soane's earliest patrons reveals the nature of his clientele. Only the Bishop and Yorke could claim descent from the higher ranks of nobility; the rest came from the affluent landed gentry (Pitt was made Baron Camelford as late as 1783). All, except Pitt and the Bishop, were under twenty-six when they met the architect. By and large, the young sons of squires or businessmen continued to provide Soane with the bulk of his private commissions. But the way was not entirely without pitfalls. Out of the seven individuals portrayed in this "rogues gallery" of Soane's first patrons (figs. 6.1–6.7), nearly half disappointed him with empty promises of work. Such a failure rate might serve as a fair index of what a talented yet still unknown late eighteenth-century architect could encounter at the outset of his career. The key to success lay less with these initial contacts than with the labyrinthine ramifications of upper-class English society. Through the people the architect met abroad he could infiltrate the entire patronage system as long as he maintained the correct professional decorum: he must be uncompromising in his standards, yet tolerant of everyone's whims; friendly in manner, yet never presumptuous; punctilious in delivering designs, yet long-suffering when it came to collecting overdue bills.[57]

In the light of Soane's activities for these clients, it is possible to speak of a consciously affected Grand Tourist manner in his early work. In these buildings and projects, more than in his later ones, he drew heavily upon his recollections from abroad. With time he would integrate the references into a more homogeneous style of his own. But for the benefit of Grand Tourist clients, he selected elements of the Continental architectural heritage that belonged to Britain, too, as a result of the advent of international tourism.

·7·

"All We Like Sheep": Guidebooks and Grand Tourism

TO A FORMER PUPIL traveling in Italy, William Chambers had the following advice to give about Naples: "You will See Some [exe]crable performances there and thereabouts...avoid them all." That remark was written in 1774. Four years later, another Chambers pupil, Thomas Hardwick, commented disdainfully on "the very wretched State of the Arts in Naples." At around the same time John Soane received a copy of Chambers's letter and passed along its warning when he wrote to a friend describing "all the works in architecture of Naples" as "miserable in points of Composition." "There is so little for an Architect to do there," echoed Soane's traveling companion, Robert Furze Brettingham.[1]

It is obvious from these quotations that Chambers had triggered a chain reaction among a younger generation which absorbed his biases as uncritically as a sponge. Singly the snatches of recorded hearsay are insignificant; together they make an interesting point. They clarify the effect that preconceived notions had upon shaping the itineraries, prejudicing the outlook, and preconditioning the reactions of English artists abroad. Seen from this perspective, any architect's travels lose their aura of uniqueness. Instead, the Grand Tour to Italy emerges less as a sequence of events, or itinerary, and more in terms of the psychology of vision and the attitudes that these events imply. We must ask ourselves not only what Soane saw, but why he saw it in the way he did, or did not. His myopic vision, a function of what he had assimilated before departure and what he read en route, explains some of the blind spots of an epoch.

On 2 May 1778, after a journey of nearly six weeks, Soane reached Rome, where he and Brettingham remained until they separated at Christmas. In his only surviving letter home, written that summer, Soane summed up his activities as "seeing and examining the numerous and inestimable remains of Antiquity."[2] A vaguer, less helpful piece of prose would be hard to imagine, especially in the absence of any other cor-

The English are like a flock of sheep; they follow each other about, always go to the same place, and never care to show any originality.

Jacques Casanova de Seingalt
Memoirs

129

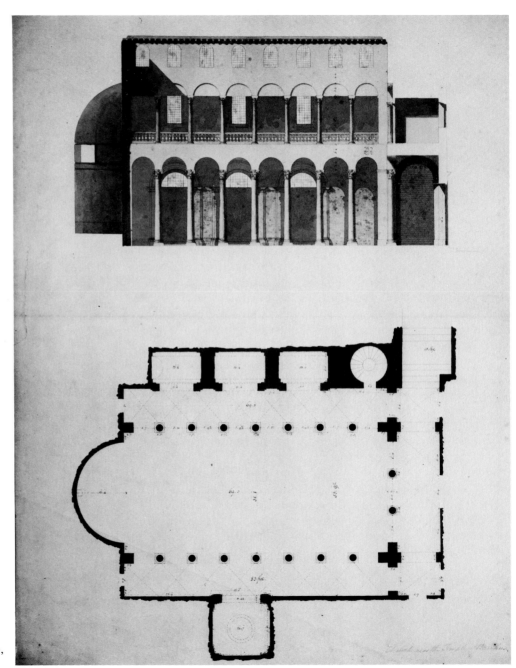

Fig. 7.1. S. Agnese fuori le Mura, Rome, plan and section, 1778 (SM, Drawer 45, Set 3, Item 3).

respondence with family or friends. Compared with the witty, informative reports of the Adam or Dance brothers, Soane's Grand Tour offers no such literary jewels. His every plodding step has to be pieced together from the evidence of drawings, sketchbooks, and the manuscript notes that go with them. At the same time they demonstrate, again and again, the sort of *idées fixes* that Soane brought with him to Rome.

Soane's first dated Roman drawing (fig. 7.1) gives a better indication of his attitude than that conveyed by his surviving writings. He drew his plan and cross section of the church of S. Agnese fuori le Mura on 21 May, less than three weeks after arrival. It remains one of his most effective early examples of draftsmanship. The plan is neat and crisp—though slightly inaccurate in places. The yellowish brown washes eloquently evoke the shadowy apse and aisles of a typical Roman basilica. The eighteenth century mistakenly took this similarity to an ancient structure as a genuine sign of Antiquity. Actually, the seventh-century church was built explicitly in honor of Saint Agnes and had not been converted from an older building. Yet Soane removed the contemporary mosaics in an effort to "restore" the interior to what he imagined its pristine appearance would have been. He regularized the columns to make them look as if they belonged to a single structure, whereas they had come from many ruined ones. With a sweep of the watercolor brush, Soane banished from S. Agnese those elements he and his contemporaries refused to see in their efforts to "antiquate" more recent monuments.

Throughout his Italian sojourn, Soane perpetrated afresh the mistakes of his predecessors. A page from his rather crude Roman sketchbook (fig. 7.2) forms a remarkable parallel with the studies of William

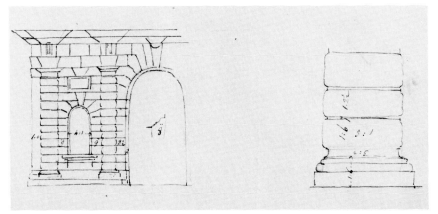

Fig. 7.2. Gateway to the Farnese Gardens, Rome, sketch elevation of the lower half of the gate (SM, Miscellaneous Sketches 1780–82, p. 154).

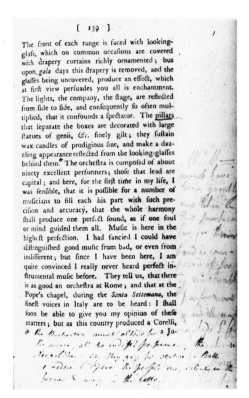

[139]

The front of each range is faced with looking-glaſs, which on common occaſions are covered with drapery curtains richly ornamented ; but upon. *gala* days this drapery is removed, and the glaſſes being uncovered, produce an effect, which at firſt view perſuades you all is enchantment. The lights, the company, the ſtage, are reflected from ſide to ſide, and conſequently ſo often multiplied, that it confounds a ſpectator. The pillars that ſeparate the boxes are decorated with large ſtatues of genii, *&c.* finely gilt; they ſuſtain wax candles of prodigious ſize, and make a dazzling appearance reflected from the looking-glaſſes behind them. The orcheſtra is compoſed of about ninety excellent performers; thoſe that lead are capital ; and here, for the firſt time in my life, I was ſenſible, that it is poſſible for a number of muſicians to fill each his part with ſuch preciſion and accuracy, that the whole harmony ſhall produce one perfect ſound, as if one ſoul or mind guided them all. Muſic is here in the higheſt perfection. I had fancied I could have diſtinguiſhed good muſic from bad, or even from indifferent ; but ſince I have been here, I am quite convinced I really never heard perfect inſtrumental muſic before. They tell us, that there is as good an orcheſtra at Rome ; and that at the Pope's chapel, during the *Santa Settemana,* the fineſt voices in Italy are to be heard : I ſhall ſoon be able to give you my opinion of theſe matters ; but as this country produced a Corelli,

Fig. 7.3. Annotated page from Soane's copy of Anna Miller's *Letters from Italy* (SM, AL, 2D).

Chambers a generation before. Both student architects, when delineating the gateway to the Farnese Gardens, omitted the top storey as if it did not exist. They had it on good authority that the upper half could not have been by Vignola, to whom they readily concurred in attributing the lower, rusticated portion. This was simply another case of mistaken identity. In a typical display of *maniera,* Vignola had designed both the top and the bottom to form deliberately contrasting stylistic accents: the one severe and restrained; the other more open and fanciful.[3] As at S. Agnese, architects were led into error by their own limited outlook. And error, once entrenched, has a bad habit of recurring, as guidebook literature so often proves.

By far the most unusual material relating to Soane's travels comes from the numerous guidebooks which he bought, annotated, and preserved for posterity. Of these, the earliest and most comprehensive is the one he must have purchased in London before leaving: Anna Riggs Miller's *Letters from Italy.*[4] It rarely left Soane's side. He had it specially vellum-bound so it could accompany him in all weathers in its own water-repellent jacket. Over a period of nearly two years he relied upon it as upon a constant companion. It also served as a catchall for the remarks he jotted down all over the margins (fig. 7.3) in preference to using sketchbook paper.[5] Strange though it may sound, Anna Miller's *Letters* became a kind of alter ego for him. It was typical of the thoroughness of the architect that he was not content to leave the relationship a one-sided one. He went a step further by addressing the authoress admiring letters of his own from Italy. He even assembled a copy of her guide with illustrations which he intended to present to her when he returned to England.[6] As will be seen, he had ulterior motives. But the case of Miller's *Letters* conveys an idea of the extent of eighteenth-century reliance on guidebooks, and the ambivalent feelings that developed toward them.

To start with, as Soane's annotations show, Anna Miller's guidebook was perfectly adequate to unlock for him the churches, museums, picture galleries, and antiquities of the Eternal City. It must have mattered little at first that she lapsed into error, ignoring whole geographical sectors, or entire artistic epochs. Later, his patience with her would diminish, and occasional corrections to her mistakes crept into the margins. For instance, when she claimed the Pantheon had lost its gilt bronze decoration, Soane retorted in the adjacent margin: "The Cornice round the Aperture is all of Bronze and part of the Gilding rem[ain]s."[7] Soane was in a position to know the facts. To prove his point he had climbed up to the dizzying heights of the oculus and made a detailed study. He

Fig. 7.4. Pantheon, Rome, detail of the cross section drawing (SM, Drawer 45, Set 3, Item 29).

incorporated the information into a meticulous cross section of the Pantheon (fig. 7.4), in which he provided measurements and annotations as to the type of interior revetment. By such daring feats of acrobatics the young students, singly, and working in teams, culled the few remaining facts that had been inaccessible to preceding generations. Part of their aim was to distinguish myth from truth. Guidebook writers like Anna Miller rarely withstood this kind of close scrutiny.

Letters from Italy reached no literary summits in its branch of the art. It formed a typical crest in a general wave of travel literature that swept over Europe in the 1770s and 1780s.[8] Like most of its kind, it was extremely derivative, as perhaps Soane began to realize once he reached Naples. Chambers notwithstanding, Soane *did* travel to that city, along with most other architects, who were lured by the fascination of a place considered taboo. Confronted with the facade of the Royal Palace there, Soane trusted to the evidence of his own eyes. Next to the printed statement that it was twenty-two bays long, he wrote the correct figure, twenty one, in the margin of *Letters from Italy*. On this and on many other occasions, Anna Miller, rather than looking for herself, had copied from the guidebook *she* had been following: Le Français de Lalande's, *Voyage d'un Français en Italie,* published a decade before. As it happened, Soane also owned the Frenchman's book.[9] By comparing the two written sources with his own observations, Soane would have been made aware of how much guidebook writers owed one another in the way of misinformation. In Naples, too, Soane recorded one of the first of his outbursts against Anna Miller when he wrote that "M- must have been greatly mistaken" in her praise of the Teatro S. Carlo, which Soane described as the "worst theatre in the world to hear music" (fig. 7.3).

Soane's heightened *esprit critique* by the time he reached Naples could be attributed to the person in whose company he traveled. Three days before Christmas, 1778, he set off for Naples with his protector, the Bishop of Derry (fig. 6.1). The two men remained together for most of the two months they spent wintering in the south. The eccentric Bishop defies any general categorizations of the eighteenth-century tourist abroad. His classical education, encyclopedic knowledge, and instinct for scientific exploration made him automatically suspicious of the half-truths most travel literature was fabricated of. In the person of the Bishop, Soane found a walking guidebook. Their outward and homeward bound journeys from Rome are remarkable examples of the Bishop's unique style of travel, which justifies his reputation as one of the most inveterate of Grand Tourists, and also proves him among the most inventive.

On Christmas Day, the pair of travelers reached an isolated stretch of the Adriatic coastline about 20 miles northwest of Terracina. Here, as has been seen, the Bishop thought he had located the supposed villa belonging to Lucullus. He and Soane even singled out what they thought to be a legendary dining triclinium mentioned in Plutarch's *Lives* (fig. 6.3). As Soane recalled in his *Memoirs:* "after wandering over those monuments of departed greatness, we determined the site of the Apollo [triclinium], and banqueted within the ruins on mullet fresh from the ancient reservoirs."[10] The Bishop, an accomplished Latinist, could fully savor this meal *al fresco* as an exact reenactment of Lucullan seafood dinners. His unusual combination of classical texts with on-the-spot investigations anticipates modern archaeological methodology. Only the looseness with which the Bishop imaginatively conflated his sources betrays a less fastidious age of scholarship.

The itinerary of Soane's return journey with the Bishop from Naples to Rome is equally amazing. They set out on 12 March 1779 and reached their destination after two weeks of painstakingly retracing the route of the ancient Via Appia.[11] On the way they recorded Roman milestones and

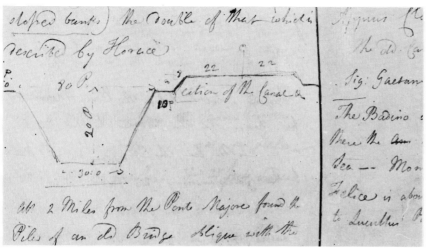

Fig. 7.5. Notebook page showing sketch cross section of the canal through the Pontine Marshes, near Terracina (SM, "Italian Sketches 1779," p. 110).

inscriptions, measured the width of the old road at various places, and tried to identify cities like Sessa, Pogia, or Mesa ad Medias, referred to by such classical authors as the geographer Strabo. While crossing the Pontine Marshes, Soane drew a cross section of the barge canal (fig. 7.5), remarking that the previous one, described by Horace, had been half the size. The Bishop was particularly knowledgeable about the Pontine Marshes, having taken personal credit for initiating the most recent papal drainage scheme, carried out by the hydraulic engineer Gaetano Rapini.[12] The Bishop may also have directed Soane's attention to the fairly lengthy discussion of the Marshes in Le Français de Lalande's guide. The passages referring to the history of the area were annotated in Soane's copy, and specific mention was made of the Horatian *Satires*.[13] One of these poems describes Horace's progress along the Via Appia and down the old canal, on his way from Rome to Brindisi. The Bishop was reconstructing, in the reverse direction, the Horatian journey of centuries before. Therefore the question of travel literature is still of paramount importance here: Le Français de Lalande was being verified; Horace could still serve as a guide.

Only the Bishop, with his intelligence and boundless energy, could have mapped out such bizarre and arduous classical tours as those he undertook with Soane. The architect followed in the prelate's wake, recording what he could of the older man's nonstop effusions. Once, taking a leaf out of the Bishop's book, Soane made a contribution of his own. It took the form of a remarkable "flashback" to his days in Dance's office. In the vicinity of Anzio, he recollected Dance saying that he had

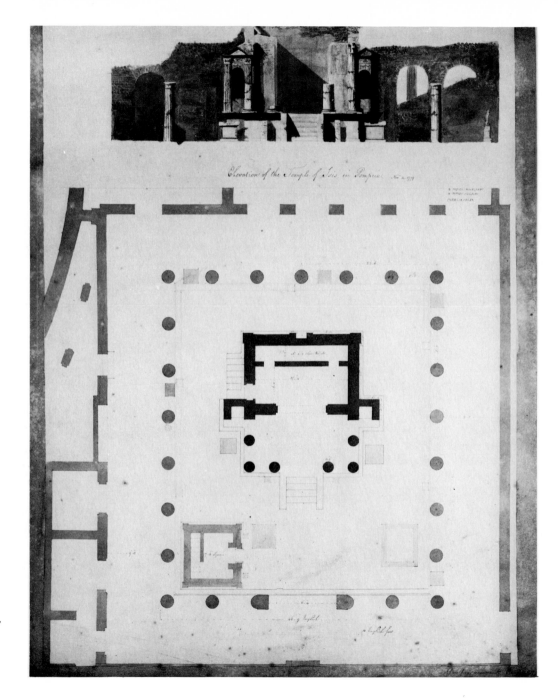

Fig. 7.6. Temple of Isis, Pompeii, plan and elevation, 1779 (SM, Drawer 45, Set 3, Item 4).

once been entertained there at the villa of the Corsini family.[14] Soane demonstrated that he, like the Bishop, could start to make original associations of ideas, unassisted by guidebooks.

By the 1770s, Pompeii had become the major attraction for visitors to nearby Naples. The excavations, after a slow start around 1750, had unearthed enough of the buried city to reveal many of the most important first century A.D. buildings. The Neapolitan state ran the site like a combination of armed camp and tourist trap. Guards had strict orders to prevent visitors from making notes or drawings. Anna Miller lamented this fact in *Letters from Italy*.[15] Determined architects, however, managed to get their measurements anyway. Soane, for one, visited Pompeii on at least three sketching parties in January 1779, the earliest occasion being the fifth of the month. At first he directed his attention to the Temple of Isis, the principal excavated site represented by artists. A number of months later, on the basis of preliminary sketches, Soane produced a finished drawing of the precinct's plan and elevation (fig. 7.6). Then, when displaying the drawing in his Royal Academy lectures, he revealed that it had been based on "sketches made by stealth by moonlight."[16] Contrary to what he told his audiences, his nocturnal measurements are all wrong on account of groping in the dark from column to column.

The interdiction on sketching at Pompeii tended to protect a band of officious guides, who told unfounded tales to unwary tourists, much as they do today. During a subsequent visit in January, Soane noted the cicerone's improbable explanation of some curious postholes in the colonnade of the gladiators' courtyard (fig. 7.7). On the basis of what he may have heard, the architect also provided a fairly plausible sketch reconstruction of the upper storey that had been destroyed by volcanic ash from Mount Vesuvius. Soane's twenty Pompeian drawings represent similar investigations by many other students, who likewise evaded detection. The law closed an eye on their infringements, in the interests of maintaining what had become a booming aspect of the Neapolitan tourist industry.

The ruined temples of Paestum, discovered by chance about the same date as Pompeii, attracted less attention because of their relative isolation and massive baseless Doric columns, which struck Soane on 15 February 1779 as "exceedingly rude." That biased statement notwithstanding, he made two recorded visits to the site.[17] On the earliest occasion, in late January, he had devoted to the three Paestum temples a series of measured sketches that included plans, elevations and even details of lofty capitals or entablatures (fig. 7.8). Each time he traveled to Paestum, he met with a group of Grand Tourists: the Bishop of Derry's party in

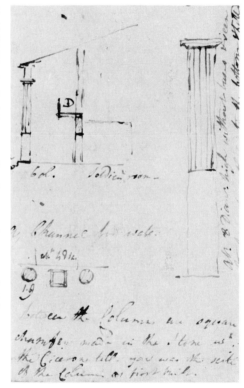

Fig. 7.7. Courtyard of the gladiators, Pompeii, sketch plan and detail of a column and reconstructed section through a barracks building (SM, "Italian Sketches and Mem.," p. 168).

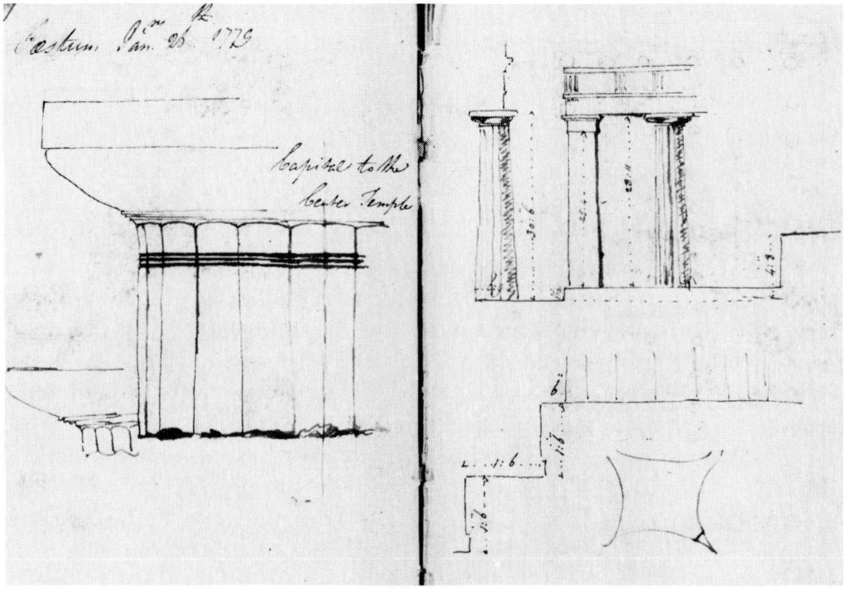

Fig. 7.8. Neptune Temple, Paestum, sketches of capital *(left)*, and stylobate *(bottom right)*, and section through the end of the cella (SM, "Italian Sketches 1779," pp. 28–29).

February; Philip Yorke and Thomas Bowdler the month before. Yorke wrote that at Paestum Soane "accompanied us thither and measured the buildings: I believe Major's views are tolerably exact."[18] The implication is that Soane was in the process of verifying Thomas Major's *The Ruins of Paestum,* published in 1768. The architect may even have had a copy of the book along with him. At any rate, some of his detailed drawings seem inspired by the format of Major's engravings. Although *The Ruins of Paestum* could certainly not be described as a guidebook in the normal sense, it still belonged to the travel literature generally consulted by cognoscenti. The popularization of the antiquities by books was a fact that a would-be explorer-architect had to contend with. In the case of Paestum, the virtually unknown spot soon became inundated with flocks of artists and tourists. By 1778, the Paestum excursion had already become institutionalized as part of a routine three-day junket.[19] Parties were herded around, a familiar enough sight in our age but a relative novelty then. Within a generation, the romantic discovery of a lost ancient city had been trampled under visitors' heels.

Among the Grand Tourists spending the winter of 1778/79 in Naples, a number of the more adventurous seriously discussed the possibility of a visit to Sicily and Malta. While by no means as commonplace as the Pompeii or Paestum trips, the one to the islands had been made numerous times before. Enough travel literature on it existed to kindle the imagination.[20] But the plan for Sicily, no sooner hatched, was set aside because those wintering at Naples preferred to attend Holy Week in Rome. This series of ceremonies was not to be missed by any Grand Tourist. In the margins of Anna Miller's description of it, Soane wrote: "Glorious and great is the effect of this spectacle."[21]

A matter of days after Easter the cancelled trip to Sicily and Malta was on again. Soane and his traveling companions (Bowdler, Burdon, Lewis, Patteson, and Stuart) started preparations to head south. The party assembled aboard ship on 21 April 1779 for a week-long sea voyage to Palermo.[22] After leaving Palermo they split into two groups. Bowdler and Stuart arrived at Naples some weeks in advance of the others' return, in early July. Fortunately, John Patteson's surviving letters establish the trip's basic itinerary as well as its underlying motive.

In his first letter from Palermo, Patteson referred his mother to her copy of a popular guidebook by Patrick Brydone, *A Tour through Sicily and Malta*. With Brydone's guidebook beside her, Mrs. Patteson could follow her son's journey from an armchair at home. He quickly reassured her that she should not believe all she read about the dangers of Sicily. Again and again he complained of the exaggerated artistic license Brydone had taken in some of his descriptions.[23] Nevertheless, the trip of the six companions was, from the outset, patently Brydonesque. Although they intended not to be taken in by "the great Mr. Brydone," yet they duplicated his circuit of the islands in reverse, empirically testing his text at every stage. And certain episodes from the beginning of their itinerary indicate the Grand Tourists had their noses buried in Brydone.

The six young travelers started by staying in the same Palermo hotel as Brydone had done, to prove that the innkeepers were not as bad as he had said. They climbed Monte Pellegrino because they wanted to show it was not as hard as he had written.[24] Soane bought a copy of the book, *Vita e miracoli di S. Rosalia*, which Brydone had not managed to obtain.[25] Finally, the entire group went off to the suburban Villa Palagonia at Bagheria, to see if it could be as monstrous as Brydone's description had made it sound. Unconsciously, no doubt, Patteson paraphrased Brydone's very words when he wrote of the villa: "The Prince of Palagonias Monsters are nothing more than the most extravagant caricatures in Stone, one cannot help laughing at them, though at the same time . . . one must blame such Folly." Patteson referred to the grostesque statues lining the approaches to the villa, one of which Soane apparently drew on the spot.[26] These instances of the six travelers' mingled reliance on and disdain for Brydone are characteristic of their relationship to his book throughout their trip.

The highpoints of the trip around Sicily and Malta all coincide with those of Brydone: Agrigento, Valetta, Syracuse, Taormina, Mount Etna, and then Naples. The only major deviations from Brydone's route were side excursions to the Temples of Segesta and Selinunte, which he had missed. There was still no escaping the omnipresent travelogues of previous explorers. Henry Swinburne, an acquaintance of Soane's, had recently returned to Rome from his own journey retracing Brydone's footsteps, and would soon publish his stirring account of Segesta. As a recent veteran of the Sicilian trip, he would have been the logical person for the young travelers to consult before setting out. When Patteson spoke of Segesta's sublime "simplicity," he might as well have been quoting from Swinburne's forthcoming book.[27]

Sublimity supplied the keynote of these Sicilian expeditions. Soane, when trying to recall his impressions of the Temple of Jupiter at Agrigento, got them hopelessly mixed up with the evocative imagery of Swinburne. The architect rephrased the guidebook writer's sentiments when he spoke to his Royal Academy audiences of "the awful and terrific grandeur of . . . the frightful ruins of that stupendous pile."[28] Unforgettable scenes awaited the travelers at every turning; this was what Patteson called the adventurous "sauce" of Sicilian travel.[29] It was the perfect antidote to the surfeit of archaeological remains around Naples. At the same time, it should not cause them to lose sight of the detective work they had set out to do. Previous opinions were all held up to scrutiny. At Syracuse Rowland Burdon took it upon himself to disprove the legend of the tyrant's "ear," faithfully reported by guidebooks. He disputed the auditory properties of a cave that had supposedly served as a prison, where the ruler of Syracuse, Dionysius, could overhear his enemies plotting. Soane recorded the position of the "ear" on a site plan he drew of the cave and the nearby Antique theater.[30]

The Syracuse drawing is one of the very few from Soane's trip to the islands. Another, representing the theater at Taormina, although dated 9 June 1779 has all the appearance of a copy from a survey already carried out in French toises rather than English feet (fig. 7.9). If the expedition was scientific in nature, then the lack of drawings, notes, or sketchbooks raises a question about the virtually blank Sicilian page of Soane's travels. One possibility is the law of chance survival and loss. A more penetrating answer would seem to lie in the undue haste with which the tour was conducted, like a race to beat the clock. The party made the tour of the islands in less than ten weeks, in order to keep pace with Brydone and Swinburne, who had taken exactly that long. But Soane was an architect, not a guidebook writer. His French con-

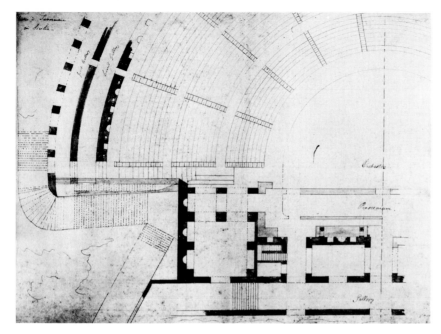

Fig. 7.9. Theater at Taormina, plan (SM, Drawer 45, Set 3, Item 21).

temporaries, like Jean-Pierre Hoüel, Louis-Jean Desprez, and Jean-Augustin Rénard, had spent months, even years, covering the same territory and measuring the monuments. Soane was in too much of a hurry to have anything comparable to show.

Soane, who styled himself as "draftsman" to his young companions, once complained to his biographer, John Britton, that "they were not persons to take a laborious and critical survey and investigation of the buildings they proposed to visit."[31] Some friction certainly existed between Soane, hurried against his will from pillar to post, and his young friends, impatient to get on with the trip and return to civilization. Although Patteson claimed that "No four young Men could have stumbled upon each other more fortunately," he went on to reveal the source of the conflict when he wrote: "Mr. Lewis and Myself see these venerable Ruins with less Passion and get many a good laugh against the others [Soane and Burdon] when they happen to admire a modern Arch for an antient one."[32] At the root of this teasing lay the whole dilemma of the architect abroad. Often he was forced to reconcile, as best he could, the demands of his profession in a competitive age and the easygoing dilettantism of the Grand Tourists he kept company with.

Of all his Sicilian companions, Soane found Burdon the most con-

Fig. 7.10. Title page of Soane's inscribed copy of Scipione Maffei's *La Verona illustrata* (SM, AL, 33C).

genial. No sooner had they returned to Rome in July 1778 than the pair began planning a trip for the month of August. This took them to the art centers of North and Central Italy and finally to Venice at the beginning of September. Along the way they certainly visited Bologna, Parma, Milan, Brescia (where they met Patteson again), Verona, and Vicenza.[33] Soane probably had his copy of Anna Miller's first volume along with him, but it has since disappeared. It would have been particularly pertinent at Parma, because there she singled out for mention the display of George Dance's drawings for the *magnifica galleria* (fig. 2.3). Her remarks on contemporary artists were extremely rare, and one imagines Dance could not have been unflattered by the honor she did him in her guide. He may have recommended it to Soane on that account.[34]

For his journey with Burdon, Soane found it necessary to augment Anna Miller's *Letters* in several ways. From some unidentified source, he compiled a long and rambling list of the principal sights to see in the Venetian state.[35] He also purchased a copy of Francesco Scipione Maffei's guide, *La Verona illustrata* (fig. 7.10). The book became very useful. Verona caught Soane's interest more than any other architectural center in the North. Maffei's scholarly text may have contributed to Soane's veneration of the Veronese buildings by Michele Sanmicheli, which he later studied (see chap. 8).

On the occasion of his trip with Burdon, but perhaps as much as a full year earlier, Soane made the tour of Umbria and the Marches, following a pattern popularized by such architects as Robert Adam.[36] Just enough of Soane's annotations exist in the second volume of Anna Miller's *Letters* to establish that he made a trip from Rome to Ravenna. Along the way he again made caustic comments in the margins of his guidebook, until he exploded in anger at the bigoted criticisms of the Santa Casa at Loreto. In response to the contention that the marble exterior was in poor taste he replied "On the contrary . . . the Statues of the Prophets are deservedly admired." He then echoed the misattribution to Michelangelo made by Le Français de Lalande.[37] Soane had begun playing his sources of information off against each other and expressing strong opinions of his own.

Nonetheless, on this same trip one of Soane's most remarkable identifications with a guidebook occurred. At Anna Miller's suggestion he stopped by the roadside to admire the so-called Temple of Clitumnus. (Once again an Early Christian church rather than a true antiquity was in question here.) While there, he sketched the little building. Later he reproduced it in a measured drawing (fig. 7.11), among his most atmospherically evocative, with its "streaky" watercolor technique and weed-

Fig. 7.11. The so-called Temple of Clitumnus, near Foligno, elevation (V&A, 3436.187).

infested masonry.[38] Later still when back in England he sent a copy to Anna Miller. In so doing, he revealed the hidden motivation behind his flattering attention to her. In one passage she had advocated facsimiles of Italian temples as ornaments for English landscape gardens. And in one of his final letters to her, Soane urged her to build a copy of the Clitumnus structure for herself. But she died in 1781, without ever meeting her extraordinary young correspondent.[39] Here was an instance of literally taking the guidebook writer at her word. In this way Soane acted out in reality the implicit relationship between those who guide and those who are guided by them.

Soane's homeward journey to England began precipitously at the insistence of his patron, the Bishop of Derry, who had succeeded to the vast estates of the earldom of Bristol at Christmastide, 1779. The season for travel was not propitious. Great Britain had declared a state of war with France. Through the Bishop's influence Soane obtained a French passport in Rome, which he had promptly to replace with an English one in Florence,[40] permitting him to travel via Germany. Soane left Rome hurriedly for the last time on 19 April 1780, but, even so, he made his final trip into a lightning-quick tour. By this time he knew the standard route to Florence well enough to act as unofficial companion for a pair of English tourists, Michael Pepper and his chaperone the Reverend Mr. George Holgate. At the Palazzo Farnese, Caprarola, they admired a demonstration of the freakish properties of the whispering chamber—the same performance repeated by generations of tour guides down to the present day.[41]

At Florence, Soane purchased another guidebook to add to his collection that already included those by Miller, Brydone, Maffei, and Le Français de Lalande. The guide in question, the *Itinéraire des routes les plus fréquentées,* by Louis Dutens, served Soane well on the long voyage home.[42] Dutens provided a close equivalent to modern automobile club route maps. He tabulated mileages between cities, recommended inns along the way, and discussed the most famous sights. Again Soane alternated between writing down impressions in his notebooks and scribbling marginalia in his copy of Dutens. Furnished with his English passport and Dutens, Soane set off for the north on 29 April. He followed a zigzag itinerary that permitted him to complete unfinished business in all directions. He used his Dutens as he passed through the familiar cities of Bologna, Padua, Vicenza, and Verona. He took in Mantua this time, settled his affairs at Parma, and stopped again at Milan, before heading for the Splügen Pass, Zurich, Basel, Cologne, Liège, Brussels, and the English Channel.[43]

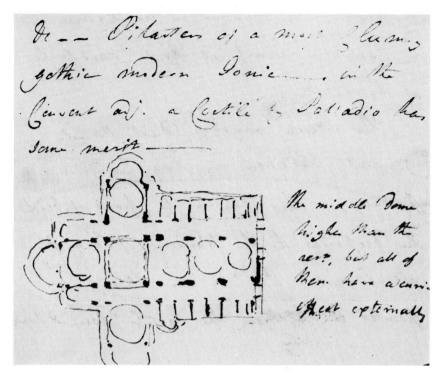

Fig. 7.12. S. Giustina, Padua, sketch plan (SM, "Notes Italy," p. 322).

Soane now knew his way about, as he had not during his earlier journeys in Italy. This sophistication made a difference to his attitude. The notebook he carried with him is, for once, coherent and full of original remarks upon what he saw around him. At Padua, for instance, he took to task the anonymous travel hints he himself had laboriously copied down the year before. According to them the church of S. Giustina was "the finest piece of Architecture in Italy."[44] Soane now affirmed (fig. 7.12) that it was not by Palladio at all and that in any case the order of architecture was "a most Clumsy gothic modern Ionic." He also started to observe things that no guidebook had ever mentioned: Palladian-style villas south of Padua (fig. 6.8), the obscure Ponte S. Michele in Vicenza, the women's apparel of Verona, the Lazzaretto there, and so forth.

The apogee of Soane's newfound sense of identity came when, against all obstacles, he persisted in making a time-consuming nine-day detour from Milan to Genoa and back. Some inner urge drove him there. Perhaps he had to say farewell to the city that had given him his first taste of Italy on his journey out in 1778. Two years later he was a changed individual. The visit to Genoa found him a seasoned traveler at the

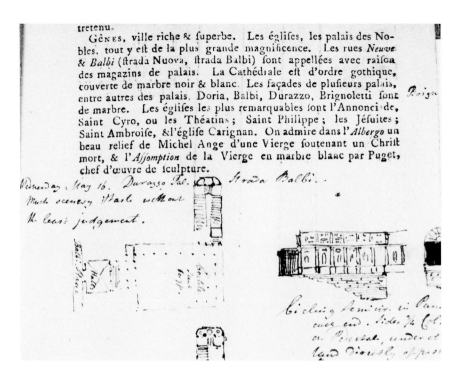

Fig. 7.13. Palazzo Durazzo-Pallavicini, Genoa, sketch plan and section of the stairhall from Soane's annotated copy of Louis Dutens's *Itinéraire* (SM, AL, 34B).

pinnacle of self-confidence. With the ease of a cosmopolite, he socialized among members of the English colony: the consul, an opera singer, and a grande dame of local society.[45] Even so, the architect's copy of Dutens was not far from reach. He copied out of it a list of noteworthy churches and palaces. Then he reminded himself to refer back to the original guidebook page where he had recorded his impressions of the Palazzo Durazzo-Pallavicini (fig. 7.13). Next to a site plan he drew a cross section of the recently completed staircase,[46] using tiny, quick, and calligraphically powerful pen strokes. What an improvement over his tentative Roman sketches of two summers before (see fig. 7.2)! Like his sketches, Soane's words carried new force. He appraised the palace as having "Much scenery and taste without the least judgement." These were strong statements compared with the quibbling remarks he had made earlier in the margins of Anna Miller's guide (see fig. 7.3).

On his departure from Genoa on 19 May, Soane noted with unusual warmth: "Left . . . at 6 o'clock in the Morn[in]g with heart felt sorrow in firm hopes of seeing it again."[47] Soane never fulfilled that hope. His consolation lay in the guidebooks he had preserved and continued to accumulate. Shelf upon shelf of them fill various nooks and crannies of

Soane's house, constituting a remarkable collection. From the comfort of Lincoln's Inn Fields, Soane had the world at his doorstep. Besides poring over his treasured old guides, he enjoyed a weakness for picaresque novels such as *Gil Blas* and *Devil on Two Sticks,* and for stories such as *The Vicar of Wakefield.* Soane's browsing library distinctly favored the romance of foreign travel and excitement of adventure that was absent from his humdrum professional life.[48] But Soane's collection was not entirely for the purpose of reliving youthful escapades. In 1805, upon his appointment as professor of architecture at the Royal Academy, all the tangible reminders of his travels came into use. Those lectures he gave were the distillation of all he had seen, heard, and read while abroad. They became an illustrated Grand Tour in capsule form. Letters to him from his pupils on their travels reflect the impression made by his vivid descriptions, some genuine, others adopted straight out of guidebooks. Now the shoe was on the other foot. Soane, a product of the eighteenth-century mania for being guided about, had, in his turn, become the guide.

On the whole, his travels justify Casanova's assertion that British tourists were "like a flock of sheep."[49] There existed such a wealth of travel tips, rumors true and false, recommendations by word of mouth, and a voluminous travel literature that it is not surprising that a herdlike mentality resulted. The Grand Tour held perils for travelers which comradeship with compatriots helped to dispel. Unversed in foreign languages, often young and immature, artists and tourists alike sheepishly followed one another about. It is reassuring to detect in Soane, however, a gradual lessening of this grip of guidebooks upon the imagination. Once he began comparing various writers' accounts with the material realities, he started more and more to question the information they had uncritically copied from one another. The disturbing tendency of such writings to derivativeness, and the uncritical way in which such information was often accepted, has a bearing on our next chapter.

Copies and Copyists

Soane borrowed Dance's d[ra]wing of the Sybills Temple and copied it, then hung it up, inserting his own name for that of Dance, as having drawn it on the spot. Byers borrowed the same drawing from Dance, copied it and sold a great number of copies of that as from his own measurement.

Joseph Farington's diary
10 February 1797

A Den of Thieves

AT TIVOLI, the ruins of the Vesta Temple, or Tempio della Sibilla, have intrigued artists for centuries. The romantic ruggedness of the cliff-top setting, above the falls of the river Aniene, provides a foil to the exquisite refinement of the temple. Architects, in particular, have made pilgrimages from Rome to this spot, hallowed by generations of their predecessors. Among them was George Dance the Younger, who visited the site numerous times between April and October 1762 in the process of carrying out a complete measured survey. In letters to his father, he noted the inaccuracies of earlier attempts, such as that by Palladio,[1] as justification for yet another effort to record the structure correctly down to the smallest detail. This boastful assertion, by a son eager to prove himself, reveals the twofold premises behind the vast output of measured drawings on the part of eighteenth-century architects studying in Italy.

Dance saw the task he set himself at Tivoli as "of the greatest service" to his personal development. With more scientific surveying techniques at his command, he hoped to penetrate to the heart of ancient architecture, to an extent never possible before. The process of accurate measurement would impart a knowledge of Roman proportion systems, an understanding of construction methods, and the hidden secrets of the orders. All this, Dance implied, would result from close examination of a supreme example like the Vesta Temple. Dance was also not blind to the fame and recognition that might result from his efforts. He told his father he had been encouraged to see the work as "not unworthy of Publication." Certain Grand Tourists had already lined up behind him to back a future book.[2] So a student architect like Dance was doubly motivated to record what he saw on his travels. As a matter of self-improvement he studied great monuments of the past to learn their design principles. But he also kept in mind the value of such studies to impress future clients, or even the general public, if the work ever appeared in print. The concepts of education, publication, and self-promotion account for what is, perhaps, the largest personal collection of eighteenth-century measured drawings—that assembled by John Soane from the time of his arrival in Italy in May 1778 until his departure two years later.[3]

It must have been shortly after reaching Rome that Soane, following in the footsteps of Dance and so many others, went to Tivoli. Soane's perspective view of the Temple of Vesta (fig. 8.1), along with several other Tivoli sketches can, on account of their relative crudeness, be placed at the beginning of his stay. No doubt Soane had seen Dance's survey so often in the office that he lacked the incentive to duplicate the effort involved. Contrary to what Soane himself later claimed, there is no evidence that he executed anything more detailed than these sketches of the Vesta Temple. Subsequently, however, the Bishop of Derry spoke about erecting a facsimile of the temple at Downhill.[4] His chosen architect, Soane, could not have achieved a scale replica without a proper survey. This may explain the anecdote from Farington's diary quoted at the opening of this chapter.

Joseph Farington elsewhere recorded Dance as saying that Soane had borrowed the Tivoli drawings after reaching London in June 1780.[5] The reason he gave Dance was the loss of his own set in an accident during his return journey. Soane proceeded to copy the drawings and brazenly display them, signed with his own name, as if he had carried them out in the first place. This part of the story, at least, is true. The copies (fig. 8.2) hang in black frames on the walls of the Soane Museum, while the originals, ironically, lie a few feet away tucked in the same drawer they have occupied since Soane purchased them from Dance's heirs.[6] A comparison proves that Soane was faithful to the originals in every respect, though less able to render their landscape settings than the more artistically gifted Dance.

Farington's diary passage goes on to make clear that Soane's actions were not as uncommon as they might seem at first. Dance explained that, years before the Soane incident, he had loaned the same Tivoli drawings to James Byres, the Scottish architect living in Rome. Byres immediately made copies and sold them without asking Dance's consent. Again the facts bear out Farington's account. An anonymous copy of Dance's elevation must be one of those by Byres, judging from its mechanical quality (fig. 8.3). Other evidence supports the idea that Byres ran a profitable business mass-producing drawings for the English tourist market or for

Fig. 8.1. Temple of Vesta, Tivoli, perspective view (SM, Miscellaneous Sketches 1780–82, p. 162).

A·GEOMETRICAL·ELEVATION·OF·THE·REMAINS·OF·A·TEMPLE·AT·TIVOLI

Fig. 8.2. Temple of Vesta, Tivoli, elevation copied after George Dance II (SM, South Drawing Room).

Fig. 8.3. Temple of Vesta, Tivoli, elevation, anonymous copy after George Dance II (RIBA, RAN 1/M/5²).

architects to pass off as their own.[7] Startlingly enough, yet another near-copy after Dance exists among the drawings of the Spanish architect Juan de Villanueva, dating from his student sojourn in Rome of 1758–64.[8]

To make matters more complicated, Dance's letters mention that he did not work alone at Tivoli. He had the collaboration of another architect, an Italian. This individual can probably be identified as Giovanni Stern, on the basis of whose measurements souvenir cork models of the Vesta Temple were made for sale in 1767.[9] Stern, for his part, may have permitted copies to be made of the joint survey. So, in the extreme case of the Tivoli drawings, the question of authorship had international ramifications involving two Englishmen, an expatriate Scot, a Spaniard, and an Italian of German extraction. Moreover, the interdependency of Dance and Stern illustrates the important role of overt or covert collaborations among architects producing measured drawings.

Soane, Hardwick, and Quarenghi

The most thoroughly documented architects' collaborative survey of the eighteenth century to have come to light is the one made by Soane and Thomas Hardwick. Though split up between two quite separate institutions, each half survives more or less intact.[10] No better illustration has so far been discovered of the way in which architects banded together on the tacit understanding that no mention would ever be made of the partnership. Hence Soane breached the unwritten pact when he inscribed the words "with Mr. Hardwicke" next to a preliminary ground plan of S. Maria Maggiore in Rome, prepared on 16 June 1778 (fig. 8.4). He thereby provided a clue to the collaboration; the only such hint in all his papers.

Although there is no proof of it, Soane and Hardwick must have known each other in the mid-1770s when both attended the Royal Academy Schools. Their presence together in Rome during the summer of 1778 prompted the former classmates to conclude a mutually advantageous arrangement. The pooling of resources they envisioned made good common sense because it obviated duplication of effort in assembling a portfolio. Moreover, the process of making measured drawings by its nature involves more than a single person if it is to be carried out efficiently. Measurements may be read aloud to check for accuracy, and turns taken at recording data on a master sheet such as that of Soane for S. Maria Maggiore.[11] The partnership principle makes a relatively easy job for two out of what would be arduous work for one. In the category of measured drawings, therefore, architects working alone

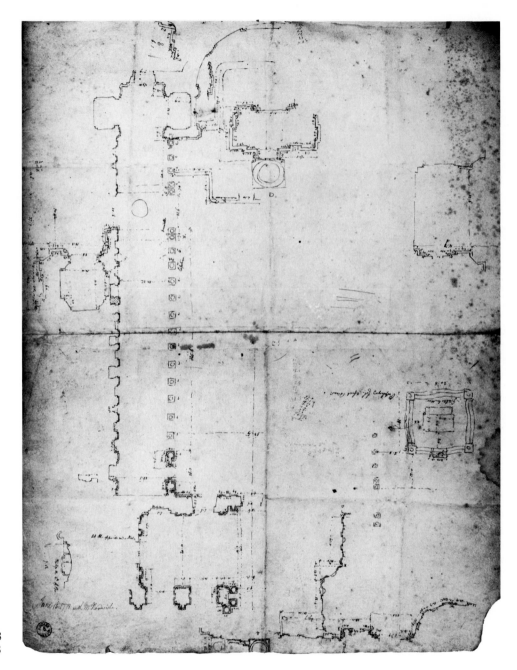

Fig. 8.4. S. Maria Maggiore, Rome, preparatory plan, 1778 (SM, Drawer 45, Set 1, Item 8 recto).

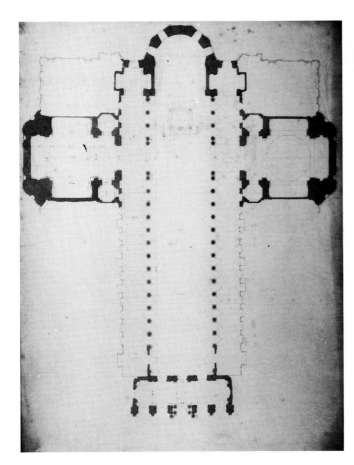

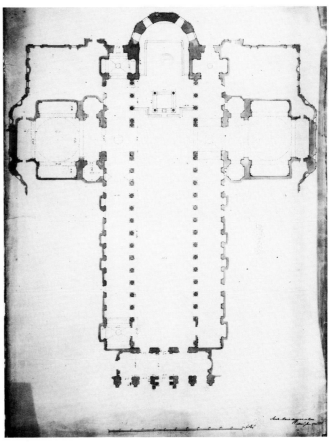

form the exception rather than the rule. Dance collaborated with Stern; Soane collaborated with Hardwick a generation later. Rarely does there exist such a thing as an entirely original drawing of this kind.[12] From the practice of sharing stems the proliferation of duplicate sets of drawings, each equally authentic. After painstaking measurements had been completed on the site, Soane and Hardwick would prepare finished drawings in the studio, based on the working one (figs. 8.5, 8.6). For some reason, Soane never signed his. But Hardwick dated his plan and initialed it, thereby seeming to take sole credit.

passed for unique products by their owners, until their collaborative aspect emerged almost two centuries later.

With a few tiny discrepancies, the finished S. Maria Maggiore plans

Fig. 8.5. S. Maria Maggiore, Rome, plan (SM, Drawer 21, Set 4, Item 1).

Fig. 8.6. Thomas Hardwick, S. Maria Maggiore, Rome, plan (RIBA, E3/37).

are identical. Nevertheless, a degree of personal expression enters even so relatively mechanical a process as this. Soane's plan has a greater number of admeasurements inscribed upon it, together with indications of vaulting in the aisles. Hardwick preferred all his drawings to look cleaner and freer of cluttering details. He strove for an attractive visual effect more than for an absolutely accurate record. Minutiae of construction concerned him less than they did Soane. This indicates a certain difference in temperament. Hardwick inclined toward the painterly; Soane remained very much the architect-engineer.

These traits recur constantly throughout the seven monuments in and around Rome delineated by Soane and Hardwick during their campaign in the summer of 1778. The unifying factor consists in the tendency to concentrate on interior spaces instead of facades. From this point of view, the group of drawings, as a whole, takes on the character of an exercise in the planning aspect of design, rather than in composition. In chronological terms the survey stretches from Antiquity to the Early Christian period, and on into the Renaissance, a representative example of which was Raphael's Villa Madama. A greater breadth of historical open-mindedness typifies academically trained students in the eighteenth century, despite certain blind spots they had, such as for the Baroque period. The rationale behind an historical and eclectic approach came from William Chambers, who admonished his students and protégés, like Soane and Hardwick, to "form if you can a style of Your own in which endeavour to avoid the faults and blend the perfections of all." On a note of urgency Chambers added, "Our students at Rome are right to make a better use of their time now than they formerly used to do, for unless they Study hard and Acquire Superior talents, they will do little."[13] Here was the voice of a mid-century architect, urging on the next generation.

The falling out of Soane and Hardwick sums up this greater competitiveness prevailing in Rome during the later eighteenth century. It will be remembered that a friend and sometime collaborator of Hardwick's, the Edinburgh architect John Henderson, drew Hardwick into his dispute with Soane over the relative originality of their designs for the Bishop of Derry's dining room (fig. 6.8). The whole idea of an artistic trial-by-jury was petty in the first place, and it should never have been allowed to contribute to an already tense atmosphere. No more is seen of Soane's working relationship with Hardwick, who departed from Rome the following spring. Yet, in 1832, Soane could still comment acrimoniously in writing about Hardwick—grudges always died hard with Soane.[14] Even so, the previous collaboration was never revealed.

The emphasis on mass coverage in the interests of eclectic designing had an adverse side to it. The young architects, in the wake of a half century of active publication on Rome, found themselves hard put to locate new material. They were forced to resort to any and all means, even copying with intent to deceive. What for Soane and Hardwick had started as a legitimate collaboration turned into the out-and-out copying of drawings that they had had no previous hand in compiling. Portfolios swelled in content and potential clients who might see them would be none the wiser. The Roman experience was turning from a pleasant finishing school into a facet of the professional race to get ahead.

To illustrate the complex problems of copying, there is no better example in the Soane and Hardwick collections than their parallel drawings of the Villa of Hadrian near Tivoli (figs. 8.7, 8.8). One of the ground plans in Soane's Tivoli series is dated February 1780, while the corresponding Hardwick mate is inscribed "meas[ure]d Nov[embe]r 1777."[15] With such conflicting data who is to be believed? Very fortunately, the garrulous diarist-painter, Thomas Jones, recorded taking part with Hardwick in a sketching expedition to Tivoli on 11 October 1777.[16] This establishes the correctness of Hardwick's chronology and also rules out Soane from taking a hand in compiling the original information. The only problem with the explanation that Soane had copied from Hardwick is that, by February 1780, Hardwick was already back in England. But Jones revealed that the 1777 sketching party included an Italian architect, whom Jones refers to simply as "Sig. Giacomo." The collaborator was none other than Giacomo Quarenghi,[17] whose difficult-to-pronounce surname had caused Jones to call him "Giacomo" for short. A watercolor in a Quarenghi album (fig. 8.9) proves his participation. It is a view of the Serapaeum at Tivoli almost identical to the one drawn by Hardwick in the bottom right corner of his sheet (fig. 8.7). Some subtle differences do exist. In the three watercolor *vedute* of the Serapaeum, the groupings of trees differ slightly between the pair of originals (cf. figs. 8.7 and 8.9). The third, that by Soane (fig. 8.8 bottom center) is a direct copy after Hardwick's arrangement, misleadingly labelled 1780, when Soane drew up his neat version. Quarenghi's is bigger and bolder in impact than the others. Already a practicing architect of note, he was ten years older than either Englishman and would soon set off for a distinguished career in Russia.[18] His *veduta*, cut out and mounted on an album leaf, may once have formed part of a larger sheet like Hardwick's, but that seems unlikely. There are almost no Quarenghi measured drawings among the hundreds scattered in North Italian and Russian collections. Quarenghi excelled as a *vedutista*.

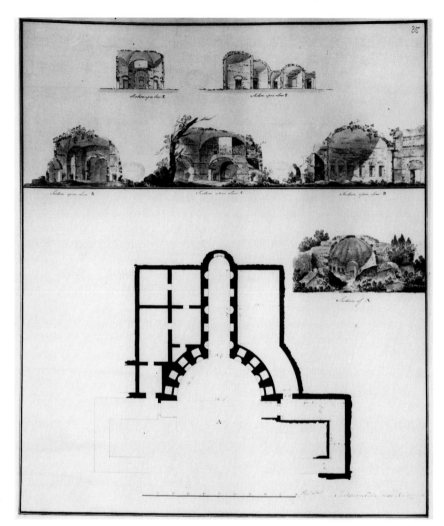

Fig. 8.7. Thomas Hardwick, Hadrian's
Villa, Tivoli *(from left to right, top to bottom)*
two sections through the Small Baths, Hall
of the Philosophers, Greek Library,
Latin Library, and the Serapaeum together
with its plan, 1777 (RIBA, E3/20).

As such he had something to teach Hardwick about rendering dry elevations into atmospheric landscape views. By the time Soane came along,
the results became watered down. And perhaps the real point here is not
so much the questionable ethics of copying as the lessened artistic conviction that it seems to entail.

Soane and Selva

In contrast to the majority of Soane's Italian drawings, one group
stands apart. They are highly technical in nature and not the least ap-

Fig. 8.8. Hadrian's Villa, Tivoli *(from left to right, top to bottom)* two sections through the Small Baths, Hall of the Philosophers, Greek Library, Latin Library, and the Serapaeum (SM, Drawer 45, Set 2, Item 27).

Fig. 8.9. Giacomo Quarenghi, Hadrian's Villa, Tivoli, section through the Serapaeum (CBB, Quarenghi Album 1, Item 2).

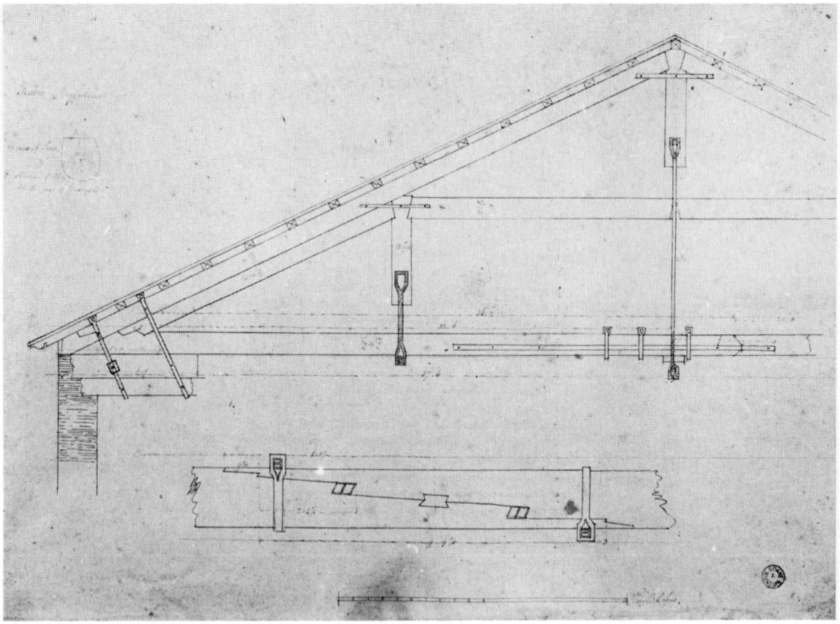

Fig. 8.10. Teatro Argentina, Rome, sketch plan of the theater and section through the roofing timbers (SM, Drawer 45, Set 6, Item 1 recto).

pealing from the artistic standpoint. They consist of cross sections and other detailed studies of Italian roofing construction (fig. 8.10). They all give the appearance of having been executed within a relatively short time of one another, because of the uniformity of Soane's handwriting, one sample of which is dated February 1780.[19] Finally, they select for study the engineering problems inherent in wide spans of wooden beam and trusswork such as found in churches and theaters with large unsupported areas of ceiling. When one considers the importance of structure to an architect, it is to be wondered that more such studies have not been found in the portfolios of Soane's contemporaries. On further reflection, these drawings seem to have a disquietingly hard and mechanical quality to them. Their polyglot inscriptions, a mixture of French, Italian, and English, leads one to suspect that there might be other such sets in existence, and that does indeed turn out to be the case.

In the Museo Correr in Venice, the drawings of the Venetian architect Giannantonio Selva include a group of eight sheets that relate to six by Soane (fig. 8.11). Unfortunately none is dated, but they can be assigned to the period from March 1778 to September 1780, when Selva was an exact contemporary of Soane's at Rome.[20] In the relatively small artistic community there, these two men might have known one another. Their

Fig. 8.11. Giannantonio Selva, Teatro Argentina, Rome, section through the roofing timbers (MC, Wcovcuh Lazzari 6318 recto).

drawings indicate some such familiarity. Selva's look more finished because of a generous use of brown and grey washes, with occasional touches of red to indicate roof tiles or the *poché* through supporting wall segments. Otherwise, five of Selva's eight drawings are virtually identical to Soane's pair of S. Maria in Campitelli, plus the three renderings he did of theaters in Rome, Bologna, and Turin—a town Soane is not known to have set foot in.[21] For that matter, Selva spent no time in Turin either, according to his student travel diary. Nor does it single out the Roman Teatro Argentina in such a way as to suggest any special acquaintance with the place on his part. It seems very likely, therefore, that neither Soane nor Selva carried out these roofing studies themselves. Instead they must have worked from two variant suites. This would explain small discrepancies among the two sets of drawings and the different scale bars and inscriptions used. A compendium of roofing studies could have existed from which Soane and Selva might copy independently of one another. The obvious precedent for this sort of structural analysis was Gabriel-Pierre-Martin Dumont's *Parallèle* of theater engravings.[22] Dumont's thirteenth plate is close in format to drawings by Soane and Selva relating to the Teatro Argentina in Rome.

Despite evidence of similar interests, Soane never mentioned Selva,

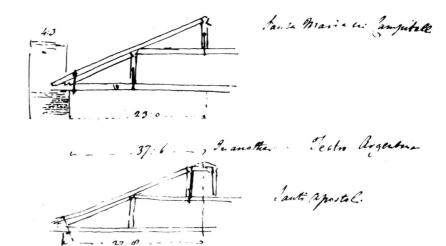

Fig. 8.12. Two sketch sections through the roofing timbers of Roman churches (SM, Soane Notebooks, 1, p. 37).

nor Selva Soane. Yet their Roman journals are among the most complete preserved. The curious thing is that, during Selva's visit to England[23] from 16 June to 1 September 1781, the relevant pages of Soane's contemporary notebook contain small-scale sketches of the Roman roofing studies that he and Selva had copied two years or so earlier (fig. 8.12). Suddenly to find this material reemerging out of context comes as an intriguing surprise. It is almost as if the topic of the roof tops of Rome had come up in conversation between two former associates when they met in London.[24] Once again, Soane and Selva were silent on the subject of a possible encounter. How are we to interpret these disquieting silences? Perhaps they are meaningless, but perhaps they imply that former members of the international artistic community in Rome avoided one another so as not to raise the topic of collaborative ventures. They all knew full well that the goings-on among architects abroad were not entirely aboveboard. On that account they may have put a guard on their tongues.

Soane and Trezza in Verona

To progressive Neoclassicists abroad, nothing could compare with discovering something new or long forgotten, and nothing could be more redundant than studying the same old things time and time again. Among "modern" architects, for instance, none had been more acclaimed earlier in the eighteenth century than Andrea Palladio. As the years wore on, however, the enthusiasm of neo-Palladians like Colin Campbell or Lord Burlington turned into the damning with faint praise of their architectural successors. The trend may be said to have been started at mid-century by the brothers Robert and James Adam. With them it became fashionable to disparage Palladio by extolling his less well-known contemporaries. Comparisons—especially controversial ones—were never odious to the Adams! During a visit to Verona, in October 1757, Robert Adam had expressed himself more favorably impressed by the Veronese architect Michele Sanmicheli's works than by those of Palladio.[25] Echoing those sentiments, James Adam, exactly three years later, wrote: "He seems to have had rather more genius than Palladio in the ornamental part of architecture, and is sometimes bold and male in his decoration." The brothers' admiration did not end with words alone. Robert spoke of unspecified "operations at Verona," and James related that he resisted "a strong *onset* from Count Pozzo and [Giuseppe] Torelli to publish" Sanmicheli's works.[26] Moreover, an autobiographical note by a young Veronese architect, Luigi Trezza, recalls that he had been set to work recording all Sanmicheli's buildings in 1769 for the benefit of a "raguardevole Personagio Inglese."[27] Someone had risen to Pozzo and Torelli's bait.

The correspondence of Giuseppe Torelli includes an interesting letter to the Bishop of Derry, written in March 1771, after a recent visit by the prelate to Verona, where he had met Torelli and Girolamo dal Pozzo, just as Adam had done a decade before.[28] Torelli wrote soliciting the Bishop's sponsorship of several publication projects. Although no mention was made of the corpus of drawings after Sanmicheli buildings, the all-inclusive nature of such a scheme would have appealed to the Bishop; one thinks of his contemporary survey of Swiss wooden bridges.[29] If the Bishop were the "raguardevole Personagio" meant by Trezza, then it is easy to see how, through this channel, other Englishmen including Soane heard of Trezza's ongoing work at Verona. Around 1771 an English architect sent Trezza drawings of the Duomo at Montefiascone as an addition to the Sanmicheli corpus.[30] Eight years later, Soane arrived in Verona probably with some prior knowledge of Trezza's undertaking. He sensed a good thing and was not averse to aggrandizing himself at someone else's expense.

Soane visited Verona at least twice, once during August 1779, when he came to the town in the company of Rowland Burdon, and again on his way back to England in May 1780.[31] Although Soane never mentioned Trezza in his notebooks or surviving correspondence—another disturbing lacuna—they must have known one another. All of Soane's supposedly original studies of Sanmicheli are, in fact, copies after Trezza's drawings, produced earlier in the 1770s. As a favor to a visitor from

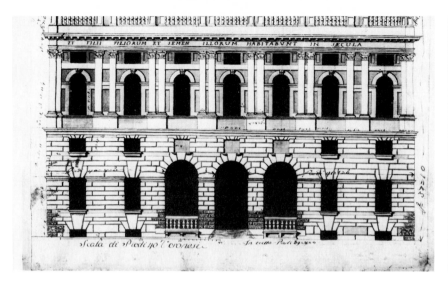
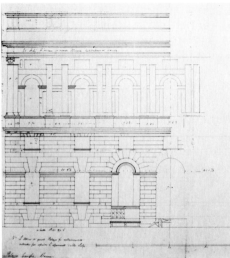

Fig. 8.13. Luigi Trezza, Palazzo Canossa, Verona, elevation (BCV, MS 1010, Folio 53).

Fig. 8.14. Palazzo Canossa, Verona, elevation (SM, Drawer 45, Set 2, Item 5).

abroad, or more likely in exchange for some remuneration,[32] Trezza put his material at Soane's disposal. These copies of Soane's included a selection of Sanmicheli's city gates, churches, and palazzi at Verona, as well as the Palazzo Grimani on the Grand Canal in Venice. There are fourteen of them in all, into which Soane managed to squeeze some twenty of Trezza's original Sanmicheli studies by using the paper more economically. Sometimes, as in the case of the elevation of the Palazzo Canossa, Soane respected Trezza's format (cf. figs. 8.13 and 8.14), but only delineated half of the symmetrical elevation. Sometimes, to save space and time, he combined several Trezza drawings on a single sheet, and sloppily applied areas of wash to indicate recessions. Everywhere there are signs of Soane's haste to get down on paper as much as he could with the intention of working up the results at a later date. In fact he never did so.

Trezza did not restrict himself entirely to the works of Michele Sanmicheli. He delineated Palladio's very Sanmichelesque Villa Sarego at S. Sofia di Pedemonte, near Verona. He also went further afield to study Giulio Romano buildings in and around Mantua, including the architect's own townhouse. Though Soane did visit Mantua once briefly,[33] he had to rely on Trezza for his detailed information. Faithfully, if in haste, Soane copied Trezza's 1774 plan and elevation of the Villa Passano at Villimpenta (figs. 8.15, 8.16), an attribution to Giulio that is still disputed.[34] Soane Italianized Trezza's French inscription, indicating that he worked from some copy other than the one now preserved in the Biblio-

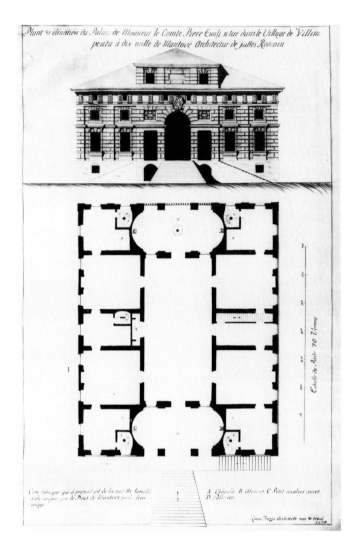

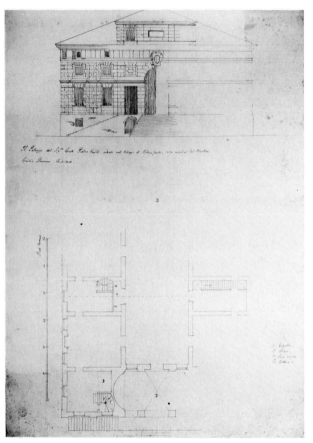

teca Civica, Verona. But the most important aspect of these drawings of Giulio's work is that Trezza, and Soane after him, started to compile a survey of the North Italian Mannerist school as a whole. It is as if he had some publication in mind that would rival Ottavio Bertotti-Scamozzi's contemporary tome, *Le Fabbriche e i disegni di Andrea Palladio*. Significantly, Soane's only mention of his North Italian studies singled out the names of Giulio and Michele along with that of Palladio.[35]

In the case of Soane, there can be little doubt that his initial amassing

Fig. 8.15. Luigi Trezza, Villa Passano, Villimpenta, plan and elevation, 1774 (BCV, MS 1784 I, Folio 15).

Fig. 8.16. Villa Passano, Villimpenta, plan and elevation (SM, Drawer 45, Set 2, Item 2).

of Trezza drawings for study purposes quickly developed into a scheme for pirating a publication on Sanmicheli. Rowland Burdon wrote Soane in 1780: "What has become of your Plan upon Verona?" thereby implying a concerted campaign on Soane's part. And Burdon was in the best position to know, having advanced the architect a considerable sum of money to help defray the cost.[36] Furthermore, when Thomas Pitt answered a subsequent Soane publication proposal, he asked him: "Have you ventur'd to introduce some of the drawings you took from the works of Michaeli St. Michaeli?—perhaps you reserve them for another work."[37] To his patrons, Soane's activities appeared perfectly bona fide. Did anyone among them realize what he was really about? Did his respectable friends know of the shadowy Trezza's existence? Could they have guessed Soane was duping him out of a publication? One thing is clear from Soane's conduct: for the Neoclassicists of the second half of the eighteenth century, the straight and narrow paths trodden by their predecessors up until 1750 would no longer suffice. The rapid development of a historicist outlook led architects to unconventional sources of inspiration. In place of Palladian purism, the more extreme Mannerism of Giulio in Mantua and of Sanmicheli in Verona became acceptable to architects like the Adam brothers, Trezza, and John Soane.

Soane and the Drawings for S. Petronio, Bologna

When Soane and Trezza met, it is possible that Trezza recommended that his English colleague see the architect Tommaso Temanza in Venice,[38] or read Temanza's series of short biographies that had appeared in a collection entitled *Vite dei più celebri architetti e scultori Veneziani.* In his life of Palladio, Temanza mentioned a unique collection of architectural drawings preserved in the archives of the church of S. Petronio in Bologna. Temanza also published a letter written to him by the Bolognese littérateur Francesco Algarotti describing the drawings. The letter mentioned the idea that "sarebbe l'intaglio de principali e più bei disegni...una...opera di assai maggior profitto per gli architetti."[39] Twenty years later Algarotti's passing remark about engraving old master architectural drawings caught Soane's attention. He was searching for just such a cache of unpublished material as he found in S. Petronio, soon after leaving Venice. With or without Temanza's personal encouragement, Soane arrived on or just before 29 September and set himself the laborious task of tracing nine of the S. Petronio drawings. Not surprisingly, he selected to copy three of the famous Palladio facade designs in the classical style (fig. 8.17). But he did not stop at that. He gathered examples from the hand of all the important architects who

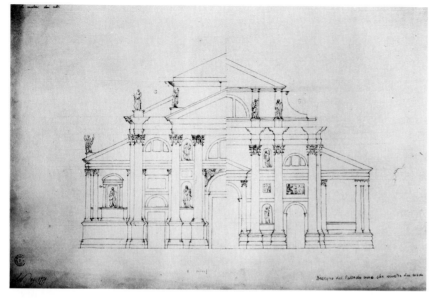

Fig. 8.17. S. Petronio, Bologna, copy of west facade design, after Andrea Palladio, 1779 (SM, Drawer 45, Set 4, Item 3).

had proposed projects for completing the medieval S. Petronio: Baldassare Peruzzi, Jacopo Barozzi da Vignola, Giulio Romano, and Girolamo Rainaldi.[40] The Rainaldi copy is historically the most important because the original early seventeenth-century plan has subsequently disappeared from S. Petronio, though the elevation still survives there. More interesting are Soane's copies of the fanciful pseudo-Gothic facade designs for the church, notably the impressive one done by Giulio Romano in collaboration with Cristoforo Lombardo (fig. 8.18). Soane's exact replica even includes a forged Giulio signature in the bottom left corner. By no means, then, was Soane attempting to pass these drawings off as originals of his own. His tactics changed in Bologna from what they had been in Verona and Rome. He sought to make a set of facsimiles with a view to carrying into execution the suggestions of Temanza and Algarotti. Still, we again encounter here Soane's preoccupation with the act of copying in all its various forms.

The copies made by Soane in Bologna and Verona, and to some extent those he collaborated on with Hardwick in Rome, harmonize into a grand scheme. He contemplated assembling a representative selection of the works of great Mannerists and proto-Mannerists like Raphael, Peruzzi, Vignola, Giulio Romano, Palladio, Sanmicheli, and even Michelangelo.[41] Only Jacopo Sansovino and Galeazzo Alessi are conspicuous in their absence from his historical survey. Bertotti-Scamozzi's

Fig. 8.18. S. Petronio, Bologna, copy of west facade design, after Giulio Romano and Cristoforo Lombardo (V&A, 3436.236).

publication of Palladio's Bolognese facade designs was still four years away. The year after that, Giovanni Stern brought out his engravings of Vignola's S. Andrea in Via Flaminia.[42] These were sporadic outbursts of the same interest in Mannerism that motivated Soane. He sensed the need for comprehensive coverage long before the appearance of Percier and Fontaine, Letarouilly, or Roncalli, to name but a few major nineteenth-century publicists. In a staggeringly rapid, almost telepathic way, a new preference spread among architects which announced the coming interest in Mannerist architecture. It is typical of Soane that he was sufficiently attuned to what was in the air to exploit the ideas of others, even if it meant wholesale copying of their work.

History always places great value on originality or pioneering efforts. This would seem especially true in the competitive world of the late eighteenth century. The Enlightenment, which had promoted the free atmosphere of inquiry in the first place, at the same time reduced the number of fresh avenues open to explore. As a result, a tenser, more guarded atmosphere prevailed in the artistic community. Soane's aggressiveness attests to the scrambling among those eager to gain an advantage. He permits a peep into the theft and sale of drawings, the plagiarism, pirating, and the picking of brains. Is it any wonder that few artists ever divulged this seamy side of international Neoclassicism? They were all implicated in the process to a greater or lesser extent. For their own protection they maintained a conspiracy of silence. Soane's unethical practices reflect the attempt among his fellow artists to defraud the art-loving public with spurious products: copied, stolen, or collaboratively produced. Never again in complete confidence can we accept at face value the measured drawings of eighteenth-century student architects.[43] The same holds true for their original work, as the next chapter demonstrates.

Soane and International Neoclassicism

Design for a British Senate-house, composed at Rome in 1779, without regard to expense, or limits as to space, in the gay morning of youthful fancy, amid all the wild imagination of an enthusiastic mind, animated by the contemplation of the majestic ruins of the sublime works of imperial Rome.

John Soane
Description of the House and Museum on the North Side of Lincoln's Inn Fields (1835)

Soane and Peyre: The Franco-British Senate House

THE ONE THING THAT SEEMS CLEAR about Neoclassicism as a style is the important part the Italian artistic climate played in liberating the Neoclassicists' powers of original composition. Soane, for one, exploded into creative activity almost upon impact with the new environment of Rome; other artists found the Roman experience so powerful as to be debilitating. The distractions of the city could have a pernicious tendency to sap the urge to create, replacing it with a *dolce far niente* attitude. The Royal Academicians had experienced such an effect upon their first traveling scholar, and they were determined it should not happen again. So to each subsequent Rome prize winner, they addressed a carefully worded letter of acceptance. Recipients, like Soane, were warned "to send home annually a Performance for the Exhibition" unless they wanted to lose their stipend.[1] Soane, therefore, wasted no time in starting to comply with this requirement. By 10 August 1778, only three months after his arrival in Rome, he produced a sketch design for a British senate house (fig. 9.1) that varied little from the one he eventually submitted to the Royal Academy exhibition of the following spring.

It will be remembered that Soane had a similar structure in mind when he proposed including it in his book *Designs in Architecture*. Like many of his grander schemes it never got beyond the proposal stage with his publisher. Nevertheless, his ideas on this score are represented by a preparatory ground plan, which he later inscribed with the words of self-mockery, "Sketch for a House of Parliament before I went abroad!" (fig. 9.2). In his own mind, he knew perfectly well the dramatic changes in his style that had come about as a result of first-hand acquaintance with ancient and modern Rome. The Soane statement calls for a comparison between the pre-Italian drawing and its August 1778 counterpart.

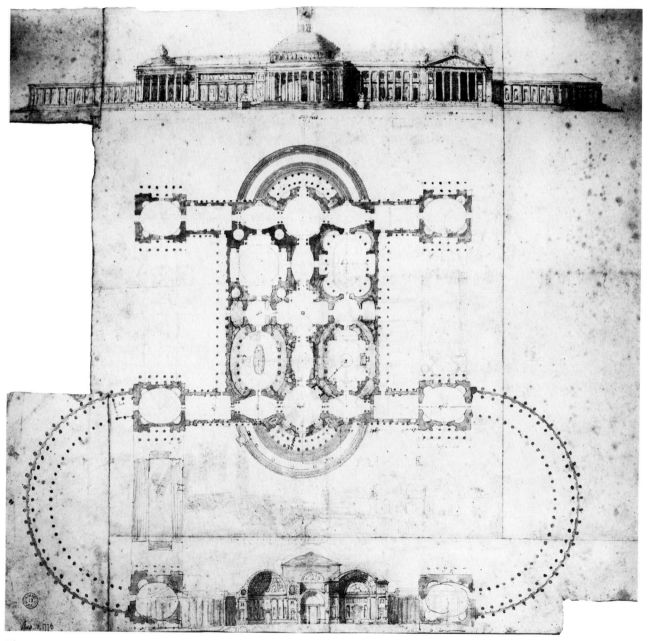

Fig. 9.1. British senate house design, plan, elevation, and section, 1778 (SM, Drawer 45, Set 1, Item 13 recto).

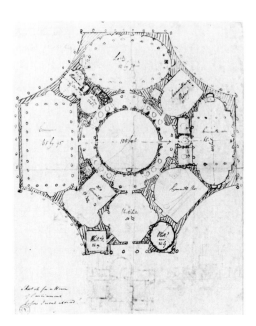

Fig. 9.2. British senate house design, preparatory plan (SM, Drawer 45, Set 1, Item 9).

As happened often while Soane attended the Academy Schools, the young architect set himself an ambitious design problem. He chose the large and complex geometric figure of an octagon, one hundred feet on one side, within which he proceeded to fit together the parliamentary chambers, like pieces in a Chinese puzzle. Around an open circular courtyard, he set an array of rooms which resemble the contorted boudoirs of his nobleman's townhouse (fig. 4.15), only much magnified. Soane did not curb this weakness for vast scale when he arrived in Rome. On the contrary, he outdid himself by proposing a megalomaniacal main facade of 597 feet across. In other ways, however, his new version of the British senate house improved upon the awkward older one.

The main difference between the two senate house schemes lies in the approach to planning. The room shapes of the later scheme dictate the overall outline, rather than the reverse, as was the case before. Despite a higher priority accorded to proper accommodation, Soane's British senate house still received a mixed reception when it went on display in London. The architect Matthew Brettingham the Younger wrote that "the design showed considerable inventive fancy and originality, but was deficient in practical acquaintance."[2] Brettingham's critique, which faulted Soane on practical grounds, missed the whole point of the Roman experience. Soane, as he himself admitted, had been carried away by enthusiastic "contemplation of the majestic ruins of the sublime works of imperial Rome." This was just as it should be. The juggling of inches, or shillings and pence, could come later; unfettered freedom of invention might happen only once in a lifetime.

With his British senate house, Soane joined the distinguished ranks of such fellow countrymen as James Adam, Robert Mylne, George Dance, and Thomas Harrison. Each of them had produced some great design or other while studying abroad.[3] Such a parliament building, museum, or public square attested to his having attended the open-air school that was Rome. Soane, like the others before him, turned to the ancient Roman baths for inspiration. The various complex spaces found there all combined happily into one complex. A similarly varied plan faced Soane when he provided houses for Lords and Commons, together with other ancillary facilities. Besides, in a symbolic sense, the togaed senators of Republican Rome were, for Soane, the obvious model for British parliamentarians. The discrepancy between a swimming pool in sunny Rome and a legislature in the north gave Soane no cause for second thoughts; he made the one as open and drafty as he had the other.

Granted the importance of Roman planning methods for Soane, the denuded ruins of the baths still offered him plenty of scope for imagination in the decoration of his British senate house. The one surviving drawing from the Royal Academy set (fig. 9.3) evokes a nobly simple arrangement. As in his nearly contemporary summer dining room scheme for the Bishop of Derry (fig. 6.8), Soane resorted almost exclusively to architectonic coffering. The House of Commons ceiling, with its unusual combination of a lozenge-shaped pattern carried on fanlike pendentives, succeeds especially well. For the rest of the interior, he relied on dramatic top lighting in the legislative chambers to alleviate any sense of coldness. The corridor in the middle is a particularly nice piece

of scenography, barely hinted at in his earlier works. A shaft of sunshine cuts across the deeply coffered vault. Beyond a columnar screen with flying entablature stands an equestrian statue representing George III and dramatically spotlighted by hidden apertures in the dome above. These breathtaking spatial sequences do not accord very well with any of Soane's surviving ground plans. Nor do the paper-thin domes seem to conform to the laws of statics. But surely an artist could be forgiven some technical oversights when the vision he created was so grand.

On the exterior, Soane settled for a continuous file of giant columns all across the elevation. The pasted-on flaps (fig. 9.1) make clear that he intended a forecourt with curving colonnaded wings to precede the main

Fig. 9.3. British senate house design, section, 1778 (SM, Drawer 13, Set 2, Item 4).

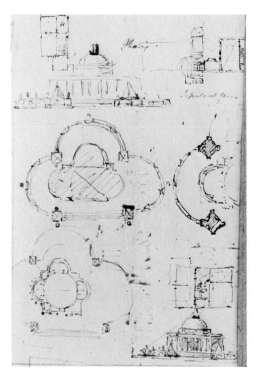

Fig. 9.4. Earl of Chatham mausoleum design, sketches (SM, OSMAS, Item 172 verso).

facade. In a later version the forecourt is symmetrically repeated at the rear as well. With its fountains and obelisks, the piazza has been seen to relate to that created by Bernini in front of St. Peter's in Rome. This may be, in fact, the ultimate source; Soane of course visited St. Peter's.[4] First-hand impressions notwithstanding, Soane continued to rely on the published designs of Marie-Joseph Peyre—designs which themselves emanated from Peyre's own stay as a *pensionnaire* of the Académie de France à Rome.[5] While in London, Soane had copied from Peyre's facade design for an academy building (fig. 4.19). In Rome he returned to the source that was to be valuable to him again and again. Peyre's plan for the same academy complex (fig. 5.15) had already assimilated many of the planning devices from the Baths and St. Peter's, which also impressed Soane. Here in Peyre were the chambers of a thermal establishment multiplied in undreamed of numbers, in the best grand-prix tradition. Here too were Bernini's colonnades, split apart and pushed to the lateral extremities of the site, ready ammunition for Soane's arsenal. It was hardly necessary to be in Rome. From a studio in the vicinity of SS. Trinità,[6] Soane could continue borrowing from Peyre, as he had done in London, especially since they breathed the same Antique air. Soane now conveyed with far greater personal conviction those ineffable qualities of majestic power and serenity that he had admired beforehand in the Frenchman's work. Direct experience at the fountainhead had taught him properly to understand Peyre.

Soane, Paine, and Harrison: The Chatham Mausoleum

On the back of a preparatory drawing for the British senate house are some sketches for another grandiose public monument, which can likewise be dated to the late summer or autumn of 1778 on the basis of similar style. The structure depicted is a mausoleum (fig. 9.4) and, as such, nothing very new in Soane's repertory. Of the several mausolea he had designed, the elevation of this one most closely resembles that commemorating James King (fig. 5.12). The King mausoleum came about as a result of Soane's ebullient mood at the time he won the gold medal at the Royal Academy. As so often with Soane's original designs, he sought opportunities to refine them. Such an opportunity came for the King mausoleum as a result of the death of the Earl of Chatham, early in May 1778, just as Soane reached Rome. Special circumstances there encouraged the idea of commemorating the Earl's career. The Bishop of Derry presided over Roman artistic circles at the time; Chatham had been his friend and idol.[7] These sentiments on the part of one of the most active patrons of the day made the Roman milieu a good place to pay tribute to

Chatham's memory.[8] Moreover, later in the year when Chatham's nephew, Thomas Pitt, arrived in town and befriended Soane, it was doubly natural that the architect should come up with a cenotaph for Chatham.

Soane's first suggestions for the exterior of the Chatham mausoleum take as their point of departure the published, two storey version of the monument to James King. The terrace, pyramids, and domed profile are all repeated. The plan, however, differs entirely. That for the James King mausoleum had been cruciform, or X-shaped (fig. 5.14), and in-

Fig. 9.5. Earl of Chatham mausoleum design, section (SM, Drawer 13, Set 2, Item 3).

spired by Peyre's *académie* design (fig. 5.15). Two years later in Rome Soane devised a concentric, trefoil configuration for the Chatham mausoleum but here again the source was Peyre. Soane based himself almost exactly upon the plan for a church that had appeared as the ninth plate in the Frenchman's *Oeuvres d'architecture*. Peyre's planning proved irresistible to Soane, despite the change of location from London to Rome.

The only surviving drawing from the Royal Academy exhibition set (fig. 9.5) introduces new elements into the consideration of the Chatham mausoleum. Initially the cross section appears to resemble that of the triumphal bridge (pl. 2). But, unlike the bridge design of three years before, the interior decoration of the Chatham mausoleum is less indebted to Peyre and is applied much more sparingly. The contrasts of light and shade are intensified, as was the case with the British senate house (fig. 9.3). Soane relied increasingly on top lighting devices which

Fig. 9.6. Earl of Chatham mausoleum design, elevation (SM, AL, Cupboard 22, Folio 1, Item 39).

were to become a hallmark of his later style. An oculus and two skylights illuminate the Chatham mausoleum. No doubt he had in mind the stronger chiaroscuro effects he encountered in Italian buildings. As for the elevation, a later copy of it depicts the innovative features. The dome has taken on the steps and low profile of the Roman Pantheon (figs. 9.4, 9.6) which Soane admired and drew. There is also a conscious reference to Italian art in the *capo di bove* frieze, based on the famous one at the tomb of Caecilius Metellus on the Via Appia. All these allusions are in keeping with the Grand Tourist style that Soane developed in Rome and continued to some extent into the early years of his London practice. The only strictly non-Italian element in the Chatham mausoleum is the baseless Greek Doric order, instead of the Roman variety. Soane may have used it earlier to support the middle tier of his James King mausoleum, though it is hard to say for certain because of the small scale of the drawing (fig. 4.11). In 1778, however, he overtly exploited the Doric's connotations of manly vigor insofar as they reflected his cosmopolitan taste, and the stoic death of Chatham.

Like so many visionary Neoclassical monuments, the Chatham mausoleum remained a drawing-board exercise.[9] Soane did not easily reconcile himself to this fate. He tenaciously clung to the supposed virtues of the design, even proposing to enlarge it into an English equivalent of the Parisian Panthéon. By the time it appeared in his *Sketches in Architecture* (1793), it had become destined for "great and virtuous characters" of the entire nation. This may explain why Soane, at the last minute, tried in vain to change the title of his entry in the Royal Academy's 1781 exhibition,[10] in order to take fuller advantage of the free publicity. When the catalogue came out, it included his mausoleum alongside a more grandiose-sounding one "for eminent characters" by

T. Park, as well as James Paine the Younger's "National Monument to the Earl of Chatham." Two years previously Thomas Harrison had exhibited his monument "occasioned," as he put it in the catalogue, "by an idea which occurred in parliament on the death of Lord Chatham."[11] And a year earlier still, when Chatham was hardly cold in his grave, John Carter suggested a Gothic-style wall tomb for him in the August 1778 issue of the *Builder's Magazine* (pl. clxxxi). Soane hated to appear so tardy, when, in fact, his design went back to 1778. Far from being derivative, it makes a notable contribution when it is seen together with the others that still survive from the Academy exhibitions. It also shows how a similar idea might occur simultaneously in the minds of numerous artists, one of whom was off in distant Italy. It would be hard to find better proof of the spontaneous nature of Neoclassicism than in the various mausolea for Chatham.

James Paine the Younger's Chatham mausoleum has come down in the form of a striking watercolor in blues and greys that depicts a storm about to envelop his imaginary structure (fig. 9.7). It has several points in common with Soane's building. Both resort to the pyramid for its symbolic mortuary connotations and its property of conveying a note of geometric purity. Both exploit the strong contrasts of light and shade

Fig. 9.7. James Paine II, Earl of Chatham mausoleum design (V&A, 9154).

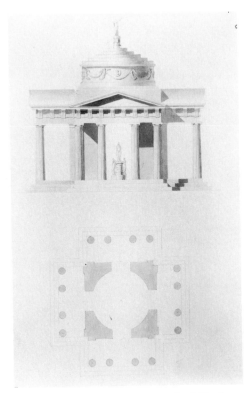

Fig. 9.8. Thomas Harrison, Earl of Chatham mausoleum design, plan and elevation (Cheshire County Museum Services, 2851).

admired in Italy. Both design on the vast scale encouraged by exposure to the Mediterranean world. (Like Soane, Paine had been in Rome for some years in the 1770s.) In Paine's case, too, the element of early Greek revivalism is forcefully introduced. Although Paine never saw the antiquities of Athens, he knew them from books, and he arranged four octastyle baseless Doric porticos like the Parthenon's. Then, in a not very happy moment of inspiration, he sent the temple fronts hurtling backward to stop just short of a vast brick cone in the center. This 30-foot-high, cloud-capped pyramid looks decidedly out of place compared with the more harmonious lines of Soane's design.

Despite the apparent novelty of Paine's mausoleum, it owes something to the slightly earlier one by Harrison, the appearance of which is recorded by a redrawing in the Harrison collection at Chester, on paper watermarked 1809 (fig. 9.8). The feature common to both designs is the motif of four porticos set around a central element. This was a favorite Harrison device; he reused it in a very similar monumental market cross scheme of around 1780, now in the National Museum, Stockholm.[12] Paine could have admired Harrison's four porticos theme at the Academy exhibition, and then substituted his own pure form cone for Harrison's more classical and dainty dome. It is hard to judge Harrison's scale, but it, too, partakes of the vogue for megalomaniacal public monuments based on Franco-Italian models. Like Paine and Soane, Harrison had spent time in Rome during the crucial decade of the 1770s. There he also caught the fever for the baseless Doric, which he employed in his mausoleum. The order became his trademark in later works. But it is the delicately swagged drum with its winged victories that gives away the 1770s date of the mausoleum's original conception, while at the same time linking with Chatham's triumph over death. His statue is presumably the one housed below. An elegant and stylish solution, it nonetheless suffers in comparison with the more substantial project by Soane, not to mention the less down-to-earth one by Paine.

Differences in qualitative terms notwithstanding, the three schemes, by Soane, Harrison, and Paine, are amazingly similar. They are united by their common sense of scale, their baseless Doric porticos, their love of dramatic contrasts, their formal purism, and their novel recombination of elements familiar from the classical past. They testify to the way three quite individual artists leapt upon the occasion of Chatham's death to present to the world their latest Neoclassical ideas on the subject. In another sense, too, they suggest that the spread of Neoclassicism had its conscious and stealthy as well as its unconscious and involuntary side. Artists were looking over their shoulders at what others were doing.

On one final occasion before leaving Italy Soane resorted to the same subject matter and to a similar approach as several of his contemporaries. But this time the design put him into direct competition with an international assortment of rival artists. It all came about because Englishmen and foreigners alike wanted some tangible recognition of their educational Grand Tour. The preferred form of distinction was a medal from one of the periodic competitions, or *concorsi,* organized by Italian academies. And no Italian academy had a better reputation for fairness 'to outsiders than Parma's; in the words of George Dance the Younger: "there could not be a better opportunity than that which offer'd itself at Parma . . . where all Italy nay all Europe may concur."[13]

George Dance's willingness "to do something to distinguish myself before I left Italy," won him the Parma gold medal for his *magnifica galleria* design (fig. 2.3). A decade and a half later, Dance's disciple, Soane, remembering his master's tales of success,[14] conceived the ambition to distinguish himself before a European audience. He took the first step in that direction when he arrived at Parma with Rowland Burdon soon after the middle of August 1779.[15] What transpired at Parma can be deduced from a rare letter by Soane written later that August to his friend, the amateur architect Thomas Pitt:

> I informed myself of the subject for the Premium in Architecture, to be given by the Royal Academy of this place in 1780 (May), for which I wish to become a candidate, if it meets with your approbation. I have therefore taken the liberty of enclosing you two designs for "*Un Castello d'acqua, decorato d'una pubblica fontana.* Si domandano il piano, l'Elevatione, et lo Spaccato d'un Serbatojo d'acqua, che in grandissima copia si supporranno in esso raccolte per comodo, ed ornamento d'una Metropoli. La Facciata adunque di questo edifizio sarà posta nel fondo d'una larga piazza, ed onerassi con tutta la magnificenza di una pubblica fontana, che si vedrà divisa in più polle scaturire da Statue, da Rupi, o da animali, come vorrà la fantasià dell' Architetto, che rappresentando qualche Favola, o qualche Istoria più distinguersi nell'invenzione. Si vuole eziandiò un aloggio unito al Serbatojo per gli Idraulici, e Custodi dell' Edificio."
>
> I must beg leave to request Your assistance to point out the most exceptionable parts, and to inform me if I have conceived it in any degree agreeable to the proposition. If you should think my request unfair, I wish you to know that I then cease to desire Your ideas on the subject, tho most sensible of the want of your assistance. I must confess the subject is entirely new to me and that I am very doubtful of the propriety of my ideas respecting it.[16]

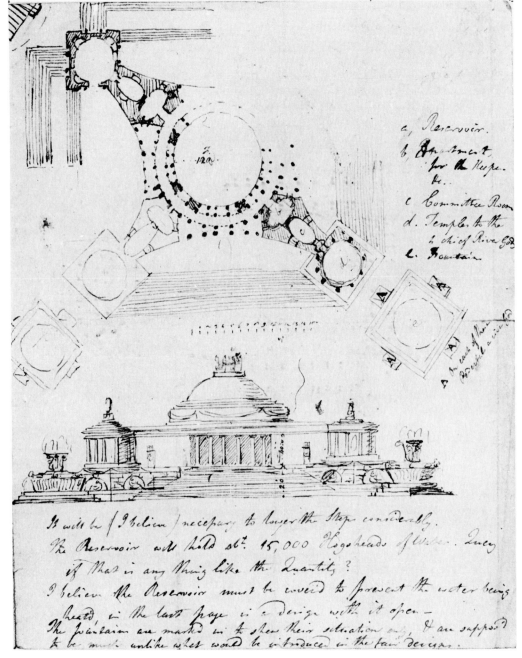

a, Reservoir.

b, Apartment
     for the Keeper
     &c..

c, Committee Room

d, Temples to the
     2 chief River Gods

e, Fountain

It will be (I believe) necessary to lower the Steps considerably.

The Reservoir will hold abt. 15,000 Hogsheads of Water. Query
     if that is any thing like the Quantity?

I believe the Reservoir must be covered to prevent the water being
     heated, in the last page is a design with it open —

The fountains are marked in to shew their situation only, & are supposed
     to be much unlike what would be introduced in the fair design.

Fig. 9.9. *Castello d'acqua*
design, first page side,
sketch plan and elevation
(SM, OSMAS, Item 184
right-hand side, recto).

Soane used his time at Parma well. He had acquainted himself thoroughly with the program of the forthcoming architectural contest. Soane's text even quotes verbatim from the official program for the *castello d'acqua,* or waterworks: a utilitarian affair with turncock's quarters and an engine room, but also intended as a civic ornament. He only omitted to include matters of detail, such as maximum size of drawings, provisions for respecting the anonymity of contestants through the use of mottos, and the all-important final date for submission of entries: 25 May of the following year. For one with nine full months in which to ponder his designs, and for one who had doubts as to the "propriety" of those designs, Soane put down on paper what he called "first Ideas" so quickly that he complained to Pitt of not having time to make copies. The reason for the rapid appearance of not one but two whole sets of sketches is that, though Soane may have thought the design problem "entirely new," his solution of it was not so (fig. 9.9).

The general outline of Soane's elevation echoes the low substructure and Pantheon-style dome of the slightly earlier Chatham mausoleum (fig. 9.6). As for the X shape of the *castello d'acqua,* Soane reused the plan of the James King mausoleum. He reasoned that the house of the dead in which he took pride might, with a few modifications, be transformed into a reservoir of life-giving water (cf. figs. 5.14 and 9.9). Who at Parma, conjectured Soane, would ever guess that he had resorted to the X shape once before, and who would recognize in it the cunning adaptation from Peyre?

Soane's grafting of an Antique-style dome onto a French Neoclassical ground plan reaffirms his adherence to the eclectic design process seen before in his other Neoclassical dream projects. More unusual are Soane's two major preoccupations as revealed in the lengthy marginalia accompanying his initial proposal. In the first place, he was concerned with the practical operation of his visionary *castello d'acqua.* Instead of the Chatham mausoleum's sepulchral chambers with sarcophagi set in gloomy loculi, Soane located such amenities as the water tank (at "a"), custodial apartments (at "b"), and committee rooms (at "c"). Soane even asked himself whether "15,000 Hogsheads of Water . . . is anything like the Quantity" needed? He went on to justify his domed centerpiece as a means "to prevent the water being heat'd" by the sun. All these precise requirements were in no way called for by the vague stipulations of the *concorso.* In the second place, Soane's annotations indicate that he had in mind stressing the *caractère* of the structure through recurrent allusions to the theme of water. Here again the Parmesan academicians did not suggest any systematic scheme of decoration—animals, piles of rockwork, or human figures were all the same to them. Soane, on the contrary, made the four spreading arms of the *castello d'acqua* terminate in statue-crowned *tempiettos* assigned to "the 4 chief River Gods" (at "d"). These, in turn, are raised on bases with reclining aquatic personifications. Set back from the projecting temples, slightly concave hexastyle colonnades permit direct access into the 120-foot-wide rotunda, where the sound of lapping water would be heard from within the reservoir. Fed from the central source are four outlying fountains (at "e"; added in later as the draftsmanship shows). On the lower pedestals of the fountains, the river god symbolism carries over (at "A"), while higher up a basin emits plumes of spray into the air. Such a carefully programmed orchestration of "characteristic" decoration accords well with Soane's often expressed desire for a logical correlation between function and ornament.

In Soane's first sketch proposal, then, the only important architectural elements entirely unprecedented in his earlier work are the *tempiettos* (perhaps intended to recall the Temple of Vesta at Tivoli). They are, moreover, the very features to be eliminated from the sketch "No. 2" (fig. 9.10) for significant reasons. Just below the numeral two on the second page side of the sketches, Soane wrote the revealing statement that "In this design the temples are omitt'd being doubtful of being at Liberty to treat the subject as an Antique Edifice." A glance at the program for the *concorso* reveals not one mention of a preferred style, either "ancient" or "modern." The Parma academicians had left Soane at complete liberty to design however he liked. Soane's casting about in his mind for alternatives to the first proposal sprang, therefore, solely from self-motivated scruples. He apparently thought that nonfunctional river god temples might be too costly a sacrifice of floor space for the sake of *all' antica* appearances. Soane ventured boldly to imply that a more successful solution to the problem existed in an up-to-date style, rather than in that of the ancients. In 1779 a man like Soane did not hesitate to unmask the myth of the incomparability of the ancients, while subscribing to the academic notion of progress in the arts as promulgated by his former teachers, Thomas Sandby and William Chambers.[17] Obviously the Antique-style pump house is the more flamboyant of the two in every detail. The second, that is, "modern" *castello d'acqua* scheme, for all its classical columns, is more tightly organized in plan than its counterpart. The river god temples vanish and in their place appears a four-square nucleus of individual machine rooms. The upper and lower pairs of pavilions are interconnected by crescent-shaped wings housing other practical facilities. The similarity of approach to that used in the fore-

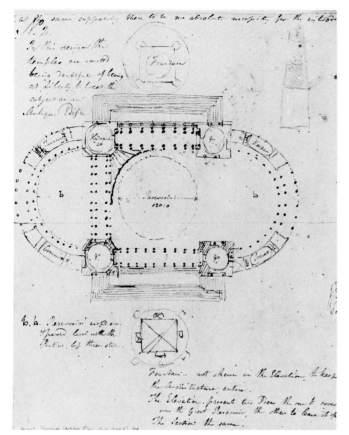

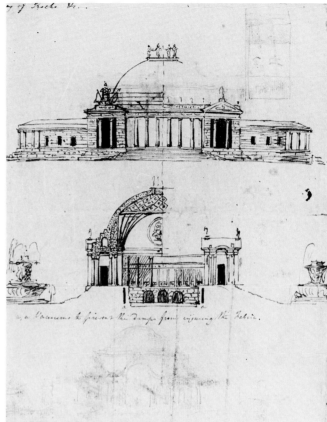

court of the British senate house comes readily to mind (fig. 9.1), as does its source in Peyre's *académie* plan (fig. 5.15).

In the dog days of a North Italian summer when the *castello d'acqua* was conceived, considerations of sufficient quantities of water and of exposure to the sun must have seemed crucial. Soane could not resolve in his mind the question of water evaporation, so when he came to his third page side of sketches he drew a pair of half elevations (above) and half sections (below) representing each possibility—domed over on the one hand, hypaethral on the other (fig. 9.11). For the first time, in the sections, he became entangled in complexities of load and support that he only weakly solved. Soane's persistent obsession with improved functioning resulted in his fussy provisions (at "a") for "Vacuums to prevent the damps from injuring the Fabric," while at the same time the enor-

Fig. 9.10. *Castello d'acqua* design, second page side, sketch plan (SM, OSMAS, Item 184 left-hand side, verso).

Fig. 9.11. *Castello d'acqua* design, third page side, sketch elevation and section (SM, OSMAS, Item 184 right-hand side, verso).

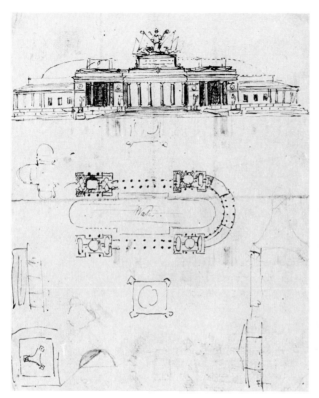

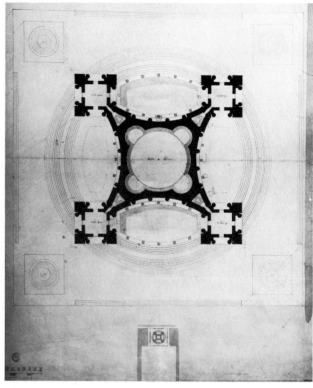

Fig. 9.12. *Castello d'acqua* design, fourth page side, sketch plans and elevation (SM, OSMAS, Item 184 left-hand side, recto).

Fig. 9.13. *Castello d'acqua* design, plan *(top)* and site plan *(bottom)* (SM, Drawer 45, Set 1, Item 22).

mously heavy and broad dome gives cause for concern as to its statical strength. Still, whatever the weaknesses of Soane's engineering, he wished for his visionary projects to *appear* practicable in every respect. As will be seen, such concerns distinguish him from many of his contemporaries.

The fourth or "last page," as Soane referred to it, contains the plan and elevation of an additional design for the *castello d'acqua* (fig. 9.12). For a variety of reasons Soane cannot have considered it very seriously. He had written, "I believe the Reservoirs must be cover'd," and yet his final scheme goes even further than the second one by uniting all three separate reservoirs into one huge tank open to the sky. (He thought better of taking such a step and lightly sketched in indications of some sort of roof.) Furthermore, the sloppiness of execution attests to Soane's lack of care with the entire proposal. Compared with the earlier ones, this last page does not convey the same convincing sense of mass and megalomaniacal scale achieved previously by quick sure strokes and cavernous inky blotches. The virtue of this crudeness lies in the fact that it reveals, in barely digested form, a reliance on the area of Peyre's *académie* plan (fig. 5.15 *far left*) heavily shaded to suggest the water in a stadium for mock naval battles.

Considering the wealth of ideas presented by the four page sides just discussed, it comes as a surprise to discover that they are only preliminary studies for a second set of Soane sketches for the *castello d'acqua*. Though very similar, these sketches, on two sides of a single sheet of paper, are later, as can be deduced from their neater appearance, their more concise marginalia, their condensed number, and from the fact that they were the ones originally attached to the letter to Pitt.[18] Also, certain points of design in question before are firmly resolved. The X-shaped plan, for instance, has its terminal *tempiettos* uniformly square, and the stairs are now treated throughout as two flights. The question of adequate water storage is solved by increasing the capacity to 55,000 hogsheads by the addition of four subterranean tanks, contrived in such a way as to form curved terraces between the four corner pavilions. Finally, the decoration is more carefully thought out. Reclining river god statues appear at the sides of the fountains in the elevation (they were only indicated on the plan previously). A triglyph and metope frieze singles out the Doric order as that now in use.

On the verso of Soane's single sheet, an alternative scheme corresponds with the third page side of the first set of proposals. But the superstructure lacks the added height of a swagged drum, its lateral extent has shrunken, four columns in the portico replace six, and the impressive trabeated recesses become a small round-headed window. If the design looked tighter, Soane's thinking, nevertheless, continued to vacillate. The dichotomy of ancient versus modern continued to plague him. As though to skirt the problem, Soane went on to say "This Idea might be applied to a Triangle."[19] This veering off to another solution was no escape. Earlier in the sketching process he had tentatively tried out triangular plans (fig. 9.12). Earlier still, he had experimented with the triangle in the humorous context of contrasting "ancient" and "modern" kennels, designed at the end of 1778 for the Bishop of Derry.[20] Soane's doghouses and waterworks prove his ability to juggle historical styles, to stand back from Antiquity with something approaching an objective perspective. His ambivalent attitude toward the past as a stimulus for the present underlies the fluctuating nature of the *castello d'acqua* designs.

From the foregoing analysis of "ancient" as opposed to "modern" designs for the *castello d'acqua*, Soane's plea to Pitt "to point out the most exceptionable parts" makes sense. Soane did not need assistance because he lacked ideas. Quite the contrary, the sketches represented a debilitating embarrassment of possibilities for him. Soane was out of his depth in a quandary of old versus new, from which he hoped Pitt would extricate him.[21]

The winter of 1779/80 in Rome gave Soane time for further reflection on the subject of the *castello d'acqua*. In a carefully prepared ink and wash plan of this date (fig. 9.13), he finally settled upon the X shape, at the same time compromising the Antique content and altering the mode of operation. The major functional change is that the central rotunda's diameter, a stable 120 feet all along, shrinks by half. Consequent loss of water capacity is counteracted by taking a step so unheralded by the earlier proposals that one is tempted to give credit for the idea to Thomas Pitt. By closing off the main reservoir entirely from the exterior, what had been lost in decreased width could simply be made up for in added height of water level within the airtight cylindrical tank. Also, in the final solution, all four sides of the *castello d'acqua* curve outward as well as inward to form segmental flights of stairs leading to ovoid terraces, occupied in two cases by reflecting pools. Ornamental outlying fountains complete a complex which, a site plan on the bottom margin shows, is for the first time placed in a piazza, as requested by the *concorso*. This harmonious reciprocity between form and function derives from an inner logic that dictates the totality of the final solution to a much greater extent than ever before in Soane's works, irrespective of stylistic considerations. This is not to say that Soane lost sight of the dichotomy of ancient and modern; rather he came to a reconciliation of the opposing poles. Soane decided to leave the problematic river god temples in the design, but he secularized them into simple vestibules above staircases that presumably lead down to the pipes and pumps. (Incidentally, the doghouse plan also called for a subterranean machine room.) In suppressing the most obvious allusions to Antiquity, Soane could still keep the more "ancient" of his formal compositions, while joining it to the most "progressive" of his planning ideas.

Nearly contemporary with the plan just discussed is a highly detailed elevation with an urban setting in the background (fig. 9.14). The fountains consist of atlantes shouldering a basin gushing water, like the ones he had admired on visiting the Villa Albani in Rome.[22] The columns feature the molded base of the Roman Doric order. Between the central three intercolumniations, water (tinted with blue wash) pours down. As if commenting on these aquatic displays below, nudes gesticulate from the edge of the roof, in the pose of Michelangelo's *ignudi* on the Sistine

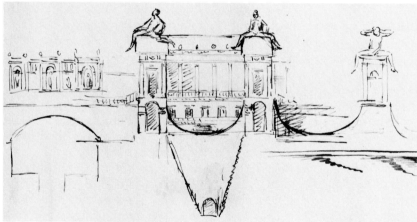

Fig. 9.14. *Castello d'acqua* design, elevation (SM, Drawer 45, Set 1, Item 20).

Fig. 9.15. *Castello d'acqua* design, sketch of a cross section (SM, OSMAS, Item 102).

Chapel ceiling. They, along with the equestrian statue above them,[23] possess a lifelike quality far beyond the powers of Soane's mediocre figure style. It seems certain that Soane, contravening the *concorso* rules on autograph work, used the assistance of his Roman friend, the painter Carlo Labruzzi. The same hand in question here sketched similar figures nimbly sitting astride a Soane hypaethral version of the *castello d'acqua* (fig. 9.15). Stylistically, these agitated little silhouettes, with areas of hastily applied wash suggesting musculature, tally well with a documented example of Labruzzi's work in Soane's collection.[24]

In another *castello d'acqua* drawing the same artistic ghost was employed again, this time for the nude maiden figures discharging the contents of urns into the open reflecting pool about which they stand (pl. 4, *bottom*). The elevation represents a building of formidable appearance, due in part to the significant changeover of architectural order to the baseless Greek Doric, a feature to be discussed shortly. The section (pl. 4, *top*) elucidates the full ingenuity of the cascades placed in the intercolumniations. They were produced simply by introducing overflow outlets in the springing level of the tank's dome. At the same time as a constant water level is maintained within, a cooling aesthetic effect is created outside by pure gravity. The plan, elevation, and section, with their neatly lettered labels in Italian, would seem to constitute the nearly completed submission for Parma Academy. Yet, on the presentation drawing of the plan (fig. 9.13) Soane, as an afterthought, sketched in pencil a larger pedestal for the central figure in the statuary groups. At about the same time and along the top margin of the original sheet, he drew a barely distinguishable figure with a maiden pouring offerings before it. Below the drawings Soane wrote an explanatory note referring to the Danube, Nile, Ganges, and La Plata, and the four continents they symbolize. So Soane, having earlier discarded a sculptural program devoted to the four rivers, now returned to the theme that fascinated him, as it had Gian Lorenzo Bernini. Soane's conception, however, owed little to the Baroque precedent of Bernini's famous fountain in Rome's Piazza Navona. Soane moved away from the already tired cliché of reclining personifications wallowing in the water. His river god statue, austere rather than frolicsome, would have sat bolt upright, like a totem pole.

While still in Italy, Soane incorporated the river god and his attendants into one final and extravagant variant of the *castello d'acqua* (fig. 9.16). To the now familiar plan, Soane added greater height onto a bizarre classicizing centerpiece with stepped pyramid, equestrian statue, and roof-top lions. Doric columns carry the heavy sill for what at first sight seems like a lunette window. Actually it is a giant sluice gate which pours out a falls of almost baby-Niagara proportions. Earlier proposals had tended to emphasize Soane's sense of restraint; this latest one adds a humorous touch of Italian bravura to a design that ranks paramount among Soane's original student works and high on any international list of Neoclassical projects.

In the minutes of a meeting of the academicians at Parma on 7 June 1780, the names of the winner and runner-up in the *concorso* were given as Auguste Cheval de Saint-Hubert and Vincenzo Poma, respectively. Soane does not appear among the seven contestants.[25] Slightly earlier in the academicians' deliberations, however, there does occur the following

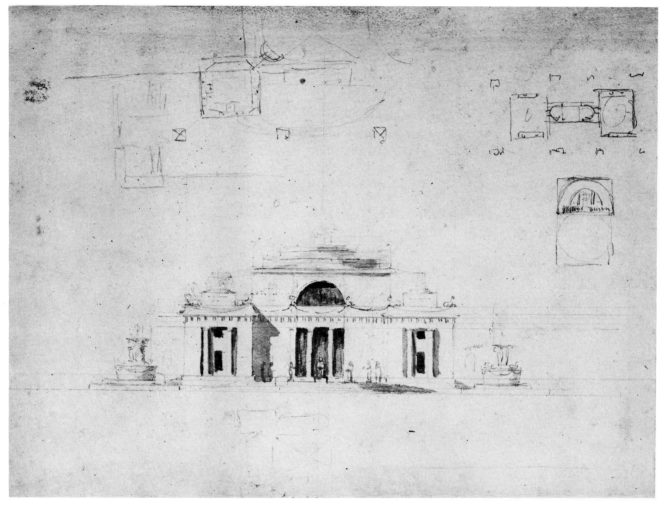

Fig. 9.16. *Castello d'acqua* design, sketch plans and elevation (SM, OSMAS, Item 136).

reference to him: "Fù esaminato il disegno d'Architettura del Sigr. Soan; e quando egli si determini ad inviare il piano, e lo Spaccato sarà fra gli Academici ammesso con piacere pel Valor suo."[26] The Parma records thus close the story of Soane's relationship with the academy on a note of compromise. Soane could not have won a premium in 1780 for the simple reason that he had quietly dropped out of the running.[27] At the same time, he obviously remained reluctant to relinquish altogether the hope he had so long cherished of equalling Dance's Parma triumph. With this in mind Soane presented the academicians on 9 May 1780 with

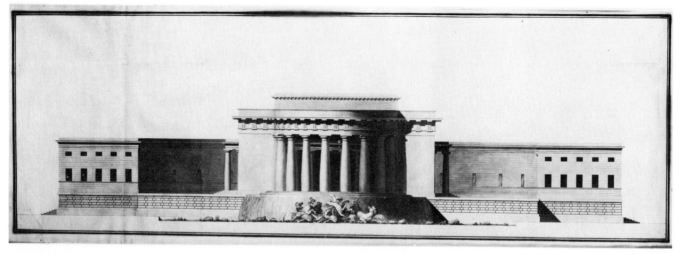

Fig. 9.17. Auguste Cheval de Saint-Hubert, *castello d'acqua* design, elevation (IPT).

(Opposite page)
Fig. 9.18. Etienne de Seine, *chateau d'eau* design for the 1777 prix de Rome competition, plan, elevations, and section (Ecole des beaux-arts, Paris).

a Greek Doric version of the triumphal bridge, as partial fulfillment of the traditional academic *morceau de réception* (fig. 4.23). His unsolicited move worked. The academicians approved of his submission, and Soane eventually received a diploma of honorary membership in Parma Academy.[28] To Soane, honorary membership was better than nothing to show for his efforts. As for the *concorso,* it would have to proceed without him. But his intended entry can be evaluated by reconstructing, with the aid of the winning designs, the competition that never was.

The first prize of the 1780 Parma *concorso* went to Saint-Hubert, a Parisian and a former pupil of the architect Louis-François Petit-Radel. He had been attached *hors de classe* to the French Academy in Rome since 1775, although he was not a full-fledged *pensionnaire.* He had once previously entered the competition at Parma, winning the second prize in 1778 with his design for a physical sciences lecture theater.[29] Vincenzo Poma, runner-up in 1780, had, like Saint-Hubert, entered the 1778 *concorso* but had been unsuccessful and therefore tried the next two years.[30] Poma, a Milanese by birth, studied under Parma Academy's professor of architecture, Ennemond-Alexandre Petitot, who had no less than three other pupils entered in the 1780 race. Parma, however, did live up to her reputation for lack of chauvinism. She admitted contestants from Bologna, Rome, and France as well and awarded the top honors to Saint-Hubert, a foreigner.[31] Thus, had Soane competed in 1780, he would have pitted talents against persons academically as distinguished as himself and from a wide diversity of backgrounds. In a stylistic sense, too, Parma provided an international crossroads.

Saint-Hubert's elevation (fig. 9.17) represents a pump house conceived as the "temple Supposé La Source de L'Eridan." In front of it, Phaeton and the sun chariot plunge to destruction in a watery, rock-strewn environment reminiscent of the Trevi Fountain in Rome. Furthermore, a statue, dimly visible among the columns, symbolizes the titular god of the Po, or ancient Eridanus.[32] The pump house proper nestles within a horseshoe-shaped piazza; the end pavilions of the screen walls project forward to either side. In a nice piece of concentric planning, of which Marie-Joseph Peyre would have approved, the interior of the inner core mirrors the form of the outer shell. The Parmesan academicians praised this "saggia distribuzione del piano"[33] and could only find fault with minute details. Little did they realize that, unlike Soane, Saint-Hubert was privy to the source of the French grand prix tradition by virtue of his association with the Académie de France à Rome. There he made friends with the *pensionnaires* and in particular with Etienne de Seine. In 1777 de Seine had been the recipient of a prix de Rome for his design of a waterworks, or *château d'eau* (fig. 9.18). When, by chance, the Parma Academy assigned the same subject for 1780, de Seine naturally advised his compatriot, Saint-Hubert.[34] The outlines of the central buildings are quite similar, although Saint-Hubert strips the ornament from his. Saint-Hubert used an octastyle portico and attached it to a virtually identical rectangular block with prominent attic. Saint-Hubert's curving colonnade and plan differ most from de Seine's. Whatever else may be said in its favor, Saint-Hubert's scheme was knowingly based on that of another artist in outright contradiction of the Parma rules. As in the copying and pirating of measured drawings, Saint-Hubert's attempt to cheat causes us to question the supposed "originality" of student-architect designs.

Unfortunately, when coming to consider the *castello d'acqua* of the shadowy Vincenzo Poma, we are left with only his colorful elevation (fig. 9.19).[35] The judges commented that Poma's waterworks were meant to be located "nelle viscere d'un'immensa Spelonca," hence the almost surreal conglomeration of rock forms evoking the bowels of a huge cave. The jury's verdict admitted the greater imaginativeness and daring of this project, in contrast to Saint-Hubert's, and praised its "grandissimo artifizio." But they mentioned the difficulty of hacking out such a work from the living rock, along with the fact that it obviously did not answer the stipulated demands of the program. Poma's scheme might work in the foothills of the Alps, they agreed, but never in the heart of the "Metropoli," for which it was destined.[36]

When, after a delay of 200 years, the designs of Soane, Saint-Hubert,

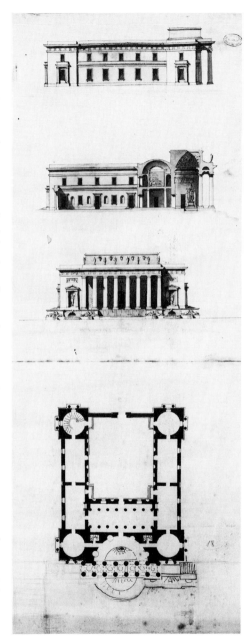

Fig. 9.19. Vincenzo Poma, *castello d'acqua* design, elevation (IPT).

and Poma are confronted in a three-way match two remarkable similarities overshadow all the differences. The trio used the baseless Doric order, and each had recourse to the theme of a rushing cascade. Given the common academic training of all three, given the identical program of the *concorso,* and given especially the widespread acceptance of certain aesthetic notions, similarities were perhaps bound to arise in the projects. These similarities in turn repay close scrutiny because they reflect upon the aesthetic notions shared by a Frenchman, an Englishman, and an Italian in 1780.

Each of the three young exponents of Neoclassicism subtly stated, in the Doric columns of his *castello d'acqua,* his personal position in the great debate over the supremacy of the Greeks or the Romans in classical architecture. Poma, the Italian, took the most ambivalent position of the three for nationalistic reasons. His order is actually a hybrid. The Greek element is the lack of base; the blank frieze, however, belongs to the Tuscan order. Poma took a middle road in the polemical argument, by intimating that the native Etruscans had as much of a hand in formulating the original order as the foreign-born Greeks.[37] Saint-Hubert went to the opposite extreme from Poma in asserting Greek superiority. His unfluted baseless shafts with gouty entasis suggest as their source the recently discovered temple of Segesta in Magna Graecia, studied by his fellow *pensionnaires* in these years and also by Soane. As this temple was extremely simple (in fact unfinished), Saint-Hubert could have taken it to represent the most archaic stage then known in the development of the Doric. In comparison with Saint-Hubert's, Soane's treatment of the Doric is somewhat less avant-garde (pl. 4). At Paestum, we remember, Soane had openly declared his aversion to "rude" archaic examples of the Doric, preferring to them the "elegant taste," as he called it, of the more svelte columns from the classical period of Greece. Even so, for an Englishman to admire the Greek Doric at all constituted a daring stance for the period.[38] And it was this element of shocking novelty inherent in the Doric that attracted all three student-architects to it, in the first place. Second, each in his own way suggested, through his use of baseless columns, the advisability of returning to the primitive origins or first principles of architecture, as advocated by such rationalist theoreticians as Abbé Marc-Antoine Laugier.[39]

The element of primitivism in the designs of Soane, Saint-Hubert, and Poma is greatly enhanced by the way they all set the baseless Doric in close juxtaposition to a rushing cascade. The *concorso* program had called for a public fountain; instead, these contestants produced waterfalls. Saint-Hubert's somewhat tame apronlike arrangement has the stream swirling right around his baseless Doric columns. Poma focused attention on the torrent through his device of a huge culvert, like the Cloaca Maxima, spewing out its contents into a rocky basin. Soane avoided the obvious naturalism of his two contemporaries. His solution is at once less literal and more telling. He made the water flow down in a tall sheet, against which the column's primitive aspects stand out.[40]

Primitivism for Soane, Saint-Hubert, and Poma had to do with an utterly simple aesthetic, on the one hand, and the oldest order of columns, on the other. Clearly, however, these two factors do not account for the cascades, nor why it is that they interact in such a powerful way to enhance the ruggedness of the Doric. The explanation would seem to be that the three student-architects had come under the spell of the potent and pervasive aesthetic concept of the Sublime. Directly or indirectly they could have been aware of Edmund Burke's writings on the psychology of the senses contained in his *Philosophical Enquiry.* At virtually the same time as Laugier, Burke explored primitivism from quite a different point of view. Burke looked back to nature in order to understand in art the operation of the Sublime, which he defined as "productive of the strongest emotions which the mind is capable of feeling." Burke found this Sublime quality where nature unleashed herself in a show of strength, as in the awe-inspiring sound of what he called "the noise of vast cataracts."[41] The roar and the sight of onrushing water produced those sensations of pain, imminent disaster, and "terror" that could overwhelm the human senses and arouse a "sublime passion." Soane,

Saint-Hubert, and Poma coupled the unusual *sight* of baseless Doric columns with the *sound* of the cascades, mentioned specifically by Burke, to produce a doubly shocking *frisson* of "terror." The terrifying elemental primitivism of their rushing water reverberated against the chronological primitivism of their order. In a superb interplay of the rational and romantic elements underlying Neoclassicism, the pure logic expressed by the columns is constrasted with the antirational theme of the brute power of nature.

For each of the student-architects, Neoclassicism was inextricably bound up with novelty achieved through their double-edged conception of primitivism. But within this general uniformity of outlook there remained room for differing national characteristics. Saint-Hubert, for instance, indulged in the French academic penchant for megalomaniacal scale and for love of columns. His formal design, on the one hand, and the use of the *castello d'acqua* as a source of water, on the other, bear little direct relationship. The pump house, for all its huge size and many columns, simply straddles a stream that meanders through it. Even more in the case of Poma, restraint is thrown aside. With an Italian love of *scenografia* he created a phantasmagoric stage set. More blatantly than the others, he introduced primitive nature to the extent that it crushes the work of man. The concept of a functioning *castello d'acqua,* if indeed Poma ever thought it out, becomes lost amid the rockwork. Stillman has pointed out the significant fact that Soane's final design (cf. figs. 9.14, 9.17, 9.19) is smaller than the others.[42] It is also a great deal more compactly organized than either Poma's or Saint-Hubert's. Soane's conception of the waterworks is imbued with a hard-headed Englishman's regard for practicality. Of the three designs only his takes seriously the theme of the *castello d'acqua* and goes on to make the operation essential to the expressive success of the total structure. If given the chance, he might conceivably have won the *concorso* against the others. With a certain perspicacity, Soane, in his emphasis on functionalism, guessed what would be the prime criterion of the Parma jury. Did they not eventually praise Saint-Hubert for his planning? Did they not blame Poma for the unrealistic aspects of his design? Obviously an awareness had dawned at Parma Academy of the necessity for a more logical adherence of the total form of a building to its intended use.

In an era of expanding horizons, artists of different nationalities became bound more closely together by the common search for answers to the architectural problems of their day. Their progressive outlook absorbed such varied influences as Greek Doric columns, Antique Roman magnificence, Italian Baroque theatrics, a "modern" Sublime simplicity,

French Cartesian geometry, English pragmatism, and even the possibility of artistic piracy on the high seas. Perhaps without being fully aware of it, Soane, Peyre, Harrison, Paine, Saint-Hubert, de Seine, and Poma all belonged to one brotherhood. In this openmindedness that defies frontiers, in this interaction of stylistic and philosophic concepts that overcomes linguistic barriers, lies the fascination of Neoclassicism as an international phenomenon.

P·A·R·T T·H·R·E·E

ESTABLISHING A PRACTICE

·10·

The Competition for the First Howardian Penitentiaries

WHILE STUDYING IN ITALY, John Soane had designed a senate house, a mausoleum, and a monumental waterworks. All were intended to serve the needs of contemporary urbanized nation states. After his return to England in June 1780,[1] he continued to set his sights on such public works projects. And, by chance, his reestablishment in London coincided with a great opportunity for him to pursue his dreams. Besides, he needed such a "main chance" to bolster his flagging self-confidence, after the debacle of his prospects in Ireland and Scotland. The great opportunity in question seemed his best hope for employment. At the same time, if he succeeded, he would save face in the aftermath of rumors about his falling out with the Earl Bishop, and the loss of his precious trunk in Switzerland.[2] Hence, from several points of view, the competition for the penitentiary houses, as they were called, engaged Soane's intense efforts for nearly a full year.

In the eighteenth century the quickening pace of developments on all fronts led to new and improved institutions. The architects played their part in evolving building types, unfamiliar before, that coped with the unfortunates and the outcasts of a more complex society. The British penal system is an example, though it fell short of its high-minded intentions. At first, radical proposals were put forward by the prison reformer John Howard. But, as so often happens, the initiative got hopelessly entangled in the irresolution that can accompany enlightened idealism. The story of the competition for the penitentiary houses forms a case study of the frustrated hopes of social reformers, and the architects who tried to turn their ideals into reality.

John Howard, humane, philanthropic, unassuming, patriotic, and fearless, was a hero even in his lifetime. To a remarkable degree his official image remains untarnished—except insofar as the fiasco of the first penitentiary houses is concerned. An abortive entry into politics first drew his attention to the plight of prisons and prisoners. His combina-

This jail is admirably constructed for its proper purposes–confinement and punishment . . . and makes the solitude become so desperate that it not only seems to have no opening for any comfort save in repentance, but it makes that almost unavoidable.

Fanny Burney's diary
Gloucester, 19 July 1788

tion of tireless effort, and a cast-iron constitution impervious to contagion, carried him through a life's work of visiting correctional institutions,[3] which led to his epoch-making book, *The State of the Prisons in England and Wales, with Preliminary Observations . . . of some Foreign Prisons.* The independently wealthy Howard brought out a first edition in 1777 at his own expense. In it he deplored the filth, disease, and cruelty he discovered in almost every prison he entered. The remedy he proposed was better "management"—a term familiar from eighteenth-century commentaries on mental illness. His prisoners' bill of rights stipulated proper food, clean water, and fresh air. Howard's book mixed religious fervor, common sense, simple prose, and cheap price, with gripping autobiographical anecdotes. It established him as an authority on penal matters, and a popular figure.

Howard's *State of the Prisons* was not without precedent. Cesare Beccaria's *Dei delitte e delle pene* had appeared in print slightly earlier. But Beccaria only referred in passing to the "disgusting horrors of a prison."[4] In contrast to his more philosophical approach, Howard attacked the question of deprivation of liberty from the down-to-earth aspect of prison architecture. A contributing factor to the practical applicability of Howard's writings was a political situation that called for swift action. After the outbreak of the American Revolution in 1776, the steady deportation of British convicts to the former colonies abruptly halted. The inadequate prisons of the mother country filled to the bursting point. The hulks of decommissioned ships were pressed into service. The convicts aboard them literally rotted to death on those floating coffins. Something had to be done about the intolerable situation. A bill was enacted to commute the sentences of transportation abroad into terms at hard labor at home. In April 1778, Howard gave evidence before a Select Committee of Parliament, appointed to improve the provisions of that act. A year later, on 1 July 1779, a supplementary act (19 George III, cap. 74) became law and provided for the construction of two "penitentiary houses." The word *penitentiary*, connoting the tasks meted out to prisoners, recalled the idea of doing acts of penance. Although this bill was written by others, it nonetheless bore the unmistakable stamp of Howard's morality. Furthermore, Howard received an appointment as one of the three supervisors whom the act empowered with seeing to the construction of the penitentiary houses.[5]

The three original supervisors could not reach unanimous agreement upon the site for the new penitentiaries. They only managed to extricate themselves from the deadlock when one of them died, thus giving Howard the excuse to resign in 1781. Howard consoled the last remaining member upon his dismissal when he wrote "we know we have got rid of a deal of trouble." This statement typifies Howard's lack of commitment when it came to the practical implementation of his theoretical reforms.[6] Howard's graceful exit finally paved the way for the Privy Council to nominate three new candidates as supervisors. Their choice, officially approved on 2 March 1781, fell upon Sir Thomas Charles Bunbury, M.P., Sir Gilbert Elliot, M.P., and Soane's friend Dr. Thomas Bowdler. Unofficially Bowdler already knew that he had been shortlisted on 20 January. Howard personally intervened in Bowdler's favor on this occasion, as he did again when the young man sought membership in the Royal Society later that year.[7]

Bowdler's appointment as supervisor of the penitentiaries immediately induced Soane to approach his former traveling companion from the Sicilian expedition of 1779. Soane's attempts to gain influence are revealed, along with much else, in a rambling and unaddressed Bowdler letter, intended for Alexander Wedderburn (Baron Loughborough), the Chief Justice of the Court of Common Pleas. Concerning "the choice of our Architect," Bowdler wrote:

> It occurred to me at first, that the best thing we could do was to make the business public, and employ the Person who could give us the best proof of his Abilities. . . . I told Mr. Soan, who was the first person that applied to me, and whom I knew intimately, that I would do nothing for him, that he might if he pleased give us a Design when we advertised for them. . . . To this he acquiesced. When Mr. Leverton applied to me, I told him the same thing . . . and recommended to him the perusal of Mr. Howard's Book, and the Act of Parliament. . . . The Person [John Howard] by whose means I was . . . made a Supervisor, recommended another Architect to me, and I have applications . . . from my Father, and my Brother. . . . One of the persons who recommended Mr. Leverton to me . . . had in a manner promised to assist me in getting an Hospital [directorship].[8]

What a picture of intrigue and influence-peddling Bowdler's letter depicts! It becomes clear that Lord Loughborough and Sir Gilbert Elliot were backing Thomas Leverton as architect. Leverton had designed Loughborough's London townhouse a decade earlier. Bowdler naturally favored Soane. Howard—still very much a power in the wings—sided with another architect, William Blackburn. The whole selection procedure had degenerated into a jockeying for position among several dark horse contenders.

On the whole, Soane's *Memoirs* corroborate Bowdler's story, the only other written account of the penitentiary competition. Soane, for his part, claimed friendship with another supervisor besides Bowdler. This was probably Sir Charles Bunbury, known for his close ties to the Royal Academy. According to Soane,

> By these Commissioners I was directed to make designs for two penitentiary houses.... Mr. Wedderburn, afterwards Lord Lough-borough, introduced Mr. Thomas Leverton to the Chief Commissioner [Sir Gilbert Elliot], by whom he was also directed to prepare plans.... I soon found Mr. Leverton's interest was too powerful for me to contend with; and shortly after the Commissioners put us both aside, and required designs by public advertisement. On this occasion I became a competitor.[9]

Despite some discrepancies, Bowdler and Soane agree on the major points. Soane and Leverton had hoped to ingratiate themselves with the three supervisors and thereby avert the awful prospect of a competition open to all comers. Disappointment lay in store for these two front runners.[10]

Bowdler's letter of 1 July 1781 had already announced to Lord Loughborough the decision to settle by competition the thorny matter of selecting architects for the penitentiaries. On the nineteenth of the month the supervisors applied for permission to grant cash premiums to the first and second prize winners in each of the two categories of penitentiary. On the same day that the permission was granted, 23 August, a description of the contest regulations appeared in *The Public Advertiser* and other London newspapers. The announcement publicized prizes of £100 and £50 for the best designs for the larger men's penitentiary; £60 and £30 were offered for the smaller women's equivalent. On or before 1 November, a complete set of floor plans, at least one section, and two elevations had to be drawn to the same 8-foot-to-1-inch scale. All applicants who presented themselves at an address on Lamb's Conduit Street would receive a copy of the site plan and "other information." In view of the rumors that had been buzzing around artistic circles in London, the supervisors felt compelled to end their advertisement with the remark "the report of an architect being already appointed...is entirely groundless; the supervisors being under no engagement to any person whatever."[11]

The "information" that was promised to aspiring penitentiary designers took the form of a broadsheet in whose combination of punctiliousness and verbosity can be detected the handiwork of the man who later bowdlerized Shakespeare. The instructions began by stressing the importance of reading the Act of Parliament, especially those pages of it that emphasized openness at the same time as security. By way of clarifying the act's legalistic language, the broadsheet explained that the penitentiaries might consist "in *many different tenements.*" In fact, the supervisors implied that a multiblock plan would be more secure. Another piece of advice given to architects was that:

> As the penitentiary houses are intended to serve as a trial of a new mode of punishment, the supervisors are of opinion . . . not to build the houses for males and females on similar designs; for which as well as other reasons, it is their intention to employ two architects: and therefore those, who chose to give in plans for both houses, are requested to make them different . . . taking the greatest care to avoid every thing which may tend to show who is the author of any of the designs.[12]

Having stressed the experimental nature of the penitentiaries, the supervisors went on to reiterate, for the architects' benefit, the key hint contained in the act. The wording referred to buildings of "*plain, strong, and substantial*" appearance, preferably built of brick for economy and strength. The broadsheet concluded with the warning that the prize winners would not necessarily become the executant architects, although they stood a better chance of being selected.

In June 1781, at the same time as the penitentiary house discussions came to a head, Soane started keeping daily notebooks of his activities. As already seen, rather than being proper diaries, these were running checklists of purchases made, letters written, bills paid and unpaid, appointments, deadlines, or duties to be performed. On rare occasions he revealed his inner motivations by resorting to Italian as a code language. So, when he wrote the words "Atto di Parlamento," and next to it the sum of one shilling and ten pence, it simply meant that he purchased a copy of the Act of Parliament on 15 July 1781, when the memorandum was dated.[13] Apart from this, and the mention of letters to Bowdler on 12 August, not one single reference exists to Soane's almost daily preoccupation with the huge penitentiaries' undertaking. It is as if he wanted to keep the proceedings a secret.

In terms of graphic evidence, however, Soane's notebooks illustrate extremely clearly the creative process involved in designing the penitentiaries. Six oblong page sides record descriptions, dimensions, plans, and elevations relating to existing prisons selected from the second, or 1780, edition of the *State of the Prisons.* Specifically, Soane concentrated upon Howard's discussion of the Belgian prisons under construction at Vilforde, near Brussels, and at Ackerghem outside of Ghent. Soane's selection was astute. These two institutions were the ones that Howard had admired most.[14] Moreover, they operated on the principle of enforced

Fig. 10.1. Maison de Force, Ghent, elevation and plan of a penitentiary design (SM, Soane Notebooks, 1, p. 68).

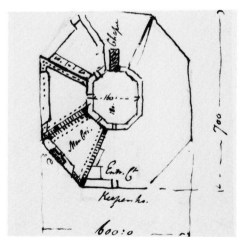

Fig. 10.2. Maison de Force, Ghent, plan (SM, Soane Notebooks, 1, p. 69).

hard labor, which underlay the Act of Parliament. The Vilforde and Ghent prisons, therefore, had a double bearing on Soane's designs, both through the *State of the Prisons* and indirectly through the legislation that derived from the book. The architect's original ideas are thus entirely tangled up with inspiration from the written sources he consulted, and must be studied in this light.

The sketches by Soane are datable to September 1781, from their place within the chronological sequence of notebook entries. They form the point of departure for any consideration of his designs. A ground plan and elevation (figs. 10.1, 10.2) copy, in simplified form, the plate in Howard's book devoted to the Maison de Force, near Ghent (fig. 10.3). The novelty of this design, evident though it was to Soane, needs emphasizing because of the fact that radial planning later became quite standard in prison layouts. For its date, the Maison de Force (begun in 1772) was the first of a kind, though others had been proposed on paper by such designers as de Neufforge, Combes, and Gisors.[15] Before this the prevalent type had been a rectangular or block plan, such as that used at Vilforde, and at Newgate, the recently constructed pride of British penal institutions. But the radially symmetrical planning of the Maison de Force put an end to the traditional courtyard arrangement. The Belgian innovation made an enormous impression on Howard, Soane, and generations of prison architects right up to the present day.

Once Soane had found his chief inspiration in Howard's engraving of the Maison de Force, he began making modifications. Directly beneath his sketch of the galleries at the Maison de Force (fig. 10.1) he devised a variant plan of his own. In the new scheme he placed within a regular octagon a Greek cross group of buildings centering upon a circular chapel. In so doing, he suggested what might have been the common source for his imaginary prison and that at Ghent. On his travels through Belgium in late May 1780, Soane paid not the slightest attention to the prisons there, nor did those anywhere else in Europe seem to interest him. But while in Milan earlier that same year he sketched the cemetery of the late seventeenth-century Ospedale Maggiore (fig. 10.4). He also made note of the Lazzaretto di San Pancrazio by Sanmicheli, which he probably visited during his stay in Verona.[16] Both North Italian structures had the peculiarity of a centric plan focused upon a place of worship. Architects like Soane and the designer of the Maison de Force could have realized the applicability of hospital and cemetery planning to prison architecture. Soane, at any rate, stuck to his placement of the chapel at the focal point, despite the fact that it had been put off-center at the Maison de Force.

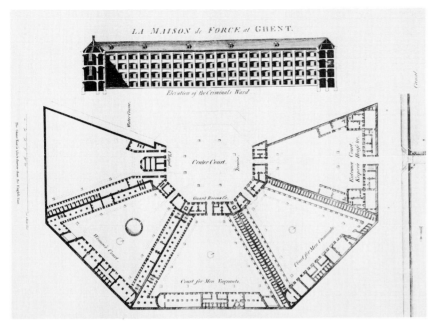

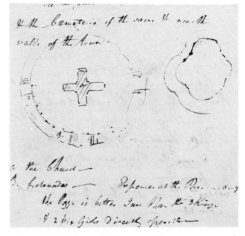

The grander scale of the men's penitentiary more readily captured Soane's attention than that for the 300 women. A small scrap of paper (fig. 10.5) served him to jot down some ideas which departed from the Maison de Force scheme and would ultimately be useful later, when he turned to the structure for women. Among these radical departures were the fifteen individual cell blocks arranged like radiating spokes (fig. 10.5 *top*). In his mathematical calculations in the right-hand corner, Soane arrived at a total length of 220 feet per block, based upon multiplying by twenty the standard cell width of 9 feet 6 inches[17] adding 30 feet more for stairwells or communal facilities. The forty prisoners on the two floors of each block made up the required total of 600. Two hasty perspective views show the long sheds converging wheellike toward a hub in the form of a domed building. These astonishing futuristic visions must not have satisfied Soane. He went on to devise an even more extraordinary geometric solution consisting of pentagonal groups of five blocks, each tangent on one side to a central circle. On the recto of the same torn piece of paper is a further alternative (fig. 10.6), quite carefully worked out. A circular building is inscribed within an equilateral triangle of slightly more than 430 feet on a side. Each side, in turn, houses two of the 600 prisoners in a pair of U-shaped complexes set facing one another across a central roadway. Soane found some in-

Fig. 10.3. Maison de Force, Ghent, engraved plan and section, in John Howard's *State of the Prisons*.

Fig. 10.4. Cemetery of the Ospedale Maggiore, Milan, plan (SM, "Notes Italy," p. 304).

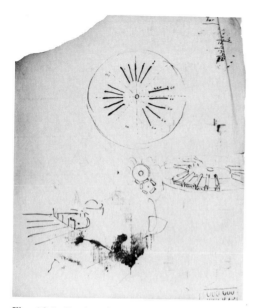

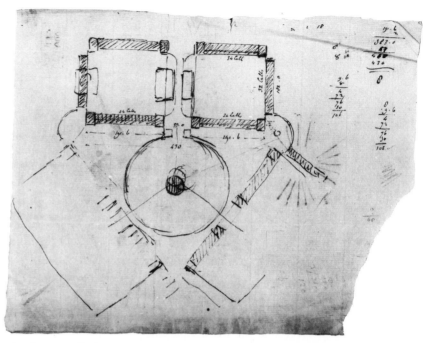

Fig. 10.5. Penitentiary design, sketch plan and aerial perspective (SM, OSMAS, Item 39 verso).

Fig. 10.6. Penitentiary design, sketch plan (SM, OSMAS, Item 39 recto).

triguing possibilities here. But he apparently felt apprehensive about the powers of his own imagination once it was unleashed. After these notable attempts to depart from the Maison de Force scheme, he fell back upon it as the one most likely to succeed.

Soane's final preparatory sketches vary little from the presentation drawings submitted to the supervisors. A ground plan, executed in pencil (fig. 10.7), may best be understood as having taken the top two-thirds of the great octagon at the Maison de Force. It is as if Soane capitulated not so much to the model of the Belgian prison itself, as to Howard's partial illustration of it (fig. 10.3). Within the borrowed outline, however, Soane substituted an ingenious internal arrangement of his own, in keeping with his recent experimental alternatives to the Maison de Force. At the expense of true radial symmetry, Soane achieved behind one outer perimeter wall three separate cruciform prisons, and a central round chapel accessible from all three. The practical reasons for this triple subdivision will be discussed. From the aesthetic point of view, the initial effect of this bold and necessary move has been to obscure Soane's reliance on the Maison de Force and on tripartite Newgate.

In Soane's two sketches for the intended elevations of the men's penitentiary (fig. 10.7), the quick pen or pencil lines enhance the impression

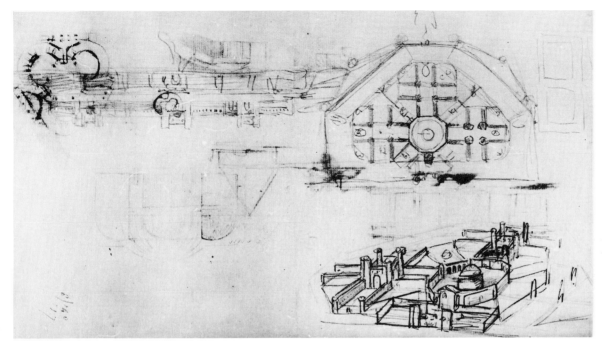

of a castlelike assembly of towers, and outer-bailey walls. Despite weak perspective, the summary draftsmanship conveys the grandeur of the conception and Soane's ability both to visualize it from various points of view and to reduce it to tiny scale. In the upper left corner a sepia plan of the chapel, drawn on the verso, shows through the paper. It resembles the trilobe proposals Soane had taken from Peyre for use in his Chatham mausoleum (fig. 9.4). In the context of a three-part penitentiary, the old idea, of course, gains a force and logic which it never had for the mausoleum. Finally, the schematic quality of the sketches endows the scheme with a dreamlike monumentality and modern starkness, not found in the drier finished drawings.

In the competition drawings of Soane, his preliminary investigations blend together with the fruits of his researches into Howard's book and the Act of Parliament. This can most readily be seen by examining the extremely complex and intricately inscribed ground plan (fig. 10.8). As the drawing bears the architect's signature, it cannot have been the one submitted anonymously, nor does its scale conform to that prescribed in the competition regulations. Still, it is probably an early copy, perhaps that exhibited by Soane at the Royal Academy in 1782. The three chief subdivisions inside the half-octagonal perimeter wall consist of Greek

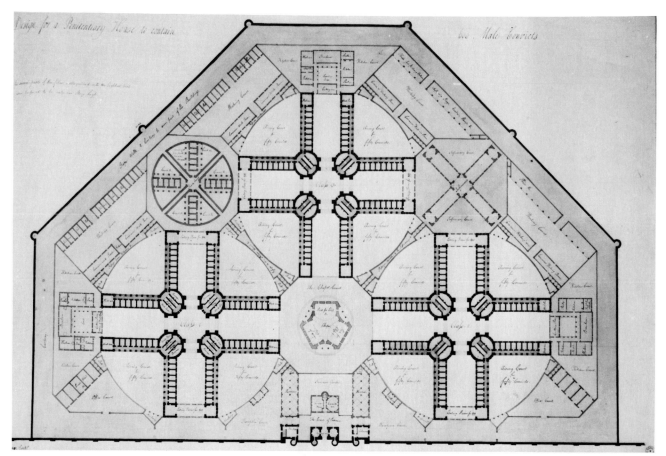

Fig. 10.8. Men's penitentiary design, plan (SM, Drawer 13, Set 1, Item 16).

crosses within a circle. They take cognizance of the act's mandatory requirements for the penitentiaries. John Howard had mentioned the three classes of convicts in the passages devoted to the Vilforde prison, which Soane had studied carefully. The framers of the Act of Parliament adopted the tripartite Vilforde system, favored by Howard, adding their own embellishments as well. In proportion to the length of sentence an inmate had served, he would progress up through the three classes, graduated according to lessening degrees of harshness.[18]

The strict classification of convicts into categories plainly implies an unavoidable element of repression in model penitentiaries. Yet Howard insisted that proper penal legislation would "correct and reform," as well as punish. The notion of "reformation," or even of salvation through faith, remained constant in the devout Howard's writings, and in the provisions of the act that stemmed from them. Specific regulations called for a chapel, a chaplain, and compulsory attendance at morning, evening, and Sunday afternoon prayers.[19] In Soane's plan the chapel in its octagonal court is at the heart of the entire complex. Inside, each class of convict receives a separate seating section to isolate it from possible corrupting influence from the others. The hexagonal shape of the chapel lent itself well to the insertion of three columnar entrances and sets of segregated pews facing toward the central pulpit.

At the bottom, the chapel looks across to the headquarters of the penitentiary administration, housed in the governor's dwelling. Howard had insisted upon the necessity of a resident governor in order for any house of correction to function smoothly. He cited as an example the model facilities at the Maison de Force (fig. 10.3). Accordingly, the Act of Parliament instructed the appointment of a penitentiary governor, and the provision of a house for ·him on the spot. To safeguard against possible graft, the law provided that an inspector and the committee of supervisors should balance the power of the governor. This explains the bicameral nature of Soane's administration building: half governor's residence and half committee room.[20]

Two octagonal courts, of identical size to that of the chapel, rest snugly in the interstices between the pairs of round cell blocks. Soane set a radially symmetrical building within each eight-sided figure. That on the right half of his plan he designated as a prison infirmary. From the outset, Howard's reform crusade had as its principal target better living conditions for prisoners. "It is a shocking thing," he wrote, "to destroy in prison . . . the health, and (as is often done) the lives of those whom the law consigns only to *hard labor* and *correction.*" In consequence of such damning statements, the model Howardian penitentiaries set up by the act sought to curb the spread of infectious diseases such as the dreaded "gaol fever," or typhus. Soane kept to the spirit of Howard's writings and the letter of the legislation by providing an infirmary, in the shape of a Saint Andrew's cross, that allowed for four open yards between the arms. This insured good ventilation, which was esteemed of the utmost importance in combatting contagion. Moreover, the location on the periphery of the penitentiary quarantined it as much as possible.[21]

Corresponding to Soane's infirmary is the "prison court," on the left half of his plan. This circular structure, divided along the lines of the British Union Jack, has eight open courts, each servicing five "dark but airy dungeons." Here Soane's inscription copies exactly the wording used on page 1399 of the Act of Parliament, where it spoke of the area set aside for troublesome convicts. Maintenance of security and order, through repressive whippings and solitary confinement, figured among the rules of the model penitentiary. The dungeons are literally the *sinister* counterpart of the infirmary. Howard had envisioned the ideal house of correction as the home of a big family—healthy but also strictly obedient.

Once a typical lawbreaker had been sentenced, he would enter the penitentiary by its single gate. He would be immediately examined by the prison doctor, bathed, deloused, issued a prison uniform, and then assigned his individual cell in the Class 1 cell block.[22] Nocturnal solitary confinement was one of the cornerstones of Howard's prison reform movement. "Solitude and silence," he argued, "are favorable to reflection and may possibly lead . . . to repentance." In consequence, the Act of Parliament specified standard-sized, "entirely separate" cells for reasons of security and to keep hardened criminals from contaminating first-time offenders. Hence, any convict in a Soane cell block would find himself with seven others on his floor whom he rarely saw, but who were continuously in line of sight of a guard in the adjacent tower. From the tower the guards could also keep watch over the four exercise yards down below. The yards, together with the baths and toilets that opened off them, answered to the importance Howard attached to cleanliness and health.

At the ends of the corridors in the cell blocks are located the so-called workrooms. Howard had stigmatized the normal English prisons of his day as "seats and seminaries . . . of idleness and every vice." He suggested work as the remedy. Enforced labor had been practiced in existing Bridewells as a prophylactic to corruption, but this rough justice had been loosely administered. On this point the 1779 Act of Parliament took an adamant stand. The model penitentiary would thrive, morally and financially, on "labor of the hardest and most servile kind, in which drudgery is chiefly required . . . such as treading in a wheel, or drawing in a capstern . . . sawing stone, polishing marble, beating hemp, rasping logwood, chopping rags, making cordage."[23] Soane derived considerable stimulus from the depressing list of tasks. Even his earliest notes copied from Howard's book had concerned themselves with the size of work spaces in the Maison de Force. Now, in the final plans, he devoted all the residual areas flanking the infirmary and "prison court" to workshops arranged around courtyards. Here the convict might spend as much as 10 hours per day toiling alone or in silent collaboration with others.

The cartway that passes between the inner and outer perimeter walk facilitates delivery of raw materials and collecting finished products. It also doubles as a ropewalk. The legislators and Howard fondly hoped that the penitentiaries would, in some measure, pay for themselves, while contributing to the rehabilitation of the inmate as a law-abiding member of society.

Adjacent to the workshops, set in separate courtyards, are the three kitchens. They have the advantage of proximity to the cartway for easy servicing. But they stand at a considerable distance from the pairs of 100 seat dining rooms, built across two ends of each of the three cruciform cell blocks. If the inmate had the misfortune to be either in the infirmary or the "prison court," the food brought down a maze of long passage-ways would never reach him warm. In almost every design decision Soane faced, the abstract concept of radial planning outweighed considerations of creature comforts, or prison security. Crosses and hexagons inscribed within circles, and circles piling up on top of one another, all look like a molecular model of some atomic structure. As an exciting geometric constellation of orbiting bodies, Soane's ground plan wins our admiration. But weaving in and out of the major organs of the grand design lie the interconnecting passages narrow to the point of occlusion, corridors so elongated as to rupture communication, important arteries of access severed. The want of proper mobility between the parts renders the organism, as a whole, nonfunctional. Furthermore, from the standpoint of security, Soane's labyrinthine network of semi-self-contained courts provided plenty of dark corners, which would have been perfect for convicts to lurk in while plotting their escape.[24]

A different but no less one-sided design prejudice permeates Soane's elevations for the men's penitentiary. With respect to the appearance of houses of correction, Howard spoke of "plainness" and "simplicity" as the most desirable qualities. From this statement, and others, Soane took the keynote of his design.[25] The austere facade facing toward the road of access (fig. 10.9) conforms in every way to the rules set down for the competition. The unwieldy scale led to a drawing over 8 feet long, formed of two sheets of paper pasted together. And the author hid his identity behind the now familiar motto "Mihi turpe relinqui est." At the same time that he borrowed the motto from Dance, he paid homage to Dance's Newgate Prison, especially to its entrance gates. At Newgate, Dance had masked the doors as fields of heavily rusticated masonry, replete with connotations of strength, impenetrability, and repression. Soane did the same. Moreover, Soane incorporated from Newgate the infamous motif of festoons of iron chains. These grisly garlands (fig.

Fig. 10.9. Men's penitentiary design, elevation (SM, Drawer 13, Set 1, Item 20).

10.10) created a truly characteristic decoration by suggesting to all those without the torment endured by those within. By imitating Dance, however, Soane committed a real faux pas. One of Howard's greatest acts of humanitarianism had been to banish leg irons and manacles from the ideal penitentiary.[26]

Elsewhere on his facades, Soane abandoned Dance's mannerist use of cyclopean masonry. Soane favored maintaining interest by simpler means, as recommended by the Act of Parliament. His penitentiary depends upon sheer physical size to convey its warning message. Blank, dreary wall surfaces, punctuated by the occasional buttress, stretch out as far as the eye can see—approximately 800 feet in all, over two and a half times the extent of Newgate. Harold Kalman has suggested that Dance sought to create at Newgate a Sublime impression, through implied vastness of dimensions. If this Burkean inspiration be so, then the argument applies better still to Soane's truly vast penitentiary, which strains the eye and mind to take it all in. "Magnitude in building" and the "artificial infinite" were concepts Burke thought would allow art to equal the "terrible" (hence Sublime) effects of nature.[27] Soane did not rely on them alone. He played off his interminably long wall against a skyline of towers that make one think of a fortress city.

The dozen towers of Soane's men's penitentiary are the most spectacular feature of the elevation drawing, and the even longer corresponding cross section (fig. 10.11). Functionally, the towers point forward to the crucial "panopticon" principle of prison design, introduced by Jeremy Bentham in 1791. (Prisoner surveillance in this type of panopticon plan emanates from a central point with optimum visibility over 360 degrees.) Aesthetically, Soane's towers, with their unmistakable connotations of a medieval castle, anticipate Louis-Jean Desprez's *Prison d'Etat* project of about 1787 and John Havilland's Gothic Revival style Eastern Penitentiary in Philadelphia (1821–29).[28] When studied in detail, however, the men's penitentiary reveals no instance whatever of real castellar details—no crenelations, no machicolations, no portcullis. Our minds at a distance *supply* the medieval flavor through the power of suggestion. The round forms and small windows of Soane's towers conjure up familiar images of keeps or dungeons. Deliberately to confuse us, his thick piers of an iron balustrade look like crenelations, until inspected more closely. What appear against the sky as observation turrets consist of giant chimney pots set foursquare and perforated by a central arch. In such a non-Gothic but medieval-looking detail, the closest parallel exists in the fantastic chimneys of John Vanbrugh's Kings

Fig. 10.10. George Dance II, Newgate Prison, London, festoon of chains (Museum of London).

Fig. 10.11. Men's penitentiary design, section (SM, Drawer 13, Set 1, Item 22).

Weston. Vanbrugh's masculine mock medievalism became for him a punning personal allusion to his own former career as a soldier who never fired a shot. Soane, an avowed Vanbrugh admirer in later years, may well have succumbed as early as 1781 to the English Baroque architect's "Castle Air."[29]

Once the gate of medievalism creaks open, associations flood in: gloomy dungeons, torture chambers, boiling oil, and muffled screams. All these clichés formed the stock-in-trade of fashionable eighteenth-century Gothic novels like Horace Walpole's *Castle of Otranto*. Soane's hint of medieval phantoms, fresh in the popular imagination,[30] added to the *caractère* of prison architecture as he construed it. Everything spoke of a long, arduous process of grinding down the recalcitrant criminal into a new man. The Soane designs set the proper fictional tone to put any potential wrongdoer in fear and trembling. On a more sophisticated level, his arched "flyovers" linking the towers forty feet above the ground might recall, not inappropriately, what Ruskin in Venice so memorably dubbed "the Bridge of Sighs."

The wording of the 1779 Act of Parliament made no distinctions between the penitentiary for 600 males and that for 300 females except for number and sex. As the broadsheet for potential competitors had rightly surmised, ambitious young contestants like Soane sought to increase their chances by submitting entries for each of the two penitentiaries. Soane's attempt to disguise by mottoes the kinship between his two designs could have fooled nobody. They share much the same bias for radial geometry. The differences that do exist imply that Soane learned from problems he had not entirely resolved in the slightly earlier and less mature men's penitentiary design.

The ground plan for Soane's women's institution (pl. 5), like that for the men's, is a splendid early redrawing of the original to a smaller scale. It clearly shows how Soane returned for inspiration to a preliminary idea he had rejected (see fig. 10.6). He took the overall concept of a circle set within a triangle formed of cell blocks. He then reduced this from six to three, took each of the U-shaped courts and turned it 90 degrees so its back faced the central triangular space with the chapel. Finally, he inscribed the entire composition within a circle of nearly 600 feet in diameter. The whole transformation occurs with an assurance not felt when Soane, like a contortionist, tried to squeeze the radially symmetrical men's penitentiary into a half octagon.[31]

As before, Soane provided only one, well-guarded entry gate, ringed by inner and outer perimeter walls, with a cobbled cartway in between. Once inside, an access route made an impressive vista directly up to the chapel, framed by the house of the governor on the right and that of the matron on the left. The matron looked out onto a court for incoming convicts, with a furnace for burning vermin-infested clothes. The governor oversaw the court set aside for delivery and warehousing of provisions. The strategic placement of houses and courts works both practically and aesthetically.

Each grade of prisoner occupies one of the sides of the triangular court in a counterclockwise succession, with the first class being located in the high-noon position. Within the identical cell blocks the other wings each consist of individual cells fronted by a light gallery. In the middle of the entry wing a vestibule gives access to an addition, jutting into the three-part green spaces, that contains the staircases and pairs of guard rooms. At the ends of the wings and in the angles between them

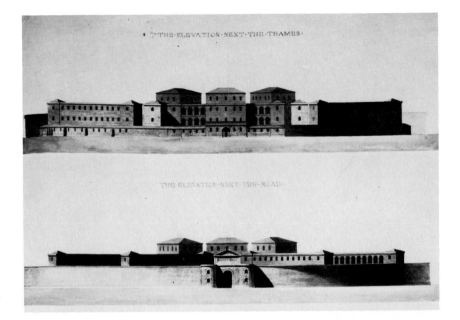

Fig. 10.12. Women's penitentiary design, rear *(top)* and front *(bottom)* elevation (SM, Drawer 13, Set 1, Item 14).

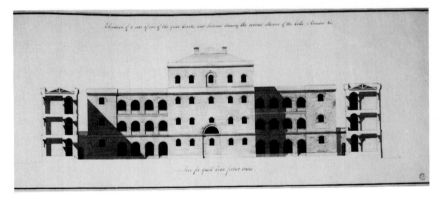

Fig. 10.13. Women's penitentiary design, section (SM, Drawer 13, Set 1, Item 18).

Soane fitted baths, privies and small work rooms, supplemented by factorylike sheds closing off the ends of the court on either side of a central dining room. The kitchens are at nine, ten, and two o'clock, while in the one o'clock position is a bakehouse and brewery court elaborately fitted up for the purpose. Because of the smaller distances and simpler plan, all these facilities are better and more conveniently interconnected than had been the case with the men's institution.

The central chapel can serve the entire female convict population at one time in its three lobes. In the words of Soane's inscription: "the three Classes are kept separate during divine Service, and indeed at all other times as the Act most justly directs them to be." Even during the rare moments of exercise Soane proudly remarked that "The great Court being subdivided . . . no more than 34 prisoners need ever be together" at a given moment. The tone of these remarks indicates that Soane, to impress the supervisors, had enforced the strictures of the act to the letter. Though Soane was obviously no pamperer, he was no out-and-out sadist either.[32] His surviving plans for the upper storeys include a master stroke of quite a different sort. The infirmary of each class sits on the roof top of the entrance wing like a penthouse. What better way of answering Howard's humanitarian plea that the sick prisoners should occupy the "airyest" situation to control communicable diseases? Soane's may be one of the first architect-designed sanitoriums of modern times.[33]

Soane's elevations for the women's institution are disappointing (figs. 10.12, 10.13), despite his presumptuous motto, *Leve fit quod bene fertur onus* ("A heavy burden well carried becomes light"). They have none of the somber grandeur of their male counterpart. Soane's puny gateway, and monochromatic watercolors indicating walls of brick, would not necessarily have prejudiced the jury of supervisors against him. He remembered the expressed preference for brick, and the implied preference for cheap and simple buildings. In place of the theatrical *terribilità* of the men's, he substituted an equally unappealing drabness. In this sense the women's penitentiary became a cut-rate alternative to the more expensive men's version. Soane probably reckoned that one or other of the designs ought to suit the supervisors. The men's penitentiary would please them if they were seeking a symbolic deterrent to would-be lawbreakers; its mate would impress levelheaded members anxious above all for economy and efficiency. The plan for the men offered a hard angularity; that for the women a feminine roundness of form.[34] Soane must have felt he had intelligently hedged his chances for success.

In the two days that intervened between the appearance of the penitentiary competition announcement, and the broadsheet explaining it, the supervisors changed the unrealistic date of submission. They moved it from the first to the twentieth of November. On 20 October they again delayed the deadline until the first of the new year, 1782. Soane, of course, had something of a head start. It is nonetheless remarkable that within the time limit, he produced two such intricate designs, and more remarkable still that his were only two among some sixty others presented at the close of the competition.[35]

Despite the large number of competitors, Soane must have rated his odds fairly high. He knew the supervisors personally, and they knew he was an architect with practical experience of new prison designing. Soane's long-term connection with Newgate Prison would stand him in good stead. He had worked in Dance's office when the drawings were being prepared and when the ground was broken for the jail. Subsequently, after the burning of Newgate by the Gordon rioters, Soane helped Dance and Peacock with estimating the cost of rebuilding the jail in May 1781. Of all the competitors for the model penitentiaries, none would have had such recent involvement with prison architecture as Soane—unless, that is, Dance himself numbered among the anonymous ranks.[36]

In the tense months that followed the closing date of the penitentiaries competition, Soane busied himself whenever he could with related matters. On 8 March 1782, he recorded expenses of sixteen shillings, eight pence, in surveying for Bowdler a potential penitentiary site in Battersea.[37] Soane may have taken the odd job as an auspicious sign. In fact, according to his autobiography, he felt convinced he would win right up to the end. He wrote:

> At length I was relieved from suspence by a visit from my honoured and esteemed friend, the first Lord Camelford [Thomas Pitt], who stated His Majesty's Commissioners . . . had selected two designs from a large number offered for that of the females, on the respective merits of which there was some difference of opinion . . . and that they had requested him to give his judgment thereon . . . which he had done accordingly; adding "the motto to the design which I consider entitled to the premium, is 'Leve fit quod bene fertur onus'"—"That, I observed, is the motto of my design." His Lordship replied, "You will hear from the Commissioners in two or three days, and until then you must not utter a word of what I have said."[38]

Soane's stupendous men's penitentiary had been passed over, but the design for the women's one looked sure of victory.

From the start, intrigue and machinations had plagued the progress of the supervisors, and this state of affairs continued until the final decision was made. Soane described that a "noble duke," hearing of the impasse about the women's penitentiary, had butted in with his unsolicited advice to the effect that neither of the designs selected by the jury could compare with another one altogether. So it happened that Soane "read in the public prints that the premium for the best design for the penitentiary house for males was adjudged to Mr. William Blackburn, that for . . . females to Mr. Thomas Hardwick."[39] The last-minute reversal must have been doubly galling for Soane who saw his hopes, that had been raised so high, dashed by an old rival like Hardwick.

On 23 March, when the four prize winners were announced as Hardwick, Leverton, George Richardson, and Blackburn, Soane's sentiments may easily be imagined. Years later he caustically commented: "a committee of taste, an honorable member of parliament, a learned barrister, a favored clerk, or any fashionable amateur armed with a little brief authority, has the power to control the architect, paralyse the best energies of his mind, and destroy his fair pretentions to fame and fortune."[40] At the actual time of his defeat, in the spring of 1782, Soane suffered an acute depression. His gloomy state of mind gave concern to George Dance who tried to cheer him up on 16 April when he wrote:

> I am uneasy that I cannot get at you, nor hear anything about your health. . . . I beg therefore when you receive this, you will give me a Line by the Post that I may be satisfied how it fares with you—above all things, "dans ce malheureux monde" remember the Motto to your Design for the Women, and forget the whole of the decision about those things (wch I hear will never be built).[41]

How right Dance was about the final outcome. Many factors conspired to doom the penitentiaries scheme. In 1783 the general climate was one of reform in the civil service and reduced government spending. As often happened in England, unwillingness to commit funds to public works projects stood in the way.[42] Impetus for change also waned when the American War of Independence ended with the Peace Treaty of Paris in 1783. The traffic in transported convicts could resume in safety. Besides, in 1770 Captain Cook had discovered Australia. The first settlement by prisoners in 1788 opened up a virgin continent for population by Britain's undesirables.

In the final analysis, an objective appraisal of Soane's penitentiary designs on qualitative grounds is impossible because of the apparent absence of his competitors' work. Without going into the whole subject of subsequent prison design, one drawing may be mentioned which does seem to relate to the competition (fig. 10.14). It is signed by Robert Baldwin, a former Dance collaborator, and a one-time friend of Soane's.[43] Baldwin's gridiron plan, intended for a site in Battersea, has eight cell blocks and workshops rigidly arranged in two sets of four, with a horizontal belt of gardens, and a vertical spine of communal facilities down the middle. If this lifeless solution is an indication of the caliber of Soane's rivals, then the gap between their creative imaginations and his was tremendous. He demonstrated common sense in practical matters, a

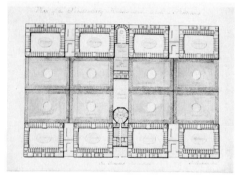

Fig. 10.14. Robert Baldwin, penitentiary design, plan (SM, Drawer 58, Set 1, Item 2).

radical bias in favor of radial planning, and created a stern language of architecture evocative of function. It was gifts such as these that eventually bore fruit when the mature Soane undertook such complex projects as the Bank of England.

As for the immediate future of England's prisons, Lord Loughborough's criticism of the Howardian penitentiaries was that "several houses of correction . . . are of more benefit than one great house . . . , they are more easily managed, better understood by the neighborhood."[44] So, as Loughborough predicted, jails did spring up along the lines suggested by Howard, but they were small and located in provincial county towns. At Gloucester (1788–90), the novelist Fanny Burney wrote with mixed piety and pitilessness: "Every culprit is to have a separate cell; every cell is clean, neat, and small, looking towards a wide expanse of country, and, far more fitted to his speculation, a wide expanse of the heavens."[45] At Dorchester (1789–95), Blackburn's "white flat facade" was described without enthusiasm in a Thomas Hardy short story *The Withered Arm*. Only at Ipswich (1787–90) and at Salford (1788–90) did Blackburn take any account of the trends toward radial planning and narrative architecture. Seen in this perspective, Soane's visionary prisons towered above the rest in terms of ingenuity of design and powerful imagery. But, in another sense, he was typical of his contemporaries' fusion of visual pleasure with physical pain. Soane's schemes for the penitentiaries reflect, mirrorlike, the ambivalent attitude of his age to the pariahs of society.

·11·

An Architect for All Classes

"The Borough Business"

FOR MORE THAN A YEAR after Soane's definitive return to London, in October 1780, there seemed a prolonged pause, when all the momentum of his first months back suddenly halted. During this trying doldrums period, Soane clung to one solitary commission. This was his urban renewal scheme for Adams Place. Ironically, it has no known connection with the elaborate network of acquaintances Soane had built up among Grand Tourists. Their names and addresses fill his first notebooks, it is true, but the sheer volume of Soane's letter writing proves his lack of immediate success in turning these connections to good account. Hidden among the numerous references to Lord Bristol, Stuart of Allanbank, Henry Bankes of Kingston Lacy, and Sir William Molesworth, there twice occurs the commonplace name of Francis Adams, once at a Bristol address and once in Lamb's Conduit Street, London.[1] When the promises of the others had vanished, leaving Soane stranded, it was Adams Place that saved the day. Otherwise the architect's order books would have been almost blank. Adams, singlehanded, kept Soane afloat until business could pick up.

Francis Adams, born in 1755, was the son of Shute Adams, a Londoner who was also the squire of Norton Malreward in the present-day county of Avon. Shute died when Francis was only ten, bequeathing him means and property, both in the West Country and in the metropolis. In 1783, however, Francis Adams severed his permanent connections with London by giving up his new townhouse in Powis Place and leasing his property on Cheapside. (Soane advertised the first for rent and did an appraisal on the second.)[2] In 1784 Francis married a girl from Corsham, Wiltshire. (Soane helped deliver a wedding present from her maternal grandfather.) Gradually, Adams shifted his base of operations to Bristol. In and around that city he served as a justice of the peace and deputy

However useful the early theoretical compositions of the young student may be . . . his judgment cannot be solely matured by such studies. . . . The delightful visions of early youth must now give place to the choice of materials and to questions of solidity and practicability of execution. He must have regard at times to the shackles of building in a great city, and always to the restraints of economy.

John Soane
Lectures in Architecture

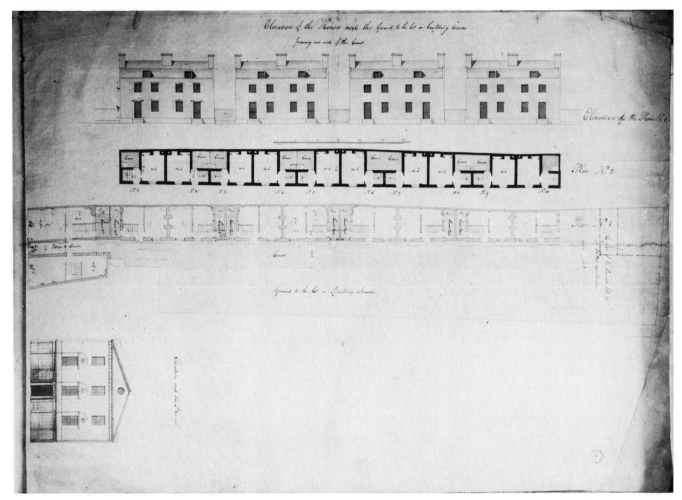

Fig. 11.1. Adams Place, London, plan and elevation, 1781 (SM, Drawer 39, Set 1, Item 6).

lieutenant until his death in 1807. He nevertheless left a permanent mark upon the face of London, in the form of a narrow cul-de-sac, which continued to bear his name until some nineteenth-century city planner with a sense of humor changed it to Eve's Place.[3]

How Soane came to meet Francis Adams remains a mystery. After the architect's first mention of his prospective client in December 1780, there is a crucial six-month gap in the notebooks. By the time they resume, the architect already had been engaged on what he called the "borough business," by which he meant the Borough of Southwark, where Adams's property was located. Whether Adams bought it or had inherited it has not been determined. He was part owner at least when Soane and Richard Jupp carried out a full evaluation of the dilapidated premises in 1781.[4] Soon thereafter, on 21 August, Soane submitted his first scheme for total redevelopment (fig. 11.1). By 2 February 1782, the previous tenants had departed, and demolition of existing structures on the site had begun. In the following autumn, work had progressed on the row of eight houses shown at the top of Soane's plan, and the two bigger ones facing Borough High Street, seen in elevation on the bottom left of the same drawing. First came the measuring of completed brickwork, then the roof, internal plastering, carpentry, and painting. Finally, on 22 January 1783, Soane rented the two shops on the High Street for £63 each. By 22 June he had collected rents for the first quarter on the row houses.[5] In the meantime, phase 2 of Adams Place, comprising the northern side, got under way. On 13 February 1783, Soane made working drawings of the plans of a public house and six more attached row houses. By August the publican paid his first quarter rents. And in a letter of 25 February 1784, Soane promised Adams the rapid completion of the remaining houses, together with a carpenter's yard that had been leased out at the far end of the property. In March only three houses were still unready for occupancy. In November of that year, Soane prepared a final breakdown of all expenses; the job was over.[6] So much, then, for the building history of Adams Place, a virtually unknown, yet exhaustively documented work. The odd thing is that Soane never referred to it, never illustrated it, or exhibited it at the Royal Academy. Probably he was ashamed to admit that his active career had begun with anything so modest. Adams Place, whatever Soane's qualms, constituted his earliest executed work. It also received his personal attention from start to finish, as he kept careful note of every step along the way. It became the model project on which he later based much of his office accounting practice.

Over the centuries, the Borough of Southwark, on the opposite shore of the Thames from the City of London, developed an autonomous and separate character. It owed its special local flavor to the strategic location as gateway to the South. For the convenience of travelers in transit, there arose the coaching inns that lined the Borough High Street, and the breweries that quenched the travelers' thirst. Side by side, and in constant competition for business, stood the George, the Tabard of Chaucerian fame, the Catherine's Wheel and a host of others (fig. 11.2). With so many busy hostelries the risk of conflageration was always high. A great fire, second only to the one that ravaged the City of London ten years earlier, destroyed much of Southwark in 1676. Somewhat in-

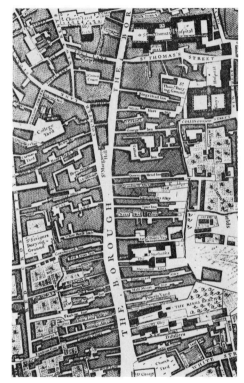

Fig. 11.2. John Rocque's 1746 map of London, detail.

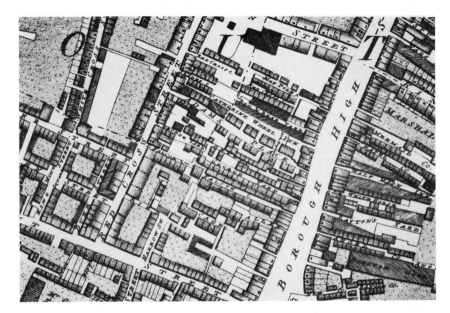

Fig. 11.3. Richard Horwood's 1799 map of London, detail.

conclusive evidence indicates that the Falcon Inn, just south of the Catherine's Wheel, was consumed in a smaller, eighteenth-century blaze. This might account for the fact that Soane levelled the site of the Falcon, when he replaced it with the Adams Place housing precinct.[7]

Adams Place, cramped as it was for space, could not depart from the age-old pattern of Southwark building. The peculiar requirements of the inns established a tendency for narrow street frontages opening onto long thin courts at the back, lined with stables below and galleried ranges for accommodation above (fig. 11.3). These galleried courtyards formed the most notable feature of Southwark topography in the heyday of British coaching. They gave Southwark its busy animation. At the Falcon Inn site, Soane faced just such a long, strung-out conglomeration of ramshackle stalls and sheds. It is no wonder that Adams's half of the total property was evaluated at only £260. Still, Soane's hands were tied by the locale. In view of Adams's intention to replace the old Falcon Inn with a new development, the architect's obvious course of action lay in adapting to the site. He set relatively innovative working-class row houses facing one another across a courtyard, in the traditional manner of tenements.[8] Such a tenement type of arrangement had a natural affinity with inns, because both featured narrow entrances into an elongated open space. The major difference was that dwellings replaced livery stables and the like. The bustle of the inn court gave way to a quiet precinct set apart from the main traffic arteries. The transition occurred so smoothly at Adams Place that the novelty of the solution and its designer's identity escaped notice.

Several factors account for the unique place of Adams's development in the annals of Soane's work, and of urban studies as a whole. Soane's poor employment prospects left him no choice but to accept the much-needed commission at Adams Place. The humbleness of the scheme was a function of the thriving, plebeian atmosphere of Southwark. Combine a young architect in search of work with a daring slum landlord, and the result is architect-designed housing-for-the-masses. But according to urban historians there was no such thing as "planned" working-class housing in eighteenth-century England.[9] They also claim that supply and demand controlled a situation left entirely in the hands of builder-contractors. Architects would shun such jobs for reasons of prestige. Because the encroachment of lower income groups could be interpreted as a threat to property owners in the better parts of town, architects hoped to protect their more lucrative source of work.[10] In face of these hypotheses, Adams Place stands out as an astonishing exception to the idea of the exclusivity of good architecture; perhaps with further research more such exceptions to the rule will turn up.

If, at Adams Place, the overall tenement type of plan arrangement ran true to form, the design of the individual units did not. The so-called back-to-back row house normally had no cross ventilation, which, despite its experimental designing, was one of its evils. Soane provided small open courts between his paired dwellings so that they were not completely hemmed in by their neighbors. In fact, the plain brick duplex houses lining the south side conceal systematic layouts behind their quite ordinary facades. Soane even offered two alternate ground plans: one with the open courts completely separating the pairs of houses, the other (drawn in black) where pairs of staircases set back to back blocked the court only at the front of the site. Such considerations of breathing space are quite atypical of normal back-to-back houses where every square inch counts. Soane seemed to be mediating between town and country. This perhaps explains the similarity of his plans to those for rural workers' cottages published in a book by Nathaniel Kent. Soane owned a copy of Kent's recent *Hints to Gentlemen of Landed Property*.[11] It mattered little that the text addressed itself to the countryman. Some confusion as to nomenclature existed at the period anyway. The urban "back-to-backs" were often euphemistically called "cottages."[12] Kent's appeal was broad enough to include the laboring class as a whole. He argued that better living conditions yielded greater productivity from the worker, be he on

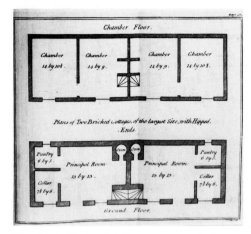

Fig. 11.4. Nathaniel Kent, engraved plans of two cottages, *Hints to Gentlemen of Landed Property*.

the farm or in the sweatshops of the city. On plan, the houses in Adams Place are really nothing more than urbanized versions of Nathaniel Kent's model cottages (fig. 11.4 and cf. fig. 11.1). Both, after all, stem from the same vernacular tradition of lower class housing. The needs were fairly standard: one or two upper and lower chambers, a chimney, a staircase, and a court or larger garden with a privy at the bottom of it.

Compared with the ordinary back-to-back houses, Adams Place obviously held greater scope for art in the stylish treatment reserved for the shop fronts on the main thoroughfare. Indeed, Soane's earliest study (fig. 11.5) specifically relates to bow windows gracefully curving into the sidewalk of the Borough High Street. This arrangement had become standard practice for shop front design, and it remained so for decades to come. To take one previous example, George Dance, in February 1777, designed a shop and residence on Fenchurch Street, London, incorporating bow windows to either side of an entrance door (fig. 11.6). Dance established a flourishing sideline in such shop designs, and it may be apropos speculatively to mention his name in connection with that of Francis Adams. Perhaps Adams, in the first instance, approached the well-known city surveyor, Dance, with his proposed redevelopment scheme. Then Dance, who always had more to handle than he cared for, might have passed the job on to Soane, whom he knew to be desperately in need of work. Whatever the truth of this quite plausible explanation, Soane remained indebted to the precedent of Dance when he first came to design the front of Adams Place. As Dance had done, he relieved the plain, pedimented main facade (fig. 11.1 *bottom left*) with a minimal amount of inset decoration. Rows of thin pilasters are similarly interspersed among the glazing bars of the shop fronts (provisionally assigned to an Irish linen draper on the right, and a Bohcah tea merchant on the left). Both architects gave a touch of high style to the humble domain of the shop in much the same way.[13] Here, as in the instance of the traditional tenement arrangement, Soane was governed by the examples of the past. But other, even more stringent, factors checked his personal expression. Soane indicated as much on his earliest sketch by preoccupying himself with mundane details, like the ten-inch projection of the bow windows and the exact position of the middle line down the party wall. Soane had good cause for paying such strict attention, as a whole body of complicated legislation regulated an architect's every move in this regard.

In 1774 a law was enacted "for the further and better regulation of buildings and party walls; and for the more effectively pre-venting...fire within the cities of London and Westminster and the

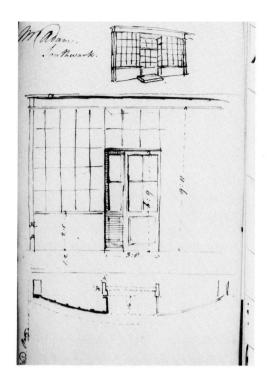

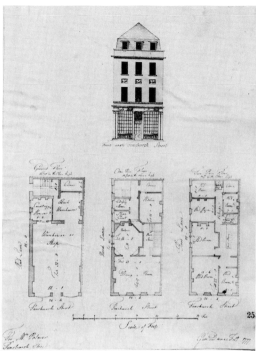

Fig. 11.5. Adams Place, London, sketch plan and elevations for the shop front (SM, Miscellaneous Sketches 1780–82, p. 21).

Fig. 11.6. George Dance II, plans and elevation of a shop and house for Mr. Palmer, 1777 (CLRO, Surveyor's Miscellaneous Plans, Item 258).

liberties thereof."[14] The legislation had been drafted for Parliament by two London architects: Robert Taylor and the ubiquitous George Dance the Younger. Unofficially stigmatized as the "Black Act," the provisions of the bill placed tight controls on speculative building in Greater London that led to a certain drabness, hence the epithet "Black." All developers had to familiarize themselves with the act and comply with it. Compliance in the case of Adams Place meant an almost exact agreement with the statutory requirements in every respect. As erected (fig. 11.7), the main building facing Borough High Street occupied an irregular site of about 1,330 square feet, cost £1,400 for the pair of shops, and rose 36 feet to a height of two storeys with a mansard attic above and basement sunk in a light well below pavement level. Hence the building clearly fell within the first of the four "rates" of structure classified by the act. The main thrust of the act, however, was directed at regulating the party walls in order to make them as fireproof as possible. Soane's preliminary sketch (fig. 11.5) and his working drawing both have dotted lines marking the middle of these party walls to indicate he had the provisions of the act in mind all along. Moreover, when Soane rebuilt the

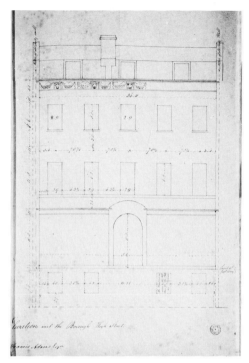

Fig. 11.7. Adams Place, London, elevation (SM, Drawer 39, Set 1, Item 4).

Fig. 11.8. Engraved samples of Coade stone friezes, 1778 (BM, Library).

existing party walls to bring them up to specification, a Mr. Richards, one of Adams's neighbors, compensated him £85.11.0 as his share of the rebuilding cost; on the debit side, Adams paid out £20 to Mr. Collins, another neighbor, for blocking two windows in the end wall of his property.[15]

Apart from the overall dimensions set down by the act, Soane's facade also took into account the limits on the use of combustible materials. His preparatory sketch shows his awareness that the bow window with its wooden glazing bars could not project outward more than 10 inches. All sash windows had to be set deep into reveals in the brickwork. Of necessity he was restricted to using brick for the most part, but he was allowed to coat it with a layer of plaster, and he may have taken up this option to render the facade of Adams Place more handsome. The act forbade altogether the use of wood for decoration, which accounts in part for the severe plainness of London facades in the last quarter of the eighteenth century. In order to avoid complete absence of ornament, architects like Soane resorted to an artificial material allowed by the act, and known commercially by the trade name Coade stone.[16]

The act of 1774 ushered in a boom period for Eleanor Coade at the Artificial Stone Manufactory she had run at Narrow Wall, Lambeth, since 1769. A printed catalogue of 1784 claimed for her fireproof terracotta material the added virtues of durability and relative cheapness. A stock list of 778 different items, ranging from full-size statues down to minute decorative mouldings, ensured customers something to their liking. But custom jobs were also undertaken, as was perhaps the case at Adams Place. At a somewhat earlier date, prints showing the sort of products available must have circulated among architects. The dated plates all come from the years 1777 and 1778. Soane found one of them that could be modified for the cornice of Adams Place (cf. figs. 11.8, 11.7). The Coade catalogue listed it as, "Ox-head, and festoons of fruit," and priced it at 12 shillings per running foot.[17]

Soane's choice of entablature fell on one that luckily had a personal significance for him. The motif of bucranes and garlands derived from the Temple of Vesta at Tivoli, one of his favorite Italian monuments (fig. 8.2). In a more general way it bestowed upon Adams Place the cachet of a high-class establishment—a "lily among the weeds," so to speak. The distinctive element of the horizontal decorative band certainly set the facade apart from the nondescript ones along the Borough High Street. Even in an 1888 watercolor (fig. 11.9), the motif of the Tivoli frieze immediately distinguished what had become the Kent and Surrey

Coffee House from its non–architect-designed neighbors. By the late nineteenth century the window frames no longer conformed to the act's regulations, but in other respects the facade was unchanged; and so it remained until its destruction around the time of World War II.[18]

Between the two imposing shop fronts, the narrow alley made its way back into the cul-de-sac lined by the two terraces (fig. 11.10). Im-

Fig. 11.9. Adams Place, London, view from Borough High Street, 1888 (Guildhall Library, City of London, S2/BOR).

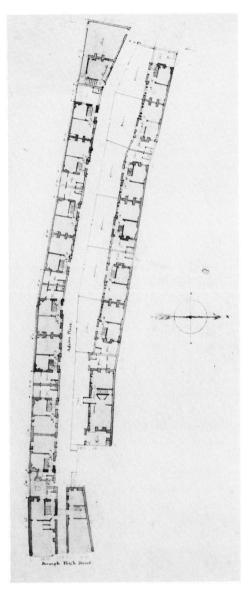

Fig. 11.10. Adams Place, London, plan (SM, Drawer 39, Set 1, Item 5).

mediately to the right was the public house and then the six semidetached houses forming the north side of the precinct. The south side consisted of four semidetached units, with slightly narrower intervening open courts than had originally been planned. At the end stood the carpenter's shop of William Reynolds. All the small brick dwellings fell within the category defined by the act as "third rate" houses: they were two storeys high, measured 4 feet, 6 inches less than the 21 foot height restriction, and exceeded £150 in cost. But the public house of John Gilbert, though the same height, covered 688 square feet, cost £400 and must therefore have been classed as a "second rate" building on those grounds.[19] Thus, from back to front and top to bottom, Adams Place reflected the "Black Act."

The documents relating to Adams Place also reveal that at each stage in the proceedings Soane, under the terms of the act, had to consult the official district surveyor, one William Meymoth. According to Meymoth's oath of office, he had to verify that work done complied with the law. In June and October 1782 and again in October 1783, Meymoth received payments of 10 guineas for his surveys. On each occasion he issed a printed certificate listing the location of the property, builder, and owner.[20] Besides all this, the Surrey and Kent sewer commissioners had to be brought in to survey the drainage Soane planned between the houses on the north side of Adams Place and the main sewer, which the plan faintly shows running along the western boundary of the property. Soane boasted the additional expense would give the houses "an advantage no other kitchens in the Borough have."[21]

The number of necessary surveys, visitations by sewer commissioners, compensations to neighbors, all tended to render building a new structure in Greater London very complex indeed. Perhaps Soane's first experience at Adams Place explains why he had so little to do with urbanism in future. Did Soane not speak about the "shackles of building in a great city" in the passage quoted at the beginning of this chapter? The act made him a mere third party mediating between the owner on the one hand and the law on the other. Adams Place succeeded as good architecture only insofar as it rose above the sea of sameness which the law, in its wisdom, had imposed. Under the circumstances, budgetary restrictions seem the least of the architect's worries, though they naturally preoccupied his client.

In 1798 Francis Adams appeared in print as an amateur economist. He published in Bristol *A Plan for Raising the Taxes Impartially and for Paying off the National Debt*. According to this pamphlet, Adams favored a new system akin to modern income tax in preference to existing levies on services and commodities. Just enough is known of Adams as a business-man to single him out as an astute capitalist. Adams Place was no philanthropic venture, but a sound money-making proposition. This was certainly the way Soane and Adams saw it, and this is still the light in which it takes on additional meaning. Their calculations of profit, and their economic forecasts, provide a full account of the shrewd mechanics behind a small-scale late eighteenth-century real estate speculation.

As an important first step, Soane provided Francis Adams with two different estimates. In phase 1 of the building program, the estimated cost would amount to £3,520: that is, £1,600 for the four duplex houses, £1,400 for the two shops and residences, £400 for the public house, and an additional £120 for paving the court. In phase 2 the owner would have to come up with £1,320 more to cover the cost of the six houses on the north side built at a cost of £220 per unit. This would bring the total estimated cost to £4,938, including extras and spread out over several years for ease in raising the capital. Following contemporary practice, Soane went on to calculate the new value of the properties at "20 years purchase"; that is, he gave their current market value, if sold, as a function of the annual rent multiplied by twenty years. He arrived at the figures of £6,650 or £5,955, depending on which of the alternative annual rents Adams decided to enforce: the higher of £21, or the lower of 16 guineas. These computations suggested that, if he wanted to, Adams could immediately turn a profit on his investment ranging from £1,200 down to £555, or anything from 10 percent to slightly over 20 percent above and beyond his actual expenses.[22]

Assuming that Adams had no carrying charges to pay on loans or mortgages and that he had inherited the land in Southwark, then 10 to 20 percent return on his money represented a better-than-average investment. Where Adams Place differed so much from similar developments was in the quality of the construction and design. The average cost of £50 for a provincial back-to-back house[23] is worth comparing with £200 per unit in Adams Place. In the long term, of course, such an outlay on materials and craftsmanship would pay off in smaller repair bills.

In black and white Soane had presented Adams with the full investment picture. On the basis of these forecasts, Adams decided to go ahead. A payment from him is among the first made into Soane's new bank account at Gosling's. In fact, it may be safe to say that Soane opened the account in August 1782 in order to handle the business with Adams and that he closed it when transactions came to an end in December 1785. The payments from Adams came in the form of drafts or notes for large lump sums drawn on the Bristol Bank. As the signers of the notes were usually Whitehead or Wilcox, the pattern of Adams's cash flow into Soane's account emerges on the credit side of Gosling's ledgers. Soane received £1,000 on 17 August 1782 and additional sums of £500 on 20 October and the following 25 February. On 8 March 1783 came £200 more, and another £800 on 29 August brought the total to £3,000. Then in 1784 on 20 May, Soane deposited a draft of £600, which brought his credits to an all-time peak of £3,744.9.9, after which they declined until he closed the account with a tiny balance of £6.7.7. Obviously the money acted as a floating fund to keep Soane abreast of outgoing reimbursements to craftsmen and suppliers. In 1785 Soane cashed £1,030 worth of notes payable over a period of months to various creditors. Meanwhile, Soane brought the final total of payments to £5,027.13.8½ by adding in various smaller sums together with the rents he had collected up to 1784, amounting to £440.[24]

Soane had estimated that by 1785 the old Falcon Inn estate could be transformed from a squalid 265 foot deep range of wheelwrights' and ferriers' premises that brought £117.6.0 in rents to a flourishing enterprise with upward of eighteen tenants, doubling if not tripling the income.[25] The success of Adams Place exceeded his predictions. The poor rate books for St. George's Parish, Southwark, act as a barometer for the steadily rising influx of new inhabitants at Adams Place. At the beginning of 1783 there were already seven, and the number rose to nine, eleven, and finally to a full complement of fourteen tenement dwellers by mid-1784. The rates started at 6 shillings for the row houses, stood at 13 for the public house, and increased to nearly a pound for the shops on the Borough High Street.[26] Adams had in the meantime opted for the higher rents proposed by Soane, and eventually got £332.10.0 per annum after taxes. For its type of accommodation, it cannot have been cheap. It addressed itself to the "aristocracy" of labor, the artisan class.

By November 1784, all the bills were in, and Soane could prepare the following itemization of the construction costs at Adams Place: carpentry £1,874.16.5½; bricklaying £1,727.1.8½; plastering £298.16.9¾; plumbing £257.8.10; masonry £249.4.0; glazing £127.12.10; painting £150.1.8; smiths' work £74.8.5½; slating £7.17.3¾; plus incidentals such as the Coade stone frieze at £27.14.0. Soane had calculated that various bills would amount to £4,840. In the final reckoning his estimate fell only £13.0.10½ short of the mark![27] The "Abstract of Bills" also preserves a remarkably complete list of the craftsmen's names. They recur with regularity in the contemporary Soane notebooks, account books, and journals, where they relate to jobs other than Adams Place. There is hardly a single artisan who does not crop up again in connection with some other Soane building. Disappointingly, from the historian's point of view, none of them decided to take up residence in Adams Place.

The plasterer William Pearce, for example, was employed in his trade at Adams Place, but also acted as Soane's clerk of works and paymaster. He held the same dual post in connection with Soane's slightly later work on the London townhouses of Wilbraham Tollemache and Philip Yorke. As for Richard Holland, the mason and general contractor, he had loaned Soane money before he went abroad and remained his lifelong friend. Not surprisingly, Holland got the lion's share of the bricklaying at Adams Place and also at the two townhouses just mentioned. In the field of carpentry, Soane likewise tended to favor another Royal Academy classmate, John Hobcraft. He engaged him to one degree or another on almost all his major early commissions. Richard Clarke and Edward Foxhall, two Soane regulars, undertook the painting at Adams Place. Clarke went on to work for Soane at the Tollemache townhouse and at Burnham and Earsham in Norfolk. Foxhall, as has been seen, became an intimate acquaintance of Soane's and assisted at Philip Yorke's townhouse and his country estate of Hammels, and at Burnham, Earsham, and Malvern, too, executing chimneypieces besides other interior carving. Ironwork was supplied by N. Beetham, who later worked at Taverham, and by the outfit of Pig and Co., whose name appears again in the accounts of Rectory Manor, Walthamstow. The slater at Adams Place, J. Tyson, covered the roofs of a large number of Soane buildings, including Taverham. Lane, the stuccatore, worked again at Letton. And Eleanor Coade supplied decorative elements at Taverham and Earsham.

The situation at Adams Place confirms what one would expect to have been the relations between an architect and a body of able craftsmen. Soane chose the artificers with care, and, if their work satisfied him, he gave them continuing opportunities. In due course these craftsmanly contacts blossomed into friendships and even family connections. Such a collaboration of designer and executant, based on mutual goodwill, remained the key to handing in accurate budgets, ensuring tight time-tables, and a dependable high standard of workmanship. In the process of building Adams Place, Soane developed for himself a crucial asset: a team of men whom he could count on to understand his requirements and work within the same specifications. At the same time, among the craftsman class, Soane became known as a demanding architect, with a watchful eye for irregularities, yet willing personally to supervise the work and ensure that the men under him received their due. Among potential clients, word would circulate that Soane could complete a job on time, within the budget, and with satisfaction guaranteed. Adams Place had been the useful proving ground.

In the accounts rendered to Francis Adams, Soane saved for the last his personal commission, which came to £251.7.0. This brought the final total cost for Adams Place to the substantial figure of £5,279.0.8½. In eighteenth-century terms this represented a considerable sum of money, especially in view of the economic situation in the early 1780s. It is common to speak of a general slump in the building trades, which by 1778–83 had reached the proportions of a full-scale recession. The theory runs that overoptimism in previous years, coupled with a crisis of confidence over the issue of the American War of Independence, had created a doubly dangerous situation. A glut of buildings already flooded the market, while tight money rendered expansion and new construction unattractive to investors.[28] How then does one account for the anomaly of Adams Place, on which its owner had spent over £5,000 during these financial hard times? Francis Adams seems to disprove the recession theory, or at least he calls for a reconsideration of its basic premises. Similarly, Adams Place requires a reappraisal of the design role of a London architect within the legalistic tangle which hemmed him in on all sides. Finally, the fond notion of the autonomy of a great architect has to undergo fresh scrutiny in the light of his reliance on the craftsmen who worked under him. The surviving Soane documents on Adams Place reveal, in its full glory, the bewildering complexity of the eighteenth-century architect's task. He must be part diplomat, part banker, part financial wizard, part gambler, part lawyer, and a gifted designer besides—all for a 5 percent commission.

The Burghers of Norwich

Soane's autobiographical *Memoirs,* after dwelling at length on his upset defeat in the penitentiaries competition, skipped over the entire episode of Adams Place, and resumed with the architect's one early triumph in the public sector: the building of Blackfriars Bridge, Norwich. He attributed his success on that occasion to his Grand Tourist friend, John Patteson, an alderman of the city, and later its mayor.[29] From him Soane learned that the old bridge had been closed to traffic late in 1782 and that a new one was to be built the following year. Thus Soane submitted his name early enough in the proceedings to win support for his design and estimate over those of others. Eventually a new stone bridge by him opened in the spring of 1784.

After Soane's early preoccupation with great civil engineering projects, Blackfriars Bridge was bound to seem anticlimactic. The river Wensum, narrow and sluggish, hardly represented a challenge to a would-be builder of great triumphal bridges, like Soane. One elliptical arch of 42 feet sufficed to cross the stream. This immediately limited Soane. The pyrotechnics of his triumphal bridge (figs. 4.18, 4.22) fizzled out for want of room to breathe. There was no scope for an elaborate program of characteristic decoration such as ships' prows or dolphins. Soane concentrated, therefore, on providing good, sound construction. Out of that he developed an unusual and plain aesthetic, very different from his visionary projects. He guessed the prevailing mood correctly. From the beginning, cost factors rather than appearances dominated the considerations of the solid, middle-class city fathers of Norwich.

The duty fell to the Tonnage Committee of the City Council to decide what was to be done about the ruinous state of old Blackfriars Bridge. In anticipation of the crucial, decision-making meeting, an open letter addressed to the committee appeared in the *Norwich Mercury* newspaper on 8 March 1783. The anonymous writer, "a disinterested citizen," timed his "Remarks on Black Friars Bridge" to coincide with the deliberations on the fate of the old bridge. He noted its weak condition as sufficient reason for demolishing it. He suggested a public subscription to raise funds for a replacement. Astonishingly, the new type of structure he specifically had in mind was to be made entirely of iron. He cited the material's durability, relative lightness, ease of construction, and "novelty" as points in its favor. Novel was the word for it. Only a matter of two years earlier, in 1781, the very first iron bridge ever built opened at Coalbrookdale, Shropshire.[30] Somehow or other the correspondent to the *Norwich Mercury* must have heard about it; he was not the only one. On the same day in March, the rival Norwich weekly, the *Norfolk Chronicle,* printed a letter to the editor from an anonymous writer who styled himself simply "a citizen." He added, as a postscript to his remarks, "I am informed Mr. Frost is ready to undertake the building of a new bridge, with a single arch, with cast iron, for £1,500." James Frost did indeed build an iron bridge at Norwich, but it had to wait until 1802, long after any "novelty" had worn off.[31] Unfortunately, nothing more is heard about this earlier proposal of his in any of the official documents relating to Blackfriars Bridge. Still, the two letters to the editor about an iron construction system that was still revolutionary is totally unexpected— especially so in a provincial newspaper.

As if oblivious to the newspaper correspondence of the previous week, the Tonnage Committee in their minutes of 12 March accepted a plan for a new bridge from the local contractor John de Carle, who estimated its cost at £950. At this juncture, Soane, tipped off by Patteson, threw his hat into the ring. Having come to Norwich on 11 March and left for Burnham, he returned post haste on 15 March, attended the General Assembly meeting two days later, and was commissioned by them to prepare rival plans and estimates, thus overriding the Tonnage Committee's original choice.[32] To smooth the waters, the assembly further instructed that "an advertisement be published . . . for other persons to deliver plans and estimates for the same [bridge] . . . and that such plans and estimates be delivered sealed up at the Town Clerk's office before the second day of April next." To all intents and purposes this public announcement was a decoy. When the advertisement appeared on 22 March in the issues of the *Mercury* and the *Chronicle,* it only called for demolition estimates and implied that a single-arch stone bridge, such as Soane's, had been virtually decided upon. The deliberately vague wording tended to discourage aspiring contenders, as did the unrealistically short deadline for submissions. Soane's friends may well have had a hand in rigging the contest for him. He had a week's lead on any others, and this, together with his prestige as a London architect and his local influence, all worked in his favor. As the front runner from the start, and probably the sole contestant, Soane never won an easier victory. His drawings, and the John de Carle estimate of £1,250 for carrying them out, received approval from the Tonnage Committee on 4 April. Three days later, the General Assembly appointed Soane as the official architect for Blackfriars Bridge[33] and de Carle as the contractor.

The contract drawings, signed 10 April 1783 (figs. 11.11, 1.10) show the bridge sandwiched between existing structures and almost totally devoid of decoration. Soane could see that a ponderous decorative scheme would have looked out of place in this workaday setting. He determined to achieve the impression of a nearly flat roadbed, effortlessly borne from shore to shore by a gently curving arch. The sheer smooth Portland stone surfaces, and the almost imperceptible rise of the road, accentuate a feeling of near tenuousness, which Soane had admired in the Swiss wooden bridges he had studied on his return from Italy. In the terms of Soane's plain aesthetic, the arch ought to appear nearly too weak to bear its load. And indeed the distance between the top of the arch and the top of the stone parapet is thin to the breaking point. Soane must have relished creating a work the engineering prowess of which seemed to undermine the apparent stability of the structure. The proof of its sturdiness is that it has stood the test of time well. Though marred by later ironwork railings, and widened with overhanging footpaths, it still carries vehicular traffic today.

Beneath the outward appearance bordering on fragility there lies a

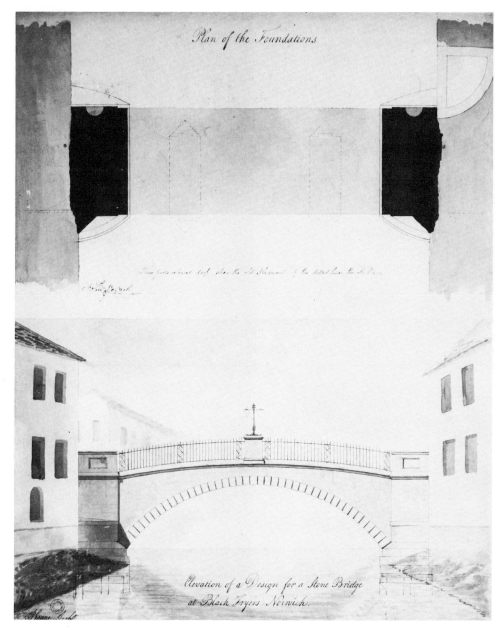

Plan of the Foundations

Elevation of a Design for a Stone Bridge at Black Fryers Norwich.

Fig. 11.11. Blackfriars Bridge, Norwich, plan of the foundations and west elevation (SM, Portfolio 3, Item 8).

carefully thought out reinforcement armature. As late as 1819 the Norwich historian John Stacy heard accounts of the "remarkable" construction techniques employed in the bridge. In particular, Stacy commented on the large proportion of metal used.[34] A little-known cross section by Soane plainly illustrates the inventiveness pointed out by Stacy (fig. 11.12). The individual voussoirs of the arch are weighted in their hollow centers with 6-pound blocks of iron. This tends to wedge them more tightly together. The joggled joints between the stones are fastened by added pressure from iron cramps. To protect them from exposure to dampness and consequent rusting, molten lead has been run into all the cavities, sealing them. As an added precaution, the contract specified that lateral tie bars encased in lead be placed under the roadbed. These can be seen in the form of dotted lines on the plan of the partitions (fig. 11.12, *top right*) and in the side elevation, too *(bottom)*. Of course, such sophisticated innovations do not make Blackfriars an all-metal bridge. Compared with the extraordinary Coalbrookdale Bridge, its reliance on rubble mixed with brick and faced with Portland stone is retardataire; compared with ordinary bridges of the period, however, Blackfriars is quite advanced.

As we have seen, Soane met with the great civil engineer Jean-Rodolphe Perronet on his way through Paris in March 1778.[35] Perronet's advice and later writings may have helped Soane design the wooden arch centering for Norwich (fig. 11.12, *bottom*). But with regard

Fig. 11.12. Blackfriars Bridge, Norwich, plan of the superstructure, section, plan of the partitions *(top row),* and elevation showing the arch centering (V&A, 3307.105).

to iron reinforcement the Frenchman does not appear to have influenced Soane as much as the carpenter-bridge builders of Teufen, Johann and Hans Ulrich Grubenmann (see chap. 5). Soane, in his Swiss travels, visited and studied two of the most famous Grubenmann examples, at Wettingen and Reichenau. The criterion Soane applied in judging their relative excellence was the degree to which metal reinforced the woodwork.[36] Like the Grubenmanns, Soane stood at the threshold of the Industrial Revolution, not daring to cross over. He remained tied to traditional masonry techniques and the aesthetic values that went along with them. This confirms his position as an architect of the old school, capable of designing elegant stone bridges. The wave of the future, however, lay with the kindred profession of the engineers, who more readily adopted the new, more versatile metal technology, because they were less hampered by age-old concepts of Beauty.

Everyone was pleased with Blackfriars Bridge, and, whatever its shortcomings in the broader historical perspective, Soane looked back on it proudly. When closing his account with Norwich Corporation, he noted with obvious satisfaction "the Court voted me their thanks," as well as a £63 commission.[37]

Soane, though an outsider, had managed to break the stranglehold on provincial jobs by local architects. He swept all competitors from the field. This is a measure of his growing reputation and the powerful interest he and his friends had among the county elite at Norwich, the commercial and cultural capital of East Anglia.[38] In the early 1780s, with business in a slump, if not a full-scale recession, one could not afford to be lax in one's dealings. Even a county-town bridge commission suddenly brought out aspiring contenders, like Frost and de Carle, in surprising numbers. Clearly, architects exceeded the volume of jobs available. Quite apart from his designing ability, Soane demonstrated the quick reflexes of a true professional on the scent of work. He had built a sound and attractive bridge on schedule and within the budget. So obvious an advertisement did him no harm in establishing a firm foothold in an affluent region.

The Dilettanti

From its foundation around 1732, the Society of Dilettanti offered its highly select membership a mixture of conviviality and scholarly comradeship with others who had made the Grand Tour. As a group, these wealthy, high-living gentlemen were poles apart from the workers of Southwark, and a cut above the burghers of Norwich. And insofar as the Italian word *dilettante* means "a connoisseur or lover of the arts," it gives

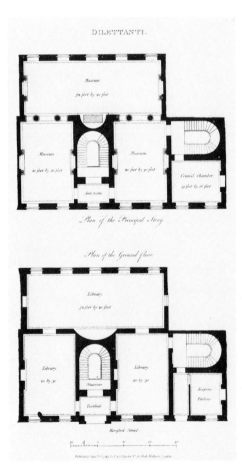

Fig. 11.13. Museum design for the Society of Dilettanti, London, engraved plans, 1789, *Plans, Elevations, and Sections.*

a good idea of the Society's goals. To a man, the Dilettanti could afford to collect. Out of this grew the long-lasting importance of the Society at the forefront in sponsoring scholarly archaeological publications.[39] As a result of the expeditions that preceded these publications, the Society became the repository of a collection of antiquities, notably statues, bas-reliefs, and inscriptions. As time went on the proper housing and display of the collection posed a problem. It was in this regard that Soane became involved with the aristocratic and well-off members.

As early as 1761, the Society resolved to play a pedagogical role by displaying its valuable possessions along with plaster casts of other sculptural examples. It would build a permanent clubhouse as an "ornament," and would open it up "in order to produce something . . . that may be beneficial to the publick." In response to this initiative, John Vardy immediately exhibited a clubhouse design at the Society of Artists' show.[40] It was the first in a whole string of abortive schemes, of which Soane's was the last. And although the Society of Dilettanti continues to thrive as a body, it is still without headquarters.

Negotiations for a clubhouse had wavered back and forth since 1747, when a London site had actually been purchased. By 1753 a design imitating the Temple of Augustus at Pola had been decided upon. In 1768, or thereabouts, William Newton submitted numerous drawings, but again no progress resulted.[41] Yet the collection continued to swell, and the intention remained the same—to share the treasures with other amateurs and artists.

Against this background of frustrated schemes, Soane's designs represent one final spurt of effort on the part of the Society, or, more specifically, one member, Thomas Pitt. Here, as elsewhere, Soane's friend and early client was the prime mover in the affair. Thomas Pitt was elected to the Society in 1763, after returning from his first Grand Tour. Some eight years later he purchased from the Grosvenor Estate the lease on two of their London properties. The location was in Hereford Street, which once ran parallel to and just south of Oxford Street in the neighborhood of Marble Arch. Pitt's townhouse was directly adjacent to the western extremity of the cul-de-sac. Any generic similarity to the plan of Adams Place ended here. Hereford Street belonged to the fashionable Mayfair district, and on Pitt's vacant lot there arose around 1777 the brick shells of two elegant terrace houses, built as part of a speculative venture by John Crunden, an architect associate of Henry Holland's. It is remotely possible, then, that Soane, in his capacity as Holland's clerk, knew the houses and their owner at an early date.[42] By 1783 Pitt had decided to dispose of the empty shells. Soane measured them, and

Fig. 11.14. Museum design for the Society of Dilettanti, London, engraved section, 1789, *Plans, Elevations, and Sections.*

in September of that year he announced their sale in a newspaper advertisement. He provided the dimensions of the unfinished rooms and informed the public of his willingness to give further details. No one showed much interest. In the same newspaper exactly nine months later, a notice of sale by auction appeared for "the two last houses on the south side of Hereford Street, Grosvenor Square, . . . the one 32 feet, the other 40 feet in front." Soane attended Christie's auction rooms for Pitt, who held a reserve bid in case the offers went too low, which they apparently did. Again no sale took place.[43]

In between the time of the first and second newspaper advertisement, Thomas Pitt, by then Lord Camelford, had had a change of heart. As a long-standing member of the Dilettanti, he knew the vexed problem of how to house the Society's collection. At some point late in 1783, he spoke with Soane about an idea he had to donate to the Society the pair of houses on Hereford Street he had recently failed to sell. He also broached the matter in a casual way with the Society's secretary, Sir Joseph Banks.[44] There was nothing casual, however, about the ambitious Soane's response. The following spring he exhibited at the Royal Academy his drawing for a "museum" for the Society (fig. 1.9) and he later engraved it on two plates (figs. 11.13, 11.14).

The total width of the rooms planned by Soane equals the street frontages mentioned by him in the advertisements. He had no intention, therefore, of changing the overall outlines or altering the position of the two existing staircases, which he retained. At the back of the site, however, he took the two rooms facing the garden and threw them into a single large space, 52 feet by 20 feet. This provided him with a sizeable library on the lower level and a "museum" up above. In fact, each room at the back connected with the two at the front to form suites of three, making extensive apartments of 2,240 square feet each. (When Soane built his own personal museum at 12–14 Lincoln's Inn Fields after 1812, he similarly exploited the back rooms of London row houses.) Apart from manipulating a few spaces, Soane's main design problem for the Society of Dilettanti consisted in creating a suitable scheme of interior decoration.

Nothing could have been more appropriate to the intended function of the building and the nature of its occupants than Soane's allusive Grand Tourist style. For the Society's main room he created a heterogeneous blend of Greek and Roman elements to reflect the archaeological tastes of his prospective clients. The pairs of columns he used as screens are based upon the Ionic north porch of the Erechtheion at Athens, a building actually published by Stuart and Revett under Dilettanti auspices. The entablature above comes from the Roman frieze of the Fortuna Virilis Temple, as illustrated by Desgodetz. Higher still, Soane placed quite unarchaeological barrel vaults, presumably of his own invention. Up the walls Soane trained his sculpture groupings. Everything had its assigned place, and, moreover, inserting the precious marbles formed a protection against possible theft.

When compared, the engraved cross section of 1788 and the earlier drawing differ (figs. 11.14, 1.9) in the actual statuary depicted, indicating that the choice was fairly arbitrary. Although the actual figures were interchangeable, their arrangement was not. A framework of aedicular niches with spiral fluted columns, reminiscent of the Clitumnus Temple (fig. 7.11), anchored the statues at set positions throughout the gallery. Around these nodal points clustered less important works or bas-relief roundels. Above the central alcove containing the horseman, Soane affixed a long processional frieze of sacrifants leading their oxen. Perhaps he intended to allude to the frieze of the Parthenon, pieces of which were in the Society's collection at the time.[45]

Soane's definite ideas about the arrangement of sculptures within a gallery came as a direct result of his travels abroad, just as much as his archaeological references did. In Rome, especially, Soane became an avid museum-goer. In his copy of Anna Miller's guidebook he noted his impressions of the Capitoline Museum; his lectures indicate his familiarity with the newer Museo Pio-Clementino in the Vatican,[46] and he drew with care the famous *gran salone* of the Villa Albani (fig. 11.15). These diverse Roman collections all shared a common method of display. As at the Villa Albani, the sculptures were grouped with an eye to their beauty of effect, in addition to didactic organization along chronological or typological lines. In the *gran salone* of the Villa Albani, the architect Carlo Marchionni set Antique bas-relief panels right into the walls or cornice.

Fig. 11.15. Villa Albani, Rome, sketch plan, elevation, and details of the *salone* (V&A, 3436.189 recto).

Fig. 11.16. Robert Adam, sketch of the proposed arrangement of his collection of Antique marbles (SM).

Fig. 11.17. Johann Zoffany, conversation piece showing Charles Towneley in his London townhouse (Towneley Hall Art Gallery and Museums).

Statues stood in niches lined with mirrors to reveal the otherwise hidden dorsal portions. The objects thus dotted about and incorporated as semipermanent fixtures became part of an overall mural design. The link between Marchionni's approach and Soane's is obvious, even though it is not possible to tell from his drawings for the Dilettanti whether Soane had any organizational rationale in mind, other than a purely visual one.[47] In any event, the Grand Tourist reminiscences in Soane's museum for the Dilettanti would not have gone to waste on the well-traveled members.

Soane was not the first in England to imitate recent Italian museological techniques. Always an innovator, Robert Adam in 1758 installed part of his personal collection of antiquities, using an aesthetic principle of arrangement based on Italian models (fig. 11.16).[48] The collector

Charles Towneley, later a member of the Dilettanti, built himself what was perhaps the best-known example of the genre at his London town-house, 7 Park Street (now 14 Queen Anne's Gate). The *mise-en-scène* can best be appreciated in the background of Johann Zoffany's conversation piece of circa 1782, showing Towneley amid the fashionable disarray of his statues and other antiquities (fig. 11.17). Bas-reliefs are set into the walls pell-mell, with a painterly eye to forming a pleasing still-life composition all its own. While the picture is not factually accurate by any means, it does evoke transplanted British examples of the Italian tradition of art display. A prophetic feature ignored by Soane in the Dilettanti museum was the skylight above Towneley's head.[49] (Soane would often resort to such lighting devices later.) But, above all, Soane's museum differed in one other important respect, which earns it the place it has long been denied in the history of British museology. Towneley's, Albani's, and Adam's galleries were all private; the Dilettanti's was conceived as having a semipublic function.

On 7 February 1785, Thomas Pitt addressed a letter to Sir Joseph Banks, reminding him of his offer of the previous year to present the Dilettanti with a clubhouse. Pitt sent Soane's drawing and, together with it, a proposal in which he stated: "We have the most noble repositorie for natural History [the British Museum] and we have establishments for encouraging of the Arts, but a Museum for what is properly call'd *Virtu* has long been wanting."[50] He envisioned a vigorous campaign to solicit funds for the clubhouse "the *whole* expence of which Mr Soane has estimated at £2,500 and would be ready to contract for the execution of it at that price." He concluded: "When the collection became an object of curiosity to the public a trifle paid by those who visited the Museum . . . for their Catalogue might assist towards the expence." Here, then, Pitt envisioned the first free art museum in Britain, excepting only the Ashmolean at Oxford.

Pitt's dream for the Society proved too grandiose. His fellow Dilettanti could see through his altruism to the self-interest behind it. Pitt could dispose of a "white elephant" by giving away the Hereford Street houses he had so far failed to sell. He could also attach some conditions to his bequest. He stipulated that the Dilettanti should assume the ground rent, but that the rear gardens should continue to belong to him; and that he should have a private entrance into the clubhouse library by means of a side door and three steps shown on Soane's drawing. When his letter, proposal, and accompanying plans were laid before the Dilettanti, they thanked him politely for his "generous offer," but refused it on the pretext of the high cost of maintenance.[51] And there the whole affair ended. Rebuffed by the Dilettanti, Pitt finally managed to dispose of the properties to private individuals.

The design for the museum of the Dilettanti, though it never materialized, had diverse repercussions. In 1784 the Society, spurred by recent suggestions, seriously turned its attention to what to do with its collections. It loaned its marbles to the Royal Academy and gave its inscriptions to the British Museum. Thus, indirectly, the Dilettanti did promote the spread of mass culture.[52] In artistic quarters, too, the discussions surrounding the Dilettanti's collection caused a stir of activity. Somehow news must have spread of the last, flickering interest the Society had in housing its treasures. After years when the building type had never been represented at all, suddenly, in 1784, three museum designs were contributed to the Royal Academy exhibition.[53] Then, just as suddenly, the number dropped off. This confirms, once again, the impression that the London and provincial building worlds were intensely competitive. As with Blackfriars Bridge, no rumor of a job, however slight, could be overlooked by an architect in search of work. And, similarly, the museum design established Soane's name, though in a very different kind of milieu from the bourgeois one of Norwich. Like the architects Stuart, Revett, and Newton before him, Soane cultivated quite a large clientele among those who were, or were to become, Dilettanti. First and foremost there was Pitt, but others followed: Sir Sampson Gideon of Belvedere, Joseph Windham, influential nephew of the owner of Earsham, Philip Yorke, William Sotheby, and John James Hamilton, the Marquis of Abercorn. All of them, aristocrats by birth or by inclination, shared the fondness of the upper class for the arts and a disposition to build lavishly.

The museum for the Dilettanti, like Adams Place and Blackfriars Bridge, could be dismissed as a mere stepping-stone to Soane's future successes. To do so would be to deny their place within his oeuvre and their importance within the history of their respective institutions. Each in its own domain contributed some innovation or other. Adams Place at an early date established a new standard for architect-designed tenement housing in the metropolis. The Norwich bridge, technically and aesthetically, looked forward to the honesty and clean lines of the best of such structures in the next two hundred years. Finally, the Dilettanti museum, in its combined emphasis on free accessibility, security, and coherent display, anticipates modern museology. Had it been built, it would have ranked among the early leaders in the grand tradition of free art galleries open to the public, one of the greatest ornaments of western civilization.

·12·

"In the Primitive Manner of Building"

WITH THE DISGRUNTLED SARCASM characteristic of his writings, the architect John Gwynn satirized in 1767 the rising tide of primitivism among his contemporaries. He thereby drew attention to a trend that a decade later affected the emerging style of the young John Soane so profoundly as to become a dominant credo in his idiosyncratic mature manner. Incontrovertible evidence of this primitivism, in its various forms, occurs among Soane's earliest commissions, earlier by several years than has hitherto been supposed.[1]

Almost the very first designs Soane received payment for depicted garden structures, intended as a gift from Lady Elizabeth Craven to Lady Penelope Pitt-Rivers (figs. 5.16, 5.17). Apart from their date of October 1781, their importance lies in the association they establish between Soane and Lady Craven, out of which grew a beautiful contemporary drawing for a rustic dairy (fig. 12.1). The architect inscribed it to his patroness in that same year. Perhaps, then, the dairy belonged to the same suite of proposals as the garden seats; it is impossible to say for certain. One thing is clear: Lady Craven, by commissioning the design, provided Soane with his baptism as an exponent of primitive buildings.

In her own right, Lady Craven was a leading high priestess of the cult of rustic naturalism. At some point soon after 1776, she used lottery winnings to construct a mock cottage on the Thames side, where the present-day Fulham Football Club now stands. At Fulham, she held fashionable tea parties in a cluster of thatched buildings that formed a perfect idyll, only a stone's throw from the expanding West End of London.[2] Craven Cottage, given its early date, is a kind of incunabulum for the flood of "cottage books" around the end of the century, and the craze for *cottages ornés* associated with them. As such, Craven Cottage introduced Soane to an existing example of a relatively new architectural fashion. Somewhat inconclusive account book entries indicate that he drew the extant Craven Cottage in 1781,[3] although he could have had

Architecture, instead of gaining ground, seems to be retreating backward . . . to a primitive, simple and truly Antique taste, composed of nothing but sticks and dirt.

John Gwynn
London and Westminster Improved

245

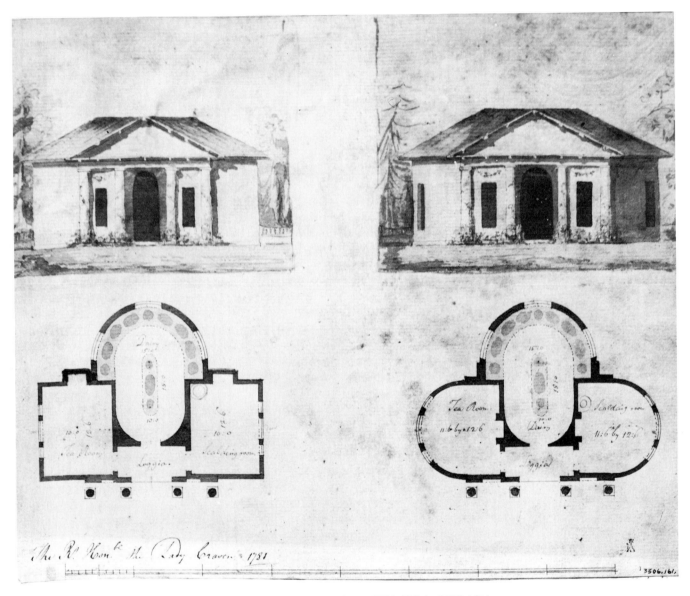

Fig. 12.1. Rustic dairy design, two alternative plans and elevations, 1781 (V&A, 3306.161).

nothing to do with the designing or construction, which probably took place while he was abroad.

Lady Craven possessed a unique quality that gave a special force to her advocacy of the simple joys of rural, cottage life. She had been raised by a Swiss governess, who taught her all the skills necessary to manage the famous dairy farms on her ancestral estate in Gloucestershire. Lady Craven did not affect an interest in country living; she knew all about it at first hand. She became a lifelong adept in the dairy,[4] hence her interest in having Soane design one for her. To some extent, she even dictated to him the style which would complement her earlier imitations of vernacular structures, like the thatched cottage.

To the prevalent quest for rustic naturalism, Lady Craven united her more personal theme of the goodness of milk and its by-products. She no doubt contributed her practical advice to Soane's planning for her dairy. The architect called for a fully functioning structure composed of three parts. The rear one was the dairy proper. Here the milk, fresh from the cow, would sit on shelves along the walls, or upon a table in the center. All-stone construction of the floors and counter surfaces would ensure the kind of even temperature essential for the cream to rise properly to the surface. Butter, cream, milk or Double Gloucester cheese could be processed in Soane's dairy. At the front of the structure, on the right hand side, was a scalding room with a fireplace and a copper cauldron beside it. This would heat the water to scald clean the utensils used in the various dairying procedures, lest harmful lactic bacteria should form and spread. Buttered tea cakes and cream buns could be enjoyed in the room across the central loggia.

Pure and wholesome milk was, in the words of one of Lady Craven's contemporaries, "the natural food."[5] In the dairy, as she conceived it, she assuaged her cravings for a better life devoid of artifice, with the practical remedy of a milk diet. Neither this health fadism, nor the rustic connotations of thatch, would be enough to make the Craven dairy an outstanding example of the trends of the times. It remained for Soane to add to these dietary and social aspects of primitivism a third, architectural kind. He achieved this by endowing with new meaning the simple vernacular elements, used previously in Craven Cottage.

In addition to the alternative plans put before Lady Craven in 1781, Soane produced another very similar, though undated, watercolor. The appearance of the dairy is virtually identical, but the drawing is, if anything, finer, more atmospherically palpable, and probably slightly later. Soane's true artistic intentions for Lady Craven are revealed by a lengthy inscription on this related drawing. Soane wrote: "The Pillars are proposed to be the Trunks of Elm Trees with the bark on and Honeysuckles and Woodbines planted at their feet, forming festoons etc. The Roof to be thatched and the ends of the Rafters to appear."[6] Then, just to be completely unequivocal in his meaning, he went on to describe the alternative round and squared-off ground plans as "two designs for a Dairy in the primitive manner of building."

When Soane wrote about the "primitive manner of building," he clearly had in mind the legendary origins of classical architecture in the trees of the forest. Along with everyone else, he thought that the authority for this belief came from the ancients via Vitruvius. According to Wolfgang Herrmann, however, "when writers on architectural theory in the seventeenth century found that Vitruvius alluded in one and the same paragraph to columns and trees, they . . . misunderstood him and believed that he was propounding a theory which fulfilled in such a perfect form their need of proof that architecture qualified as an imitative art."[7] Soane's dairy perpetuated the same mistaken interpretation. His bark-covered tree trunks reflect those that had supposedly first inspired man with the concept of the column. Rooted to the ground in their natural state, festooned with creepers growing wild in the woods, these uprights formed the vertical support system for Soane's portico. The horizontal branches became metamorphosed into his exposed beams and rafters. A covering of greenery, in the form of reeds, acted as the dairy's thatched roof. By extension this natural analogy supplied the concrete architectural form that underlay Soane's dairy: the so-called primitive hut. The idea of a primeval manmade habitation had first been put forward in Abbé Marc-Antoine Laugier's *Essai sur l'architecture* of 1753. Two years later, in a graphic representation quite similar to Soane's dairy, Laugier's hut theory inspired the frontispiece of the English translation of his book (fig. 12.2). Replace the engraver's band of prehistoric natives by Lady Craven's milkmaids, and there is Soane's dairy design, thatch, projecting beam ends, and all.

For the design of the Craven dairy, Soane need not have consulted Laugier, let alone the specific English edition of it, though he later came to own numerous copies of the book.[8] By 1781 Laugier's hut imagery had become fairly widespread. While the Craven dairy predates the previously held beginnings of Soane's primitivism,[9] it postdates by several decades the introduction of hut designs into English pattern books. Most such illustrations tended to skirt the theoretical issues raised by Laugier's polemical hut, but they could still draw on him for visual stimulus. In 1759 William Chambers introduced illustrations of huts into the first plate of his *Treatise,* a book familiar enough to Soane from his

Fig. 12.2. Frontispiece engraving of a primitive hut from Laugier's *Essay on Architecture.*

school days. Chambers did not, however, subscribe to Laugier's radical proposal of the hut as the prototype for a rationalized modern architecture. Existing on a parallel but lower rung to the *Treatise* were the pattern books promoting the "twiggy" vogue for branch and root structures—texts like Charles Over's *Ornamental Architecture* (1758) and Paul Decker's *Gothic Architecture Decorated* (1759).[10] Another possible source for Soane's dairy was William Wrighte's *Grotesque Architecture*, a book which he had resorted to on a previous occasion (fig. 5.8). Wrighte introduced as his first plate a hut intended to represent the "primitive state of the Doric Order." Reading further in Wrighte's text, one comes across numerous references to "trunks of trees twined about with ivy." Soane with his dairy simply changed the genus of plant. "Henceforth," as Joseph Burke has written, "woodbine and its satellites, honeysuckle and the briar rose, were to adorn the cottage."[11] Smothered in a sweet-smelling bower, Soane's Craven dairy would have been abuzz with honeybees.

Mock cottages and fantastic root houses had been built in the British Isles before Soane's time;[12] so had dairies. A splendid precedent for Soane existed in the rustic structures planned by Robert Adam. One of these, a dairy with attached farm court for Anthony Chamier, is datable to around 1765 (fig. 12.3).[13] Justifying his reputation as a pacesetter, Adam adumbrated in his drawing most of the genre's essential features. He deftly sketched in thatch, old-fashioned mullioned windows, and a simple columnar porch. Seen in the light of Adam's contribution, Soane obviously had little new to add. What he did accomplish with the Craven dairy was to unite allied yet disparate aspects of a common philosophical impetus. The return to nature via the rustic cottage was one of the aspects, the milk fad as an expression of the simple life was another, and the notion of prehistoric primitivism in architecture was a third. The Craven dairy-cum-cottage, disguised as a Laugier hut, formed an excellent compendium of advanced ideas that were part and parcel of Neoclassicism's search for the origins of things.[14]

Despite the engaging drawings related to Lady Craven's dairy, the delectable little structure was never built as originally proposed. A year or so after its demise, however, Soane resuscitated the scheme and this time carried it into execution. At the end of January 1783, Soane visited George Dance, and together they drew up a dairy proposal. The intended location was the Hertfordshire estate of Hammels, belonging to Soane's early patron Philip Yorke. Several days later, Soane consulted a certain "Webber," probably the painter John Webber whose rustic scenes Soane later collected. Webber's somewhat faulty perspective technique

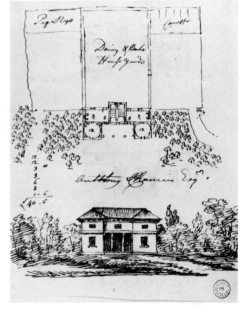

Fig. 12.3. Robert Adam, dairy and farm design, sketch plan and elevation (SM, Adam Drawings, Volume 54, Series 7, Item 179).

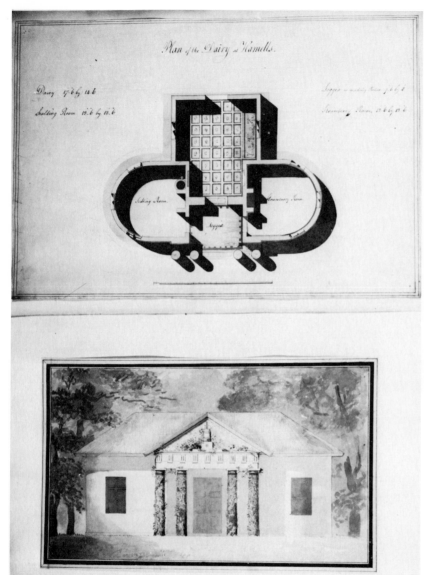

Plan of the Dairy at Hamels.

Dairy 17.6 by 14.6

Scalding Room 10.6 by 13.6

Supper or resting Room 9.6 by 9

Strawbery Room 10.6 by 10.6

Milking Room

Strawbery Room

Nugget

Dairy & Pronaos to be paved with White footiles.
Strawbery Room boarded
Scalding Room paved with Red tile

Fig. 12.5. Hammels Park dairy, sketch elevations (SM, Soane Notebooks, 7, p. 20).

Fig. 12.4. Hammels Park dairy, plan and elevation (SM, AL, Designs for Various Buildings by John Soane, Architect, 1789–1794, Items 6 and 7).

can be recognized in a charming artist's rendering of the dairy that was most likely the one delivered to Philip Yorke in March of that year (pl. 6).[15] A swaying milkmaid, her pail on her head, passes between the pairs of bark and vine-covered columns, recalling the prehistoric primitivism Soane had so clearly articulated for Lady Craven. The empty spaces left open between the triglyph blocks reinforce reminiscences of the all-wood huts that supposedly preceded the dawn of stone temple architecture. The tree trunks, standing flush with the ground, announce a proto-Doric era.[16] The plastered walls, thatched roof, and latticed windows call to mind the virtuous ways of country folk. Who could resist such a delightful vision: part erudite textbook exercise, part romantic appeal to the blood and soil ideology?

Philip Yorke and his young bride were captivated by Soane's dairy proposal for Hammels. Work was ordered to begin in the spring of 1783, and the dairy may have already been functioning by the end of that summer. The whole cost amounted to about £550. The building only measured 23 feet across (fig. 12.4 *top*); yet Soane recognized the capital importance of the work in the evolution of his style. He exhibited a drawing of the dairy at the Royal Academy that April, and published it in his book of 1788.[17]

The Hammels dairy as executed is virtually the same as the one for Lady Craven, right down to the measurements. Presumably, then, the assistance of Dance and Webber had nothing to do with the architectural side of the design. A slight change occurred when Soane replaced the tea room of Lady Craven with one for eating strawberries and cream. Otherwise the shape remains more or less identical, with the exception of a rectangular dairy room instead of a curvilinear one. Soane's Hammels ground plan does give some indication of the interior decoration, and this is borne out by detailed sketches for the fitting up (figs. 12.5, 12.6). He wanted a white tiled floor for the dairy room and for the loggia, or "pronaos," as he put it. Red tiles were to cover the scalding room. The wooden floor of the strawberry room complemented decorative panelling along the walls. The sketch shows the marble-topped wooden counters on which the milk jugs would stand underneath a coffered barrel vault, indicated on the ground plan.

In specifying these dainty, rather feminine interior decorations, Soane would seem to have recognized the dairy as a domain of the ladies. This had been very much the case with the design for Elizabeth Craven. She was not unique. In one reference to Hammels, Soane singled out Lady Elizabeth Yorke as the recipient of sketches for the fence in front of her dairy. In another note Soane reminded himself to draw a copy of the

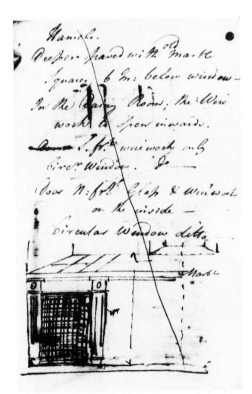

Fig. 12.6. Hammels Park dairy, sketch of a counter for the storage of milk jugs (SM, Soane Notebooks, 7, p. 21).

Hammels building for Lady Harrowby to inspect.[18] More pertinently, from the design point of view, Soane had knowledge of the dairy of yet another aristocratic milkmaid, Lady Hillsborough. Her husband had entrusted the landscaping of Hill Park, Kent, to the firm of Lancelot Brown between 1772 and 1775. So, while employed by Brown and Holland, Soane copied down various bills relating to construction work on the property, indicating his familiarity with it. He also came to possess a Henry Holland sketchbook containing a 1777 sectional drawing of the dairy actually built for Lady Hillsborough (fig. 12.7) sometime before her death in 1780.[19] Holland's sketch, confirming his authorship of this unknown work, has a special bearing on Soane. It depicts milk jars on shelves along the wall in a manner entirely analogous to that Soane adopted six years later at Hammels. The Brownian dairy for Lady Digby at Sherborne, Dorset, which still has its marble counters intact, would be another precedent that Soane could easily have drawn upon when designing Hammels.[20] The custom of keeping dairies was obviously fashionable among aristocratic ladies. But Soane, more brilliantly than most of his predecessors, exploited, in architectural terms, the romantic aspirations these women had to emulate the simple life.[21]

For the exterior of the Hammels dairy, Soane stipulated whitewashed plaster. The walls themselves would be "set with small Stones," a pebble dashing technique aimed at heightening the rustic cottage flavor.[22] Within the smooth plaster of the Antique pediment, he set the oval medallion of a cow (pl. 6). In a rejected alternate proposal, a butter churn occupied the same position (fig. 12.4, *bottom*). These delightful notes of characteristic decoration proclaimed the purist function, while not detracting from the temple front's rational exposition of prehistoric primitivism. Soane's use of the term "pronaos" on one of his sketches underscores the scientific aspect of his search for the relationship between the hut and temple architecture. Even the coy-looking thatch has a logical reason for being here. From Lady Craven and others, Soane learned of the excellent insulating properties peculiar to thatch.[23] The roof had the advantage of insuring an even temperature, thus providing a natural refrigeration system appropriate to milk products. At Hammels, Soane combined, with surprising homogeneity, the themes of milk, cottage industry, prehistoric primitivism, and functional rationalism.

Not far from the site of the vanished Hammels dairy stands a pair of Soane gate lodges at an entrance to the park. Less literal in their primitivism, they are equally effective once their intent is understood. They occupied Soane during the winter of 1780/81 when he had precious little other work. They cost only £400 plus the architect's 5 percent

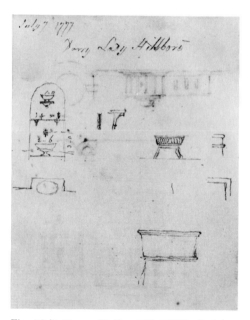

Fig. 12.7. Henry Holland II, Hill Park dairy, sketches of shelving for milk jugs, 1777 (SM, Miscellaneous Sketches 1777, p. 50).

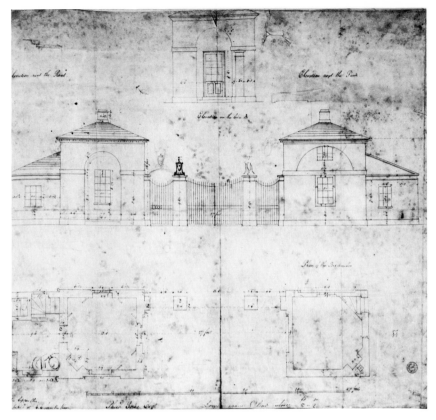

Fig. 12.8. Hammels Park gate and lodges, plan and elevations (SM, Drawer 62, Set 8, Item 32).

fee and traveling expenses. His trips recur with greatest frequency between August and December 1781, and this activity must relate to the main building campaign. Delivery of John Machell's iron lamp standards for the gates dragged on into the following year.[24] The single surviving drawing of the project must date from just before the start of construction (fig. 12.8). Nothing more is known about the evolution of the design: nothing, that is, except its direct source of inspiration. In the same Henry Holland sketchbook containing the cross section of Lady Hillsborough's dairy are a Holland plan and elevation for an unidentified pair of lodges (figs. 12.9, 12.10). They are strikingly like their later Soane counterparts. Holland called for the larger of his two lodges to have a 12 foot square interior with canted corners; so did Soane. Holland added a shed-type "washhouse" at the rear, complete with hot-water boiler and back stairs; so did Soane. The younger architect's reuse of his one-time employer's design would amount to total unoriginality, were it not that

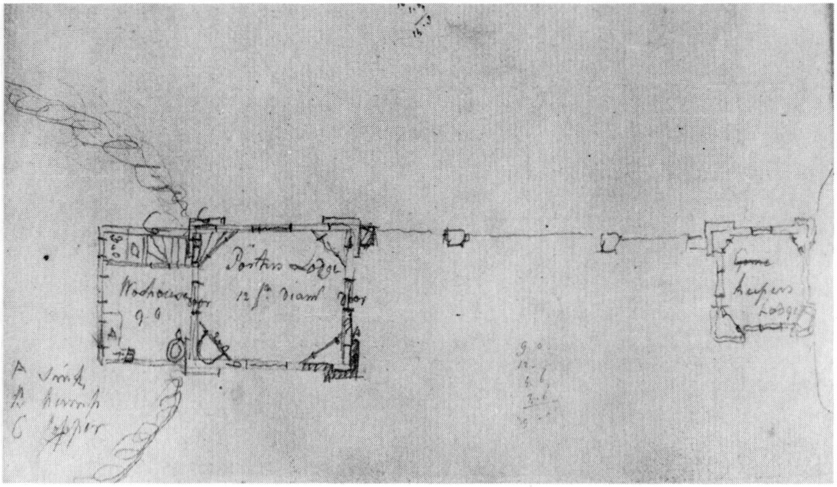

Fig. 12.9. Henry Holland II, gate lodge design, sketch plan (SM, Miscellaneous Sketches 1777, p. 12).

Fig. 12.10. Henry Holland II, gate lodge design, sketch elevation (SM, Miscellaneous Sketches 1777, p. 13).

he changed Holland's elevation significantly in the process. Soane stripped away any obvious classical elements by removing Holland's four gables with their split pediments. They evoke a lingering neo-Palladian vocabulary. Holland's interplay of small, tightly organized elements is replaced by Soane's proportionally large areas of unbroken wall surface. The utter plainness is relieved by the shallow, arched depressions around the windows, no deeper than 5 inches—the thickness of a brick. The simple relieving arches suggest a subtle peeling back of layers that emphasizes mass at the same time that it hints at thinness. This tension, between weightiness and apparent weightlessness, is something typically Soane's, as remarked elsewhere at Blackfriars Bridge.

Soane's approach, while radical in its severity, owed much to the traditional treatment given to lodges on eighteenth-century country estates. The firm of Brown and Holland had a good deal to offer Soane in this respect. Apart from the unidentified sketches by Holland, just referred to, Brown on his own produced an unexecuted lodge design for Blenheim Park around 1765. He featured high relieving arches and an otherwise smooth surface, except for quoins along the corners. In 1775–76, when the Brown-Holland partnership flourished, and Soane acted as their clerk, these rejected Blenheim lodges were executed at Trentham, Staffordshire. They still survive, incorrectly attributed to Joseph Pickford of Derby. This mistaken attribution is understandable, for Pickford submitted two variant designs of his own,[25] and they share with the ones erected the common tendency to reduction of decoration and reliance on the relieving arch motif. John Miller's *Country Gentleman's Architect* published several plates illustrating lodges in a similar vein. William Chambers's gate lodges at Milton Abbey, Dorset, resort to exactly this language, adding a plain dentil cornice. So Brown and Holland had no artistic monopoly on the simple treatment they deemed suitable to a rural lodge. They and others developed an English equivalent to the *caractère mâle,* of which Chambers's teacher, Blondel, had so often spoken in his *Cours d'architecture.* Soane, at Hammels, fastened onto these ideas, pushing them in the direction of overt primitivism.[26]

In the Hammels lodges (fig. 12.11), the only thing that could pass for ornament is the in-and-out rhythm created by the cornice directly under the eaves. By laying header bricks so as to project out from the normal stretchers, a pattern is established reminiscent of classical dentils. Many unpretentious examples exist throughout the British Isles from the beginning of the eighteenth century onward. There is nothing novel about this English brickworking technique, called dentilation,[27] except for Soane's consistent exploitation of it in the context of Hammels and elsewhere. In the hands of a trained architect, dentilation served expressive purposes. Chambers at Milton Abbey realized the appositeness of a simple cornice to the boxy shape of his lodges there. He used heavy stone dentils as his only decorative device. Soane went a step further at Hammels. The all-brick construction of his lodges had the virtue of sturdy cheapness, which one associates with rustic buildings. Besides, a bricklayers' trick like dentilation was a direct outgrowth of the shape of the bricks themselves. A truthfulness to the material could be achieved.

Fig. 12.11. Hammels Park gate and lodge.

From the theoretical standpoint this added to a closer resemblance between brick and the wooden construction of the primitive hut, in which all features expressed the nature of the material itself. The exposed and projecting beam ends of Soane's Craven and Hammels dairies recalled, in a direct way, the structural system of the primitive hut. No less effectively, Soane's dentilation of the lodges resembles it too (cf. figs. 12.1, 12.11). What John Summerson has called Soane's "primitive 'entablature'"[28] conveys to the knowing eye a complex association of ideas by the most economical of means. No wonder Soane often reused so unemphatic, yet potentially sophisticated, a motif in a whole range of rustic or utilitarian building types. And when, later on, the lodges at Hammels received an upper storey to the lean-to sheds (cf. figs. 12.8, 12.11), the anonymous builder respected Soane's intent. Not only did he extend Soane's "primitive 'entablature'" onto the new portions, but he introduced it around the top of his new, off-center chimney, in which position it seems to convey Soane's meaning better than even the architect himself had previously done.

If there is any doubt about Soane's artistic motives at the Hammels lodges, the pair at Langley clears it up (fig. 12.12). "Multiple-choice" proposals of a rather ornamental kind had gone out to the patron for consideration in September 1784 (figs. 1.14, 1.15). In November another design followed. By the next April the choice had been made, working

Fig. 12.12. Langley Park gate and lodges.

drawings were sent, and construction got under way in the summer.[29] The lodges as they stand, reaffirm Soane's decision to favor a primitive simplicity in the large majority of his utilitarian structures in the country. What had been embryonically primitive in the Hammels dairy, implicitly so in the nearby lodges, became explicit at Langley with the introduction of baseless Doric columns.

According to the evolutionary theories generally believed by Soane and his architectural contemporaries, the tree-columns of Vitruvian fame formed the proto-Doric, the first step toward a proper order. This transitional phase led to the true Doric, an imitation in stone of its wooden antecedents. Up to this point everyone was in agreement. A dispute developed, however, over whether the Doric at this stage already had a base. Chambers, and many of like persuasion, held that it did. Their concept of the primitive hut included hand-hewn uprights, placed upon blocklike archetypal bases to prevent rot. Abbé Laugier, Ribart de Chamoust, and others carried their researches further back, almost to the point of being preadamite. For them, the primitive hut had started with a chance formation of living trees, a God-given gift of Nature. Antediluvian man had only to transform what he found growing wild. Therefore, it was obvious that the rooted tree had developed into a baseless column.[30] Whether or not Soane understood all the scholastic fine points of the opposing schools of thought, he advocated the baselessness of the

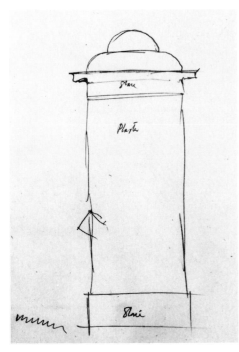

Fig. 12.13. Tendring Hall gate piers, Raymond Erith sketch elevation (Author's Collection).

Doric on numerous occasions as has been seen. In the case of lodges, moreover, it made special sense for the humble function to adopt the most basic form of the simplest order. This was a straightforward application of the Vitruvian rules of decorum. The wisdom of Soane's choice can be seen at Langley.

The lodges of Langley were executed in the local Suffolk white brick. Yellowish in hue, despite the name, Suffolk "whites" tend to lack the stronger coloristic values of red bricks, and they increase the volumetric quality of the building itself. The simple geometric shapes of cube and isosceles triangle, bluntly juxtaposed at Langley, would have been thrown off balance by the intrusion of a more ornate order of architecture. The lack of base to the column was enough strongly to suggest the same appropriate primitive overtones hinted at by the dentilation of the Hammels lodges. Baseless Doric primitivism united with a rustic structure to produce, once and for all, a clear statement about the way Soane visualized such buildings.

The Langley experiment was not repeated. The slightly later set of Soane gates on the same property are astylar. Perhaps the crudeness with which the local craftsmen had interpreted Soane's drawings of the baseless column and Doric entablature persuaded him to simplify his approach in future.[31] By the 1790s at the Tyringham gate lodges the baseless Doric columns have been reduced to pure cylinders, with only a vestigial capital remaining. But there were earlier signs of this tendency to geometricize the primitive aspects into a formal as well as an expressive language. For instance, engravings and eyewitness accounts convey an idea of the lodges at Tendring Hall.[32] The lodges themselves, begun in 1785, resembled the earlier Hammels ones, complete with "primitive 'entablature.'" Soane refined the prototype by setting the Tendring lodges diagonally on the site, thus accentuating the dichotomy of cube below, pyramidal roof above. The gate piers in particular had the character of an exegesis in miniature on the use of geometry for primitive ends (fig. 12.13). Square in section on the lower level, they ended in a pure hemispherical "bubble" of stone.

Soane's geometric primitivism reached expressive heights in a series of early utilitarian buildings that perfectly epitomize Robert Morris's engaging verses:

> A little structure built for use alone,
> Requires no dress nor ornament of stone,
> The plainest, neatest method is the best,
> One simple modus governs all the rest.[33]

A notable example of this tendency to simplification in Soane's rustic work is the Burn Hall cow barn (fig. 1.6). The patron was George Smith, whom Soane met in County Durham through their mutual friend, Rowland Burdon. The commission was given to Soane on 19 June 1783, with an agreed fee set at 6 guineas in payment for the two drawings he produced. As no further mention of the project occurs in the architect's accounts or notebooks, it may be presumed that the work was carried out without his personal supervision.[34] Its present condition suggests that certain changes have occurred (cf. figs. 12.14, 1.6). In the course of construction, Soane's low end pavilions with their diminutive haylofts were raised an extra storey in height, without unduly spoiling the composition. The central pavilion has suffered most. Soane's "Great Arch" is cluttered by partitions that jut out into what the architect intended as a shadow-filled, eye-catching void. It happens that this design feature is the one which indicates the source for the cow barn. Once again, Soane found inspiration from the period of his association with Brown and Holland. For their client the Hon. Robert Drummond, they planned the new mansion house at Cadland in Hampshire, together with a model home farm complex identified by the inscription on a drawing of July 1777 (fig. 12.15).[35] Significantly, the handwriting on the sheet is Soane's, contemporary in date with his freelance schemes for St. Luke's Hospital (cf. fig. 3.10). The idea for Soane's "Great Arch" at Burn Hall came from the similar arches at Cadland, which acted as passageways slotted in from the sides. The motif resembles a gouged-out version of the familiar relieving arches delicately cut into the surfaces of contemporary Brown and Holland gate lodges. It could be that Soane himself took on responsibility for the Cadland farm, in which case he developed his own ideas at Burn Hall. By 1783 Soane was no newcomer to transforming humble agricultural buildings into eloquent statements of his advanced geometric type of primitivism.

A tradition of enlightened farm design was promoted by a series of pattern books stretching back into the eighteenth century. Daniel Garrett started the movement in 1747 with his *Designs and Estimates for Farm Houses.* William Halfpenny, that prolific publicist, followed quickly on his heels two years later with *Twelve Beautiful Designs for Farm Houses.* Timothy Lightoler collaborated with Halfpenny on the *Modern Builder's Assistant* (1757), and then brought out his own *Gentleman and Farmers' Architect* in 1762.[36] The designs for farm houses and farm courts took on a variety of styles—neo-Palladian, Gothic, Chinese, and mixtures of all three. It was only with John Carter's *Builder's Magazine* of the 1770s that anything approaching primitivism appeared in this type of structure. On

Fig. 12.14. Burn Hall cow barn.

several occasions Carter incorporated the menial Tuscan order, or tree trunk-columns, connoting the unaffected goodness of rural life.[37] At Burn Hall, Soane's cow barn profited from the pattern book examples as distilled by Brown and Holland.

Out of the banal rectangularity and watered-down Palladianism of the Cadland farm, Soane developed a design for Burn Hall that attempted to be something new and unusual. He utilized a type of semielliptical plan that he favored in other contemporary designs, notably those for St. Luke's. Then he carried the pure geometry over to the elevations, focusing on the well-proportioned main pavilion with a round arch, triangular pediment, and rectangular base. Stark simplicity, as Soane realized, had served barns and farm structures perfectly well in the past. By geometrically accentuating this utilitarian quality, Soane discovered a "primitive" logic. His conscious economy of means admirably suited the rustic character of the little building; "wholesome" on account of its bovine inhabitants, but "unstylish" in its use.

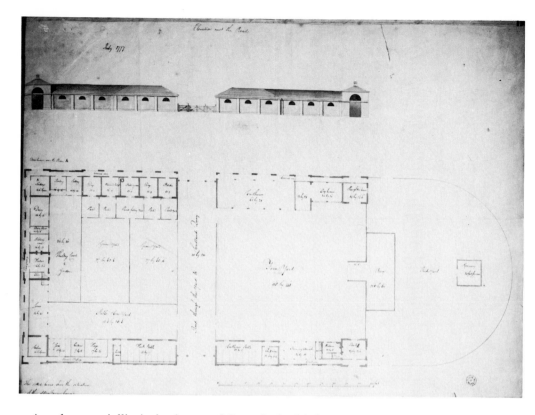

Fig. 12.15. Cadland home farm, plan and elevation, 1777 (SM, Drawer 64, Set 6, Item 41).

Another semielliptical scheme of Soane's, had it been erected, would have rounded out the examples of the architect's geometric variety of primitivism. It had to do with a model village project for Hammels, commissioned from Soane in September 1784, and intended to be called Yorke Place after its owner (fig. 12.16). Consisting of five semidetached houses, it was organized on a regular plan, which Soane went so far as to stake out, but proceeded no further with.[38] In this overlooked work of the architect's, he entered fully into the philosophy of primitivism as it applied to housing for workers on the land.

England pioneered the notion of the model village in the eighteenth century, and a hundred years later developed it into the modern concept of the garden city. The earliest recorded example of the trend occurred in 1699 at the Castle Howard estate in Yorkshire. It ushered in a whole sequence of such schemes, notable among them: Chippenham, Cambridgeshire (1702); New Houghton, Norfolk (1729); Cardington, Bedfordshire (1763); and Milton Abbas, Dorset (1773–79). The motives of

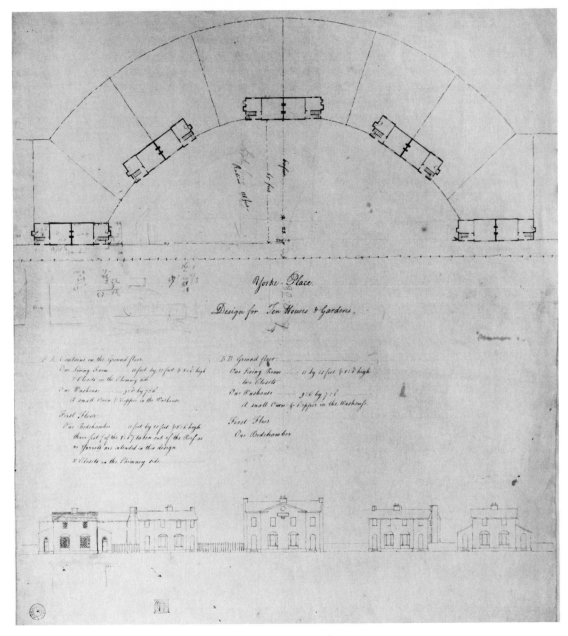

Fig. 12.16. Hammels Park, design for Yorke Place, plan and elevation, 1784 (SM, Drawer 64, Set 6, Item 16).

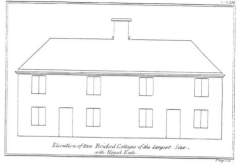

Fig. 12.17. Milton Abbas model village.

Fig. 12.18. Nathaniel Kent, engraved cottage elevation, *Hints to Gentlemen of Landed Property.*

the landowners differed as much as the nature of the projects themselves.[39] At Cardington, for instance, the philanthropist John Howard had the welfare of his tenants first and foremost in mind. At Milton Abbas, on the contrary, Joseph Damer swept away an entire market town, to move it out of sight of his mansion. Once again it was Brown, in succession to William Chambers, who served as Damer's architect at a time when Soane was working in the office. Brown relocated the villagers on a long curving street (fig.12.17), regularly lined with uniform, thatched duplexes of brick, rendered with plaster to look like traditional cob construction.[40] The inhabitants must have wondered why a London architect had to be called in to imitate the vernacular Dorset cottage. In their innocence they missed the whole point! Damer and Brown believed in the moral power of architecture to improve mankind. They tried to return people to a Rousseauesque state of nature—a state they had never left in the first place. Tidy peasant houses, conducive to rural virtues, would theoretically insure sobriety, goodness, and perhaps greater productivity too. Some of this ideology must have rubbed off on Soane from his exposure to Brown.

It is surely not coincidental that Brown's name comes up in correspondence from John Stuart to Soane regarding the landscaping for Allanbank House. In September 1782, Stuart wrote Soane about ideas he had in mind for creating a new village on his property, composed of cottages with a battlemented public building at the center. Soane responded with what the letters describe as a semielliptical plan—the germ that later blossomed into Yorke Place. In August 1783, Soane submitted his bill for 5 guineas, after which no more is heard of the Allanbank scheme.[41] So he felt no harm could come of reviving the plan a year later for Philip Yorke. The elliptical layout offered advantages over the previous model villages with their houses dead set in straight rows. Around the perimeter of his spacious elliptical village green, Soane spaced wide apart the five double cottages of Yorke Place. The individual cottages, despite alternate elevations, shared the same basic plan that had much in common with the houses at Adams Place (fig. 11.1). Yorke Place similarly derived from Nathaniel Kent's *Hints to Gentlemen of Landed Property.* In fact, Kent's book had specifically addressed itself to people of Stuart and Yorke's station in life.

The proposed elevations for Yorke Place differ from Kent's childish, unsophisticated designs (fig. 12.18). Nevertheless, Kent had advocated simple cottages, not "fine or expensive" ones, and Soane, in response, maintained plain but well-proportioned masses throughout his housing scheme. He limited classical references to a pediment over the central building. As at St. Luke's Hospital, seven years before (fig. 3.8), Soane incorporated the so-called Wyatt window for his ground floor openings, simplifying them still further. At Yorke Place, the undecorated mullions and filled-in lunettes added to the bold geometric quality of the elevations. In this skeletal version, the Wyatt window did not detract from the bare bones of architecture. On the contrary, it evoked what Kent described as cottagers' "more primitive lives . . . free from vice."[42]

Whether humanitarian motives or worker exploitation really lay behind Yorke Place, it deserves honorable mention among the forerunners of the garden city concept. It also indicates new departures in Soane's later work. Together with the adjacent lodges and the dairy at Hammels, it would have formed an essential part of Soane and Yorke's outdoor experimental laboratory. Patron and architect explored the different types of primitivism appropriate to the sorts of buildings found on a rural estate. The dairy was an instance of humorous prehistoric primitivism, like a child's proto-Doric playhouse. The lodges' geometric primitivism avoided the dairy's romantic sentimentality in favor of conveying a more rigorous though similar meaning by pure, formal means. Out of the two solutions Soane began to develop in the workers' houses a primitivism that was progressive aesthetically and socially, but also flexible enough for him to accommodate a wide range of building types over the rest of a lifetime. Whatever his debt to former teachers, or to pattern books, Soane's originality was to lie in the way he adopted the subtle nuances of primitivism's quest for the simple and basic as his guiding aesthetic principle.

Pl. 1. Pitzhanger Manor, Ealing, perspective view from the northeast, probably by J. M. Gandy and A. van Assen, after Soane, 1800 (SM, New Model Room).

Section through the Center Building.

Pl. 2. Triumphal bridge design, cross section through the central pavilion (SM, Drawer 12, Set 5, Item 7).

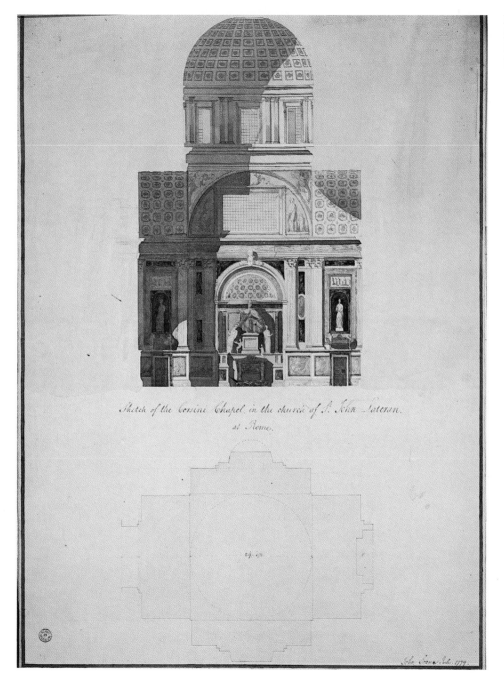

Pl. 3. Corsini chapel, S. Giovanni in Laterano, Rome, cross section, 1779 (SM, Drawer 45, Set 2, Item 23).

LO STACCATO D'VN DISEGNO PER VN CASTELLO D'ACQVA

L'ELEVAZIONE D'VN DISEGNO PER VN CASTELLO D'ACQVA

Pl. 4. *Castello d'acqua* design, cross section and elevation (SM, Drawer 45, Set 1, Item 21).

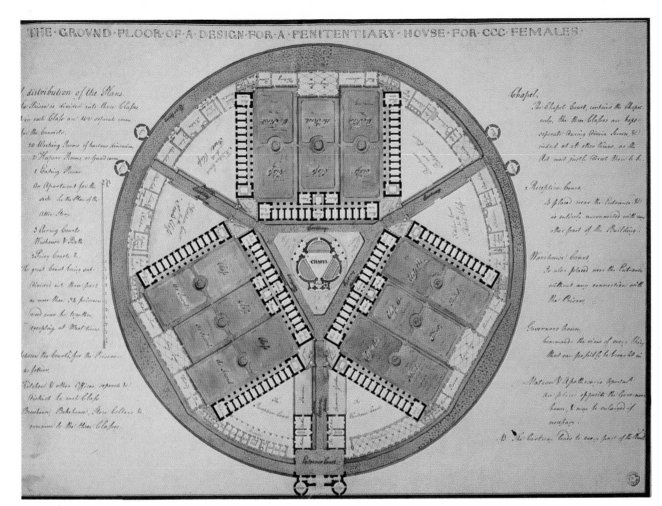

Pl. 5. Women's penitentiary design, plan (SM, Drawer 13, Set 1, Item 11).

Pl. 6. Hammels Park dairy, perspective view, probably by J. Webber, after Soane (V&A, 3306.163).

Pl. 7. Saxlingham Rectory, north facade.

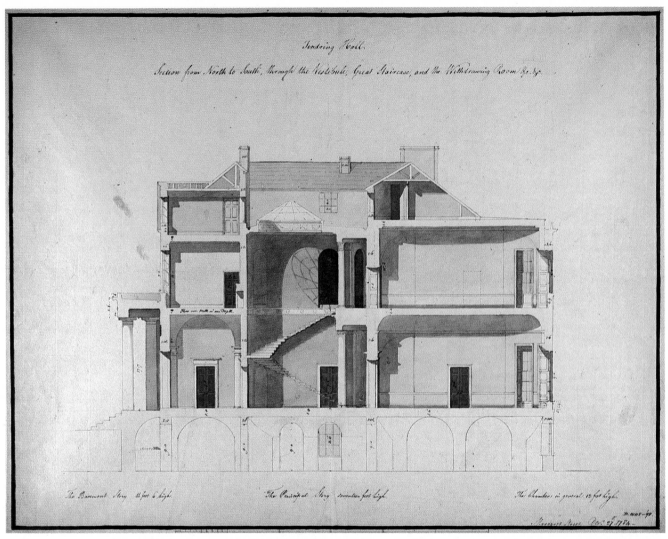

Pl. 8. Tendring Hall, cross section on the north-south axis, 1784
(V&A, D.1445-'98).

·13·
Soane's Place in the Genesis of the "Villa"

The Meaning of "Villa"

WITH THE WORDS, "the idea of the *villa*," John Summerson concluded his second Cantor Lecture in 1959, and announced the title of his third one, given the following week. Two decades later, his analysis of plan types and his tabulations of building statistics still faithfully chart the growth rate and development of the eighteenth-century English country house. Although he only touched upon the period of Soane's activity in his search for the archetypal villa, he indicated the desirability of a more "detailed study."[1] Subsequently, Sandra Blutman followed Summerson's lead and extended the scope of consideration from 1780 until 1815.[2] The present chapter dealing with Soane's country house planning is greatly indebted to both these scholars' analytical method of inquiry. It must be mentioned, however, that some possibility for confusion arises when they introduce alongside the eighteenth-century notion of a "villa," a usage of the same term to designate a specific squarish plan-type, divided into nine internal units.[3] Hardly a scrap of written evidence supports such a restrictive, Palladian interpretation of "villa" among Soane's contemporaries or immediate predecessors. On the contrary, their terminology was in a state of near-anarchy, as a further investigation will reveal. Yet, as Summerson has indicated, the "villa" concept remains central to understanding domestic architecture throughout the youthful period of John Soane's career. In order to grasp the position of his early country house practice, some yardstick must gauge his contribution to a domain already well established. The key is locked in the meaning that the word "villa" had for him.

Etymologically speaking, "villa" came into the English language as a response to renewed interest in the classics during the seventeenth century. The early examples cited in the *Oxford English Dictionary* all seek to draw parallels between contemporary English life or architecture and

Thus, by the end of the [eighteenth] century, the great Palladian mansions were already seen as hulks stranded from the past.... The typical and representative country house of the last three decades of the eighteenth century was ... smaller, its contrivances for "conveniency" greater and its sense of "parade" much modified. As to architectural character, this varied considerably.... But behind it was a single, positive idea ... the idea of the villa.

John Summerson
"The Idea of the Villa"

the sumptuous country estates of ancient Romans, like Pliny the Younger. The writings of Pliny made the greatest impact on later readers because of his vivid descriptions of the luxurious establishments he had at Laurentinum by the sea, and Tusculum in the foothills of the Apennines. These descriptions stimulated the imagination of authors and architects from the Italian Renaissance onward. The various reconstructions of these villas form a study unto themselves, beginning with Michelozzo, continuing with Raphael, Palladio, Scamozzi, Félibien, and the Englishmen Robert Castell, Edward Stevens, and Thomas Wright, the "Wizard of Durham."[4] Of all the attempted reconstructions, none was so thorough, lavish, and scholarly as that published by Castell in his book *Villas of the Ancients Illustrated* (1728). Significantly, the folio had a dedication to Lord Burlington, to whose propagandistic program for a second, post-Inigo Jones, "villa" revival it was to have belonged. But neither Burlington's own Chiswick House nor Colin Campbell's Mereworth Castle was called "villa" in the period, though both were modelled after Palladio's neo-Antique buildings. Tempting though it is to base a picture of "villa" on these examples, to do so is to start from a weak premise. No one, except perhaps Thomas Wright, seems to have paid much attention to Castell's archaeological approach, or tried to put it into effect. This did not hamper the "villa" concept from spreading quickly into nonarchitectural parlance where the trouble with terminology really began. The nomenclature passed from the hands of a few classically educated authors into the fashion-conscious vocabulary of the beau monde. "Villa" became synonymous with all that was chic, petite, à la mode, or dernier cri, despite the fact that early dictionary definitions by Samuel Johnson and Ephraim Chambers make no reference to smallness as a characteristic. As a reaction to this trend, satirical connotations set in. Alexander Pope's fictitious "Timon's Villa" served as a literary device to ridicule nouveau riche folly and extravagance. Two generations later Fanny Burney mocked "mighty pretty neat little villas."[5] At mid-century Francis Coventry invented the buffoonish parvenu, Squire Mushroom, for whom a "modish villa," half Gothic and half neo-Palladian, seemed the perfect habitation. As Coventry concluded: "if one wished to see a coxcomb expose himself in the most effectual manner, one would advise him to build a villa, which is the *chef d'oeuvre* of modern impertinence."[6] Whether used allusively by classicists in an Augustan Age, pejoratively by guardians of public morals, or flippantly by everyone else, "villa" had no precise definition. Modern critics have tried to supply one, but it is based on their own preconception of what a "villa" ought to look like: smallish, blocky, set in ample grounds.

Given the number of houses that supposedly might fall under the rubric "villa," the facts about its architectural usage come as a surprise. The term appears infrequently in the printed architectural literature of the period and when it does it is often employed in a self-contradictory sense. In order to determine more clearly the meaning of "villa" in the eighteenth century, a sampling was taken of architectural literature bracketed by the publication of *Vitruvius Britannicus* (1715) on the one end and the appearance of Soane's *Plans, Elevations, and Sections* (1788) at the other.[7] Only twenty-six titles *likely* to have included the "villa" building type were consulted in this selective and necessarily incomplete survey. Of the twenty-six, eight made no mention of the term, though many compact houses that might have been considered "villas" were illustrated. Another five books had only a single reference, usually in the form of a title to an engraved plate. In several of these instances the term "villa" was restricted to houses for part-time inhabitation near the metropolis. Writers like the Adam brothers and Gibbs, who had had training abroad were aware of the Italian subcategory of *villa suburbana* and referred to it in their descriptions. Much more unusual and interesting are the interpretations of the word by English architects who lacked acquaintance with the Italian tradition.

In the case of Thomas Collins Overton, who illustrated six so-called villas, he gave a number of them a distinctly castellar appearance. The Norwich architect Thomas Rawlins, more than any other writer, based himself literally on the Palladian meaning of "villa" to connote a "country estate" rather than the building built upon it. His application of the term "villa" is nevertheless haphazard. Sometimes he described one design as a "villa," but not another, nearly identical one. Such wooly thinking reaches its climax in John Crunden's popular book *Convenient and Ornamental Architecture, Consisting of Original Designs . . . Beginning with the Farm House, and Regularly Ascending to the Most Grand and Magnificent Villa.* First published in 1768, it went through at least two subsequent reprintings. Crunden's class-conscious "ascent" by building type became nebulous precisely when it reached the "villa" category. Seven "villas" are mentioned, a large number by the standards of contemporary literature. The designs come in all shapes and sizes, and the plans look quite dissimilar except for the attached wings. This diversity, worthy of a many-sided personality like Palladio himself, negates the notion of a fixed "villa" prototype. Plans and elevations varied, as did designations. In two examples by Crunden, one is simply called a "house," whereas another is called a "small villa" (see figs. 13.1, 13.2). To be sure, the presence of wings in one case conferred certain properties of "villadom"; neverthe-

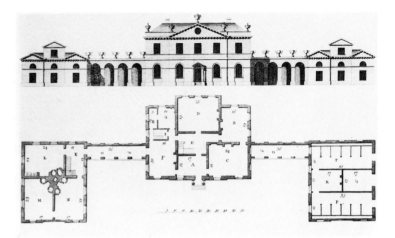

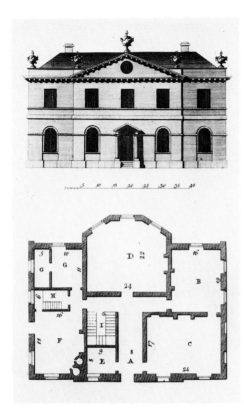

Fig. 13.1. John Crunden, house design, engraved plan and elevation, *Convenient and Ornamental Architecture.*

Fig. 13.2. John Crunden, villa design, engraved plan and elevation, *Convenient and Ornamental Architecture.*

less, Crunden himself pointed out that the plans were identical. In Crunden's case, the denomination "villa" looks quite arbitrary and reflects the confused, extremely relative terminology of his age.

For William Pain, author of the *British Palladio* (1786), a villa could be as wide as 271 feet. For James Peacock (alias José MacPacke) the villa was seen as best suiting "gentlemen of moderate fortune." For James Lewis the villa had to stand isolated on its own and could be treated "in a greater style" or less elaborately. Hence the villa became all things to all men. No rational growth pattern of the word's usage emerges; no gently rising curve on a graph portrays its increased popularity or a deepened understanding. The illogical state of affairs persisted into the 1790s and the early decades of the next century, when villas are mentioned in almost all the contemporary books devoted to the smaller houses favored in the period. All that can be said for certain is that no one had any firm definition of the word artistically, let alone linguistically. Everyone spoke about villas and designed them without really knowing what was meant. It did not seem to matter.

The widespread popularity of the villa concept is more clearly demonstrated by a similar survey made of the first seventeen Royal Academy exhibitions. Up until 1785, the closing year for this study, only one show, the tiny first one of 1769, had no representative of the villa class.[8] In all the others villas appeared, always constituting a significant proportion of the total architectural exhibits. The average representation was 15.7 percent, rising from a low of 3.2 percent in 1783, to a high of 29.4 percent in 1778. It managed to hold its own pretty well against a steady numerical increase in the overall size of the shows and the architectural component of them. The only discernible pattern that can be recognized in these fluctuations is that years of feast were often followed by years of famine, when it seemed the market for villa designs had been saturated. The constant factor throughout this cyclical ebb and flow was the evident desire among younger exhibitors to keep pace with what they thought were the fashions of the times. John Soane, when still relatively unknown, submitted one villa design to the exhibitions of 1773 and 1785. Thomas Leverton, slightly better-placed and older, submitted the most villa designs (nine) over the same period; John Plaw submitted five and later distinguished himself as the most prolific publicist of the building type. On the average, then, villa designers tended to be young architects just starting up, or students anxious to seem abreast of the latest taste. The established architect-academicians like Dance, Chambers, Sandby, and Gwynn, or rising stars like James Wyatt, rarely used the term villa for their catalogue entries, though there is no telling whether they chose to show work of a villa nature. Thus, even with architectural drawings, where the number of printed references to villas is far greater proportionally than in books, the same dilemma quickly recurs: what was actually *called* a "villa," and what *looks* like one to the modern critic's eye have, of necessity, no correlation.

In light of the ambiguities and conflicting associations inherent in the word "villa," a working resolution to the problem would be to select as a substitute the term "smaller house." Eventually this term could even be quantified in a mathematical way. At the same time it does not question the obvious value of a plan typology. The assumption of certain norms of design helps to align Soane alongside his contemporaries.

Theme

Soane's "gentleman's villa" design, listed at the Royal Academy in 1773, unfortunately does not appear to survive. After this first known attempt at a villa, he did not exhibit another in the space of the next dozen years. But in the interim, the 1781 exhibition included a related type of structure by him, entitled in the catalogue a "hunting casino." In this case the word "casino," which copies the Italian diminutive for *casa,* or house, was not even accepted by the standard eighteenth-century English lexicographers. As far as one can tell, however, "villa" and "casino" were used more or less synonymously, except that a casino connoted a smaller house still and came to conjure up images of gambling or illicit assignations at the bottom of a garden. At the Royal Academy in the 1770s casinos were all the rage. During the decade, nine of them appeared at intervals, as opposed to thirty-one of the even more popular villas. The interesting statistic is that, until 1779, the casino as a building type was the complete monopoly of the Chambers office. The master himself showed only one, that for Marino (fig. 5.2), but his pupils Thomas Hardwick, Edward Stevens, and John Yenn were recurrent exhibitors of them. And, as we have seen, Soane kept a sharp weather eye on any prevailing breezes that might come from Chambers's quarter.

In 1781, when the craze for casinos had somewhat abated, Soane exhibited his (fig. 13.3). The drawing's high degree of polished presentation had been perfected over several years with two quite different academies in mind. The earlier hunting casino was dated October 1779 according to a nineteenth-century source.[9] This plan and elevation remained behind in Italy as Soane's *morceau de réception* given in fulfillment of the Florentine Academy's conditions for honorary membership. The second, presumably very similar, hunting casino is the one that went on display in London two years later. The surviving drawing agrees well in its soft watercolor style with an early 1780s date (cf. figs. 13.3, 12.1). Keeping aside the elevation and turning to the plan, it can be seen to reproduce in reverse the scheme for a casino previously published by Soane in 1778 (fig. 5.22). Apart from the compactness associated with such small-scale structures, they share in common a central swelling curve, like the front of a bombé chest of drawers. The rounded feature, a crucial and often repeated motif in Soane's country houses from this period on, has never been remarked upon, either in his mature buildings, or here at its inception in the late 1770s and early 1780s.

As already mentioned, the immediate source behind the hunting casinos was Chambers. The closest precedent for Soane's planning is a Chambers design produced at Rome in which the same bombé effect occurs (fig. 13.4). One also finds it a year earlier in the 1753 scheme which Chambers called a "villa composed in the style of Balthazar Peruzzi," when he exhibited it at the Society of Artists a dozen years later.[10] Notwithstanding the reference to the Italian Peruzzi and some Cinquecento decorative trimmings, Chambers's two plans were basically French in inspiration, as might be expected from his background.

William Chambers's studies in Paris under Jacques-François Blondel coincided with a new phase in the development of the bombé and canted-bay plan treatment. This device had a distinguished pedigree in France but was not practiced much in Italy. Its French roots reached back to a great country house like Vaux le Vicomte (1657–61). There it had been employed on a grand scale to express externally a large oval salon situated directly behind the curved facade. The central swelling projection, related to internal function, enjoyed considerable popularity

Fig. 13.3. Hunting casino design, plan and elevation (SM, Drawer 45, Set 3, Item 6).

in the Rococo period. In harmony with effervescent Rococo interior decoration, it acted as a leavening agent in the doughy wall mass of the traditional château. It reached a stage of crystalline perfection at mid-century in the more restrained and geometric work of Ange-Jacques Gabriel. His petite *rendez-vous de chasse* for Louis XV at Le Butard arose in the late summer of 1750, just at the moment Chambers was preparing his departure for Italy.[11] The designing of Le Butard, located close to Paris, could not have failed to create a stir in the capital. Its plan, with a polygonal bow on the garden side (fig. 13.5), is reflected in the Roman casinos of Chambers, and even more closely by those of Soane. (Coincidentally, the Soane and Gabriel buildings both catered to the pleasures of the hunt.) Although it was never published, Gabriel's masterful rendition of the casino at Le Butard went on to influence a considerable number of designs and buildings in France, small and enlarged, metropolitan and provincial.[12] After Chambers's arrival in England in 1755, the knowledge of the Le Butard plan-type was spread among the architect's pupils and in Academy circles. It also entered independently into Robert Adam's ingenious planning repertory. His Green Park ranger's lodge, built in 1768 (fig. 13.6), was literally across the street from the offices of Henry Holland where Soane worked in the next decade. The undulating plan-type of Le Butard fitted in with the Adam brothers' theory of rising and falling "movement," and their expressed admiration of French planning.[13]

Overlapping this imported French tradition of planning is an existing English one, which Summerson believes relates to the activities of the Burlingtonian group early in the eighteenth century.[14] Subsequent dated manifestations take the form of a rounded bay or a polygonal facade projection. Examples are the end pavilions originally designed for Sir Thomas Robinson's Rokeby Hall in 1725, those at Isaac Ware's Wrotham Park of the 1750s, the contemporary Nuthall Temple, and John Carr's Constable Burton of the following decade. These scattered, relatively isolated instances cannot compare with the single-minded exploitation of the theme by Robert Taylor from the 1750s onward. In a series of smaller houses, of which Asgill, on the Thames at Richmond, is the masterpiece, he played with the polygonal form incessantly (fig. 13.7). Taylor worked in the still fashionable neo-Palladian idiom of rusticated basements, severe *piano nobile,* and carefully balanced proportions. The canted bays he employed in juxtaposition to the flat walls, provided a successful volumetric counterpoint to the staccato rhythms all in one plane.[15] In view of its natural affinity to Palladio's vocabulary, it is curious that he never once used it in any of his designs.

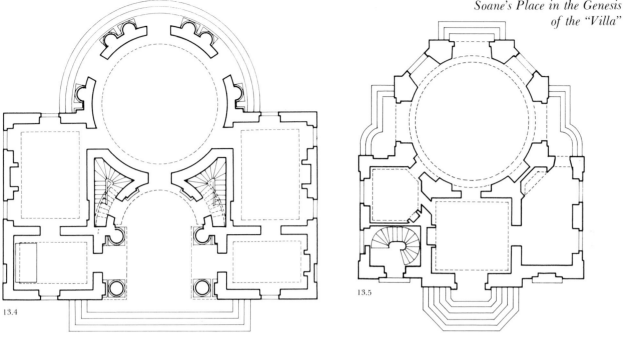

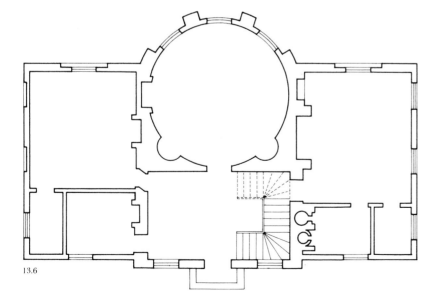

Fig. 13.4. William Chambers, casino design, plan (after V&A, 3359).

Fig. 13.5. Ange-Jacques Gabriel, Le Butard hunting pavilion, plan (after C. Tadgell, *Ange-Jacques Gabriel*).

Fig. 13.6. Robert Adam, Green Park ranger's lodge, London, plan (after R. and J. Adam, *The Works in Architecture*).

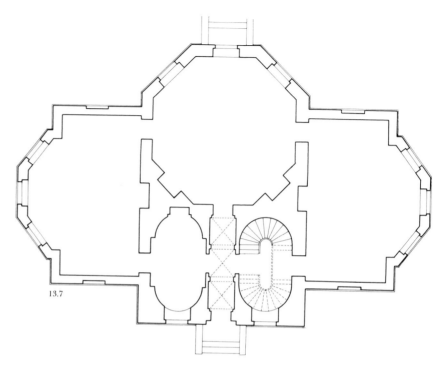

Fig. 13.7. Robert Taylor, Asgill House, Richmond, plan (after J. Woolfe and J. Gandon, *Vitruvius Britannicus* 4).

Fig. 13.8. Villa design for Mottram, plan (after J. Soane, *Plans, Elevations, and Sections*).

13.7

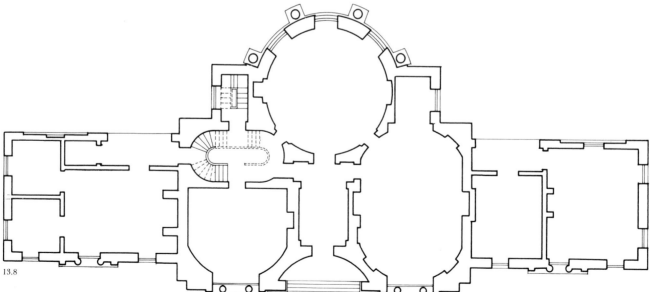

13.8

Once pioneering designers of country houses such as Taylor had sanctioned the bow-fronted or canted-bay plan-type, others followed. A typical lesser exponent from the third quarter of the century, John Johnson, designed Sadborrow in Dorset, built in 1773–75.[16] Here he resorted to a bombé garden facade, but related it so awkwardly to the principal rooms and main axis that he missed the underlying logic. He had mimicked a motif without understanding the rationale behind it. He demonstrated the pitfalls attendant upon aping fashion. In this respect, Soane, with his hunting casino (fig. 13.3), came closer to grasping the full potentialities, both in planning terms and for external visual effect. He responded to an entrenched trend among the second-generation neo-Palladians, by reinforcing it with injections of spirited Gallic taste conveyed through Adam and Chambers. By any token, Soane had been quite tardy in discovering the virtues of the bowed front or canted bay. He could have received inspiration from any one of a number of sources, foreign and native, or from a combination of them. His virtue was to lie in his long-protracted experimentation with the theme starting in 1778. Ten years later he metamorphosed what had been a modest casino into what he termed a "villa" at Mottram, Cheshire (fig. 13.8).[17] All he needed to do was add low wings to the original bombé-fronted core. In this "villa" disguise, the hunting casinos of 1778 and 1781 overtly entered into the mainstream of Soane's published designs for smaller houses.

Comparing the elevations of Soane's two hunting casinos (figs. 13.3, 5.22), it will be seen that in 1781 he either suppressed altogether the dome of his 1778 version, or else hid it from sight behind a triangular pediment. The more even spacing of Doric columns, coupled with this pediment, convey the intended illusion of a peripteral classical temple. In a later publication, Soane gave the revealing description of the design as "a Roman temple altered into a casino retaining the general character of the exterior of the ancient edifice."[18] Between 1778 and 1781, a demonstrable change had taken place in Soane's thinking. The intermediary stage in the development can be traced to a sketch that occupies a prominent place at the beginning of Soane's Downhill Notebook (fig. 13.9). Datable to the year 1780, it immediately suggests a connection with the building schemes for the Bishop of Derry in Ireland. It stands midway between the other two casinos. It retains the low, Pantheon-style dome of 1778 on one facade, while including the temple front effect on the other. Antiquity and the more relaxed fashions of modern times merge in a Janus-faced way instead of remaining distinct as they had in his *castello d'acqua* (fig. 9.9). The aspect of a habitable temple, still a

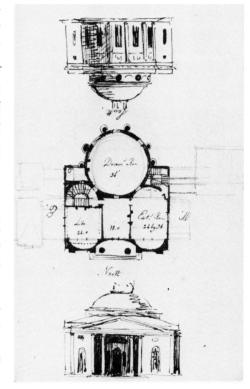

Fig. 13.9. Casino design, sketch plan and elevations (SM, Downhill Notebook, p. 7).

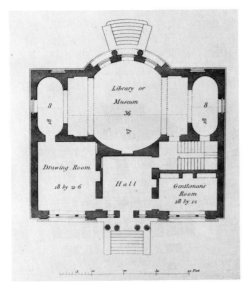

Fig. 13.10. Spencers Wood, design for a house, aquatint plan, 1793, *Sketches in Architecture.*

novelty in England despite earlier garden structures, points to the Bishop's taste for archaeological references. Whether or not he consulted the Bishop, Soane certainly acknowledged advice on the designs from two other amateurs, Thomas Pitt and Henry Bankes.

The period of Pitt and Bankes's presence in Italy coincided with the Bishop of Derry's renewed activities in Ireland and with a drawing of Soane's done in Rome on 11 November 1779.[19] This further variation on the theme of the casino enlarges the plan to that of a five-bedroom house, adds a full decastyle row of columns across the entrance front, and stipulates the cornice of the Temple of the Sun at Baalbec for the semicircular bow on the garden front. The spirit of exactitude implied by the insistence on a specific cornice moulding again recalls the erudite dabbling of the Bishop. And, as it happens, the prelate had under way at the time a small banqueting house in the gardens of his episcopal palace at Londonderry. The accounts refer to it as a casino. In all likelihood, then, Soane improved upon his casino design of 1778 with both the Florentine Academy and the patronage of the Bishop in mind.[20] When that patron abruptly removed his protection, Soane turned to the London Royal Academy. These were the first steps in a lengthy period of gestation that finally freed him enough to vary the themes he had borrowed.

Variations

The earliest smaller house by Soane to copy the plan of his hunting casinos was the one he designed in late 1780 or early the next year for a member of the Burdon family circle (fig. 6.15). Its far-reaching implications have been already hinted at, but its connection with the casino plan-type remains to be emphasized. From the sketch stage on (fig. 6.13), this larger dwelling incorporated the bombé garden facade. With the exception of the Italianate attached wings, the central core remained close to the casino format with minor variations. One of the preliminary designs calls for a house slightly more compact, but otherwise identical. A second sketch is more spread out, with an ovoid reception room, and it begins the drift away from the prototype. In the final presentation drawing (fig. 6.15), the gradual process of elongation reaches its full extent of just under 60 feet. In other respects, the plan is faithful to the original conception: corner rooms clustered around an axial arrangement of entrance hall and bowed drawing room beyond. Thus the organization of the casino, based on models like the pavilion at Le Butard, persisted in Soane's first plans for a model smaller house and continued as a constant factor thereafter.

Fig. 13.11. Spencers Wood, design for a house, aquatint elevation, 1793, *Sketches in Architecture.*

Covering the period from 20 October until 10 November 1781, a critical gap occurs in Soane's contemporary notebook. In the space of those few undocumented days he took two important steps in his professional development. With the first of these, a commission from Lady Craven, Soane entered the realm of garden architecture (fig. 5.16). The second commission, from William Sotheby, held even greater promise because it entailed designing an entire country house. As it happened, Soane would have to wait another two years till such an opportunity came his way again; whatever the reasons, this initial chance slipped through his fingers. He charged Sotheby only £21 for the unused drawings and estimates for a house at Spencers Wood, near Reading, Soane's boyhood home.[21]

From motives of innate frugality, Soane stored up for future use this, his first country house design. In 1793 he published its plan and elevation as belonging to "a villa designed for a gentleman in Berkshire" (figs. 13.10, 13.11). No early drawing exists for the elevation, but ground plans for Sotheby's house, dated December 1781, agree fairly well with the printed version.[22] They corroborate such elements in the aquatint as the placement of the door and windows on the lower storey. Certainly the house has the small proportions commonly associated with the villa concept. The facade measures only 60 feet across, and is nearly as deep. In this respect, as well as others, it compares closely with Soane's hunting casinos, which fall a few feet short of the same dimensions. Another point in common is the internal planning. Basically the arrangement of rooms is the same at Spencers Wood. Although the center of the garden facade does not bulge outward as conspicuously, its gentle swelling suggests, in embryo, the form more fully developed in the hunting casinos. Their polygonal or circular reception rooms are enlarged into a complex, three-part cruciform chamber. An ovoid central "crossing" is flanked by the arms of a cross-vaulted "transept," beyond which are smaller, apsidal-ended extensions. On plan this spatial sequence constitutes the most exciting domestic interior before the ones Soane produced for the library and yellow drawing room at Wimpole early in the 1790s.

The room that occupies the entire garden front at Spencers Wood is designated as a library or museum and reveals the scholarly inclinations of its intended owner. William Sotheby was a poet, playwright, and a member of the Society of Dilettanti. In 1780 he had married Mary Isted of Ecton Hall, an heiress from Northamptonshire.[23] William Sotheby's literary pursuits would explain the presence of a book room that displaced many normal amenities found in a smaller house. And Soane's only other museum of the perid was the one he designed for the collectors' society to which Sotheby belonged (fig. 11.14). The erudite sophistication of Soane's elevations also suited Sotheby's accomplishments as traveler and translator of the classics. In his best Grand Tourist style, Soane organized a row of giant Corinthian pilasters carrying an elaborate frieze across Sotheby's facade. The motif of the swags is picked up by the aedicular porch in front of the entrance door. The tripartite form is, in turn, echoed by the so-called Wyatt windows in the outer bays of the main storey. The recurrent tertiary rhythms, and Antique decorative motifs, unite the composition and give it its studied flavor. The elevation has no great originality. But into a small space Soane crammed a great deal of elegance without overloading the total effect unduly. Throughout there prevails a feeling of thinness and delicacy, accentuated by fragile ornaments and timid relieving arches. Soane eventually transformed the indecisiveness into a powerfully plain expression. Such was his persistence that he could found a personal style on elements such as these, lacking in real inspiration. In one form or another, the Spencers Wood solution would continue to crop up in Soane's work.

The first evidence of the reuse of the Spencers Wood scheme occurs in a drawing dating from 3 January 1784 (fig. 13.12), for the "intended

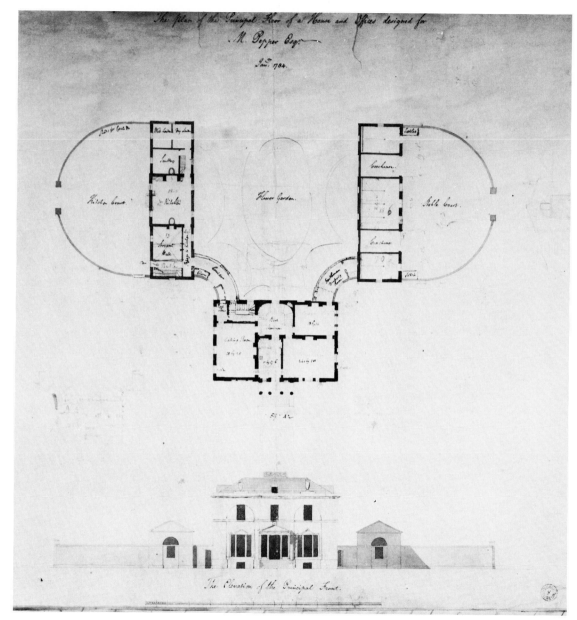

Fig. 13.12. Great Dunmow, design for a house, plan and elevation,
1784 (SM, Drawer 4, Set 3, Item 8).

villa" of Michael Pepper. A previous drawing had been done on 24 December 1783, following a visit the architect had made to "examine situations" at Great Dunmow, Essex.[24] Comparing the elevation to that originated for William Sotheby, one can see that during the intervening two years the design improved. Some of the underlying harmony became intensified; some of the disquieting fussiness was removed. Soane, for instance, dispensed with the giant pilasters and disengaged the relieving arches from around the windows, taking them right up through the two storeys of the facade. The Wyatt windows then assume a pedimented central light, so that they reflect even more closely the entrance porch—a virtually identical feature to the one in the Sotheby scheme. Relieving arches in the two low service blocks repeat nicely the similar arches on the facade. Pretentious classicizing elements disappear, to be replaced by a subtle manipulation of wall mass in proportion to apertures, all on a small scale. The villa in this case has almost the same 60-foot dimensions of the one for Sotheby. It looks more compact and unified because Soane chose to tone down the Grand Tourist references, although Michael Pepper had every right to them.

Pepper, son and namesake of Michael Pepper, a merchant of Stanstead Thele in Essex, stood to inherit the manor of Bigods, near Great Dunmow, which his father had purchased in 1763. Young Michael had made the Grand Tour in the company of the Reverend Mr. George Holgate. Soane met them both in Rome and traveled with them from there to Florence in April 1780.[25] The case of young Michael Pepper reconfirms the extent to which Soane initially relied upon the contacts he had made abroad. With Pepper, as with others, the careful grooming of a potential client, and the overtures of 1783/84, only amounted to the same £21 fee for unused designs that the architect had charged Sotheby.

In designing Michael Pepper's villa, Soane departed somewhat from the pattern established by the hunting casino and William Sotheby's house. Externally, the garden front for Pepper no longer includes the bombé effect. From the point of view of the interior, however, the impression of a bow is still conveyed by the curving inner walls of the stairhall. It is as if the bulge had been retracted into the body of the house itself, rather than dispensed with altogether. Soane felt a need to express curvilinear forms inside, outside, or preferably in both places. This ingrained tendency stretched back to the period of his training under Henry Holland and his exposure to Holland's use of circular rooms like the so-called tribune. The stylistic connection is reinforced by the overall disposition of rooms, service blocks, and curving wings at the Pepper villa which recalls Berrington, Herefordshire, by Holland.[26]

A further stage in Soane's development of an ideal smaller house plan came at Burn Hall in County Durham. The owner, George Smith, had first intended a simple cow barn on the property (figs. 1.6, 12.14). Soane's arrival at Burn Hall on 22 July 1783 probably had to do with laying out this farm building, but at the same time he took a measured plan of the existing "premises."[27] Out of this grew a scheme to rebuild, extend, or replace an existing mansion nearby. The letterpress accompanying Soane's published plan of 1788 (fig. 13.13) is characteristically unclear. It states that "the eating room had been built for some time" but does not say whether it was the one designed by Soane or another predecessor. By 1785 an elevation of the intended structure was in existence and went on display at the Royal Academy (fig. 13.16). Meanwhile, Soane had purchased for Smith the Piercefield estate in Monmouthshire, where he proceeded to build a house. This acquisition made a total of three Smith properties in different parts of Britain in different stages of construction. His mania for building was his undoing and led to the sale of Burn Hall. According to Soane,[28] the Burn Hall scheme had been abandoned long before.

Soane's elevation for Burn Hall ranks among the boldest examples of his early domestic architecture. The grandiose appearance is misleading, attributable in part to the rather strident watercolor draftsmanship, probably by a Soane apprentice. This is still a smaller type of house. As with Spencers Wood and the Pepper villa, the magic dimension at Burn Hall is 60 feet on a side. Perhaps Soane need not take complete blame for the facade if it was a question of extending the mansion. For his sake one would happily excuse him from responsibility for the round-headed statuary niches blocking the light from a rectangular window, or the disproportionate centerpiece. Here, on a larger scale than at the porch of Malvern Hall,[29] he tried to convey the appearance of the Vesta Temple at Tivoli but miscalculated the ponderous effect it would have.

The real significance of the centerpiece at Burn Hall is the way it relates to what lies behind. In the arrangement of the interior, Soane joined back-to-back two versions of his favorite hunting casino. The arrangement in this case becomes, of necessity, more complex. The circular entrance vestibule communicates with a curving stairhall, and culminates in the bow of a large drawing room, creating for the first time a long processional axis. A less well defined lateral axis also exists here for the first time. It stretches from the stairhead via a "corridore" to the lady's round-ended dressing room, or to a semicircular balcony overlooking a view of the valley below. The essence of the plan prepared the way for Tendring Hall, Soane's largest country-house commission of the period (see chap. 14).

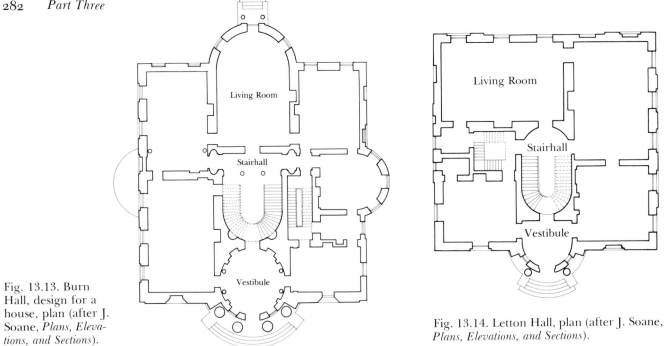

Fig. 13.13. Burn Hall, design for a house, plan (after J. Soane, *Plans, Elevations, and Sections*).

Fig. 13.14. Letton Hall, plan (after J. Soane, *Plans, Elevations, and Sections*).

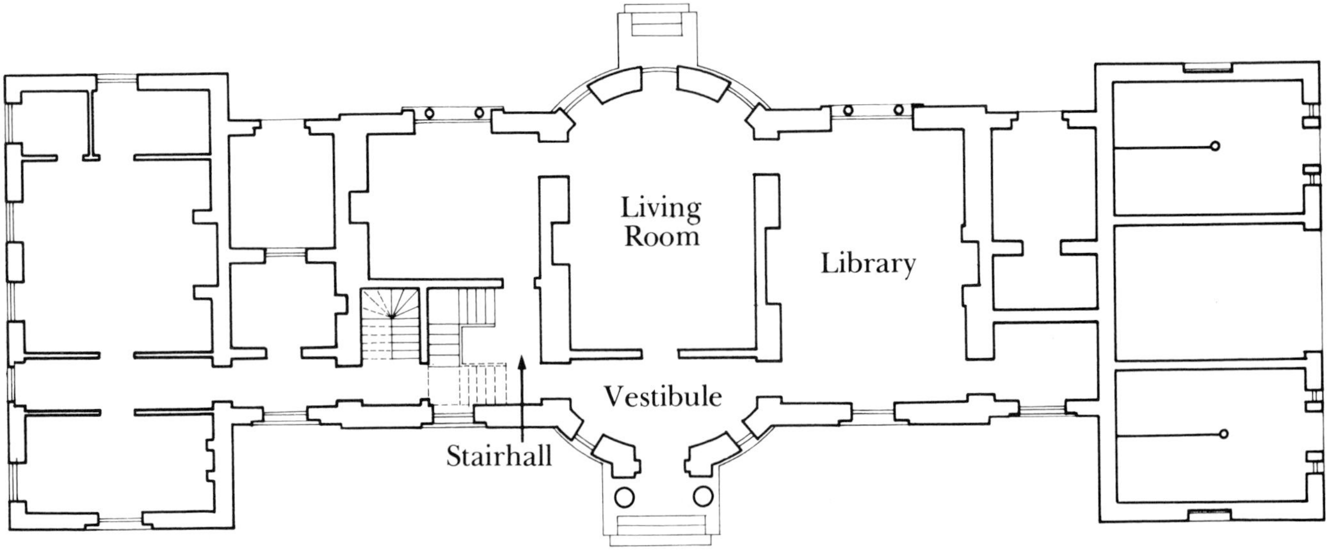

Fig. 13.15. Saxlingham Rectory, plan with proposed wings (after J. Soane, *Plans, Elevations, and Sections*).

Fig. 13.16. Burn Hall, design for a house, elevation (V&A, 3306.172).

Soane's next smaller house, the one for Dillingham Brampton Gurdon Dillingham, began modestly enough. The two met in May 1783, the patron no doubt having heard of Soane's increasing prominence in East Anglia. On one of Soane's frequent trips to Norfolk, he made an excursion from Norwich on 11 July 1783 to Letton Hall. The old mansion house, near Shipham, had passed to Brampton Gurdon from his father Thornhagh. Brampton subsequently added on his maternal grandfather's surname to his own in order to qualify for an inheritance under the terms of Theophilus Dillingham's will[30] of 1768; hence his long patronymic. At first, having chosen a location, Soane set about making various plans for new stables on the property. His references to "drawings" and "designs" in August and September are tantalizingly vague. But his earliest dated drawing, the first of more than forty preserved for Letton, relates to the semicircular stable design, and so does the estimate enclosed in a letter to Dillingham of 28 February 1784.[31] No sooner had all this been settled upon, than the decision was entirely reversed. Perhaps the change had been brewing for some time. In the course of dealings with Dillingham, the architect must have won the client's confidence and brought him around to the idea of remaining in the old mansion house until a completely new one could be built. Obviously, Soane had had drawings in readiness for such a move, though none of the preliminary ones is dated. On 19 April, while Soane was at Letton, Dillingham finally abandoned the stables scheme, proposing instead that: "The old House . . . be changed into Stables." More important still, at the same meeting they agreed "The new House to be begun in three weeks."[32]

It was more like three months than three weeks before digging for the foundations of the new Letton Hall commenced 1 July 1784. By this time a fairly definite agreement as to the outside dimensions of the house must have been reached with Philip Barnes, who contracted to build the brick shell for the sum of £2,837.[33] At some point prior to this decision, Soane had supplied Dillingham with a set of "multiple-choice" ground plans to choose from. One of them, numbered 3 (fig. 13.17), repeats the familiar casino pattern Soane continuously experimented with in these years. The drawing numbered 4 differs only by a few feet in either direction. The alternatives 1 and 2 are lost, probably because they were used to form the basis for the house as built. Soane managed to retain from 3 and 4 the magic number of 60-feet square. Within those confines, however, subsequent plans show him relinquishing more and more of his graceful, repetitive curves.

By degrees, Soane capitulated to various cost-related contingencies that impinged on his ideal curvilinear proposals. Another of the early schemes is far closer to the one executed (fig. 13.18). To judge from some pencil annotations in the area of the semicircular stable court, it may date from as early as the winter of 1783. The squarish plan is missing the curving bow front on the garden side. Soane compensated for it by creating the circular tetrastyle porch on the entrance facade. A drawing closely contemporary in style suggests a full-scale portico treatment for the porch with a giant order of Doric columns and antae.[34] The idea was quickly dropped in favor of greater simplicity.

Within his 1783 plan, Soane arranged for a curved and top-lighted stairhall. Then, as an afterthought, he contemplated changing the square entrance hall into a double apsidal-ended chamber, to carry on the theme of the repeated curves begun on the porch. The peculiar solution of placing both stairhall and the drawing room at right angles to the main axis, diverges from Soane's normal tendency to bilateral symmetry along the central spine of the building. To some extent, he rectified the confused impression when he came to the final solution (fig. 13.14). In the ground floor of Letton as built, Soane arranged to line up his ovoid stairhall and the bowed vestibule, even though the rectangular dining room at the end of the axis remained off center.

A good deal of Soane's desired spatial effect can still be sensed at

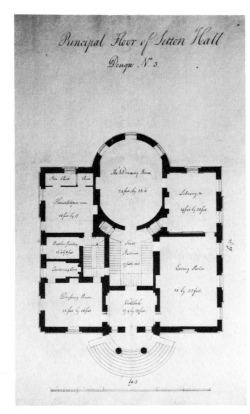

Fig. 13.17. Letton Hall, plan (SM, Drawer 28, Set 7, Item 7).

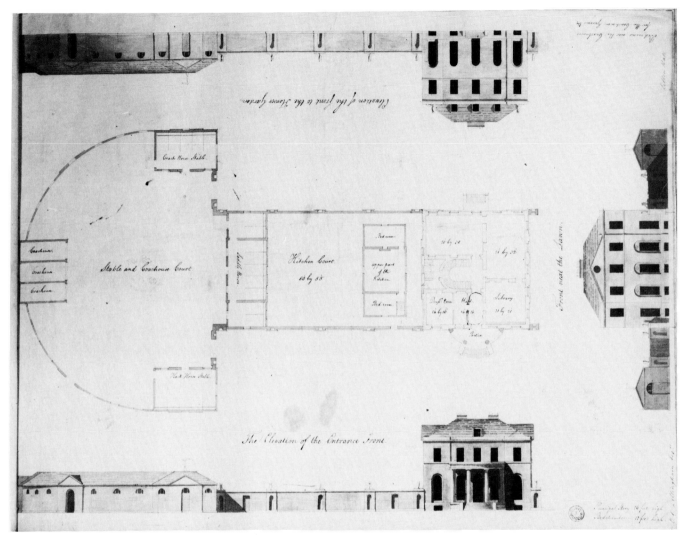

Fig. 13.18. Letton Hall, plan with proposed stable court and elevations (SM, Drawer 28, Set 7, Item 3).

Letton, despite alterations. A view along the main processional axis (fig. 13.19) captures the impression that the architect desired to make. Upon entering the house through the front door, the visitor has behind him walls that curve gently backward. Straight ahead, through the pedimented doorway, is an incomplete glimpse of the stairhall, the curving end wall of which is echoed by the curving cantilevered ramp of the treads and risers. The closed door immediately beyond the stairs

Fig. 13.19. Letton Hall, view from the vestibule into the stairhall.

leads to the dining room and hides the anticlimactic rectangular space to be found there. In terms of the sophisticated internal geometry of Soane's earlier schemes, the final solution at Letton cannot have entirely satisfied him. It lacked the full ingenuity and subtlety of approach he had developed as a result of the many false starts at Spencers Wood, Burn Hall, and elsewhere.

The elevations as originally proposed do not differ greatly from the ones executed, especially on the east and south sides (fig. 13.18 *top* and *right* respectively). The main change is the addition of an attic storey throughout, which detracts from the impression of compactness. As for the west, or entrance front, its appearance is best reconstructed from a Soane elevation (fig. 13.20) of January 1785. By that time, all but a few details, such as the indented corners, had been settled. In this drawing the attic is already present, and it helps create the same vertical accent that the original proposal had called for in the slightly projecting end bays. The semicircular portico in the final scheme extends the hall space forward. It ceases to be freestanding and, as a result, it integrates better with the entire composition of the west facade. Above the Doric portico

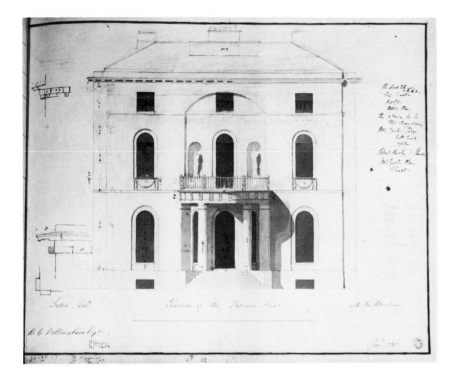

Fig. 13.20. Letton Hall, elevation of the west facade, 1785 (SM, Drawer 28, Set 7, Item 16).

Fig. 13.21. Letton Hall, west facade.

he harmonized into a consonant whole a series of circles. He grouped round-headed niches to either side of an arched window within an arched reveal. He then set the whole against the background of a giant segmental relieving arch. The top of it can just be made out behind an insensitive balustraded addition (fig. 13.21) of relatively recent date.[35] Before it was marred, this subtly handled play with shapes and surfaces testified to Soane's mastery of layers, masses, and textures.

The January 1785 elevation (fig. 13.20) documents in an interesting way the last stages in the designing of Letton. Having decided to keep the drawing as a rough copy, Soane used the lower left-hand margin to jot down a column of personal expenses. Above, in what was probably a memo to his apprentice, Sanders, Soane listed other drawings required from him for the Hammels lodges, or the more recent pair at Langley. On the right-hand side of the sheet Sanders crudely sketched in the treatment of the brick dentilated cornice at Letton that was executed by Philip Barnes later that year when he completed the brick shell. As late as 27 January 1789, however, Soane continued to send drawings for mouldings. Small modifications kept him occupied until 1792. Finally,

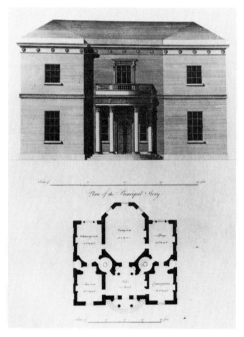

Fig. 13.22. William Thomas, casino design, engraved plan and elevation, *Original Designs in Architecture.*

he received his 5 percent commission on the total £6,000 cost, in addition to compensation for forty-two journeys to Letton made by himself or his assistants.[36]

At Letton, as time went on, delegation of duty became the order of the day. It would be physically impossible for Soane to master major works with the same personal attention his smaller ones had received before. The architectural office, with its opportunities for sharing work and collaborating with others, was the natural outcome of all Soane had struggled to achieve alone. For its moderate cost, Letton still showed a high degree of Soane's "personality" because of the way he had nurtured it himself over the years it took to build. But this achievement should not be overrated.

It comes as a shock to compare the west facade and plan of Letton with a very similar and exactly contemporary "design for a casine" from William Thomas's book (fig. 13.22). Thomas, a fairly undistinguished architect, seems to have had many of the same ideas as the more illustrious Soane. The notion of a compact house plan, compatible with a sparsely elegant facade having curvilinear or polygonal highlights, must have become common coinage among the architectural brotherhood in London. Once more Soane is seen to be in step with his contemporaries, rather than strides ahead of them. Soane and Thomas drew their designs from the same sources. Thomas subjected his to a process of congellation; his shapes are frozen hard and reminiscent of the second-generation neo-Palladians at their most glacial. Elsewhere he introduced curved porches and spaces that are somewhat at variance with his otherwise rectilinear geometry. His casino design has all the weaknesses of a mixed metaphor. Soane's approach, in contrast, remained much more fluid, even when he came to publish the Letton designs. In his book of 1788, he included plans and elevations as built, as "intended," and as "originally proposed." Although these do not vary enormously one from another, nonetheless they show Soane's continued flexibility and willingness to experiment. Soane was not afraid to display openly the evolution of his ideas. Ultimately, Letton in its finished form demonstrated those subtle areas in which Soane excelled as a country house designer.

At virtually the same moment as Soane had contracted for Letton, he entered into similar negotiations with the Reverend Mr. Gooch, recently appointed to the living of St. Mary's Church, Saxlingham Nethergate, near Norwich. In many ways Letton and Saxlingham Rectory are related and can be viewed as a natural outgrowth, the one from the other. Common planning principles unite them, as does a similar approach to the simple treatment of facades. Both underwent a similar process of simplification. Yet another similarity stems from the construction of the two Soane buildings. Philip Barnes, the contractor for Letton, laid the same Suffolk white bricks at Saxlingham. John de Carle, Soane's close associate at Blackfriars Bridge, Norwich, did the masonry for both houses. James Wilkins plastered the interiors, and Thomas Marks installed the plumbing. To their very bones, Letton and Saxlingham, despite differences in size, were made with the same materials and put together by the same hands.[37]

The Reverend John Gooch, M.A., came from a distinguished line of aristocratic East Anglian clerics. The Gooches had acted as rectors of Earsham on the Suffolk-Norfolk border early in the eighteenth century. The most notable member of the clan, Sir Thomas Gooch, D.D., had risen to hold consecutively the bishoprics of Norwich and Ely. The Bishop's second son, John, was rector of a living in Cambridgeshire. The Bishop's first son and heir, Sir Thomas, was the father of our John Gooch who succeeded his grandfather's chaplain in 1782 as the rector of Saxlingham. He later became an archdeacon. His patron was his brother, the wealthy fourth baronet, who also subsequently became a client of Soane's.[38] While John Gooch was staying at Christ Church, Oxford, from which he had received his degree, Soane sent him two designs on 26 March 1784. On 25 April the architect made a rough map of the location (fig. 13.23), and on July the second the drawings had been decided upon; the work of demolition began the following Monday.[39]

The major construction work at Saxlingham lasted until the end of 1786. Decorative details, over which Gooch was very particular, remained unsettled for another year. In the spring of 1788, when the final bills were in, the total came to £2,500, plus Soane's 5 percent commission.[40] The costs were less than half those of Letton and were kept low, in part, by the reuse of a considerable amount of old material from the previous rectory. That building, described as "good and convenient" in 1781,[41] stood to the west of St. Mary's churchyard as seen on Soane's site plan. It was obviously not good enough for a new incumbent with the name of Gooch. Soane measured the existing premises on 15 April 1784 and chose a location for the new replacement nearby. That same evening he returned to Norwich and dined with the Dean of the cathedral there.[42] This concurrence of events makes it likely that Gooch had applied to his diocese for a mortgage under the terms of Gilbert's Act of 1777 "to promote the residence of parochial clergy, by making provision for the more speedy and effectual building . . . of houses."

Gilbert's Act (17 George III, cap. 53) sought to remedy one of the prevalent ills of the Anglican church: pluralism, whereby clergy could

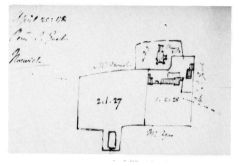

Fig. 13.23. Saxlingham Rectory, sketch site plan (SM, Soane Notebooks, 11, p. 15).

hold several geographically dispersed livings simultaneously, often resulting in absenteeism. The parliamentarian reformer, Thomas Gilbert, in his Clergy Residences Act, made it possible for decayed or substandard housing to be certified as such by a competent architect or contractor, torn down if the incumbent's superiors were in agreement, and paid for by mortgaging the parish tithes for the next twenty-five years. Penalties would be levied upon those who resided less than twenty weeks of the year with their pastoral flocks. The act initiated a spate of new parsonages,[43] of which that at Saxlingham was probably one. It may be that Gooch, in view of his rich relatives, did not need to borrow against his future income. Soane's survey and subsequent visit to Gooch's Dean would suggest otherwise. And if Gooch were far from indigent, money matters were not his strong point either. He did not pay off the full amount of Soane's fee until nearly a decade after the completion of the rectory.[44]

To return to Soane's four preparatory designs for Saxlingham Rectory, they fell into two categories according to plan type. For simplicity's sake the architect numbered them 1 through 4. The first of the originals exists in elevation only, dated March 1784 (fig. 13.24). The plans of the second, fourth, and third are known from a single sheet on which they are arranged in that descending order from top to bottom (fig. 13.25). On the one drawing, dated April 1784, the client could assess the relative merits according to his means and needs. (He was still a bachelor at the time and would remain so for the next seven years.) The rectangular plans at the top and the bottom have elements in common with Letton on a scale half as large. The middle alternative must, by process of elimination, correspond with the missing elevation numbered 4. It is a fascinating, slightly elongated version of Soane's original hunting casinos. In this case, even the dimensions of 46 feet × 24 feet are close. In contrast to the outcome at Letton, at Saxlingham the curvilinear solution was adopted. After years of unsuccessful trying, Soane succeeded in persuading a client to execute his favorite plan type. What had started as a sportsman's shooting box came into being under a clerical guise. One wonders whether Gooch was one of the proverbial hunting parsons.

The elevation numbered 1 (fig. 13.24) distinctly recalls the facade originated for the connoisseur-owner of Spencers Wood (see fig. 13.11). It is by far the most elaborate and costly of the four proposals submitted to Gooch. The second, third, and fourth in the series are all a good deal closer in spirit to the plainness of the existing rectory. The third one was faithfully reproduced in an engraving, where Soane described it as the

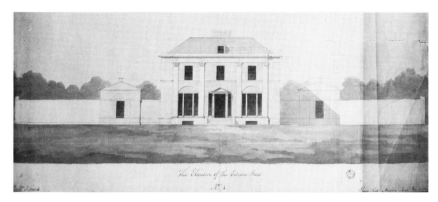

Fig. 13.24. Saxlingham Rectory, elevation of the north facade, 1784 (SM, Drawer 28, Set 1, Item 4).

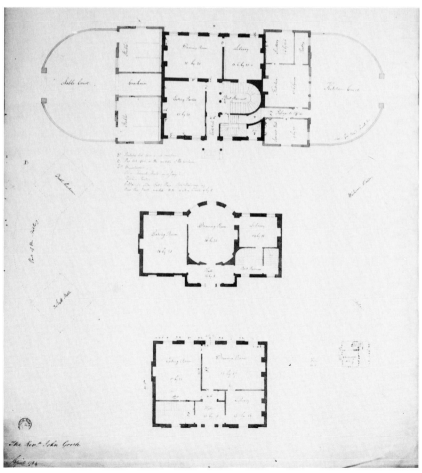

Fig. 13.25. Saxlingham Rectory, three alternative plans, 1784 (SM, Drawer 28, Set 1, Item 12).

"first design proposed."[45] A recessed center is flanked by salient and pedimented outer bays. In the second proposal the emphasis is merely switched from the ends to the middle. The lost fourth proposal—nearest of all to the executed version—would have been similar, with an even bolder central projection on the entrance facade. They all three share the characteristic astylar, simply treated wall mass. In this respect they foretell the rectory eventually erected—one of Soane's simplest, yet most prophetic smaller houses. The contributing factors that motivated Soane in the direction of stark simplicity would include the client's taste, the element of cost, and the limited abilities of local Norfolk craftsmen. The benefits to be derived from this enforced economy of means must slowly have dawned on Soane. At a certain point, his separate aspirations toward architectural primitivism and neoclassical elegance merged into a single objective. The common ground was provided by smaller, "low budget" dwellings, such as the one Soane proudly exhibited at the Royal Academy in 1785 under the title "a villa designed for a gentleman in Norfolk."[46]

As early as June 1784, the appearance of the north or entrance front to the rectory had been determined (fig. 13.26). In contrast to the earlier proposals, this facade now incorporated a gently curving bowed central bay. Constructed in Suffolk white brick—at one point stucco rough-casting had been suggested[47]—the whole composition takes on an air of stark, solid geometricality (pl. 7). In this context, the central bay can be read as a tower or silo-type form that surges forward from the flat wall surfaces to either side of it, enlivening them. Soane introduced his much-favored relieving arches to break the monotony and proposed to carry them up into the upper storey. The idea, along with the only hint of decoration, three bosses or paterae above the windows, was dispensed with, leaving the textural and coloristic values of the bricks to speak simply but eloquently for themselves.

Aspects of the garden facade remained unsettled in the form proposed in June 1784. The plan called for narrow window frames, 6 inches wider than those on the north side. But by 12 April 1786, working drawings were sent for what Soane called "Venetian Windows."[48] Actually these apertures are of the variety introduced by James Wyatt which lack the arched central light of the traditional Serlian, or Venetian, window (fig. 13.27). In contrast to the unadorned masses of the southern facade, these Wyatt windows, as recently restored, add a welcome note of classical refinement. They also suggest the lightness and openness of the interior, in the way they give onto the lawn that stretches down to the public road.

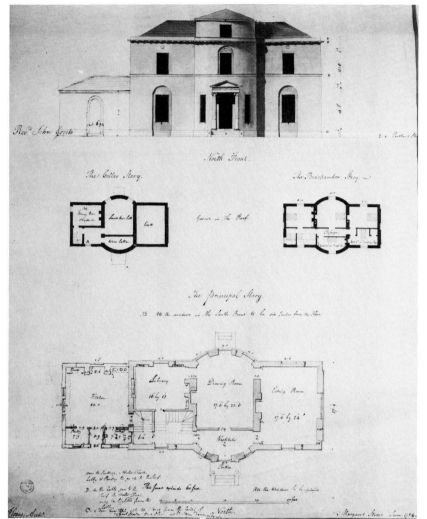

Fig. 13.27. Saxlingham Rectory, south facade.

Fig. 13.26. Saxlingham Rectory, plans and elevation of the north facade, 1784 (SM, Drawer 28, Set 1, Item 7).

As far as the plan of Saxlingham Rectory is concerned, it had been essentially determined in the June 1784 drawing (fig. 13.26). Only a few details remained to be cleared up. The treatment of the service courts is a case of an unresolved problem. When Soane published his plan and elevation, he remarked that the "offices" as shown "were entirely changed" in execution (fig. 13.15). A long history of proposals and counterproposals lies behind this statement.[49] Obviously his preferred

Fig. 13.28. Saxlingham Rectory, living room looking south.

solution from the start had been for service blocks attached to the core of the rectory and extending laterally by means of semicircular open courts. The elegant wings, besides detracting from the purity of the isolated central block, must have proved too expensive for the Reverend Mr. Gooch. In freehand addenda to the drawing of June 1784, Soane sketched in the position for a small kitchen extension which must have been erected along these lines, modified in Victorian times, and then demolished during the recent restoration and renovation. In almost every other respect, the rectory stands today much as Soane drew it and engraved it. It is a rare survival of his early work.

At Saxlingham, better than anywhere else, it is still possible to savor the end product of Soane's youthful evolution as a country house designer. The rectory took from the hunting casino prototype its compactness, the bombé facade treatment, and the device of the processional axis. In his parsonage Soane overcame the inherent problems of convenient spatial organization and cost with a single master stroke. He simply took the circular room he had been juggling in different combinations and sliced it across the middle with a dividing wall. The northern segment formed the entrance vestibule. Its curving walls continued the theme the visitor had first experienced outside in the towerlike central projection. From this point the processional axis, greatly reduced in length of course, headed off in one direction to the south. Passing through the partition wall, the spatial sequence resumed with a living room almost in the mirror image of the previous space (fig. 13.28). The curving end wall bows into the garden, inviting the gaze in a continuous sweeping motion down the walls, round the bow and to the out-of-doors beyond. This is not all. As had been announced by some of Soane's earlier plans, especially that for Burn Hall, the entry vestibule acts as a cross roads. Another processional axis (fig. 13.29), at right angles to the first, leads the visitor's attention off to the sides where, if doors remain ajar, he has a vista of the curving main staircase or the window in the end wall of the present-day library, bathed in western sunlight. In this modest building Soane had distilled down to manageable proportions the essence of his thinking. What had started with ambitious and fashionable villas for the rich, had ended up with an inexpensive parsonage for a cleric who could not pay his bills on time. The amazing thing about the whole process is that it changed Soane's outlook so little. He simply "packaged" the same ideas he had had in ever smaller and more humble-looking parcels. At the same time this slow scaling down of objectives forcibly liberated him from some of the hackneyed conventions of fellow beginners. Having to think realistically led him to investigate an approach in which the elegant planning and the radically simple elevations of the age might combine and point toward new directions in architecture.

Fig. 13.29. Saxlingham Rectory, view from the stairhall looking west.

Postmortem for Tendring Hall

There seems to be something ill-omen'd to you in the whole of this Tendring Hall business, and I advise you to be very careful how you venture upon a ladder or scaffold there for fear of accidents.

Thomas Pitt, Lord Camelford to Soane
16 February 1786

WITH THE DEMOLITION OF TENDRING HALL in 1955,[1] a little-recognized masterpiece disappeared. It never attracted the kind of attention bestowed on other country houses. Soane himself did not exhibit drawings of it, as he usually did with his major buildings. Guidebook writers overlooked it, except for one who mistakenly attributed it to James Wyatt.[2] Its location naturally reinforced its obscurity, tucked away near Stoke-by-Nayland, in a quiet rural corner of Suffolk. Even the painter John Constable, who immortalized in his landscapes Stoke, Dedham Vale, and the neighboring villages, apparently never recorded Tendring, though it was a prominent enough landmark (fig. 14.1). A giant hole in the ground marks the spot where the house once stood overlooking the River Stour. All that survive are four columns of the entrance porch, a gaunt cenotaph worthy of a war cemetery or concentration camp. Despite the total obliteration, Tendring lives on in the memory of those who can still vividly recollect it. And, like a ghost, it returns to haunt us in an eerie series of photographs taken by Avery Colebrook as a record before the destruction.[3] Through the medium of Colebrook's art, the appearance of Tendring can be recaptured, as well as something of the spirit that earned it a special, if neglected, place in Soane's oeuvre.

Tendring was the largest Soane commission begun before 1785, and the costliest besides. The estimate for the new house, stables, lodges, park enclosure wall, and various outbuildings ran to six pages, and totalled £12,050—nearly twice as much as Letton, Soane's biggest comparable early house.[4] The project began in the summer of 1784, and work continued until 1790. Some fifty-seven surviving drawings document all phases of construction. Their evidence, coupled with voluminous accounts, notebook entries, an Act of Parliament, and two lawsuits portray the enormous complexity of undertaking a country house in the eighteenth century. An impressive machinery had to be in place before such a job could be hazarded. Letton, with whose construction Tendring

Fig. 14.1. Tendring Hall seen from the southeast.

overlapped, provided the necessary trial run. This chapter seeks to analyze the organizational abilities and design techniques seen in full force for the first time at Tendring, while at the same time seeking to evoke its appearance in words and pictures.

In contrast to the slow maturation of ideas at Saxlingham and Letton, Soane's contemporary Tendring projects evolved without the least hesitation. The first mention of Admiral Rowley (later Sir Joshua) occurs in Soane's notebooks on 28 April 1784, without preamble or explanation.[5] There is no indication of how this professional seaman, recently retired with an undistinguished record, came to hear of Soane. Nor is there any indication that Admiral Rowley, his wife, or their eldest son, William, were particularly devoted to the arts. But they obviously had a great fondness for the ancestral estate where the Admiral had chosen to spend his last days ashore, and near to which the present baronet, Sir Joshua, still lives. Soane immediately presented designs for a new Tendring Hall, dating them on 3 May 1784 (fig. 14.2). A glance at the ground plan explains how he could respond with such speed to a patron's first overture. He returned to the familiar theme of the hunting casino.

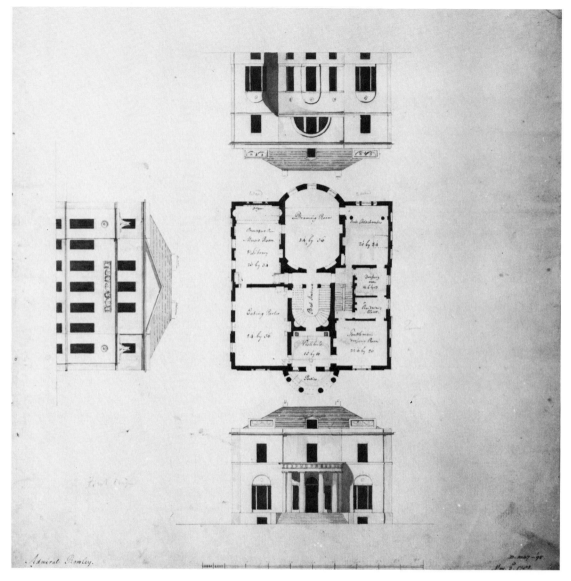

Fig. 14.2. Tendring Hall, plan and elevations, 1784 (V&A, D. 1447-'98).

As finally built, the ground plan hardly differs at all from the original design (fig. 14.3, and see figs. 13.3, 13.13–13.15). By trial and error, Soane had arrived at a personally pleasing formula, one that was acceptable to clients of moderate fortunes. The bombé garden facade and the processional axis down the center of the house are repeated here. Soane included the lateral axis he had experimented with at Saxlingham, the curved stairhall he had used at Letton, and he suggested, in pencil, a reciprocal curving projection in the entrance vestibule as at Burn Hall. Nothing was wasted with Soane. The dimensions only exceeded those at Letton by a matter of several feet. It was the main facades of Tendring that were the areas most open to modification, perhaps in response to the site. The location, while less dramatic than the one at Burn Hall, still far exceeded the possibilities of the relatively flat terrain the architect had faced at Letton and Saxlingham. To the north lay a gently rising plateau, to the south the hill slope fell down to the banks of the Stour. The natural contours suggested to Soane the ridge as the obvious position for the house. It may also have influenced him to aggrandize the south facade somewhat and play down the northern one, which would only receive early morning sunlight. On his first trip to the site, 8 May 1784, Soane visited the existing mansion house of the Rowleys with a measured plan in hand. Begun about 150 years earlier in a half-timbered style, it had fallen into disrepair. The architect determined that the "old house must come down."[6] He then left Tendring on 11 May in order to resume work on his estimate and drawing of the facades.

Very soon after seeing the hillside at Tendring, Soane increased the height of the bow on the south, or garden side to a full two storeys (fig. 14.4). This gave prominence to the facade which, in any event, would be the one first seen across the park as the London road approached Stoke-by-Nayland from below. Internally, the advantage of the extra storey was that it made possible a large dressing room above the saloon, both of which dominated a panorama off in several directions over the park and river valley. In the grounds Soane had determined the quality of the clay during his first visit. All the bricks for the new mansion were eventually baked in kilns set up within the Tendring estate. The local Suffolk white bricks impart a neutral tone to the architecture. At Tendring, as at Saxlingham (pl. 7), Soane achieved a curving, towerlike effect by the simplest means. But here at Tendring, the striking device is accentuated by being viewed from below (fig. 14.4). The sense of smooth roundness and height are increased. Complete absence of ornament focuses attention on the geometric interplay of shapes, while keeping down the cost.

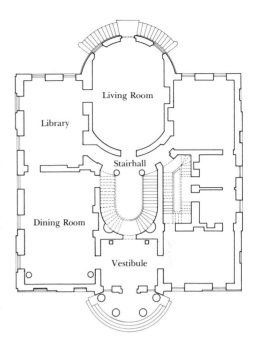

Fig. 14.3. Tendring Hall, plan (after J. Soane, *Plans, Elevations, and Sections*).

Fig. 14.4. Tendring Hall, center of the south facade.

Soane returned to Tendring on 28 May 1784, with the uncle of his future bride, George Wyatt. The two men examined the old house, and the proposed new site. Between them they devised a careful, itemized estimate; George Wyatt later subcontracted for much of the brickwork and masonry on the new house.[7] The need for Wyatt's second opinion had to do with the complex legal tangle surrounding Tendring and the Rowleys. Admiral Sir William Rowley, the father of Joshua, died in 1768, leaving an entailed estate in the hands of trustees. The trust was established so that the half-wit eldest son would be cared for until death. Joshua and his son, William, wanted to alter the terms of the trust so that large sums of money could be released for the building of a new mansion. In order to do so a private member's bill had to be introduced into the House of Lords. The professional opinions and estimates of Soane and Wyatt would add necessary weight to the Rowley's case in the eyes of their trustees. Soane had to attend the committee meetings at the House of Lords on 8 June and again on 9 July to provide evidence under oath and show his drawings.[8] Sworn in as one of the "skillful and experienced surveyors," Soane produced his estimate, countersigned by the Rowleys, father and son. After the first and second readings of the bill, Lord Camelford, Soane's friend, reported on 15 July for the Committee of Lords. The Lords agreed the bill should be engrossed with one amendment. As later litigation shows, Lord Bathurst expressed doubts about the competence of Soane's estimates. The amendment legally bound Soane to build the house for the cost stipulated in those estimates, within four years. The amendment was accepted by all parties, and thus Soane became appointed contractor as well as architect. Therein lay the root of all his future difficulties with the trustees and the Rowleys themselves.[9]

Once the Rowleys' private member's bill had received approval, events moved quickly. In mid-September, Soane went to Tendring to supervise the digging of the foundations. A month later he returned for the foundation laying, which marked the end of the first season's building campaign. Meanwhile, Soane was preparing a set of contract drawings for Admiral Rowley to sign (fig. 14.5).[10] The one of the north facade has the client's signature in the bottom right-hand corner, below which is the date 19 December 1784, and a note in Soane's writing to the effect that the bas-relief panels to either side of the Doric entrance porch had been added as an approved afterthought. The panels—probably in Coade stone—would have added a touch of elegance to an otherwise severe elevation. They help to enliven the effect, but were omitted from the house as executed. The similar ones intended for Letton (fig. 13.14) were also not carried out. Judicious tree planting, as suggested in the

drawing, did much to soften the harsh lines and plainness of the building (fig. 14.6). Leafy branches frame the vista down the Tendring carriage drive, while shrubs conceal some of the attached service areas. Early morning sun rakes the relatively shallow projections that subtly divide up the wall plane. Soane had to abandon the Wyatt windows he had originally envisioned (fig. 14.2) in favor of ordinary ones. The semi-

Fig. 14.5. Tendring Hall, contract elevation of the north facade, 1784 (V&A, D. 1435-'98).

Fig. 14.6. Tendring Hall, north facade.

Fig. 14.7. Tendring Hall, view from the entrance vestibule looking south.

circular porch, later altered to a rectangular plan, gave the only hint of the curves abounding on the interior. Doric columns shown in all the early drawings have been replaced with Ionic ones, which seem less in keeping with the austere facade—strong and stern as a man-of-war.[11]

Standing at the entrance, with the doors ajar (fig. 14.7) it was possible all at once to sense the processional axis at Tendring, and some of the surprises that Soane had in store along the way. In the middle distance the shafts of distant columns could be distinguished. Luminous patches at the far end announced the outer limits, at the same time permitting a glimpse of the fields and river valley beyond. "He keeps the structure simple," writes Colebrook, who knew Tendring well, "but one turns a corner—and something suddenly opens up. . . . Here is the *frisson*."[12] Soane's exterior was therefore conceived as a simple vessel to hold the precious commodity of the space it contained. One left the outdoors behind, only to find it recreated indoors in the open, light-saturated stairhall.

On the threshold of Tendring, Soane made clear his realization of a typical dichotomy in most contemporary country houses. Quite simply the dichotomy involves the treatment of interiors as opposed to exteriors. Often the two were treated quite separately by different individuals. Soane never resorted to this practice. Nevertheless the same dichotomy existed at Tendring. Its simple external massing, lacking the neo-Palladian rhetoric of rusticated basement and smooth *piano nobile*, could in no way prepare the visitor for what he experienced inside. Organization and decoration of interior spaces meant at least as much to Soane as the plan and elevations. Just how much time he devoted to this branch of his profession is proven by the surviving drawings. Of the forty-seven sheets for the house, fourteen relate to decorative details. The roofed shell of Tendring Hall was just the beginning. It was the part of the design that usually went smoothly, and as fast as experienced bricklayers could set one course upon another. At Tendring, however, the normal process came to a standstill in February 1785. The Rowley trustees began making difficulties for the architect-contractor. They demanded receipts which he felt questioned his integrity, and they counteracted his refusal to comply by cutting off all funds for a while. The dilemma need never have arisen, had not the Act of Parliament confused the bounds of authority vested in the trustees as opposed to their architect. Soane sought legal advice.[13] He turned over his accounts to a lawyer; hence, perhaps, the total absence of them for the year 1785—the same year in which his notebooks mysteriously cease. The temporary delay caused by the trustees had been resolved by 3 July 1785, when Soane prepared a working drawing for the framing of the upstairs floor. In January of the following year accounts resume with Soane insuring the unfinished carcase for £4,000. Slates for the roof and glass for the windows arrived in August 1786.[14] The shell would be complete by the winter, and the work of interior decoration could begin in earnest.

The batch of contract drawings prepared in December 1784 included two sections through the east-west and north-south axes (pl. 8). A sectional drawing, as a rule, goes one step beyond geometrical and ichnographic representations. It makes explicit what the others leave implicit. It integrates the information they provide. It also gives the architect his first opportunity to suggest color schemes, decorative mouldings, and his treatment of spaces by means of evocative shadows cast from the skylight. Soane took full advantage of all these effects in the section along the processional axis. He tinted the entrance vestibule and stairhall aquamarine, the main apartment on the garden side green, and Lady Rowley's dressing room above it a canary yellow. He also indicated a progression of architectural orders from Doric, in the vestibule, to Ionic and Corinthian, above each other in the superposed columns of the two-storey-high central hall.

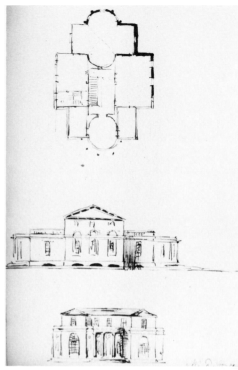

Fig. 14.8. George
Dance II, Cranbury
Park, view into the ball-
room.

Fig. 14.9. Sketch plan
and elevations for a
country house (SM,
Miscellaneous Sketches
1780–82, p. 9).

The spatial progression from low and dark rooms to higher and
brighter ones is a classic architectural solution, which still gives plenty of
scope for personal expression. Robert Taylor understood the technique
and used it at Sharpham, Devon; so did James Paine the Elder at Wardour
Castle, Wiltshire, though the end results differ. Summerson mentions
the stairhall by Holland at Berrington in connection with Tendring.[15]
Soane's acquaintance with these specific buildings is a matter of conjecture. A much stronger documentary case can be made for George
Dance's Cranbury Park in Hampshire. Within an existing shell, Dance
organized a sequence of spaces that Nikolaus Pevsner has described as
"an unforgettable experience"[16]—and so it is. Despite frequent, awkward right-angled turns, the suite at Cranbury—culminating in the ballroom (fig. 14.8)—plays upon our feelings of constriction and of release
in a remarkable way. Columnar screens create artificial bottlenecks
through which we must pass. Low lobbies and antechambers are illumi-
nated by unexpected skylights. Finally, the great ballroom opens up
before us, a so-called starfish motif splayed out across the intricate plas-

ter ceiling. This brilliant piece of Dance's decorative invention found echoes in a number of Soane ceilings in later years. Soane could have known the design from drawings. He even assisted Dance in a modest way with the final stages of Cranbury's interior decoration.[17] What is more, the same early notebook in which he wrote of Cranbury records a Soane journey to Lymington on the Hampshire coast. As Thomas Dummer, the recently deceased owner of Cranbury, was M.P. for that borough, it seems likely Soane went there on the widow Dummer's business. Nothing would have been easier, or more proper, than that he take in a visit to Cranbury on his way back to London.[18]

Personal familiarity with Cranbury would have established in Soane's mind a high standard to emulate. Some evidence for such emulation is reflected in a page from Soane's "Miscellaneous Sketches 1780–82" (fig. 14.9). The lower margin has the inscription "Mr. D. from me." It was written at a time when Soane did not yet have clients with that initial, so it could only refer to Dance. It is known that on later occasions Dance borrowed Soane's ideas for country house plans,[19] so the interchange of ideas may have stretched back further in the two men's careers. Soane's ideal ground plan, while different from Cranbury, pays homage to Dance, whose starfish ceiling is recalled in Soane's groin-vaulted saloon. Soane merely takes Cranbury as a point of departure for an extraordinary new configuration, best described as two of his bombé-fronted houses set back to back. In his early work, the closest he ever came to realizing such dramatic spatial transitions was at Tendring.

In Soane's cross section of Tendring, his main processional axis started off on the north with a groin-vaulted entrance vestibule with Doric columns placed in the corners. The later engraving in his book,[20] and modern photographs, show that the idea was rejected in favor of a transverse barrel vault, coffered in a similar manner to the ceiling of the slightly earlier music pavilion at Earsham. In consequence of this decision, Soane moved the Doric columns back into the stairhall to replace the Ionic ones on the lower level. Emerging from the relatively dark vestibule, under the ramp of the cantilevered stone staircase overhead, the full height of the central hall was finally revealed (fig. 14.10). The use of an ornamented Roman Doric order supplied richness (fig. 14.11). Whether it was originally intended to marbleize these freestanding shafts and their responds is hard to say. They made the top-lighted hall more somber at its lowest level. The enriched entablature introduces Soane's favorite motif of the bull's head from the Temple of Vesta, Tivoli, but in an original combination with groups of flutes (fig. 14.12). The entire composition seems without exact classical precedent. It points

Fig. 14.10. Tendring Hall, view looking up the stairhall.

Fig. 14.11. Tendring Hall, stairhall.

Fig. 14.12. Tendring Hall, detail of the Doric entablature in the stairhall.

for the first time to Soane's familiarity with the whole range of Antique mouldings, and his willingness freely to experiment with them—a trait particularly apparent in his idiosyncratic mature decorative style, where this process of omission and tendency to three-dimensional boldness reaches a climax.

The change in Soane's interior decoration did not transpire all at once; he accomplished it by gradual, almost imperceptible stages. The general mood in the interior of Tendring remains fashionably light, particularly in the stairhall (fig. 14.10). The extreme thinness of the cantilevered stone treads is repeated in the balustrade, but the ironwork differs much in its simplicity from the more elaborate types employed by Soane's immediate predecessors. Time and again Soane used the plain

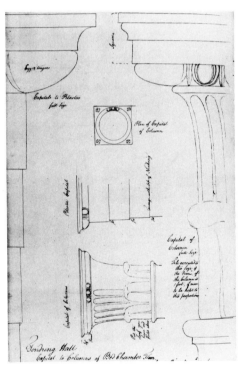

Fig. 14.13. Tendring Hall, detailed elevations and moulding profiles for the Ionic order in the stairhall, 1786 (SM, Precedents in Architecture 1784, fol. 75 verso).

motif of vertical bands of lozenges alternating with straight bars. The balustrade was installed in the autumn of 1786; there is a reference to modifications to it on 28 October.[21] What makes the stairhall at Tendring unusual is the repetition of the ironwork in front of arched openings on the bedroom floor. These act as miniature balconies, from which to observe the stairs. The act of ascending or descending the steps thus takes on the attributes of a theatrical performance, watched over by a potential audience installed in private boxes around a horseshoe-shaped stairwell. At Tendring, Soane had arrived at a solution midway between the ordinary staircase and the nonfunctional "tribune" favored by Henry Holland and later by himself. Some of the theatrical properties of the space were realized, while its practical role was unimpeded.

In the stairhall, Soane skillfully combined the circular forms he preferred; curved columns and balustrade, arched balcony openings, and the oculus with skylight above it. Soane devoted minute attention to areas such as the decorative frieze of bull's heads (fig. 14.12). Soane had used it elsewhere before and at Tendring included a slightly different version in the cornice of the library. He also worked out the details of the Corinthianesque columns on the upper landing with meticulous care. A drawing of them (fig. 14.13), partly done to full scale, was prepared for William Pearce, Soane's clerk of works, on 27 May 1786. The capital derives from the order at Spalatro, published by Robert Adam, and introduced by him into so many of his works.[22] The Adam brothers' approach to interior decoration made an impact on England, the reverberations of which could still be felt in the early years of Soane's career. He, like many others, followed the Adamesque fashion for delicate motifs of Antique derivation employed for mural decoration, ceilings or chimneypieces. The architect must have felt ensnared by these accepted ornamental conventions, his young wings pinioned by the parsimony of his clients. The line of least resistance for him was to conform to the prevailing norms of design in a diluted Adamesque vein. Yet here and there, tucked away at Tendring (figs. 14.12, 14.11) are rows of egg and dart, disembodied from, and a vestigial reminder of, a normal cornice. The isolated moulding, blown up to a bigger scale than usual, simply runs along as a continuous decorative band, emphasizing surfaces and contours with no relation at all to classically ordained precedent. These were the sorts of liberties that earned him so much derision later on. They constituted part of the "defiance hurled at Rome and Greece" that one early Soane critic wrote about.[23]

Plaster ceiling design was at least as highly developed a branch of English eighteenth-century architecture as decorative mouldings. In

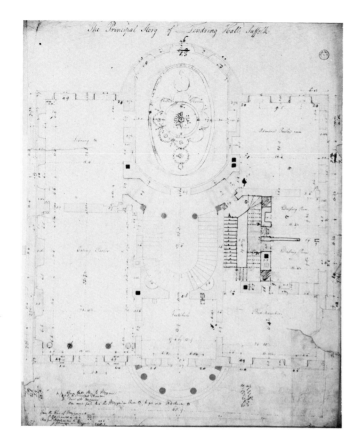

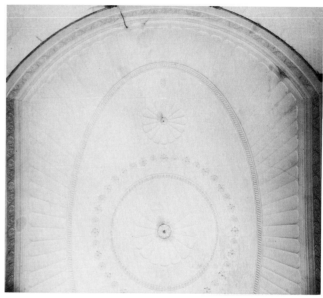

comparison to the many variations upon ceiling patterns evolved by the Adams, Chambers, and Wyatt, Soane had not much originality in this field. Ultimately he found his way to a few treatments, such as the starfish ceiling, that he repeated over and over again. Early in his career, however, he floundered around unsuccessfully in search of an expression he could adopt and feel at home with. At Tendring he had his biggest opportunity for experimentation, but the results were disappointingly unoriginal. One of his working drawings of the house gives a rare indication of his method of arriving at a ceiling design (fig. 14.14). With a hasty sketch he proposed to treat the flat surface of the bowed room on the garden facade in a fairly insipid arrangement of concentric circles within an oval border. The fact that he specified the reuse of the same border in the ceiling of the adjacent library does not say much for Soane's fertility of invention. Furthermore, the resemblance of this

Fig. 14.14. Tendring Hall, plan of the principal storey (SM, Drawer 28, Set 2, Item 5).

Fig. 14.15. Tendring Hall, ceiling of the living room.

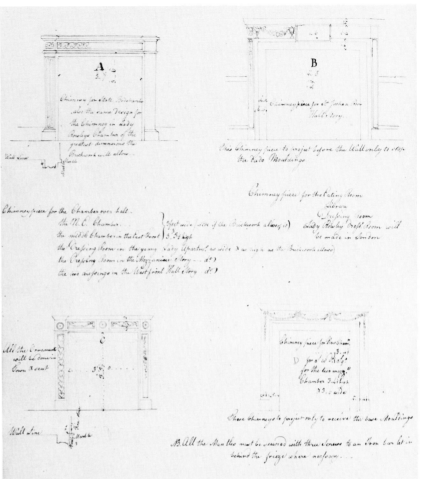

Fig. 14.16. George Richardson, engraved chimneypiece design, 1780, *A New Collection of Chimney Pieces.*

Fig. 14.17. Tendring Hall, elevations of four chimneypieces in the upper storeys of the house (SM, Precedents in Architecture 1784, fol. 77 verso).

Tendring ceiling to that of Claremont is notable (fig. 2.6), and not entirely surprising. Soane had traced decorative motifs by Henry Holland when working for him, and ten years later returned to them. All along Soane had little native ability in the decorative domain, either at the free-lance drawing or the designing of it. At Tendring he had not yet admitted the fact fully to himself. In its executed form, the ceiling there (fig. 14.15), even before it had become stained and cracked, lacked dynamic energy. The flat elements drift about apparently unrelated to one another. The plasterers he employed, such as William Lee and Thomas Holloway,[24] were obviously not of high enough caliber to supply inspiration where it was wanting in the first place. Soane learned that the elimination of decorative plaster ceilings altogether, or at least their drastic simplification, would ultimately prove the best remedy.

In that other great mainstay of English interior decoration, the realm of the chimneypiece, Soane excelled almost as much as he fumbled with his early ceilings. In his designs for ornamental fireplaces he quickly established a preferred pattern quite different from the manner generally in favor. During roughly the first half of the century there was a preference for heavy chimneypieces, the most sumptuous examples of which were in statuary marble and incorporated caryatids or sculpted figures. Gradually the fashion shifted to a more delicate treatment, less boldly three-dimensional, flatter, and more decorative. The old architectonic divisions between columns or pilasters and the entablature they carried over the fireplace opening also fused together. The Adam brothers could claim responsibility for the new emphasis. The taste they helped establish forms the background against which Soane's contributions ought to be considered.

Adam-style chimneypieces varied a lot among themselves, but, as with the ceiling patterns, the variety resulted from a skillful manipulation of a few recurrent elements.[25] The infinite permutations can easily be studied from the designs published by George Richardson (fig. 14.16), which appeared in 1781 as Soane was setting up practice. Richardson, a one-time Adam co-worker, devised chimneypieces of the typical sort that influenced Soane to begin with. In some designs for John Patteson (fig. 6.16) Soane mimicked the Adamesque language of garlands, paterae, bell flowers and so forth. The metamorphosis in his repertory occurred in a sporadic way. Two dated chimneypiece designs of November 1782 for the Hon. Elizabeth Pery's Berkeley Square townhouse are more accomplished.[26] The thyrsus motif is added to Soane's arsenal, but otherwise there is no departure from the ornamental quality. It persists in two designs for Richard Holland, dated 12 January 1784, although in this case there is a notably greater use of architectural fluting and less reliance on naturalistic elements.[27] Further signs of change occur later that same year. In December, Soane prepared a drawing of a marble chimneypiece which took place within a twelve-month period.
strigilation in place of capitals, and several bull's eye motifs on the entablature. This design cannot be located anywhere at Earsham,[28] but an extremely similar one, without the ribbons on the fasces, was executed for John Patteson (fig. 6.18), as has been seen. It is a lovely and quite original indication of Soane's versatile mastery of the art of the chimneypiece which took place within a twelve-month period.

Fig. 14.18. Tendring Hall, dining room chimneypiece.

At Tendring, a drawing (fig. 14.17) made shortly after Admiral Rowley's creation as a baronet in June 1786 gives no less than four possible types of wooden chimneypiece for the upstairs bedrooms. Of the four, *A*, *B*, and *D* reutilize the Adamesque formulas, while *C* is more prophetic in its use of the bull's eyes. Annotations indicate that the framework would be constructed on the job, whereas the plaster ornaments would be sent up from London separately. As for the marble chimneypieces in the reception rooms, they would be shipped from the capital ready for installation. The one in the dining room at Tendring (fig. 14.18) is a mature and starkly simple statement of the preferred type of chimneypiece Soane was developing in these years. Other contemporary examples are at Saxlingham (fig. 13.22) and at Letton (datable to late 1786).[29] The proliferation of the characteristic Soane chimneypiece was under way. With time, Soane would drop even the plain fluting and bull's eyes in preference for a style whose blocky, unornamented massiveness he made inimitably his own.

By no means all the decorative elements of a Soane building were architect-designed. At Tendring, for example, surviving photographs of the principal rooms show that most of the marble chimneypieces looked quite different from the one in the dining room. They would have been ready-made, instead of made-to-order. An account records one of them to have cost £28 from a statuary named Davies, possibly Samuel. Another, for Mrs. Rowley's upstairs dressing room, was supplied directly by James Nelson, the mason at Tendring, for £30.[30] The practice of utilizing "off-the-peg" items extended to other areas as well. The London firm of Keir and Co. supplied a prefabricated round iron skylight at Tendring, just as their costlier oblong model had been installed earlier at Letton. Soane could order directly from their sales catalogue, of which he owned a copy, as he must also have done from Eleanor Coade's artificial stone company.[31] It stands to reason that, to some extent, he would accommodate his designs according to a firm's standard specifications. This was certainly the case with Joseph Bramah's recently patented flush toilets. At least one, if not two, went into Tendring at the usual fee of £11. Bramah provided other water closets for Letton and at Rectory Manor, Walthamstow.[32] More such evidence may come to light when Soane's later works are studied in detail. Enough is already known strongly to suggest that he no longer designed a house in the time-honored way of his illustrious predecessors, like the Adam brothers. They took responsibility for personally designing a house down to the smallest fixtures. For Soane, cost factors would argue against such labor-intensive pursuits, especially with the middle-income sort of house that he was mostly engaged in. At Tendring, the contract drawings even specified the reuse of mahogany doors from the old house, as a cost-saving measure.[33] In one sense such factors as existing doors, standardized water closets, and the like, cut down on the architect's artistic freedom. Soane seems to have acceded willingly to such constraints. Branches of architecture such as fittings and furnishings hardly interested him at all. Compared with the Adams his output in this area was tiny and uninspired. So, from ready-made skylights down to door handles, Soane used short cuts in the design and construction process. Inevitably, a Soane house would pay the price of a certain loss of individuality in exchange for relative standardization. A sameness underlies not only their design, but their details and fitting out. Soane worked with what he knew to be readily available on the market. One senses with him that the era of handcraftsmanship is beginning to draw to a close in the face of rapid industrialization by the building trades. Without apparent resistance, Soane accepted in principle the concept that led to the mass-produced housing of the future.

In his dual capacity as contractor and architect, Soane dealt directly with the craftsmen of Tendring and the suppliers of goods or raw materials. His position was not enviable. He had some pretty difficult customers to contend with: on the one hand, a mason, Richard Payne, who demanded more payment than Soane thought "that rascal" was entitled to;[34] on the other hand, an aging client, eager for results and somewhat capricious. The Admiral forced the architect to lower the windows in Mrs. Rowley's dressing room in 1786, much to the detriment of the garden facade (fig. 14.4).[35] Soane had to placate the patron, and maintain confidence with the many people advancing goods and services on credit. At the same time he fought a rearguard action with the Rowley trustees. Their slow and sporadic financing posed the constant threat of a work stoppage. Early in 1789, Soane calculated that the sums they had advanced him only totalled £9,469, as against the expenditures of £12,050. Assuming Soane was on target with his budget, as he usually was, then he needed an additional £2,500 to complete his final payments.[36] When Thomas Pitt warned Soane "to be very careful how you venture upon a ladder or scaffold," he said so more than in jest.[37] The situation at Tendring was potentially dangerous. It combined, in an explosive mixture, restive owners, insubordinate workmen, suspicious trustees, and increasingly impatient creditors.

To make matters worse, Admiral Rowley died at Tendring on 26 February 1790. His successor, Sir William, apparently refused to pay Soane his fee and expenses. In 1791, the architect once again turned over the troubled Tendring accounts to a lawyer. Counsel Norris of Lincoln's Inn recommended the formation of a board of arbitration on which George Dance sat as Soane's representative. In the end Soane was awarded £992.13.9 exclusive of his legal fees. The proceedings emphasize the precarious nature of Soane's professional transactions, founded as they were on a principle of mutual trust. Bankrupt architects were not unheard of at the period.[38] Clearly, architecture had become such a demanding business that the best possible financial and legal advice was necessary every step of the way.

It cannot be a coincidence that the formation of Soane's architectural office coincided with the twin commissions for Letton and Tendring coming in quick succession. The pressure of work, which had been building up for some time, reached a crest in that summer of 1784. On 1 September, John Sanders became Soane's first articled apprentice. John McDowell, sixteen years of age at the time, followed early in 1786. Thomas Chawner, David Laing, and Frederick Meyer joined the ranks of pupils in 1788, 1790, and 1791, respectively. Alongside them worked paid clerks like Thomas Neill, Edward Cocker, and Robert Woodgate.[39] In the later phases of the design and construction of Tendring, their names take on an ever bigger proportion of the day-to-day office duties. Drawings begin to appear that lack the master's touch. Account book entries are made in a variety of handwritings. Of the twenty-nine recorded on-site inspections of Tendring, an increasing number fall to the lot of these pupils and clerks. Thus Tendring comprises a microcosm of these essential assistants' activities. In 1780–84, the picture had been entirely different. Up until the articling of Sanders, Soane was alone. By a superhuman effort of determined will he managed by himself an ever enlarging business. Drawings, accounts, letters, visits to clients, inspections; he carried them all out himself. There was a limit to this sort of overextension, and Soane had reached it in 1784. Thereafter, the architect kept tight control, but the questions of collaboration and compromised standards enter in which could not have occurred before.

Tendring Hall, initiated before 1785, was Soane's final solo performance. It raised the curtain on his collaborative activities within the framework of an architectural office. For all that, it remained one of his typical smaller houses. Although room dimensions and designations fluctuated, the contract drawings provide a general physical description that runs something like this: capital brick mansion 68 feet 9 inches wide by 62 feet 9 inches deep; 4 reception rooms and 2 stairs; 19 bedrooms; 11 closets and dressing rooms; 2 water closets; vaulted kitchen; servants hall; cellars, etc. In fact the accommodation was less spacious than it sounds, because of the high ratio of bedrooms to reception areas. As far as can be determined, only three or four bedrooms were set aside for visiting guests; all the rest belonged to the large Rowley household, to the various members of which Soane assigned them. The Admiral's apartments were on the main floor; Mrs. Rowley's appear to have been upstairs. The entire attic storey was turned into a warren of bedrooms where the lower servants slept dormitory style, with separate rooms set apart for the housekeeper, butler, and head maid. Then came the Rowley children, seven in all, four boys and three girls. Master Joshua and Master Charles Rowley lived at the top of the house adjacent to the housekeeper. They were fifteen and fourteen, respectively, at the time construction began. William, the eldest son, and Captain Bartholomew Samuel, the next in line, were both in their early twenties. For them Soane set aside a bachelor apartment on a mezzanine, sandwiched between the main floor and the principal bedroom storey above. When William married in 1785 he presumably moved out. Arabella, Sarah, and Philadelphia Rowley had a suite of interconnecting rooms to themselves, though Sarah married in 1787 and left home. They, and their elder brothers located just below them, were the only ones provided with new-fangled water closets. It is interesting to note about Soane's planning that the children, old and young alike, were concentrated along with servants in the garrets and on one side of the house. Principal access to their rooms was by the common back stairs. The girls were nearest to their mother, but had to reach her through a network of indirectly connecting passageways. This arrangement, which Soane in his book singled out to praise for the privacy it provided, was perhaps the forerunner of the separate nursery wings of the next century. Things had not yet reached that degree of segregation at Tendring. It still serviced an entire household, servants and all, that slept under the same roof; hence the relatively compact size without sacrifice of privacy. This would soon change.

On a visit to Tendring in July 1787, Soane actually slept in the unfinished house. It must have been fully habitable soon thereafter, although the construction of offices, stables, and greenhouses dragged on for several years longer.[40] This was not the completion of the Tendring story, just the end of one of its phases. By late Victorian times, it had grown to almost twice its original size with the addition of sprawling wings off to the sides to accommodate the weekend hunting parties fashionable in that era. More reception rooms and separate servants quarters swelled Tendring.

From its peak of elephantine grandeur, around the turn of the century, Tendring began its long and steady decline along with the fortune of the Rowleys. During the Second World War the house was requisitioned for troops, a fate from which it never recovered. The tender mercies of the armed forces, coupled with the effects of deterioration that those years of neglect had brought on, made a sad wreck of a once fine house. At one point the late Raymond Erith, the architect, proposed valiantly to save the house by removing the later accretions, lopping off the decayed attic storey, and reducing the living space to manageable proportions.[41] The effort failed; Tendring is only a fading memory. With a strange prescience Thomas Pitt had written Soane that "There seems to be something ill-omen'd to you in the whole . . . Tendring Hall business." And he turned out to be right.

Conclusion

The House That Jack Built

UNLIKE MOST MAJOR ARCHITECTS OF HIS DAY, Soane had few material advantages to start life off with. It was only luck that blessed him as a child with a home environment conducive to book learning. It was an even greater stroke of luck that brought him to the attention of Dance, whose brilliant example first awakened in Soane the ambition to distinguish himself as an architect. Although he lacked Dance's manual gifts and genteel background, Soane aspired to combine Dance's suave artistry and amiable disposition. But the element of struggle to push himself forward naturally doomed Soane's whole effort. His aggressive side was to be further developed under Brown and Holland, who personified the business sense that Soane had found lacking in Dance. The two partners also introduced Soane to Robert Adam, perhaps the most gifted architect of his generation, and certainly the most calculating. Later still, Soane met the influential Chambers, friend of the king. The prosperity, prestige, and social respectability of these men fueled Soane's drive to get ahead; the extreme competitiveness of the Royal Academy Schools, and the scramble for patronage on the Grand Tour, only confirmed it.

An outcome of Soane's apprenticeship in the ways of the world was his openness to new ideas. This initial receptivity to the exploration of different styles, or to an outré order like the baseless Doric, earned him an ambivalent position in the hierarchy of British architecture. Reared in a thoroughly orthodox academic manner, later to become a pillar of that same establishment, his style eluded traditional categories and his thorny individuality lost him ready acceptance by fellow artists. He became controversial in spite of a yearning for universal admiration, manifest in his aggrieved reaction to criticism of his work, and in his love for applause by the public press. A predisposition to paranoia, perhaps aggravated by years of strain and overwork, increased as people or events turned against him when he ceased to be the star pupil and became

The story of Soane is, therefore, the story of the construction of a career: a career as integral, as precise in detail, and as deftly planned as any of his buildings.

John Summerson
Georgian London

317

instead a rival to his former mentors. The economic situation of his youth also reinforced Soane's disposition. In the depressed circumstances of the early 1780s an architect needed to be more aggressive than usual to make a start. Soane overcame an inauspicious climate by his willingness to work hard at any task, however small, by his ability to undertake new design problems however complex, and by his performance on the job.

Soane's rise to prominence was premeditated, but not unprincipled. He had achieved success the hard way himself, and we are sometimes inclined to forget that he always maintained a sympathy for the underdog, giving a helping hand to old acquaintances whom fortune had passed by. The moralizing James Peacock had instilled in him as a youth a strong ethical code. Mutual respect, Peacock argued, ought to underlie architects' relationships. This sense of common decency served as a golden rule to Soane when he was setting up business on his own. His behavior toward craftsmen and clients was exemplary. Lasting friendships with patrons and artisans often ensued. The basic ingredient of Soane's harmonious business transactions was his enviable reputation for integrity and reliability. The trouble with Soane was that he could also be quite intolerant of others' poor workmanship, laziness, or overcharging. This explains why he came to be on bad terms with many of his brother architects. They fought back by finding the flaws in Soane's armor, particularly his sensitivity on the subject of his humble origins. As a form of self-protection a certain deviousness crept into his nature at an early age. He began altering his signature, covering up facts, or distorting historical dates to support his claim to fame or to foil what he suspected was a collective plot against him. As I have shown, these tactics typify an age of more laissez-faire attitudes to artistic advancement than our own. It is easy to judge Soane harshly, harder by far to fathom the troubled inner wellsprings that gave rise to the deep sense of threat Soane felt during his entire career.

A part of Soane's furtive streak extended to what he regarded rightly as trade secrets. Are we not entitled to interpret his silence on the subject of his motivation and artistic inspiration as a sign of intentional reticence? The principles of his design theory only emerge indirectly from a detailed consideration of his works, rarely from his writings. Soane avoided committing his ideas to paper except in the form of revealing sketches or the occasional code word. There may even be a sense in which his theories were in part subconscious or at least not worked out methodically. He was quite outspoken, however, on the topic of "character." From Dance, Peacock, Chambers, and Professor Thomas

Sandby, Soane learned by word of mouth about the way in which appropriate expression might narrate a building's usage. Soane took the somewhat trite notion of "character" and applied it with characteristic rigor to all his work. He investigated the subtle nuances that "character" might take in a whole variety of structures, from dairies and dog houses to a triumphal bridge. He tried to involve the "character" directly with the building's smooth function, which was always of practical concern to him, whether in a cow barn or a great public waterworks.

Another fundamental element of Soane's designing was its eclecticism. An eclectic approach often typifies architectural beginners, and this was especially true in the Royal Academy Schools, where designing in that manner was encouraged. At its worst, the idea of recombining stylistic traits from the past can lead to extreme derivativeness. In the case of Soane, such ill-effects can be seen in his first book, rushed to meet a deadline and crammed with pastiches of Chambers's style. The eclectic ideal, however, can connote an educated and even witty picking and choosing from among approved examples. It also emphasizes original end products in which the artist's genius acts as a catalyst to unify diverse elements. At his best, Soane could absorb borrowings and produce designs of real distinction that hold up well in comparison with analogous works by such contemporaries as William Newton, Poma, Saint-Hubert, and James Paine the Younger.

In contrast to the conscious, rational eclecticism of the Royal Academy, there was an antirational theme contained in the teaching as well. Thomas Sandby exposed Soane to it when he introduced him to the aesthetic theory of the Sublime. Soane found in it justification for responding to a sweeping composition, or admiring the dramatic interplays of light and shade. Soane's emotional nature, largely kept in check by his strict professional demeanor, sometimes welled up in unexpected and ecstatic utterances about the power of an Alpine cascade or the splendor of an Easter procession in papal Rome. An architect might legitimately hope to capture some of this sublimity in the chiaroscuro effects of his own stairhalls, or in his processional axes. The Academy had handed down to Soane apparently conflicting credos. In a spirit of rational investigation he sought intellectually to construct a style of his own based on the best from the past. At the same time, in a spontaneous way, he sought to abandon himself to grandiose flights of the imagination that might rival the majesty of the elements. Soane inherited all the scientific rigor of a Neoclassicist, to which he added the increasingly strong surge of pre-Romanticism that would develop fully in the next century.

The young Soane's designs also reveal his "primitivist" persuasion. Seen in the broadest cultural perspective, primitivism can best be understood as an empirical preoccupation with the origins of things. Soane was a product of his times in his need to establish basic truths with his own eyes. He had to remeasure, to check his guidebook sources, and to probe beneath the surface. In a more restricted architectural sense, Soane's search led him back for inspiration to a prehistoric primitivism. At first this expressed itself literally in the form of imitations of Laugier's primitive hut. Ultimately he extended the principle to affect his production as a whole. On the basis of primitivism, with its implicit lack of preconceptions, he built up a style of his own. He grasped the fact that from a primitive touchstone, which assumed few or no conventions, true "novelty" might develop.

Why did the doctrine of primitivism strike such a fundamental chord of response in Soane's artistic makeup? My own conviction is that he adopted the credo so wholeheartedly because of an awareness of his limitations. His native gifts were not as startling as those of a Wyatt, a Dance, or an Adam. He had a definite weakness when it came to an eye for drawing, though he compensated with his head for figures. His inability to cope with inventing or rendering naturalistic ornament and his crude attempts at the human figure convinced him that discretion surely would be the better part of valor. He came to the realization that the route he should pursue lay in the direction of greater simplicity. He therefore rejected the fashionable Adamesque interiors of his day, in favor of a paring down of ornament to a few easily drawn geometric patterns like the bull's eye motifs in his distinctive chimneypiece designs. This tendency to "minimalism" found fully mature expression in the taut surfaces, pure geometry, and "negative," incised decoration of later works. It has also convinced some critics that Soane is a pioneer of "modern" architecture. Be that as it may, I have preferred to place him within his own milieu, in order to establish his progressiveness relative to his own day.

As has already been remarked, the young Soane had a prodigious facility for imitating styles. Early biographers mentioned his gift for picking up languages, and this ability seems to have extended into the realm of art. While working under Dance he learned the master's versatile grand manner. In the office of Brown and Holland, he familiarized himself with curvaceous planning and integrated decorative schemes. He began to master the styles appropriate to the range of utilitarian structures just becoming part of a trained architect's concern. In the Royal Academy and while abroad, Soane perfected the grand-prix approach to designing which he carried off with more than ordinary conviction. In itself, of course, this process of accumulating information would have led to a dead end had not Soane scrutinized the ideas he received. He was constantly sifting through the material to find what he could use as a means of self-expression. This explains why he settled on a few themes to exploit. The casino plan type was such an instance where Soane selected the house with a bombé facade as expressing the future trend toward greater compactness and elegance without loss of convenience. Soane hardly wavered from it throughout his long practice in domestic architecture. In this singleminded, persistent consistency Soane discovered the virtue of economy of means. Each new project offered an opportunity to test out and perfect his preferred plan type. Soane was in pursuit of an ultimate solution; there was no room for complacency, nor for capricious acceptance of new fads. Soane worked in a similar manner when honing down his exterior elevations until there was nothing left but sharp edges, clean-cut lines, and uncluttered surfaces. His preference for simple geometric shapes probably stemmed from the same predilection he had for lack of ornament. At one point, with his Grand Tourist designs of the early 1780s, Soane came close to a weak and affected manner. This was a momentary detour from the path he had chosen before he went abroad. His executed country houses are more indicative of the future turn of events. Some would dismiss these structures as simple to the point of dullness. Such an over-hasty judgment ignores the fact that all the ingredients were present for the later stripped-down, avant-garde style commonly associated with Soane's name. Through the study of his early period an awareness dawns that the mature and idiosyncratic Soane intensified ideas present before 1785.

In the less than thirty-three years covered by this book Soane had achieved a great deal even by reference to the "success stories" of his contemporaries. Not least of all he combined a levelheaded, businesslike attitude with his aspirations to great art. He had at his command accounting techniques learned from his early employers and then systematized into a kind of science. The effort and discipline required by his multiple bookkeeping procedures all written in his own hand demonstrates Soane's enormous capacity for hard work. Soane took balancing his books just as seriously as maintaining in good order his network of contacts with craftsmen and clients. There was, of course, a limit of endurance to these time-consuming personal activities. By 1784 he had reached the breaking point. He would have to relinquish to his staff more and more of the attention to detail he had made the hallmark of his success. But he modelled his office structure on the principles and the procedures he had laid down while working on his own. He thereby established a tight-knit office organization that would be the key to future achievement as his reputation grew. In this very direct sense everything that followed reflected the early experience he had gained: Soane's ambitious drive, code of ethics, design theory, radical style, and organizational ability would all culminate in the foundation of an efficient office. When his later works come to be studied in detail, they must be evaluated both in the light of the collaborative nature of his output after 1785 and in terms of his ideas formulated before that crucial year.

From an historiographical viewpoint, Soane's later triumphs—fascinating in their own right of course—are incidental to his early career, to which this study is devoted. What it loses in one regard it compensates for because his obsession with preserving even the tiniest scraps relevant to his past has made him beyond doubt the best representative example of a young eighteenth-century architect's life and times. And whenever comparative material does come to light, it constantly seems to confirm Soane's conduct as typical of his age: he reflected contemporary ethics, or the lack thereof; his deceitful plagiarisms and his pirating of others' works were common enough, as I have shown; his travels even followed a fairly routine pattern; and his domineering ambitiousness can be found as part of the ruthless atmosphere prevailing at home and abroad. The intensely competitive spirit that had arisen may also be related to a heightened historical self-awareness characteristic of the young architects we have studied. They seem to have been conscious of their place within a broad chronological framework. They saw themselves as distinct from the "ancient" past by virtue of developing a progressive "modern" art. To an unusual extent they have been shown to be aware of one another as well. Only such an explanation could account for the rapidity with which ideas passed from one artist to another. Perhaps there existed among these kindred minds an attunement so fine that it set off sympathetically a hum of artistic creativity.

In the final analysis, Soane's early career discloses the basic "modernity" of the eighteenth century. His career touches upon the foundation of our architectural profession with its uniform qualifications and standardized fees. His work in the public sector anticipates the growing role of government in great building works and the dawn of bridge engineering as a separate enterprise from architecture. At the other end of the spectrum, he gives us insights into the origins of housing for lower-income groups, or for the farm and the shop. His researches brought him into contact with such emerging institutions as the art museum, the penitentiary, and the psychiatric hospital much in the form we know them. Soane's uniquely preserved, richly varied legacy is enhanced by its broad applicability to concerns which continue, in a remarkable way, to unite him with us after the passage of two centuries.

Appendix 1

Sir John Soane's Family Tree

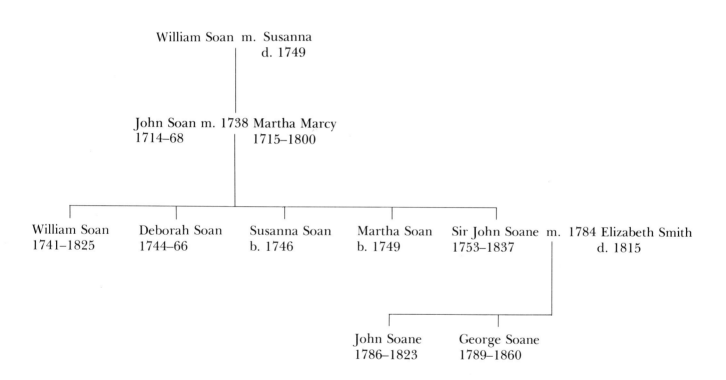

Appendix 2

Soane's Exhibits at the Royal Academy, 1772–85

Year	Catalogue Number	Title of the Drawing (with spellings modernized)
1772	315	*Front of a Nobleman's Townhouse*
1773	281	*Front, Next the Thames, of the Royal Academy, from Actual Measurements in 1770*
	282	*Garden Front of a Gentleman's Villa*
1774	296	*A Garden Building, Consisting of a Tea Room, Alcove, Bath, and Dressing Room to the Bath*
1775	298	*Elevation for a Townhouse*
	299	*Section through the Hall*
1776	289	*The Principal Facade and Plan of a Design for a Royal Academy*
1777	330	*Elevation of a Mausoleum to the Memory of James King, Esquire*
1779	308	*Plan, Elevation, and Section of a British Senate House*
1781	471	*Design for a Dog House*
	488	*Elevation of a Mausoleum*
	489	*Design for a Mausoleum*
	498	*Plan of a Mausoleum*
	524	*Plan and Elevation of a Hunting Casino*
1782	534	*Elevation of a Design for a Prison*
1783	362	*Design for a Gateway*
	367	*Design for a Dairy*
	388	*Design for an Observatory*
1784	420	*Gateway at Brancepeth Castle*
	471	*Blackfriars Bridge, Norwich*
	485	*Design for a Mausoleum*
	489	*Offices at Burn Hall*
	500	*Design for a Museum*
1785	496	*Front of a Villa Designed for a Gentleman in Norfolk*
	563	*Entrance Front of Burn Hall, the Seat of George Smith, Esquire*

Notes

LIST OF ABBREVIATIONS

BCV   Biblioteca Civica, Verona
BM   British Museum, London, Department of Manuscripts (unless otherwise stated)
BQS   Biblioteca Querini-Stampalia, Venice
CBB   Civica Biblioteca, Bergamo
CLRO   Corporation of London Record Office
FD   Joseph Farington diary (When available the volumes of the incomplete printed edition were used; otherwise the typescript in the BM, Prints and Drawings Department was referred to.)
GBB   Gosling's Branch, Barclays Bank, London
GLC   Greater London Council
HBLB   Hervey-Bruce letter book
HMST   Harrowby Manuscript Trust, Sandon Hall
IPT   Istituto Paolo Toschi, Parma
MC   Museo Correr, Venice
NNRO   Norfolk and Norwich Record Office, Norwich
PRO   Public Record Office, London
RA   Royal Academy, London
RCHM   Royal Commission on Historical Monuments
RIBA   Royal Institute of British Architects, London, Drawings Collection (unless otherwise stated)
SDSA   Society of Dilettanti Archives, Society of Antiquaries, London
SLW   St. Luke's Hospital, Woodside, London
SM   Soane Museum, London
  AL   Architectural Library
  CC   Correspondence Cupboard
  GL   General Library
  OSMAS   Original Sketches Miscellaneous Architectural Subjects
  PC   Pamphlet Cupboard
  SNBT   Soane Notebook Transcripts
SRO   Scottish Record Office, Edinburgh
V&A   Victoria and Albert Museum, London, Department of Prints and Drawings (unless otherwise stated)

1. SM, Soane Notebooks, 1–13, cover the period June 1781 until the end of 1784. The Downhill Notebook (SM, AL, Sir John Soane's Case, Shelf A) should be seen as a part of this series. It begins in late June 1780 and continues into the early months of the next year. I have referred to the originals throughout and have devised a pagination system for them. The entire group of nearly two hundred notebooks were transcribed in the form of a typescript (SNBT), which may be consulted in the Soane Museum and which I have used only for references after 1784. The transcription is both inaccurate and incomplete and therefore should be used with caution. The only comparable documents I know of the careers of contemporary architects are the printed diaries of Robert Mylne, published in A. E. Richardson's *Robert Mylne, Architect and Engineer* (London, 1955), and *The Virginia Journals of Benjamin Henry Latrobe* (2 vols.; New Haven, 1977). Latrobe would use foreign words to conceal personal remarks as did Soane.

2. The records of the Soans or Soanes of Swallowfield and Whitchurch are preserved in the parish registers of those villages, and I am grateful to the vicars concerned for making the relevant information available to me. An enclosure document of as recent a date as 1858 relates to John and James Soane of Shinfield near Swallowfield. (See the Berkshire Record Office Q/RDC. 91.) The case of Joseph Soanes, carver of chimneypieces, is better known because of his involvement with such houses as Audley End, Essex (Rupert Gunnis, *Dictionary of British Sculptors, 1660–1851,* p. 361), and Benham Park, Berkshire (SM, Copies of Bills 1785, pp. 78–80). It is an interesting fact that John Soane and Joseph his kinsman should have both been working on the same Berkshire building simultaneously, in their different capacities.

3. As an elderly man, Soane became sufficiently interested in his roots to make a pilgrimage to Basildon near Goring, where he "exd. register," presumably to see the birth notice of his mother. See SM, SNBT, 13, p. 76, entry for 4 September 1830. Most of the references to the births and marriages of the Soans of Goring are contained in Walter Money's *Stray Notes on the Parish of Basildon.* But the Vicar of Goring has helped me to enlarge upon Money's information.

4. Many, many instances of "corrected" Soane signatures exist among his papers, drawings, and books, and they prove very helpful for purposes of dating designs or library acquisitions. One of the *last* instances I have found of a dated autograph signature without the final *e* is on a drawing of 20 July 1784 (SM, AL, Cupboard 26, Folio 5, Item 15). After that the spelling "Soane" is uniformly accepted by architect and clients.

5. Parish register of St. Peter's Church, Chertsey, entry for 6 February 1800. See also the entry for 1 December 1825, recording the death of William Soan.

6. FD, p. 2028, entry for 12 May 1803, recorded the anecdote about young Soane from Thomas Daniell, artist and brother of the innkeeper of the Swan at Chertsey.

7. RA, Royal Academy Students Register 1769–1829, entry under S for 25

October 1771. Soane himself once wrote: "an accursed day, my birthday" (entry for 10 September 1818, SM, SNBT, 10, p. 67). For the various accounts of Soane's birthplace, see my *John Soane's Architectural Education,* p. 384, n. 6.

8. SM, CC 1, Division 2, T(14), Items 11–12, refer to the rental by a "Mr. Soane" in 1761 of a property belonging to Timothy Tyrrell. Item 13 in the same group is the letter from Soane to Tyrrell quoted at the beginning of this chapter. It is one of the rare Soane pieces of correspondence preserved in the Soane Museum and was presented by A. N. L. Munby in 1945. Soane and young Tyrrell probably were classmates and friends at Mr. Baker's Academy in Reading, which is supposedly where Soane was educated (see Thomas Leverton Donaldson, *A Review of the Professional Life of Sir John Soane,* p. 9). I am indebted to Mrs. Frances Jackson for sending me the Tyrrell family tree and other information pertaining to her ancestor Timothy Tyrrell (1753–1832), Rembrancer of the City of London.

9. SM, Soane Notebooks, 11, pp. 53 (used Tyrrell's horse), 55 (ate with Tyrrell); 13, p. 5 (paid Tyrrell for "Jack's school[in]g"). Jack Sanders's articles of apprenticeship, dated 27 November 1784, are witnessed by Tyrrell. See SM, CC 2, Division 15, C, Item 1 (cf. Arthur T. Bolton, *Architectural Education a Century Ago,* p. 12; on p. 17, Bolton notes that Tyrrell's son Charles also became a Soane pupil in 1811).

10. SM, Ledger A, pp. 40–41; Account Book 1781–86, p. 51, both record construction of this "new office."

11. John Soane, *Memoirs of the Professional Life of an Architect,* p. 11. The reference to Peacock and Chertsey also occurs in SNBT, 7, p. 54, entry for 26 July 1809. John Soane, *Lectures on Architecture,* p. 191, praised Peacock as "my late worthy and intelligent friend."

12. The text of the original marriage register was published by Arthur T. Bolton, *The Portrait of Sir John Soane,* p. 5. It was copied from the original records in the parish church of Christ Church, Blackfriars Bridge, London, which were subsequently destroyed by enemy action during World War II. The register index, however, is preserved in the GLC Record Office and confirms that the Soane-Smith wedding took place there and not in Surrey (as Bolton vaguely wrote), nor Lambeth (as stated by Dorothy Stroud, *The Architecture of Sir John Soane,* p. 24). Elizabeth Levick, who along with George Wyatt acted as witness at the wedding, was a daughter of Wyatt's niece Ann Levick. Ann inherited a property and sum of money under the terms of Wyatt's will (see n. 14 infra) and this in turn passed to Elizabeth, who kept in touch with Soane until her death in 1826 (SM, CC 2, Division 13, Part 1, A(19), Items 1, 3, 7, 8).

13. I know nothing of the background or parentage of Elizabeth Smith, later Mrs. John Soane. She died in 1815, aged 54 or 55, according to the pedigree prepared by Walter Spiers, curator of the Soane Museum and deposited in a letter file marked "Soane Personal." It appears she had a brother who died 23 May 1784 (SM, Soane Notebooks, 11, p. 35, "Brother of Miss S. died this morn"). Soane's courtship of "Eliza" and other details concerning the George Wyatts are furnished by Soane Notebooks, 10–12, passim. The sittings for her picture to

"Mr Dance" occurred on 4 and 6 May 1784. This would be "Mr [George] Dance" says Dorothy Stroud, *George Dance, Architect, 1741–1825,* p. 144. I think it more likely, however, that the architect's brother William, a miniaturist, is in question here. A miniature, traditionally identified as Mrs. Soane, is preserved in the Soane Museum, Strong Room, and, though it is faded, its style agrees well with a documented William Dance miniature that I have seen in the possession of the Misses Patteson. A miniature of Mrs. Soane by William Dance certainly did exist because John Jackson based his posthumous portrait of her upon it according to John Soane, *Description of the House and Museum* (1835), p. 21. Whether the 1784 sittings are to be identified with the badly faded miniature remains a moot point.

14. John Soane, *Plans, Elevations, and Perspective Views of Pitzhanger Manor House,* p. 3. George Wyatt's will of 15 December 1789 is PRO, P.C.C. 111 Bishop (PROB. 11/1189). Although Wyatt's obituary writer in the *Gentleman's Magazine* 60 (1790), pt. 1, p. 186, believed the deceased was a brother of the architect James Wyatt, this does not seem to have been credited by other writers of the period such as Donaldson (*Review of the Professional Life,* p. 14). Nor has it been accepted in the recent study by John Martin Robinson, *The Wyatts: An Architectural Dynasty* (Oxford, 1979), p. 55.

15. Donaldson, *Review of the Professional Life,* p. 9.

16. Soane, *Memoirs,* p. 19. For early signs of Soane's paranoia, see John Stuart's letter to the architect of 5 September 1780, in SM, CC 1, Division 4, S(3), Item 2, published in Bolton, *Portrait,* pp. 38–39.

17. SM, Soane Notebooks, 11, p. 3.

18. Stroud, *Dance,* p. 179, mentions the 1784 hanging committee. Almost certainly the "discourse" mentioned by Soane had to do with the cause célèbre of that year's exhibition. When the hanging committee refused to give pride of place to Thomas Gainsborough's portrait of the royal princesses, Gainsborough withdrew all his entries in a huff. See William T. Whitley, *Artists and Their Friends in England* (2 vols.; London, 1929), 1:400–401; and RA, Council Minutes, vol. 1, p. 358, entry for 11 April 1784.

19. Starting in mid-summer 1781, Soane rented a first- and second-floor apartment at 53 Margaret Street near Cavendish Square (SM, Soane Notebooks, 1, p. 5). For his subsequent moves, see Stroud, *Architecture of Sir John Soane,* pp. 23–24.

20. RA, General Assembly Minutes, vol. 1, p. 138.

21. *Royal Academy Exhibition Catalogue* (London, 1775), pp. 5, 18, listed stable buildings exhibited by William Blackburn and Thomas Leverton, respectively. These stables form a separate class of structure and are not farm buildings in the full sense that Soane's cow barn was.

22. See my article, "Oblivion for Soane's Cow Barn?" *Country Life* 159 (1976):84. But cf. Stroud, *Architecture of Sir John Soane,* p. 157, concerning Marlesford. The important topic of farm buildings was first discussed by Eileen Spiegel Harris, "The English Farm House: A Study in Architectural Theory and Design" (Ph.D. diss., Columbia University, 1960). Recently the scope of

research has been broadened by John Martin Robinson in his article "Model Farm Buildings of the Age of Improvement."

23. SM, Soane Notebooks, 6, pp. 6, 31. This Soane mausoleum design illustrated by me is in no way dated, but I ascribe it confidently to 1783/84 on the basis of style. A C. J. Richardson watercolor rendering of it, dated 1830, is in the V&A, 93 E.19, no. 3307.16. John Summerson, "Sir John Soane and the Furniture of Death," fig. 2 reproduces another version dated 1800.

24. For a list and exemplary discussion of mausolea exhibited at the RA, see Damie Stillman, "Death Defied and Honor Upheld: The Mausoleum in Neo-Classical England." Stillman, however, omitted Soane's 1784 mausoleum from his otherwise complete list.

25. Soane planned wings for Downhill in Northern Ireland, Allanbank in Scotland, and executed such extensions at Taverham in Norfolk, and at Malvern Hall. All these precede his first full house.

26. On Sanders at Malvern Hall, see SM, Soane Notebooks, 13, pp. 40, 46, entries for October 1784. It is interesting to observe that even before his official articles had been signed (see n. 9 supra), Sanders was working for Soane on a trial basis.

27. John Soane, *Plans, Elevations, and Sections of Buildings,* pl. 43. In the accompanying letterpress, Soane excused the lack of symmetry at Blackfriars on the grounds of the peculiar site.

28. Stroud, *Dance,* p. 143, gives an instance of Soane's "furtive streak," as she aptly describes it.

29. SM, Soane Notebooks, 12, p. 17, copying from the *Morning Chronicle* for 27 May 1789. I have been unable to locate a copy of the newspaper issue in question. The Brancepeth lodges were apparently never built. Certainly I saw none when I was kindly driven there by Dr. Peter Willis. The 1784 design, however, was resuscitated by Soane in 1796 as lodges for Lord Ducie, but again never constructed. The Ducie drawing is SM, Drawer 62, Set 8, Item 28, and has been discussed by Stroud, *Architecture of Sir John Soane,* p. 160.

30. SM, Soane Notebooks, 12, pp. 29–50, 52–53. And see Soane Notebooks, 13, pp. 24–35, for an example of a later and even more taxing Norfolk trip.

31. Taylor's habit of taking catnaps while en route was mentioned in his anonymous obituary in the *Gentleman's Magazine* 58 (1788), pt. 2, pp. 930–31. On James Wyatt's charges per mile, see FD, p. 278, entry for 2 January 1795; p. 914, entry for 2 November 1797; entry for 16 October 1805. These references are quoted in Frances Fergusson, "The Neo-Classical Architecture of James Wyatt" (2 vols.; Ph.D. diss., Harvard University, 1973), 1:39. Note should be taken, however, of Mrs. Soane's amazingly disloyal, if perhaps perceptive statement: "Mr. Soane was not to be compared with Mr. Wyatt as to ability, but had taken more pains than Mr. W. would do." See FD, p. 1529, entry for 29 March 1801.

32. SM, Soane Notebooks, 12, pp. 38, 45, gives details of the Branthwayte dinner party and the address of the Beauchamp-Proctors. Downhill Notebook, pp. 84–94, passim, lists Soane's desperate daily outpouring of letters in 1780 solicit-

ing work from clients whose addresses are often noted down.

33. SM, Soane Notebooks, 12, p. 47; 13, pp. 34, 50. See also Account Book 1781–86, p. 39, Ledger A, pp. 44–45, 98–99. On Langley's gate lodges, see Dorothy Stroud, "The Early Work of Soane," p. 122, and idem, *Architecture of Sir John Soane,* p. 32.

34. See the further accounts of this work in SM, Account Book 1781–86, p. 35; Journal 1, p. 128 left; Ledger A, p. 38. Stroud, *Architecture of Sir John Soane,* p. 157, suggests the stables were probably built. I tentatively agree with her. There is on the property today a half-ruined stable building of semicircular shape, comparable in style to Soane's curving Burn Hall cow barn. As at Burn Hall, Soane's designs could have been carried out by workmen locally. My researches among the Jerningham Papers at the Henry P. Huntington Library, San Marino, California, turned up only the fact that Sir William Jerningham was an avid sportsman.

35. Soane is given complete credit by Stroud, *Architecture of Sir John Soane,* pp. 31–32, and idem, "Early Work of Soane," p. 122. But Soane himself had written in *Plans, Elevations, and Sections:* "This edifice . . . was originally intended for a greenhouse, and completed for that purpose, but . . . since converted into a music room." Soane's annoyingly imprecise prose makes unclear the degree of his responsibility for the greenhouse. Howard M. Colvin, though he maintains a general attribution to Soane in his *Biographical Dictionary of British Architects, 1600–1814,* p. 768, in a letter to me of 13 July 1976 supports my interpretation of the exterior as being pre-Soane. Major Meade most courteously put up with my visits to Earsham. SM, Abstract of Bills 1782, pp. 24–25, Account Book 1781–86, pp. 45–46, and Ledger A, p. 122, cover the main entries relating to Earsham.

36. James Peacock (alias José MacPacke), *Oikidia; or, Nutshells,* p. 55. This statement on models is paraphrased by Soane, *Plans, Elevations, and Sections,* p. 6. Purchases of wooden models are recorded as follows: SM, Account Book 1781–86, p. 21 (Letton) and p. 47 (Saxlingham); Ledger A, p. 118 (Taverham); and the model of the Blackfriars Bridge centering is mentioned in Soane Notebooks, 6, p. 51 and billed for in Account Book 1781–86, p. 7. In the case of the models of Letton and the Taverham dining room, their London maker was named William Cooke, and he charged £6.11.4 and £0.16.8 for them, respectively. All this adds to the information in John Wilton-Ely's "The Architectural Models of Sir John Soane," *Architectural History* 12 (1969):5–38.

37. SM, Ledger A, p. 3.

38. For an example of Soane's social visits to clients, take the case of his outings to Rectory Manor, Walthamstow, at the invitation of the owner, William Cooke (SM, Soane Notebooks, 10, pp. 5, 27, 38, 40). Soane reciprocated with several dinner parties to which he invited the Cookes (SM, Soane Notebooks, 10, p. 31; 11, p. 1).

39. Soane's letter to Windham, of 3 January 1785, and his plan for redesigning the Earsham kitchens are SM, Drawer 4, Set 3, Item 1 verso and recto, respectively. Soane continued to work in various capacities for Windham until the

client's death in 1789. Elsewhere reference is made by Soane to a "Statue of Venus on a pedestal" in "chiar oscuro," and this surely refers to de Bruyn's painting either in the house or in the music pavilion (Soane Notebooks, 13, p. 50). Geoffrey Beard, *Georgian Craftsmen and Their Work* (London, 1966), p. 87, refers briefly to de Bruyn's career.

CHAPTER TWO

1. The earliest source for the date that I am aware of is George Richardson's *The New Vitruvius Britannicus* (2 vols.; London, 1802–8), 2:9. Richardson's informant was probably Soane himself, the owner of the house at the time of publication. Other information is contained in Arthur T. Bolton, *Pitzhanger Manor, Ealing Green* (London, n.d.); Mrs. Basil Holmes, *The Home of the Ealing Free Library: Notes on the History of the Manor House, Ealing Green* (Ealing, 1902), pp. 5–17; Dorothy Stroud, *George Dance, Architect, 1741–1825*, pp. 87–89; and Harold D. Kalman, "The Architecture of George Dance the Younger," pp. 76–78.

2. John Soane, *Plans, Elevations, and Perspective Views of Pitzhanger Manor House*, p. 5.

3. SM, AL, Sir John Soane's Case, "Extracts Hints etc. for Lectures on Architecture by J. Soane 1813 to 1818," p. 135.

4. Ibid., pp. 134–35. The Soane passage, quite unusually revealing for him, refers all in one breath to Ealing, the Arch of Constantine, Kedleston, and Italian villas. I am indebted to Susan G. Feinberg, "Sir John Soane's 'Museum': An Analysis of the Architect's House-Museum in Lincoln's Inn Fields, London," pp. 29–30, for bringing these manuscript references to my attention. Soane's personal knowledge of the Villa Medici can be deduced from Robert Furze Brettingham's letter to him of 22 December 1778. See SM, CC 1, Division 1, B(13), Item 2. The lion statues in the round, which Soane transformed into roundels, are discussed by Glen M. Andres, *The Villa Medici in Rome* (New York, 1976).

5. Stroud, *Dance*, p. 93, mentions that the owner of Cranbury was a noted coin and medal collector. It occurs to me that the medallic character of the Cranbury facade roundels has escaped notice as a typical instance of "narrative" architecture such as Dance used in other of his buildings. For a discussion of the roundels, see C. F. Bell, *Annals of Thomas Banks, Sculptor* (London, 1938), p. 54. And for a discussion of Soane's knowledge of Cranbury and his role in its completion, see chap. 14.

6. FD, entry for 2 August 1809, "Soane's admiration of Dance was excessive . . . , Soane always expressed a difficulty in opposing Dance."

7. Stroud, *Dance*, p. 88, quotes Mrs. Gurnell's letter to Dance. See also Harold D. Kalman's entry in *Catalogue of the Drawings Collection of the Royal Institute of British Architects*, vol. C–F (Farnborough, 1972), p. 61 [26].

8. An inscription, to the effect that Soane was residing on Chiswell Street, is on the back flyleaf of his copy of John Ward's *The Young Mathematician's Guide* (2d

ed.; London, 1713), which is in SM, AL, 34J. This address remained that of the Dance family home until 1775 according to Stroud, *Dance,* pp. 132–33.

9. Thomas Leverton Donaldson, *A Review of the Professional Life of Sir John Soane,* p. 9, implied Soane could not afford the expensive premium that an articled pupil paid to a master to take him on.

10. Arthur T. Bolton, in his official capacity as curator of the Soane Museum, strenuously opposed the idea that Soane had acted in a servile capacity for Dance. See Bolton's *Works of Sir John Soane,* p. xxii, and his letter to James Greig, editor of the published version of *The Farington Diary* (8 vols.; London, 1922–28), 4:46. All this notwithstanding, Farington recorded from the lips of Nathaniel Dance what to Bolton was a damnable statement: "He well remembered Soane, being a Servant in Dance's House when a youth and had himself been with Him often in the Kitchen when He was cleaning the Shoes etc." See FD, entry for 12 November 1806. Reprehensible though Farington's slanderous motives may have been, I tend to accept the *essential* truth of these anecdotes.

11. CLRO, Repertories, 172–74 (1768–70), simply record the order for setting up the Guildhall for the annual banquet, and give no details that help pinpoint a dating for Soane's drawing. Kalman, "Dance," p. 23, first drew attention to it, but errs in giving to Soane the written inscription on the sheet addressed to his superior, William Mountague. The handwriting of the instructions is not Soane's.

12. John Soane, *A Statement of Facts,* p. 5.

13. Soane, as will be seen, preempted Dance's motto on several occasions for a personal watchword.

14. The classic discussions of Soane and Dance were written by John Summerson, "Soane: The Case-History of a Personal Style," and idem, *Sir John Soane.* Georges Teyssot, *Città e utopia,* has interpreted some of the same evidence in a different way.

15. This key Dance statement, made with reference to Thomas Hope's house in London, was recorded by Dance's friend, Joseph Farington in FD, p. 2286, entry for 31 March 1804.

16. The verdict of the Parmesan jury, now lost, is recorded by Samuel Angell, "Sketch of the Professional Life of George Dance, Architect, R.A.," *Builder* 5 (1847):334. Soane's comments on All Hallows are contained in his *Lectures on Architecture,* p. 53. For Cockerell's appreciation of Dance, see FD, p. 1087, entry for 10 November 1798.

17. James Peacock's *Subordinates in Architecture,* is facetiously dedicated to Dance "after whom the author had the honor of carrying the hod for more than forty years." For other instances of Peacock's mocking self-denigration, see Arthur T. Bolton, *The Portrait of Sir John Soane,* p. 98.

18. John Soane, *Memoirs of the Professional Life of an Architect,* p. 11. Stroud, *Dance,* p. 89, suggests Dance and Peacock knew one another before the 1768 Pitzhanger commission, and I agree with her.

19. James Peacock (alias José MacPacke), *Oikidia; or, Nutshells,* pp. 3–4. For an appreciation of *Oikidia*'s importance, see Sandra Blutman, "Books of Designs for

Country Houses, 1780–1815," *Architectural History* 11 (1968):26. In James Peacock's *Proposals for a Magnificent and Interesting Establishment* (London, 1790), pp. 22–23, he takes responsibility for the anonymous pamphlet entitled *The Outlines of a Scheme for the General Relief, Instruction, Employment, and Maintenance of the Poor, etc.* (London, 1777). I have found a copy in Columbia University Library and the pronounced, distinctive style of writing seems similar to me to that of the *Essay*. A review of the *Outlines* appeared in the *London Review of English and Foreign Literature* 8 (1778), pt. 2, pp. 156–62.

20. Compare, for example, the following close paraphrases: "if . . . I should *seem* to make a few digressions, I beg the reader's indulgence, and flatter myself he will not find them wholly foreign to the point in hand" (*Essay*, pp. iv–v); "it is hoped, the step or two he may take out of the main path, may lead him to something, not totally uninteresting, or unconnected with the matter in hand" (*Oikidia*, pp. 51–52).

21. Peacock, *Subordinates*, p. 86, makes similar points about the supply of inferior materials without, however, resorting to any word-for-word self-plagiary.

22. The *Essay* had been first attributed to Dance by Richard Pennington, "Dance the Younger and the Architectural Profession," *Journal of the Royal Institute of British Architects* 42 (1935):648. This attribution has been accepted in the subsequent literature. Harold D. Kalman, "Newgate Prison," p. 59, n. 13, has so far been the only scholar to question Dance's authorship. Teyssot, *Città e utopia*, p. 158, notes Kalman's tentative attribution to Peacock rather than Dance. But Kalman, in a letter to me of 25 July 1969, went so far as to give the text outright to Peacock.

23. *Essay*, pp. 17–18; the italics are mine, but otherwise this is a substantially correct quotation by the essayist from Sir Henry Wotton's *The Elements of Architecture* (London, 1624), p. 23. That members of Dance's office liked to tease him is borne out by SM, Soane Notebooks, 1, p. 25, in which Soane quotes a 1781 punning allusion to the print after Nathaniel Dance of the ballet master Vestris, called in a quatrain "le dieu de danse." See David Goodreau, *Nathaniel Dance, 1735–1811* (London, 1977), item 45 in the catalogue, who illustrates and discusses Nathaniel Dance's print, but is not aware of the punning poem quoted by Soane (the text was published by Arthur T. Bolton, "St. Luke's Hospital, Old Street," p. 200). I should point out that Wotton's maxim is also quoted by Peacock, *Oikidia*, p. 66, where it is ascribed to Dr. Thomas Fuller. Here Peacock may allude to a physician named Thomas, whose *Gnomologia: Adagies and Proverbs; Wise Sentences and Witty Sayings, Ancient and Modern, Foreign and British* (London, 1732) is an unindexed volume of 6,496 adages. Seeking to verify Peacock's contention was like finding the proverbial needle in a haystack. More likely Peacock was referring to Dr. Thomas Fuller, D.D. If so he was mistaken, because Fuller's early aphorisms "of building" contain no such statement. See Fuller's *The Holy State and the Profane State* (London, 1642). I am still at a loss to explain how the author would cite the *correct* source in the 1773 *Essay,* and a *different* one in *Oikidia*. I do not consider this sufficient reason to exclude Peacock from authorship of the *Essay*.

24. Kalman, "Newgate Prison," pp. 51 and 59, nn. 13–14, summarizes the history of the Newgate dispute and the respective roles played by Dance, and his two assistants Peacock and Robert Baldwin, both of whom claimed the right to succeed Dance in his post. Baldwin's candidacy appeared in *The Morning Chronicle and London Advertiser,* no. 1,347 (16 September 1773) and in a broadsheet of the twenty-first of that month he replied to Peacock's own hostile broadsheet. I am grateful to Jeffrey Cook for a copy of the latter, the original of which is SM, CC 1, Division 3, D(5). In the event, Dance withdrew his resignation.

25. *Essay,* pp. 10–11.

26. Ibid., pp. 13–14. These passages are extensively quoted in Barrington Kaye, *The Development of the Architectural Profession in Britain,* pp. 48–49. Donaldson, *Review of the Professional Life,* p. 8, commented on Soane's ability as a linguist. In proof of this, see Soane's annotated copy of Jean-Jacques Rousseau's *Julie ou la nouvelle Hélöise* (SM, GL, 26H).

27. *Essay,* p. 38. Peacock's now-lost epitaph, as quoted by Stroud, *Dance,* p. 246, described him as a man of "great talent, inflexible integrity, universal benevolence, Christian piety and unaffected humility." Peacock's later letters to Soane combine paternal solicitude with a punster's joviality. See SM, CC 1, Division 2, P(5), Items 1–7. Peacock's "virtues and moral excellence" were paid tribute to in Joseph Gwilt's introduction to his edition of William Chambers's *Treatise on the Decorative Part of Civil Architecture* (4th ed.; London, 1825).

28. Soane, *Memoirs,* p. 11.

29. Stroud, *Dance,* p. 137 and pl. 43b; see also Harold D. Kalman's relevant entries in the *Catalogue of the Drawings Collection of the Royal Institute of British Architects,* vol. C–F (Farnborough, 1972), p. 60 [3, 7].

30. Peacock, *Oikidia,* p. 68.

31. Soane, *Memoirs,* p. 11.

32. Ibid., p. 29, Soane attributed the reason for not being appointed Surveyor of St. Paul's Cathedral to his having been "brought up as a hack in Mr. Dance's office." See also FD, p. 254, entry for 10 October 1794, where the humor takes a sadistic turn: "Soane the architect was foot Boy to George Dance, who encouraged an inclination He discovered in him for drawing. The remembrance of his former situation in *Dances Office* among the young men, rendered his situation rather unpleasant. He removed to Holland and was his Clerk."

33. John Soane, *Description of the House and Museum* (1830), p. 40. This amount of salary seems to be confirmed by the account of Henry Holland and Son, as well as the personal accounts of both father and son, which are among the bound ledgers of the GBB, vols. 47, 50, 54, 58 passim.

34. The earliest surviving letter from a client to Soane is addressed to Henry Holland's on Hertford Street and is franked 4 July. The correspondent was John Stuart of Allanbank, and the year can be supplied as 1780 on the basis of a reference to the recent loss of Soane's trunk in Switzerland. See SM, CC 1, Division 4, S(3), Item 75.

35. For these commissions, see Dorothy Stroud, *Henry Holland, His Life and*

Architecture, Howard M. Colvin, *Biographical Dictionary of British Architects, 1600–1840,* and my n. 19 of chap. 12 regarding Hill Park.

36. Stroud, *Holland,* pp. 31–32, and idem, *Capability Brown,* p. 168.

37. FD, p. 275, entry for 14 December 1794. As for Soane, his only remark about his move to Holland's office was a perfunctory one. Otherwise he remained virtually silent about the years spent with Brown and Holland.

38. Stroud, *Holland,* pp. 32–34 quotes from the documentation in SM, Copies of Bills 1785, pp. 23–37 and 38–42. The originals of the two estimates for Claremont are also in SM, CC 1, Division 4, W(9ª), Items 3–4.

39. SM, AL, Sir John Soane's Case, Shelf A, "R. Pearce Price Book"; "Soane Price Book 1772–82."

40. "Soane Price Book 1772–82," pp. 90–124, 126.

41. SM, CC 2, Division 14, B(1), Items 1ª and 1ᵇ (letters of ca. 1776 and of 1 August 1778); cf. Bolton, *Portrait,* pp. 15–16.

42. See n. 38 supra. The interior estimate is undated, but presumably quite late in the building campaign because it explicitly describes the entrance hall, which Soane claimed a part in.

43. John Soane, *Designs for Public and Private Buildings* (1832), p. 39, and see his *Memoirs,* p. 15, where he seems to take complete credit for the design.

44. Arthur T. Bolton, *The Architecture of Robert and James Adam 1758–1794* (2 vols.; London, 1922) 1:172, discusses Harewood. But see the recent guide to the house for the repainting of the columns. Damie Stillman, *Decorative Work of Robert Adam,* pp. 71–72, deals with Newby and cites Adam's general opinion on the propriety of Doric in halls. Geoffrey Beard, *Georgian Craftsmen and Their Work* (London, 1966), pl. 115, gives the date for Newby, which is confirmed by John Cornforth, "Newby Hall II" *Country Life* 165 (1979):1918–19.

45. Stroud, *Holland,* p. 34.

46. SM, AL, Sir John Soane's Case, Shelf A, "Extracts from various Authors on Architecture," p. 44, and see also pp. 44–45, for other precepts learned at Claremont.

47. Soane, *Lectures,* p. 149; and see idem, *An Appeal to the Public,* p. 30.

48. John Summerson, *A New Description of Sir John Soane's Museum,* p. 64.

49. Robert and James Adam, *The Works in Architecture of Robert and James Adam,* introduction to vol. 1 (London, 1773). For a discussion of some of these concepts, see David C. Huntington, "Robert Adam's *Mise-en-Scène* for the Human Figure," *Journal of the Society of Architectural Historians* 27 (1968):249–63.

50. The drawing was first published by Dorothy Stroud. It is one of two. The other has flat pilasters and a more decorative mural treatment. See "A Capability Brown Discovery," *Country Life* 121 (1957):60–65. I was kindly permitted to consult the album by Lady Mary Clive of Whitfield, Herefordshire, and I have reproduced both schemes fully in my *John Soane's Architectural Education, 1753–80,* pls. 9–10.

51. Stroud, *Holland,* pp. 37–38, still remains the clearest discussion of the tribune. See also Sandra Millikin, "The Tribune in English Architecture," *Bur-*

lington Magazine 112 (1970):442–46. The derivation of the term *tribune* comes from the "Tribuna" room in the Uffizi, Florence.

52. *Essay*, p. 35.

CHAPTER THREE

1. Charles Newenham French, *The Story of St. Luke's Hospital*, pp. 10–30, is based on St. Luke's records of the first building. And see also Dorothy Stroud, *George Dance, Architect, 1741–1825*, pp. 49–50, which stresses information from the minutes of the City Lands Committee. Of more marginal interest is Courtney Dainton's *The Story of England's Hospitals* (London, 1961).

2. French, *St. Luke's*, p. 23; Stroud, *Dance*, p. 141, and SLW, General Committee Book 1775–1804, entry for 1 May 1776.

3. Michel Foucault, *Histoire de la folie*, p. 104.

4. SLW, General Committee Book 1775–1804. French, *St. Luke's*, pp. 27–28, gives a substantially correct account. Like his father before him, George Dance the Younger reputedly worked without fee.

5. On the subject of the Blackfriars Bridge competition, see Robert Scott Mylne, *The Master Masons to the Crown of Scotland and Their Works* (Edinburgh, 1893), pp. 264–65. See also Edward McParland, "James Gandon and the Royal Exchange Competition, 1768–69," *Journal of the Royal Society of Antiquaries of Ireland* 102 (1972):58–72.

6. *The Public Advertiser*, nos. 13,270 and 13,273 (25 April and 29 April 1777); *The Daily Advertiser*, nos. 14,460 and 14,487 (22 April and 23 May 1777).

7. According to *The Royal Academy Exhibition Catalogue* (London, 1777), p. 3, John Alefounder the Younger showed a "design for a lunatic hospital." The opening date of the exhibition was 24 April, and thus it occurred at exactly the moment of the first *official* announcement of a St. Luke's competition. But Alefounder's father was at the time district surveyor of the parish of St. Luke, Old Street (see Howard M. Colvin, *Biographical Dictionary of British Architects, 1600–1840*, p. 64). Hence the younger Alefounder may unofficially have gotten wind of an impending competition.

8. *The Daily Advertiser*, no. 14,500 (7 June 1777).

9. Gandon's memoirs are published in Thomas J. Mulvany, *The Life of James Gandon*, pp. 37–39 and 220. Gandon also exhibited designs in the *Royal Academy Exhibition Catalogue* (London, 1778), p. 10. But Gandon's vague nomenclature confused Edward Geoffrey O'Donoghue, *The Story of Bethlehem Hospital*, pp. 310–12; Maurice Craig in his unpaginated introduction to the reprint edition of Mulvany; and also Frank Jenkins, *Architect and Patron*, pp. 155–56.

10. Mulvany, *Gandon*, p. 38.

11. See Colvin, *Biographical Dictionary*, p. 518.

12. The attribution to Dance is maintained by Stroud, *Dance*, pp. 141–42, who produced a dating of 1781–82. Only Harold D. Kalman, "The Architecture of George Dance the Younger," pp. 104–5, indirectly suggested an earlier dating by drawing attention to James Lewis's designs of 1777.

13. See O'Donoghue, *Bethlehem Hospital,* and M. I. Batten, "The Architecture of Dr. Robert Hooke, F.R.S.," *Walpole Society* 25 (1936–37):83–113, especially pp. 91–92.

14. *The Daily Advertiser,* no. 14,517, announced that all contestants might collect their drawings and "receive their answers to the same."

15. I am grateful to Dr. Edward Teitelman, M.D., for showing me a copy of Bevans's letter to William Tuke of 27 February 1794 and for discussing with me the development of the moral treatment window from that of St. Luke's. References to the Retreat may be found in Helen Rosenau, *Social Purpose in Architecture,* pp. 73–75; Nikolaus Pevsner, *A History of Building Types,* pp. 148–49; John D. Thompson and Grace Goldin, *The Hospital: A Social and Architectural History,* pp. 71–74.

16. The printed *Catalogue of the Drawings Collection of the Royal Institute of British Architects,* vol. L–N (Farnborough, 1973), p. 142 [79], simply lists Newton's drawing as for "a prison or lunatic asylum."

17. William Battie, *A Treatise on Madness,* p. 93. For a general discussion of Battie's principles, see Richard Hunter and Ida MacAlpine, *Three Hundred Years of Psychiatry, 1535–1860,* pp. 402–8.

18. Charles Lucas, *An Essay on Waters* (London, 1756), p. 218. An interesting if coincidental precedent for Newton's bathhouse is an unpublished Serlio design, which appears in the facsimile edition of his sixth book, *Sebastiano Serlio on Domestic Architecture* (Cambridge, Mass., 1978), pl. 33.

19. On baths and bathing in asylums, see O'Donoghue, *Bethlehem Hospital,* p. 224; French, *St. Luke's,* p. 13, who mentions a bill of £13 in 1752 for fitting up a cold bath; and Hunter and MacAlpine, *Three Hundred Years of Psychiatry,* pp. 254–56, 309, and 325–26, who quote from various early accounts of hydrotherapy in the treatment of mental illness. See also Foucault, *Histoire de la folie,* pp. 162–70.

20. Battie, *Treatise on Madness,* pp. 91–92 and 96. But cf. Hunter and MacAlpine, *Three Hundred Years of Psychiatry,* p. 405, who speak of Battie's "blunt strictures on contemporary methods." In reply to Battie, Dr. John Monro brought out *Remarks on Dr. Battie's Treatise on Madness* (London, 1758). Monro praised outright the "excellent effect" of cold bathing (quoted by Hunter and MacAlpine, p. 416).

21. Algernon Graves, *The Society of Artists,* p. 148.

22. SM, AL, 5D, *Original Designs in Architecture* (London, 1780 and 1797), is Soane's copy of Lewis, with caustic marginal comments by him about the author's fear of novelty.

23. Ibid., key to plate on p. 14 of vol. 2.

24. Battie, *Treatise on Madness,* pp. 90–91.

25. Arthur T. Bolton, "St. Luke's Hospital, Old Street," pp. 197–201, first drew attention to and illustrated Soane's two schemes, and saw correctly the relative chronology of them. But Bolton, despite suspicions of a competition (p. 198), dated Soane's schemes together with those of Dance to the years 1781–82. Bolton (pl. op. p. 200) redrew the elevations of Soane's two schemes and in-

cluded a third, quite out of place, which was Soane's design for a female penitentiary (see my chap. 10).

26. *Reasons for the Establishing of St. Luke's Hospital for Lunatics together with the Rules and Orders for the Government thereof* (London, 1751), rule 35; Battie, *Treatise on Madness*, p. 68.

27. John Summerson, *A New Description of Sir John Soane's Museum*, pp. 19–20, gives details of Soane's purchase of the *Rake's Progress*. For further details, see Ronald Paulson, *Hogarth: His Life, Art, and Times* (2 vols.; New Haven, 1971), 1:326–27.

28. Mulvany, *Gandon*, p. 39.

29. John Summerson, *Georgian London*, pp. 119–20, discusses the growth of London's hospitals, as does A. G. L. Ives, *British Hospitals* (London, 1948).

30. The handwriting by Soane on this drawing (SM, Drawer 62, Set 10, Item 3) matches exactly the style of his 1777 St. Luke's inscriptions. For the Middlesex Hospital, see Thompson and Goldin, *The Hospital*, p. 91 and figs. 98–99.

31. David Watkin, *Thomas Hope*, pp. 245–49, provides a useful list of early revivals of the baseless Doric order in Europe (he does not mention Soane's St. Luke's scheme).

32. Antony Dale, *James Wyatt, Architect, 1746–1813* (Oxford, 1936), pp. 32–33, defines the Wyatt window-type. It made a notable appearance in the Radcliffe Observatory at Oxford, begun by him in 1773.

33. Margaret Whinney, *Sculpture in Britain, 1530 to 1830* (London, 1964), p. 49, and p. 247, n. 8, maintains the traditional attribution of these statues to Caius Gabriel Cibber, despite Robert Hooke's diary entry mentioning Thomas Cartwright as the sculptor.

34. The quotation is by Ned Ward the satirist writing around 1700. See Edward Ward, *The London Spy: The Vanities and Vices of the Town Exposed to View* (London, 1927), p. 52.

35. The other drawing, SM, Dance Cabinet, Slider 4, Set 1, Item 2, is less complete. As yet no evidence exists to tie possible St. Luke's entries with specific architects. In a circumstantial way, however, I feel it likely that John Dotchen and Thomas Whetten also contributed designs. Whetten showed a "hospital" at the Royal Academy in 1778 and Dotchen showed a "design for a lunatic hospital" four years later. See *Royal Academy Exhibition Catalogue* (London), p. 25 (1778) and p. 17 (1782).

36. The motif of a spiral strigilated topknot is also used by Soane in *Designs in Architecture*, pls. v, xvi, which derive from such precedents as Chambers's Franco-Italian Album (V&A 93.B.21) Item 342.

37. John Soane, *Appeal to the Public*, pp. 44–45, and idem, *Memoirs of the Professional Life of an Architect*, p. 21.

38. See n. 24 of my chap. 8.

39. John Soane, *Description of the House and Museum* (1830), pp. 37–38. The passage, which is quoted more fully on the first page of this chapter, refers to the "Million Churches" competition of ca. 1818. Soane claims to have made the statement in one of his Royal Academy lectures. This would be the fifth lecture

according to Gerald Carr, "Soane's Specimen Church Designs of 1818: A Reconsideration," *Architectural History* 16 (1973):50, n. 43. No such reference appears in the published version of the lectures.

40. On Soane's indebtedness to Dance, see in particular John Summerson, "Soane: The Case-History of a Personal Style," 83–91; idem, *Sir John Soane;* and Helen Rosenau, "George Dance the Younger," *Journal of the Royal Institute of British Architects* 54 (1947–48):502–7.

41. Georges Teyssot, *Città e utopia,* p. 160, was lead incorrectly to identify the drawing SM, AL, OSMAS, Item 169, as being for St. Luke's (a note to that effect was inscribed on the drawing in Arthur T. Bolton's hand). The verso is addressed to Soane at Henry Holland's on Hertford Street in London and is franked from Reading, Berkshire. The natural conclusion is that the drawing pertains to toilets at Benham, near Reading, of which it is known there were two (see SM, AL, Copies of Bills 1785, p. 65, for an estimate dated 1775).

42. Invitations to Gandon to apply for the Royal Academy Rome prize in 1772 and again in 1790 are recorded in RA, Council Minutes, vol. 1, p. 135; ibid., vol. 2, p. 95 (also see Mulvany, *Gandon,* p. 120).

CHAPTER FOUR

1. Nikolaus Pevsner, *Academies of Art Past and Present* (Cambridge, 1940), pp. 140–42, gives the vital statistics on the growth rate of eighteenth-century academies.

2. The standard histories are: William Sandby, *The History of the Royal Academy of Arts* (2 vols.; London, 1862); John Evans Hodgson and Fred A. Eaton, *The Royal Academy and Its Members, 1768–1830* (New York, 1905); Sidney C. Hutchison, *The History of the Royal Academy, 1768–1968* (London, 1968).

3. RA, Council Minutes, vol. 1 (1768–84), pp. 111–12. See also, Sidney C. Hutchison, "The Royal Academy Schools, 1768–1830," p. 137.

4. Arthur T. Bolton, *The Portrait of Sir John Soane,* p. 10, alludes to Dance's tardiness in joining the Royal Academy. John Soane, *Memoirs of the Professional Life of an Architect,* p. 30, obliquely hinted at what he saw as this discredit to Dance's reputation.

5. On the probability of a probationary period in the Academy Schools, see Humphrey C. Morgan, "A History of the Organisation and Growth of the Royal Academy Schools . . . to 1836" (Master's thesis, University of Leeds, 1964), pp. 36–39.

6. The announcement of the silver medal subject was made 7 January 1771 (RA, Council Minutes, vol. 1, pp. 95–96), by which time Somerset House was already described as the Royal Academy headquarters.

7. Letter from John Deare to his father, 24 March 1777, cited in John Thomas Smith, *Nollekens and His Times,* ed. Wilfred Whitten (4th ed.; 2 vols.; London and New York, 1920), 2:237.

8. John Harris, *Sir William Chambers,* p. 105, and Sidney C. Hutchison, *The Homes of the Royal Academy* (London, 1956), p. 10.

9. Henry Lemonnier, ed., *Procès verbaux de l'académie royale d'architecture* 9:51, notes a student complaint of 1781 about small drafting space and large-scale drawings.

10. RA, Council Minutes, vol. 1, p. 119. I am not inclined to follow my friend John Wilton-Ely's somewhat negative appraisal of architectural teaching in the Schools, as voiced in his "Rise of the Professional Architect in England," *The Architect: Chapters in the History of the Profession*, ed. Spiro Kostof (New York, 1977), pp. 191–92.

11. Joshua Reynolds, *The Letters of Sir Joshua Reynolds,* ed. Frederick Whiley Hilles (Cambridge, 1929), p. 23. The RA, Cash Book, vol. 1 (1769–94), carries the references to Chambers's book buying expedition (21 May 1774 and an undated entry for 1775, which lists some titles).

12. RA, Council Minutes, vol. 1, p. 162, entry for 22 October 1773, states: "that the Day of the Library being open be changed from Wednesday to Monday."

13. This humorous vignette of Academy life, reported by a former student, John Bannister, is published in Henry Angelo's, *Reminiscences of Henry Angelo, with Memoirs of His Late Father and Friends* (2 vols.; London, 1828–30), 1:254–55. Richard Wilson was Academy librarian from 1776, when he succeeded Francis Hayman, until his death in 1782.

14. John Summerson, *A New Description of Sir John Soane's Museum*, p. 73.

15. These books are all in SM, AL, 34 I or J. On the flyleaf of another, Benjamin Martin's, *The Young Student's Memorial Book, or Pocket Library* (London, 1736), Soane signed himself "Philom[ath]."

16. For a general idea of Soane's book collection as it stood around 1783, see appendix B of my *John Soane's Architectural Education, 1753–80*. Certain architectural titles were presented as gifts to the architect. These include Vitruvius's *De Architectura* (SM, AL, 42C) and Palladio's *I Quattro libri dell'architettura* (SM, AL, Sir John Soane's Case, Shelf B), both presented in 1778 by the Bishop of Derry; Matthew Brettingham the Younger's *The Plans, Elevations, and Sections of Holkham* (SM, AL, 4B), presented by its author.

17. SM, AL, 15, inscribed "John Soane [*e* added] 1780" and "Pd. for Soane 3 Gui[neas]."

18. SM, AL, Sir John Soane's Case, Shelf A. The notebook must date from before 1773 because at the end of it is a bill referring to ca. 1772–73 work on the Chandois Street London townhouse of Henry Holland's brother-in-law, Leonard Tresilian (see SM, Copies of Bills 1785, pp. 82–84, and Westminster Public Library, St. Paul's Covent Garden Rate Books, 1770–74, p. 10, for alterations to Tresilian's house).

19. Take, for example, the aphorism Soane quoted from Ganganelli: "There are two rocks to be shunned; that of believing too much and that of not believing enough." See SM, AL, Sir John Soane's Case, Shelf A, "MSS. Extracts from various Authors 1776. J. Soane," p. 15; and compare Giovanni Vincenzo Antonio Ganganelli, *Interesting Letters of Pope Clement XIV (Ganganelli)* (2 vols.; Lon-

don, 1777), 1:123. SM, GL, 28G, contains the copy of this edition actually used by Soane.

20. Soane, "Extracts from Various Authors on Architecture," p. 17 ("Mr. Sandby says that the Doric Order should have its Mutules, the Ionic its Dentils, and the Corinthian and Composite their Modiglions"). See also n. 18 supra.

21. Extracts from a Sandby letter of 4 September 1769, asking William Chambers's advice were published in the catalogues of the autograph dealers, Maggs Brothers, of London, in 1925 and 1927. At a meeting of 7 October 1769, Sandby read the text of his first and second lectures which were approved (RA, Council Minutes, vol. 1, p. 42). Copies of the lectures were to be left on deposit for consultation, and the first course began 9 October 1769 (ibid., p. 41).

22. *Daily Advertiser*, no. 12,436, 3 November 1770, gives the dates of the second architectural lecture as 5 November 1770, and from this the 8 October date can be deduced, because the various professors gave lectures in rotation. On Chambers's lectures, see n. 32 infra.

23. SM, AL, 31B, Sandby Lecture 1, pp. 74–75. This volume, copied from the one in the RIBA Library, contains the full series of six lectures transcribed by Soane and his assistants in preparation for Soane's own lectures as RA Professor of Architecture.

24. RIBA, Library, Sandby Lecture 2, p. 36.

25. SM, Sandby Lecture 6, p. 4, refers to Burke indirectly as a "very ingenious Gentleman." I have discussed Sandby's reliance on Burke in my review of John Harris, *A Catalogue of British Drawings for Architecture . . . in American Collections,* in *Studies in Burke and His Time* 15 (1974):305–9. Burke championed the Royal Academy and maintained a close friendship with William Chambers (Harris, *Chambers,* pp. 96–98).

26. John Soane, *Lectures on Architecture,* p. 91.

27. Edmund Burke, *A Philosophical Enquiry into the Origin of Our Ideas of the Sublime and Beautiful,* pp. 96–97. Sandby's original side elevation, stretching 16 feet in length, is discussed in the Council of Europe's exhibition catalogue *The Age of Neo-Classicism,* p. 622, and *Catalogue of the Drawings Collection of the Royal Institute of British Architects,* vol. S (Farnborough, 1976), p. 18 [3]. Though first exhibited in the Royal Academy show of 1781, it seems to have been in existence earlier judging from Soane's comments (see n. 26 supra).

28. For Soane's impressions of the Alps, see SM, AL, Sir John Soane's Case, Shelf A, "Sir John Soane's Notes Italy and Italian Language," pp. 300–299, and Soane's underlined contemporary copy of Rousseau's *Julie ou la nouvelle Hélöise* (3 vols.; Amsterdam, 1775), 1:75 (SM, AL, 26H). The Norfolk snowstorm was mentioned by Soane in SM, Soane Notebooks, 10, p. 16.

29. SM, Sandby Lecture 1, p. 61.

30. Ibid. 6, p. 19. Compare the Sandby quotation with an extremely similar statement in Jacques-François Blondel's *Cours d' architecture,* 2:229: "Toutes les différentes espèces . . . de l'architecture doivent porter l'empreint de la destination particulière de chaque édifice . . . . Il ne suffit pas que ce caractère distinctif

soit seulement designé par les attributs de la sculpture." The similarity of these passages suggests that Sandby actually referred to the *Cours* volume some time after the 1771 date of publication. Robin Middleton has shared with me his knowledge of this subject. See his "Jacques-François Blondel and the Cours d'Architecture," *Journal of the Society of Architectural Historians* 18 (1959):140–49.

31. Marc-Antoine Laugier, *Essai sur l'architecture,* p. 155.

32. RA, A. E. Richardson Collection of Chambersiana (sheaf marked "R.A. Lecture Notes"). These are Chambers's notes for the lectures he gave in 1769/70. On Chambers's connections with his master Blondel, see Harris, *Chambers,* pp. 5–6, which also discusses Chambers's lectures together with extracts from them (pp. 18, 128–29, 140–41, 168). Chambers refers to Laugier in his *Treatise on Civil Architecture.* For a discussion, see Wolfgang Herrmann, *Laugier and Eighteenth-Century French Theory.*

33. The whole topic of *caractère,* "narrative" architecture, and *architecture parlante* needs further investigation. A key text is Emil Kaufmann, "Three Revolutionary Architects, Boullée, Ledoux, and Lequeu," *Transactions of the American Philosophical Society,* n.s. 42 (1952):433–564. More recently the matter has been discussed by John Archer, "Character in English Architectural Design," *Eighteenth Century Studies* 12 (1979):339–71. Archer puts new emphasis on Morris's contribution, but perhaps discounts too much Kaufmann's pioneering work. Unfortunately, I was able to study only briefly an advance copy of my late mentor Donald Egbert's *Beaux-Arts Tradition in French Architecture* (Princeton, 1980). Egbert's section on "character" (pp. 121–38) promises to be the fullest discussion so far.

34. See Morris, *Lectures on Architecture,* pt. 2, p. 132. Peacock's *Oikidia* (pp. 68, 73), echoes Morris on "characteristic" beauty. Peacock's signed copy of Morris's *Lectures* is in SM, AL, 36B. I disagree on textual grounds with Dianne Ames's attribution of *Critical Observations* to James Stuart in her reprint edition (Los Angeles, 1978).

35. Soane's dated but unannotated copy of Whateley's *Observations* is in SM, AL, 32E.

36. Soane, *Lectures,* p. 178.

37. I disagree with Colin Rowe, *The Mathematics of the Ideal Villa and Other Essays* (Cambridge, Mass., 1976), pp. 67–69, when he argues that "character" was anti-academic. In theory, at least, this contradicts the use of the concept by Sandby and Blondel, among other academic spokesmen. But, in practice, Rowe may be right to suggest that "character" had a tendency to "atomize" academic-idealist order. See also Rowe's "Character and Composition; or, Some Vicissitudes of Architectural Vocabulary in the Nineteenth Century," *Oppositions* 2 (1974):41–60.

38. Hutchison, "Academy Schools," passim, lists the enrollment of Soane's various friends into the Academy.

39. John Soane, *Description of the House and Museum* (1830), p. 41, gives the correct date for this portrait, which is often misstated to have been painted in Rome three years later. Soane referred only once more to Hunneman in a June

1783 reference to the purchase of sheet music (SM, Soane Notebooks, 8, p. 1).

Notes to Pages 71–74   345

40. John Soane, *Description of the House and Museum* (1835), p. 89, includes Soane's tribute to Matthews. In the RA exhibition catalogues he is listed as a pupil of Robert Mylne's. For Brettingham, see Walter Brettingham, "The Brettingham Family of Norfolk," *Blackmansbury* 6 (1969):51–55.

41. RA, Council Minutes, vol. 1, p. 115, entry for 8 November 1771, and see Soane, *Memoirs*, p. 11. The winner of the silver medal was Thomas Whetten.

42. The James King mausoleum design has recently figured in two valuable articles: John Summerson's "Sir John Soane and the Furniture of Death," and Damie Stillman's "Death Defied and Honor Upheld: The Mausoleum in Neo-Classical England." For my discussion of the sources of the James King mausoleum, see chap. 5. There is no notice of King's burial in the records of St. Alphege Church, Greenwich, near to which the accident is said to have occurred. I have this information thanks to the assistance of the Vicar of St. Alphege.

43. Flaxman's drawing was first brought to my attention by the exhibition catalogue *Follies and Fantasies* (Brighton, 1971). SM, AL, Sir John Soane's Case, Shelf C, OSMAS, Items 86, 96, are further Flaxman sketches related to the same mausoleum scheme. More sketches in this same album may be attributed to George Dance and others. See my *John Soane's Architectural Education,* pls. 77–81. Soane's will (PRO, PROB. 11, 1888, Norwich, fols. 167 verso–172 verso) clarifies somewhat his relations with C. J. Richardson, one-time owner of the Flaxman drawing. In the original document of 11 May 1833, Richardson received a small bequest. But in a second, undated codicil (fol. 172 verso) Soane nominated Richardson to be assistant curator under George Bailey. I strongly suspect that Richardson imposed himself upon his old and ailing master, and helped himself to a choice selection of architectural drawings, including several by Flaxman. The attributions to Flaxman are in Richardson's hand.

44. RA, Council Minutes, vol. 1, p. 124, entry for 11 January 1772.

45. RA, General Assembly Minutes, vol. 1, pp. 71–72. Also reported in the *Gentleman's Magazine* 42 (1772), pt. 2, p. 593.

46. Joshua Reynolds, *Discourses,* p. 82, spoke of "a mischevious tendency . . . to an ambition of pleasing indiscriminately."

47. *Catalogue of the Drawings Collection of the Royal Institute of British Architects,* vol. O–R (Farnborough, 1976), p. 173. Differences of measurement between this Rudd drawing and Soane's (fig. 4.13) show they were prepared independently. Rudd was one of the numerous pupils of William Chambers enrolled in the Schools (Harris, *Chambers,* p. 11, n. 41, and Hutchison, "Academy Schools," p. 138).

48. RA, Council Minutes, vol. 1, pp. 124, 169, entries for 11 January 1772 and 31 December 1773.

49. Ibid., pp. 173–74, 176, entries 21 March and 9 April 1774. The Council's decision was ratified by the General Assembly on 2 May 1774 (ibid., General Assembly Minutes, vol. 1, p. 85).

50. *Abstract of the Institution and Laws of the Royal Academy of Arts in London* (London, 1797), p. 34.

51. Harris, *Chambers,* pp. 36–38, 213, pl. 29. It still stands moved to a different location in the grounds.

52. Ibid., pp. 226–27. Melbourne House was nearing completion in 1774.

53. This drawing (fig. 4.16) is close to the one first attributed to Chambers in the catalogue *Architectural Drawings from the Collection of the Royal Institute of British Architects* (London, 1961), p. 7, which has been accepted in subsequent publications as a scheme by him related to Melbourne House. This resemblance to Melbourne House is clear, but the project seems to me adapted to a civic rather than an aristocratic structure (note the Tyche statues symbolic of cities atop the pediment). The present drawing has been described as an unfinished version of its mate in the *Catalogue of the Drawings Collection of the Royal Institute of British Architects,* vol. C–F (Farnborough, 1972), p. 20. This is incorrect. The drawing is quite complete, and different enough from the other in details and draftsmanship to merit separate consideration. Furthermore, a marked similarity in handling and presentation exists between the more elaborate of the two townhouses and another one, signed by Edward Stevens in 1763 while he was still working for Chambers. See *Catalogue of the Drawings Collection of the Royal Institute of British Architects,* vol. S (Farnborough, 1976), p. 112 [3], and pl. 85. The derivation of both elevations from Melbourne House relates them to pupils in Chambers's office. In this connection it is worth noting that John Ride displayed a townhouse design 120 feet wide at the 1773 Academy show. See *Royal Academy Exhibition Catalogue* (London, 1773), p. 21.

54. RA, General Assembly Minutes, vol. 1, p. 94, entry for 19 December 1774.

55. RA, Council Minutes, vol. 1, p. 214, entry for 5 February 1776.

56. Soane, *Memoirs,* pp. 13–14.

57. RA, Council Minutes, vol. 1, p. 226, and RA, General Assembly Minutes, vol. 1, p. 106, entry for 2 December 1776.

58. RA, General Assembly Minutes, vol. 1, p. 108.

59. Anonymous, "Memoir of John Soane," p. 5. Arthur T. Bolton, *The Works of Sir John Soane,* p. 5, suggested that the author of the memoir was James Northcote. Johannes Dobai, *Die Kunstlerliteratur des Klassizismus und der Romantik in England,* 3:792, offers the same attribution but mistakes the date of publication for 1818. See also Thomas J. Mulvany, *The Life of James Gandon,* p. 24, where Gandon's warm reception is described when he won the first gold medal in architecture in 1769.

60. The literature on the triumphal bridge theme is extensive and dispersed. Dorothy Stroud discussed the tradition with special reference to Soane in "Soane's Designs for a Triumphal Bridge," pp. 260–62. The Italian forerunners form part of the subject of Werner Oechslin's *Bildungsgut und Antikenrezeption des frühen Settecento in Rom* (Zürich, 1972). The contributions of the various French *pensionnaires* have been summarized in the recent Académie de France à Rome exhibition catalogue *Piranèse et les français, 1740–1790.* Chambers's part in the dissemination of the triumphal bridge is reviewed by Harris, *Chambers,* p. 90, and appendix 8 where, among Chambers's sales catalogues, is listed a lot containing bridge designs, possibly Franco-Italian ones. Chambers vividly described his

concept of a triumphal bridge in the *Explanatory Discourse by Tan Chet-Qua* appended to his *Dissertation on Oriental Gardening* (2d ed.; London, 1773), p. 134.

61. *London and Westminster Improved,* pp. 10, 95–96. Soane in his *Lectures,* p. 165, praised this book by "poor neglected Gwynn."

62. The similarity between Soane's triumphal bridge and Peyre's *académie* design was originally noted by Nikolaus Pevsner and S. Lang, "Apollo or Baboon," p. 278. Harris, *Chambers,* p. 183, lists Peyre's *Oeuvres* as being in Chambers's library. No copy was in the library of the Academy when Stothard made his shelf list of it in 1815.

63. On the basis of previous winners of the silver medal, I have compiled the following list of eligible candidates for the 1776 gold medal competition: William Blackburn, John Haywood, Richard Holland, William Hunter, Thomas Malton, William Moss, John Rudd, John Soane, William Wickham. Joseph Farington heard from Malton himself that he was one of Soane's competitors (FD, p. 254, 10 October 1794). This is further supported by Malton's submission of a "superstructure of a triumphal bridge," to the *Royal Academy Exhibition Catalogue* (London, 1784), p. 16. But the anonymous drawing illustrated here (fig. 4.20) is surely far too weak and crude for the gifted Malton (see his design for a bath in the Roman manner, RIBA, CC7/2, first attributed to him by John Summerson, "Soane: The Case-History of a Personal Style," p. 91, n. 7).

64. According to Robert Scott Mylne, *The Master Masons to the Crown of Scotland and Their Works* (Edinburgh, 1893), p. 265, Chambers's now-lost Blackfriars Bridge elevation of 1759/60 was 6 feet 4 inches long.

65. Anonymous, "Memoir of John Soane," p. 5.

66. FD, p. 279, entry for 21 December 1794. RA, Council Minutes, vol. 1, p. 135, entry for 14 May 1772, illustrates how, in normal practice, all eligible gold medalists had to be canvassed each three years when a traveling fellowship became available. See my n. 42 of chap. 3 concerning the case of James Gandon.

67. Soane, *Description* (1830), p. 40.

68. RA, General Assembly Minutes, vol. 1, pp. 116–18. RA, Council Minutes, vol. 1, p. 246, entry for 31 December 1777, confirms Soane's appointment and orders that a letter of approval be sent to him.

69. The Royal Academy's quarterly payments to Soane, plus his traveling money out and back, are all tabulated in appendix D of my *John Soane's Architectural Education.*

70. SM, AL, Precedents in Architecture 1784, fol. 2 verso–4 recto. This is a partial transcription of a now-lost account by Soane of his visit to Paris. The extract preserves a record of his conversation with Perronet.

71. SM, AL, 34B, Louis Dutens, *Itinéraire des routes les plus fréquentées,* p. 53, marginal note by Soane, written in late April 1780.

72. Emil Kaufmann, *Architecture in the Age of Reason,* pp. 51–52.

73. Soane, *Description* (1835), pp. 82–83.

74. John Soane, *Plans, Elevations, and Perspective Views of Pitzhanger Manor House,* p. 3.

1. SRO, GD18/4777. Damie Stillman kindly took the trouble to provide me with the proper reference to this important letter of 4 July 1755, by Adam to his brother James alluding to Antoine Desgodetz's *Les Edifices antiques de Rome* (Paris, 1682), which Adam proposed republishing.

2. The full prospectus is printed in Arthur T. Bolton, *The Portrait of Sir John Soane*, p. 14. Despite many attempts to locate the original, I have still been unable to trace it.

3. The drawing for this title page is SM, AL, Sir John Soane's Case, Shelf C, OSMAS, Item 166 recto. It is reproduced as fig. 45 in my *John Soane's Architectural Education, 1753–80*. Fig. 46 shows the verso of this same sheet on which is a Gothic-style house, dated 1777, obviously the lone survivor of those schemes rejected from *Designs in Architecture*. The plan is nearly identical to that of my fig. 5.22. See chap. 13 for a further discussion of Soane's early planning.

4. Soane's departure for France at 5 A.M. on 18 March 1778, is recorded in SM, SNBT, 13, p. 91, entry for 18 March 1831. Just two days earlier the British ambassador at Paris had been recalled in preparation for declaring a state of war that would effectively have closed off the Franco-Italian route to Soane.

5. The anonymous inscription quoted here appears on the flyleaf of the V&A, library copy of *Designs in Architecture*. Other citations referred to in this passage are Thomas Leverton Donaldson, *A Review of the Professional Life of Sir John Soane*, p. 12; Bolton, *Portrait*, p. 13; John Summerson, *Sir John Soane*, p. 16; Johannes Dobai, *Die Kunstlerliteratur des Klassizismus und der Romantik in England*, 2:624.

6. See Chambers's *Plans, Elevations, and Sections*, pls. 31, 33.

7. John Summerson, "The Idea of the Villa: The Classical Country House in Eighteenth-Century England," p. 584, and more recently Dobai, *Kunstlerliteratur*, 2:624, both mention Jean-Charles Delafosse's *Nouvelle iconologie historique* (Paris, 1768) and Jean-François de Neufforge's *Recueil élémentaire d'architecture*.

8. John Harris, *Sir William Chambers*, appendix 12, provides a checklist of the contents of the Franco-Italian album. That Yenn used it can be demonstrated by comparing his lake pavilion design of 1774 (RA, Yenn Box 7, D7) with Item 125 in the album.

9. Harris, *Chambers*, pp. 19–20, 29, and see also Werner Oechslin, "Pyramide et sphère: Notes sur l'architecture révolutionnaire du XVIIIeme siècle et ses sources Italiennes," *Gazette des beaux-arts* 77 (1971):201–38. Richard G. Carrott, *The Egyptian Revival: Its Sources, Monuments, and Meaning, 1808–1858* (Berkeley, 1978), p. 33, briefly mentions Soane's pyramid within the broader context of Egyptomania.

10. Soane's unannotated copy of Carter is in the SM, AL, 41A. A connection between the two men is implied by Emil Kaufmann, *Architecture in the Age of Reason*, p. 57, and he is followed in his belief by Dobai, *Kunstlerliteratur*, 2:614, 624. I myself find no exact parallels between the *Builder's Magazine* and *Designs in Architecture*. Borrowings there may be on Soane's part, but, if so, they are either very general or very well disguised.

11. For a partial listing of contemporary books, see my n. 7 of chap. 13, and also Dobai, *Kunstlerliteratur*, vol. 2.

12. The topic of Soane's triangular designs in relation to Laugier is discussed by Kaufmann, *Architecture in the Age of Reason*, p. 57; Wolfgang Herrmann, *Laugier and Eighteenth-Century French Theory*, p. 183; and Arthur T. Bolton, *The Works of Sir John Soane*, p. 16. Kaufmann cites Carter's *Builder's Magazine*, pls. 62 and 65, and William Halfpenny's *A New and Complete System of Architecture* (London, 1749), pl. 44, as possible additional sources. Howard M. Colvin, *Biographical Dictionary of British Architects, 1600–1840*, pp. 450–51, discusses Jacobsen's triangular designs and notes the interesting fact that the engraver's plates for them are in the Soane Museum. This may be just a coincidence. The *Catalogue of the Royal Institute of British Architects Drawings Collection*, vol. G–K (Farnborough, 1973), p. 149, refers to Thomas Hunt's triangular house of 1765, a most awkward affair judging from the plan (fig. 89).

13. Soane's library contains the second, or 1790, edition of Wrighte's book (AL, 3B). But this does not preclude Soane's earlier knowledge of the work. On Chambers and Wrighte, see Dobai, *Kunstlerliteratur*, 2:619.

14. Charles-Joseph de Ligne, *Coup d'oeil sur Beloeil et sur une grande partie des jardins de l'Europe* (Paris, 1922), p. 24, has a note by the editor, Comte Ernest de Ganay, referring to a pre-1788 map of Beloeil drawn by the Comte de Ségur. I have to thank M. de Kersavond, estate manager of the present Prince de Ligne at Beloeil for allowing me to study the map. Although the vignettes on it are presumably in de Ségur's hand, the garden buildings they represent must reflect Belanger's ideas.

15. Douglas Richardson has observed to me that perhaps Soane had in mind a humorous allusion to the cow that jumped over the moon from the Mother Goose nursery rhyme.

16. *Royal Academy Exhibition Catalogue* (London, 1776), p. 8, lists a Chambers mausoleum. Chambers, in turn, may well have based his finial ornament on an identical one drawn by J. H. Müntz in Rome, and datable to the period 1749–50, just before Chambers's own arrival in that city. For an illustration, see Michael J. McCarthy, "Johann Heinrich Müntz: The Roman Drawings, 1749–76," *Burlington Magazine* 119:335–40, fig. 17. On Chambers's other sources, see Harris, *Chambers*, pp. 24–25, 29, and also the Académie de France à Rome exhibition catalogue *Piranèse et les français, 1740–1790*, pp. 155, 158.

17. According to Soane's ambiguously worded account books, the designs for Lady Craven were probably intended by her as presents to a friend, "Lady [Penelope] Pitt-Rivers," of Strathfield-Saye, Hampshire and the Villa Pitt, near Lyons, France (see SM, Journal 1781–1797, p. 9, Ledger A, p. 157). The verso of my fig. 5.16 bears the inscription "Sketches for Garden Seats Octr 19th 1781," which agrees with dated account book entries relating to Lady Craven. Lady Pitt-Rivers obtained designs for Villa Pitt from Claude-Nicolas Ledoux according to letters published in John W. Oliver, *The Life of William Beckford* (London, 1932), p. 172.

18. See n. 33 of my chap. 2, and n. 41 of chap. 3.

19. See pl. 19 of Robert Morris's *Rural Architecture: Consisting of Plans and Elevations for Buildings in the Country* (London, 1750), revised five years later as *Select Architecture: Being Regular Designs of Plans and Elevations well Suited to both Town and Country.* A copy of each book is in Soane's library and appears to have been so from an early date; see appendix B of my *John Soane's Architectural Education, 1753–80*, p. 359.

20. David Watkins's *Sale Catalogues of Libraries of Eminent Persons, Architects,* vol. 4 (London, 1972), gives details on the libraries of Chambers, Robert Adam, George Dance, and Robert Smirke and shows that none of these contained a copy of *Designs in Architecture,* at the time of their dispersal.

21. Franklin Toker, *The Church of Notre Dame in Montreal: An Architectural History* (Montreal, 1970) gives a history of O'Donnell's career before he came to work on Notre Dame and illustrates the 1798 drawing by him. When I drew Toker's attention to the Soane derivation he generously supplied me with the photograph I reproduce here.

22. A John Yenn design for a monument at Blenheim, Oxfordshire, to the memory of the Fair Rosamond Clifford includes such a loculus specifically inscribed as a "Spherical Arch" (RA, Yenn Box 1, A4, verso). The date of the drawing is a late one, 1786, but the implication is that a tradition stands behind it that goes back to Chambers, and to similar arches in de Neufforge, *Recueil,* supplementary vol., pl. 178.

23. On Plaw, see Colvin, *Biographical Dictionary,* pp. 642–43.

24. John Plaw, *Rural Architecture: Consisting of Designs from the Simple Cottage to the More Decorated Villa* (London, 1785), p. 8. See also n. 3 supra for discussion of an earlier version of the Soane plan copied by Plaw.

25. Soane's incomplete copy of Plaw's *Rural Architecture* is in SM, AL, 27A.

26. John Soane, *Plans, Elevations, and Sections of Buildings,* p. 11.

27. See Coxe, *Travels in Switzerland,* pl. opposite p. 132. Detailed background information is provided in my "Eighteenth-Century English Sources for a History of Swiss Wooden Bridges." I owe the discovery of the Soane engraving (fig. 5.23) to the friendly interest and quick eye of Douglas Richardson. At the time I wrote my article I was unaware of the plate in Coxe's book and was at a loss to explain how a similar one had appeared in a Swiss publication without Soane's knowledge. Coxe provides the missing link. Copies of the first and fourth editions of Coxe's book signed by the author are in SM, GL, 7A.

28. Candidus, "Fasciculus iv," *Architectural Magazine* 4 (1837):117. Susan Feinberg, "Sir John Soane's 'Museum': An Analysis of the Architect's House-Museum in Lincoln's Inn Fields, London," p. 280, n. 105, identifies "Candidus" as Soane's one-time collaborator, William Henry Leeds. On Leeds, see Colvin, *Biographical Dictionary,* pp. 510–11, and Bolton, *Portrait,* pp. 416–19.

29. *Architectural Magazine* 4 (1837):157–60.

1. RIBA, Library, MS DA1/1 (Dance Letter Book), p. 19. See John Fleming, *Robert Adam and His Circle*, p. 245, for an edited version of this important letter of 3 February 1762 from Nathaniel Dance to his father.

2. BM, Egerton MS 1970, fol. 26 (letter from John Brown to John Strange, 14 August 1779).

3. For the career of a typical tour guide in Rome, see Brinsley Ford's account of "James Byres Principal Antiquarian for the English Visitors to Rome," *Apollo* 99 (1974):446–61.

4. The standard biography, William Shakespeare Childe-Pemberton's *Earl Bishop*, has recently been augmented by Brian Fothergill's *Mitred Earl*. Both books need to be compared with the typescripts of the Hervey family letters deposited among the Wharncliffe Papers in the Sheffield City Central Library.

5. An inscribed copy of Andrea Palladio's *I Quatro libri dell' architettura*, given by the Bishop to Soane, proves that they knew one another by October 1778. This is not a rare first edition, as was once thought, but a copy of Pasquali's 1768 Venetian facsimile edition. See also n. 16 of chap. 4.

6. See Brinsley Ford's entertaining article, "The Earl Bishop, an Eccentric and Capricious Patron of the Arts," *Apollo* 99 (1974):426–34.

7. Pitt's arrival in Rome and his reception by the Bishop is recorded by Childe-Pemberton, *Earl Bishop*, 1:226. See also Vere Foster, ed., *The Two Dutchesses* (London, 1898), pp. 68–69.

8. A typescript of Pitt's correspondence with Soane throughout the late 1780s and early 1790s was kindly made available to me by Michael J. McCarthy. See SM, CC 1, Division 4, P(2), Items 1–37. Perhaps by coincidence Pitt met Soane's teacher, Dance, in a similar student capacity in Rome. Dance remarked on Pitt's "extraordinary fine sense," RIBA, Library, MS DA1/1 (Dance Letter Book), p. 17, letter from George Dance to his father, 7 October 1761. Pitt's architectural accomplishments are discussed by Michael J. McCarthy, "The Rebuilding of Stowe House, 1770–1777," *Huntington Library Quarterly* 36 (1973):267–98.

9. BM, Add. MS 35,378, fol. 261 verso, letter from Philip Yorke to his uncle, 31 October 1778.

10. Ibid., fol. 305 verso, letter from Philip Yorke to his uncle, 31 January 1779. In the same letter Yorke called the Paestum temples "magnificent," whereas it was more common to deprecate them. On the return journey via Pompeii he wrote (fol. 304 verso) with remarkable perspicacity of the "agreeably new" sensation "of finding oneself in an ancient street existing in the same state it was upwards of 1700 years ago."

11. See my "John Soane, Philip Yorke, and Their Quest for Primitive Architecture."

12. Childe-Pemberton, *Earl Bishop*, 1:230, publishes the Bishop's unkind remarks about Bowdler. The young man was in Rome by 7 November 1778, when he addressed a letter to John Strange, British resident at Venice, in which he mentioned both Philip Yorke and the Bishop (BM, Egerton MS 2,001, fol. 216).

For Bowdler in his career as expurgator, see Noel Perrin, *Dr. Bowdler's Legacy: A History of Expurgated Books in England and America* (New York, 1969). Professor Perrin and the National Portrait Gallery, London, assisted me in the fruitless search for a likeness of Bowdler.

13. HMST, vol. 94, 3d series, fol. 51, letter from Bowdler to Lord Loughborough, 1 July 1781. See n. 8 of chap. 10 for a further discussion.

14. BM, Egerton MS 2,002, fol. 39, letter from John Askew to John Strange recommending Burdon, 30 September 1778. Burdon's movements and his friendship with Bowdler are mentioned in the latter's correspondence with Strange (BM, Egerton MS 2,002, fol. 16). A. Paul Oppé, ed., "Memoirs of Thomas Jones," p. 88, records Burdon's commission from Jones of a landscape of Naples, implying the patron's visit there early in 1779.

15. NNRO, Patteson Box 3/12, letter from John Patteson to his mother, 11 June 1779.

16. Soane and Burdon's joint travels in North Italy are referred to by the architect in his *Memoirs of the Professional Life of an Architect,* p. 15.

17. For Patteson, see Isabella K. Patteson, *Henry Staniforth Patteson: A Memoir* (Norwich, 1899), pp. 9–17; and Basil Cozens-Hardy and Ernest A. Kent, *Mayors of Norwich, 1403–1835* (Norwich, 1938), p. 140.

18. NNRO, Patteson Box 3/12, letter of 29 April 1779, and see also, letter of 12 April 1779, for a reference to Bowdler and Martineau.

19. Oppé, "Memoirs of Thomas Jones," only mentions Soane three times, and his name appears once in Sidney Charles Herbert, ed., *Henry, Elizabeth, and George (1734–80),* pp. 273–74.

20. NNRO, Patteson Box 3/12, letter of 12 April 1779, refers to "poor [Richard] Bosanquet." Soane also makes mention of him in some manuscript travel hints (SM, CC 2, Division 14, B(1), Item 11). See also my *John Soane's Architectural Education, 1753–80,* p. 374 (appendix G) and p. 162 n. 43.

21. BM, Egerton MS 2,002, fol. 18, letter from Thomas Bowdler to John Strange, 10 June 1779, clarifies the itinerary of Bowdler and Stuart. Biographical details of Stuart, and his controversial marriage to his Coutts cousin, are given in Ernest Hartley Coleridge, *The Life of Thomas Coutts, Banker* (2 vols.; London, 1920).

22. The close friendship between Soane and the Stuarts is alluded to in a letter to the architect from Rowland Burdon. See SM, CC 1, Division 3, B(2), Item 1 (see also Arthur T. Bolton, *The Portrait of Sir John Soane,* pp. 27–28). Bolton, however, omitted the letter in which Stuart reprimanded Soane for meddlesome behavior. See SM, CC 1, Division 4, S(3), Item 12 ("it is the height of impropriety for any person unconnected to interfere with family affairs," letter of 8 January 1781). This probably refers to Soane's falling out with John Coxe Hippisley, who had married Stuart's sister in Rome.

23. NNRO, Patteson Box 3/12, letter from John Patteson to his mother, 11 June 1779, mentions "Mr. Lewis." Henry Greswolde Lewis's hotel bills from Naples are preserved in the Warwickshire County Record Office (CR 1291/323/1–2; and 322/12–20).

24. For Soane's alterations to Tollemache's properties at Hyde Park Corner, at Combe near Kingston, Surrey, and at Steephill Cottage, Isle of Wight, see Dorothy Stroud, *The Architecture of Sir John Soane,* pp. 157, 159.

25. Soane's activities as artistic middleman are revealed in his correspondence with Rowland Burdon (n. 14 supra) and with John Patteson, see SM, CC 1, Division 2, P(1), Item 1; and Bolton, *Portrait,* pp. 29–30.

26. NNRO, Patteson Box 3/12, letter of 12 April 1779. The sketches referred to in the letter could not be found.

27. SM, CC 1, Division 4, S(3), Item 1, letter of April 1780; and Bolton, *Portrait,* p. 26.

28. HBLB, vol. 1, p. 30, letter of 22 July 1778, from Michael Shanahan to the Bishop.

29. The account is given in Soane, *Memoirs,* p. 15; and idem, *Designs for Public and Private Buildings* (London, 1832), pp. 39–40, has another version of the same anecdote. Subsequent to my article "Soane and Hardwick in Rome: A Neoclassical Partnership," more information on Henderson has been published in Howard M. Colvin's *Biographical Dictionary of British Architects, 1600–1840,* p. 412. Also from Alistair Rowan's *The Buildings of Ireland: North West Ulster* (Harmondsworth, 1979), p. 245, I have learned that Robert Adam prepared a scheme for the Downhill dining room. No source for this information is given.

30. Soane, *Memoirs,* p. 15.

31. Childe-Pemberton, *Earl Bishop,* 1:178, explicitly mentions a cast of the Apollo Belvedere. On a later occasion, Soane specifically took into account the size and placement of a William Pars copy of Guido Reni's *Aurora,* intended for the ceiling of the Bishop's gallery at Downhill. See SM, AL, Sir John Soane's Case, Shelf A, Downhill Notebook, p. 30, and Oppé, "Memoirs of Thomas Jones," p. 88.

32. Plutarch, *Plutarch's Lives* (London, 1914–26), 2:603, 605. Plutarch, however, never connected his anecdote about Lucullus with any specific house owned by the Roman.

33. SM, AL, Sir John Soane's Case, Shelf A, "Italian Sketches 1779," p. 174.

34. I have dealt with the early and late phases of Soane's artistic involvement with the Bishop in two articles: "Soane and Hardwick," pp. 52–53; and "'Je N'Oublieraj Jamais': John Soane and Downhill."

35. Soane, *Memoirs,* p. 16.

36. The drawing is SM, Drawer 5, Set 3, Item 1, recto and verso.

37. A copy of Soane's letter to Stuart is in SM, CC 1, Division 4, S(3), Item 4.

38. The visit of the party of travelers to the Villa Palagonia is documented by NNRO, Patteson Box 3/12, letter of 29 April–2 May. An account of the extraordinary architecture is provided by Anthony Blunt, *Sicilian Baroque* (London, 1968), pp. 42–43. Concerning the mirror-encrusted furnishings, Alvar Gonzalez-Palacios has written "The Prince of Palagonia, Goethe and Glass Furniture," *Burlington Magazine* 113 (1971):456–60. An earlier account, useful for illustrations, is Karl Lohmeyer's *Palagonisches Barock das Haus der Laune des Prinzen von Palagonia* (Frankfurt a.M., 1943).

39. John Soane, *Description of the House and Museum* (1830), p. 53, referred to "the wonderful performances of the Prince of Palagonia." He also corresponded with Rowland Burdon in 1819 on the subject of their visit to the Villa. See SM, CC 1, Division 3, B(2), Item 14; and Bolton, *Portrait,* p. 305.

40. SM, CC 1, Division 4, S(3), Item 6, letter of 5 December 1780.

41. Ibid., Item 7, Soane to Stuart, 11 December 1780; Item 69, Stuart to Soane, 20 August [1782]. It seems clear that no wings, at least, were ever added to Allanbank House. An early nineteenth-century watercolor of it by Stuart's talented son, James, shows none. I am grateful to Lady Naomi Mitchison for showing me the Stuart family album, now at Carradale House, Argylshire.

42. SM, AL, Sir John Soane's Case, Shelf A, Downhill Notebook, pp. 38, 40. Soane's Journal 1781–1797, p. 15, lists some of the charges involved in carrying out the minor alterations at Castle Eden.

43. John Soane, *Sketches in Architecture,* pl. 26.

44. Yorke's remarks are preserved in an almost illegible journal which he kept in Rome (BM, Add. MS 36,260, fol. 95 verso). His guide on the occasion was James Byres (see my n. 3, supra).

45. SM, Journal 1781–1797, p. 11. This bill also refers to Soane making a drawing for Yorke of an unspecified "Ancient Monument near Capua." Probably the famous so-called conocchia, or distaff, is in question. Neither of the original watercolors once in Yorke's possession has been located. It is worth noting the existence of another sectional drawing of the chapel, along its ritual east-west axis, signed and dated 1779 by the Italian architect Camillo Buti. See the *Catalogue of the Drawings Collection of the Royal Institute of British Architects,* vol. B (Farnborough, 1972), p. 147. It seems to me quite possible that Soane in some way copied from or collaborated with Buti.

46. SM, CC 1, Division 2, P(1), Item 1, letter of 6 April 1780; and Bolton, *Portrait,* p. 30.

47. Soane, Downhill Notebook, p. 84 to the end, passim, makes reference to letters written to Patteson and small commissions performed for him.

48. The documents relevant to the chimneypieces for Surrey Street are found in SM, Journal 1781–1797, pp. 3, 34 (Patteson and Foxhall accounts respectively). In Soane Notebooks, 1, p. 58, there also occurs reference to a £20 payment to Foxhall on behalf of Patteson. The following two page sides are those containing the chimneypiece sketches reproduced here (figs. 6.16, 6.17). A painter named Hamilton (probably William, R.A.) supplied two ornamental chimney boards (see Soane Notebooks, 2, p. 30, and 3, p. 2).

49. Dorothy Stroud, "The Country Houses of Sir John Soane," p. 782.

50. Damie Stillman, "Chimney-Pieces for the English Market: A Thriving Business in Late Eighteenth-Century Rome," *Art Bulletin* 59 (1977):85–94.

51. In a letter to Horace Mann of 17 September 1778, Horace Walpole commented sarcastically on Pitt's departure for Italy to regain his health. Letter quoted by Tresham J. P. Lever, *The House of Pitt: A Family Chronicle* (London, 1947), p. 204.

52. SM, AL, Sir John Soane's Case, Shelf C, OSMAS, Item 182; and Bolton, *Portrait*, pp. 22–23.

53. The Claremont bathroom, among others, is commented on in a brief and witty historical sketch by Mark Girouard, "Country House Plumbing 2," *Country Life* 164 (1978):2218–20.

54. A similarly rich underground bathroom of 1782 was that of the Hotel Bézenval in Paris, now dismantled. It is described in Jacques Silvestre de Sacy's monograph, *Alexandre-Théodore Brongniart, 1739–1813: Sa vie, son oeuvre* (Paris, 1940), pp. 60–62. Its first bather is reputed to have died of a chill.

55. Warwick County Record Office, CRO 299/578, has a plan of Malvern's basement on which a manuscript note in an unknown hand has been made to indicate the removal of the bathroom from the scheme. A memorable investigation by flashlight of the Malvern cellars revealed no trace of the room. My thanks to Miss Joyce E. Griffiths for arranging the subterranean tour.

56. Dorothy Stroud, "Soane Barn"; and idem, *Architecture of Sir John Soane*, p. 81.

57. SM, Ledger A, p. 87, records that John Stuart's debt to Soane had still to be settled when the Scotsman died in 1817.

CHAPTER SEVEN

1. The original of Chambers's letter, written to Edward Stevens on 5 August 1774, is preserved in SM, CC 1, Division 1, C(7), Item 1, which also contains Brettingham's letter to Soane, B(13), Item 2, 22 December 1778. See Arthur T. Bolton, *The Portrait of Sir John Soane*, pp. 10–13, 19–20, respectively. On Soane's travel hints, see Bolton, pp. 18–19. Thomas Hardwick's journal quotation is from RIBA, H1/4, fol. 20 recto.

2. SM, CC 2, Division 14, B(1), Item 1[b] (letter of Soane to Henry Wood of 1 August 1778); and see Bolton, *Portrait*, p. 16. RA, Cash Book, vol. 1 (1769–94), confirms the date of Soane's safe arrival at Rome on 2 May.

3. Chambers's drawing of the gateway is V&A, Box Q2C, E.3268-1934. A Soane drawing measured in *palmi* rather than feet agrees with his sketch in omitting the top storey (SM, Drawer 45, Set 4, Item 17). Francesco Milizia aided the general misapprehension about Vignola's authorship by voicing it in his book *Le Vite de' più celebri architetti* (Rome, 1768), p. 265.

4. SM, AL, 2D.

5. For an example of Soane's integration of sketchbook entries together with his guidebook marginalia, see SM, AL, Sir John Soane's Case, Shelf A, "Italian Sketches and Mem.," p. 181.

6. On 12 July 1780, Anna Miller wrote Soane: "of all the compliments I have ever had made me that of inserting views in my letters is the greatest." See SM, CC 2, Division 13, Part 2(23), Item 2; and Bolton, *Portrait*, pp. 36–37. The letter goes on to imply that Soane's intended gift was among his belongings lost in Switzerland.

7. Miller, *Letters,* 2:194.

8. Two of the rare general discussions I know of concerning travel literature are Ludwig Schudt's *Italienreisen in 17. und 18. Jahrhundert* (Vienna and Munich, 1959), and R. S. Pine-Coffin's *Bibliography of British and American Travel in Italy to 1860* (Florence, 1974).

9. In a number of places Miller can be shown to have borrowed her information (and misinformation) directly from Joseph-Jérôme le Français de Lalande, *Voyage d'un Français en Italie.* For example, compare Miller, *Letters,* 2:138, with Le Français de Lalande, *Voyage,* 6:126 (Soane's copy of *Voyage* is in SM, AL, 33B).

10. Soane, *Memoirs of the Professional Life of an Architect,* p. 15 and also SM, AL, Sir John Soane's Case, Shelf A, "Italian Sketches and Mem.," pp. 192–91.

11. SM, AL, Sir John Soane's Case, Shelf A, "Italian Sketches," pp. 93–128, covers the entire extraordinary progress of this journey.

12. The Bishop's claim to personal responsibility for the renewed interest in draining the marshes is contained in a letter of his dated 1800 (see William Shakespeare Childe-Pemberton's *Earl Bishop,* 2:600).

13. Le Français de Lalande's *Voyage,* 6:2, may have put the Bishop in mind of Horace's fifth satire.

14. SM, "Italian Sketches," p. 118 ("The Cardinals Villa at Nettuno, the ancient Antium"). See RIBA, Library, MS DA1/1 (Dance Letter Book, letter of 6 May 1762), for Dance's account of his reception at Anzio.

15. Miller, *Letters,* 2:93, and cf. also BM, Add. MS 35,378, fol. 304 recto, letter of Philip Yorke, 31 January 1779. See the Académie de France à Rome catalogue *Piranèse et les français, 1750–1790,* passim, for the Pompeii activities of Frenchmen, such as Louis-Jean Desprez.

16. John Soane, *Lectures on Architecture,* p. 50.

17. SM, "Italian Sketches," pp. 60–61. See my n. 38 of chap. 9 for further discussion.

18. BM, Add. MS 35,378, fol. 305 verso, letter of 31 January 1779.

19. The same standard itinerary is described by Soane in his travel hints (see n. 1 supra), by Thomas Bowdler (BM, Egerton MS 2,002, fols. 5–6, letter of 26 January 1779), and by Thomas Hardwick (RIBA, H1/4, fols. 16 verso–17 recto, entry dated 17 May 1778, "staid . . . abt. 2½ hours"). But Soane stayed longer than most and in this he was unusual.

20. Abbé Jean-Claude Richard de Saint-Non's *Voyage pittoresque ou déscription des royaumes de Naples et de Sicile* (4 vols.; Paris, 1781–86) and Jean-Pierre-Laurent Hoüel's *Voyage pittoresque des isles de Sicile, de Malte et de Lipari* (4 vols.; Paris, 1782–87). Trips to Sicily were undertaken by such Englishmen as Robert Mylne (1757), Richard Payne Knight (1777), and Henry Swinburne (1777).

21. Miller, *Letters,* 2:179.

22. The dates are provided by NNRO, Patteson Box 3/12, letter from John Patteson of 29 April 1779, and BM, Egerton MS 2,002, fol. 18, letter of Thomas Bowdler, 10 June 1779.

23. NNRO, Patteson Box 3/12, letter of 29 April–May 6 1779.

24. Ibid.

25. Soane's copy of this book by Juan de San Bernardo is in SM, GL, 30B. Originally written in Spanish, Soane's is the Palermo, 1693 edition.

26. NNRO, Patteson Box 3/12, letter of 29 April 1779, finished 6 May. Patteson paraphrased Patrick Brydone, *A Tour through Sicily and Malta,* 2:100. Similar criticisms of the Villa Palagonia were brought up retrospectively by another member of the party, Rowland Burdon, when he wrote Soane 40 years later. See SM, CC 1, Division 3, B(2), Item 14; and Bolton, *Portrait,* p. 305. Burdon also referred to Soane's drawing of the Palagonia monster statues in the same letter.

27. NNRO, Patteson Box 3/12, letter of 23 May 1779. See also Swinburne's *Travels in the Two Sicilies,* 2:233. Soane in his "Italian Sketches," p. 79, made reference to the Swinburne family, and later suggested familiarity with them by copying down the touching epitaph to their daughter in the English College at Rome. See SM, CC 1, Division 2, S(30), Item 1. On Martha Swinburne's wall plaque, see Terence Hodgkinson, "Christopher Hewetson, an Irish Sculptor in Rome," *Walpole Society* 34 (1952–54):42–54.

28. Soane, *Lectures,* p. 83, paraphrasing Swinburne, *Travels Sicilies,* 2:288.

29. NNRO, Patteson Box 3/12, letter of 29 April–6 May 1779.

30. The Swiss naturalist Charles Bonnet complimented Burdon: "vous avé sagement fait de couper cette oreille du fameux Tyran de Syracuse." The letter of 27 August 1779 is in the Bibliothèque publique et universitaire, Geneva, Correspondance Bonnet, vol. 75, fol. 215 recto. Soane's drawing showing the "ear" is SM, Drawer 45, Set 1, Item 6. I have illustrated it as fig. 209, in my *John Soane's Architectural Education, 1753–80.*

31. John Britton, "Sir John Soane," p. 5.

32. NNRO, Patteson Box 3/12, letter of 11 June 1779.

33. Burdon and Soane's friendship and travels are referred to by Soane, *Memoirs,* pp. 15–16, and by Burdon in a letter of 13 August 1836, inserted in a bound volume of congratulatory messages (SM, AL, Sir John Soane's Case, Shelf D; see Bolton, *Portrait,* p. 532). Burdon discussed the itinerary in a letter to John Strange of 16 August 1779 (BM, Egerton MS 2,002, fol. 28). Other evidence is provided by A. Paul Oppé, ed., "The Memoirs of Thomas Jones," p. 90. NNRO, Patteson Box 3/12, letter of 25 September 1779, records Patteson's meeting with his two friends at Brescia.

34. Miller, *Letters,* 1:276–77. The passage praising Dance is quoted by Soane, *Lectures,* p. 132.

35. I have published the tips on North Italian sightseeing given to Soane in appendix H of my *John Soane's Architectural Education* (the original is in SM, "Italian Sketches," pp. 78, 82–92).

36. John Fleming, "An Italian Sketchbook by Robert Adam, Clérisseau and Others," *Connoisseur* 146 (1960):186–94.

37. Miller, *Letters,* 2:307. She had written: "This casing is loaded with . . . sculpture all heavy and ill-done." Cf. Le Français de Lalande, *Voyage,* 7:376 ("toute cette sculpture est . . . de l'école de Michel Ange"). In respects other than attribution she copied Le Français de Lalande's wording.

38. Soane, *Lectures,* p. 61, briefly discussed the temple. The lecture diagram

(pl. 16) of it is a later redrawing of the original reproduced here.

39. Miller, *Letters,* 2:298, 256, discussed the Clitumnus temple and English garden structures. She wrote Soane on 12 July 1780: "Accept my best thanks for the sketch of the Temple . . . if ever I put it in execution I shall adhere strictly to your advice." See SM, CC 2, Division 13, Part 2(23), Item 2; and Bolton, *Portrait,* p. 36.

40. Soane's two passports are in SM, CC 2, Division 14, A, Items 2–3.

41. SM, AL, Sir John Soane's Case, Shelf A, "Notes Italy and Italian Language," pp. 328–29 records Soane's departure date from Rome, and his expenses en route to Florence via Caprarola.

42. Ibid., p. 329, gives the purchase price of Soane's copy of Dutens, *Itinéraire,* whose pp. 102, 110, give in summary form the route of his return journey from Florence to London.

43. The dates of Soane's numerous stopovers between 29 April and late June 1780 are given in my *John Soane's Architectural Education,* pp. 292–337.

44. Soane, "Italian Sketches," p. 85. Soane added the words "very false" to the earlier notes he had made.

45. Soane, "Notes Italy," pp. 307–11, makes clear that Soane met the English Consul, John Bett; an English physician Dr. William Batt; the soprano Cecilia Davies, whom he heard perform; and he was received by the expatriate English hostess Mme Cilesia with her two daughters. On the Cilesia family, see Joseph Baretti, *A Journey from London to Genoa* (2d ed.; 2 vols.; London, 1770), 2:335. Soane, although he apparently did not own this work, may have known it, because he certainly possessed the same author's *Account of the Manners and Customs of Italy* (London, 1768), inscribed by Soane with the date 1777 (SM, GL, 7A). As Soane's correspondent Antony Gibbs put it with reference to Genoa, the architect "meant to plunge head and ears into the Noblesse." See SM, CC 2, Division 14, B(1), Item 4, Gibbs's letter of 5 June 1780; and see Bolton, *Portrait,* p. 34.

46. Soane's sketch helps to provide a terminus ante quem for the new staircase by Andrea Tagliafichi, usually dated ca. 1780. See Piero Torriti, *La Galleria del Palazzo Durazzo Pallavicini a Genova* (Genoa, 1967).

47. SM, "Notes Italy," p. 307.

48. Soane's sometime assitant George Wightwick has left us the pathetic vignette of the near-blind Soane having *Gil Blas* read to him over and over again. See Wightwick's "The Life of an Architect," p. 404.

49. Jacques Casanova de Seingalt, *Memoirs* (6 vols.; New York, 1959–60), 6:362.

CHAPTER EIGHT

1. RIBA, Library, MS DA1/1 (Dance Letter Book), pp. 28–29, letter of 30 October 1762. Dance was referring to the views of the Tivoli temple in Palladio's *I Quattro libri dell' architettura.*

2. RIBA, Library, MS DA1/1 (Dance Letter Book), p. 21, letter of 10 April 1762. Dance was encouraged by a Mr. Hinchliffe, probably John, later Bishop of Peterborough.

3. John Soane, *Lectures on Architecture,* p. 115, recommended to his students the practice of making measured drawings to "form in his mind an inexhaustible magazine of ideas."

4. Ibid., p. 57, acknowledged the excellence of Dance's survey indirectly. But Soane, *Description of the House and Museum,* (1830), p. 23, claimed his Tivoli elevation (fig. 8.2) was "made in Rome in 1778." See my "'Je N'Oublieraj Jamais': John Soane and Downhill," pp. 18–19, concerning the Bishop's Tivoli replica in Ireland.

5. FD, entry for 4 March 1810: "On Soane's return from Italy He told Dance that after He left Rome He lost His sketches owing to the bottom of his trunk coming out. He afterward borrowed Dance's drawing of the Sybils Temple at Tivoli and copied it, and hung it up in His House with John Soane written under it, as if the drawing had been originally made by Himself. This being remarked to him He claimed originality for this drawing, saying that He borrowed Mr. Dance's drawing only to compare it with his own."

6. SM, Dance Cabinet, Slider 3, Set 1, Items 1–6.

7. Another instance of Byres's sale of drawings is represented by the plans of various *terme* in Rome, inscribed "da Sigr. Byers Copia" inserted in the so-called Hardwick Albums. Thomas Hardwick later made enlarged versions of these plans without acknowledging Byres. See the *Catalogue of the Drawings Collection of the Royal Institute of British Architects,* vol. G–K (Farnborough, 1973), p. 93 [29–32].

8. Fernando Chueca Goitia, *La Vida y las obras del architecto Juan de Villanueva* (Madrid, 1949), pl. 16, illustrates the Tivoli drawing in question, now in the Madrid Academy.

9. See S. Rowland Pierce, "Thomas Jenkins in Rome," *Antiquaries Journal* 45 (1965), pt. 2, p. 222. The cork model maker from Naples, Giovanni Altieri, carried out the work. An example is in the Soane Museum's New Picture Room; it is signed by Altieri and dated in the 1770s (the last digit has been effaced).

10. I have dealt with this subject in "Soane and Hardwick in Rome: A Neoclassical Partnership." The catalogue published there remains complete with the exception of Soane's finished plan of S. Maria Maggiore, which I chanced upon later and which is reproduced here for the first time. My discussion of all the Hardwick drawings from Italy appears separately in the *Catalogue of the Drawings Collection of the Royal Institute of British Architects,* vol. G–K, pp. 89–95.

11. The late Raymond Erith kindly described architects' measuring procedures to me.

12. John Fleming, *Robert Adam and His Circle,* passim, mentions the use by the Adams of nameless hired "myrmidons." This practice insured the existence of a single master copy, but it was costly and hence not often utilized by student architects.

13. See n. 1 of my chap. 7.

14. John Soane, *Designs for Public and Private Buildings* (1832), p. 39.

15. Compare SM, Drawer 45, Set 3, Item 5, and its Hardwick mate in the *Catalogue of the Drawings Collection of the Royal Institute of British Architects,* vol. G–K, p. 94 [40].

16. A. Paul Oppé, ed., "Memoirs of Thomas Jones," pp. 64–65.

17. I am grateful to Ian R. Hooper for suggesting Quarenghi's name to me in a letter of 14 May 1973. I had completely overlooked the possible identification in my earlier catalogue of the RIBA drawings (n. 10 supra). But Hooper did not publish his astute guess when he wrote the Quarenghi entries for the *Catalogue of the Drawings Collection of the Royal Institute of British Architects,* vol. O–R (Farnborough, 1976), pp. 109–10.

18. Apart from the five Quarenghi albums, of which I illustrate one leaf (fig. 8.9), the CBB holds a corpus of photographs of Quarenghi drawings in North Italian collections and in the Hermitage Museum, Leningrad. Renzo Mangili, assistant to the director, Gianni Barachetti, was most helpful in putting this entire archive at my disposition. Another Quarenghi album leaf (Album I, no. 19) relates to Hadrian's Villa, but it has no mate among the Hardwick Tivoli drawings in a sketchbook owned by John G. Dunbar, who kindly communicated this information to me. See his "An English Architect at Naples," *Burlington Magazine* 110 (1968):265–66. See also the exhibition catalogue, *Disegni di Giacomo Quarenghi* (Vicenza, 1967), and Sandro Angelini's publication *I Cinque album di Giacomo Quarenghi nella Civica Biblioteca di Bergamo* (Bergamo, 1967).

19. SM, Drawer 45, Set 6, Item 1 verso, "Il Teatro Tordinona Roma. Feb. 1780," a rafter study and sketch plan of seating capacity. The entire group of Soane's drawings is discussed and most of them are illustrated in my *John Soane's Architectural Education, 1753–80,* p. 288.

20. Elena Bassi, *Giannantonio Selva architetto Veneziano* (Padua, 1936), p. 9, gives the relevant information about Quarenghi's friendship with Selva, both of whom were pupils of the Venetian architect, Tommaso Temanza. Bassi, pp. 4–11, discussed the few details then known about Selva's student period. But Bassi, "Napoli nel 1780," *Studi in onore di Roberto Pane* (Naples, 1969–71), pp. 443–55, published extracts from Selva's MS journal, which had in the meantime been deposited in the BQS. (MS cod. 35, no. 1175). I am grateful to Antonio Fancello, assistant to the director, Ugo Ruggeri, for making the Selva journal so readily available to me.

21. The following list is a concordance of the identical Soane and Selva drawings not otherwise mentioned or illustrated in my text: Rome, S. Maria in Campitelli, cross section and detail of beam (SM, Drawer 45, Set 6, Item 2 recto; and MC, 6314 verso); Rome, S. Maria in Campitelli, 7 details of metal clamps and tie bars (SM, Drawer 45, Set 6, Item 3; MC, 6314 recto); Bologna theater, cross section (SM, Drawer 45, Set 6, Item 4 recto; MC, 6313); Turin Theater, cross section (SM, Drawer 45, Set 6, Item 4 verso; MC, 6318 verso). Other Selva roofing studies are listed by Bassi, *Selva,* p. 129. Only two further Soane drawings are identified. They are: Rome, SS. Apostoli, section and beam detail (SM,

Drawer 45, Set 6, Item 5 recto); Rome, Teatro Tordinone, section and detail of beam (SM, Drawer 45, Set 6, Item 2 verso).

Notes to Pages 159–64 361

22. Dumont, *Parallèle de plans des plus belles salles de spectacles d'Italie et de France, avec les détails de machines théatrales* (Paris, 1763).

23. BQS, MS cod. 35, no. 1175, fols. 31 recto–40 verso, covers the period of Selva's English visit. His own journal information can be augmented by two other manuscript accounts: BM Egerton MS 2,002, fols. 96–97, letter of William Lock to John Strange, 27 July 1781; and MC, P.D. 785/C/7(6), Item 11, report of the Venetian resident in London, 1 September 1781.

24. Arthur T. Bolton, "St. Luke's Hospital, Old Street," p. 199, discusses entries in SM, Soane Notebooks, 1, pp. 19, 28–34, which he relates to the Italian roofing sections. He draws the conclusion that Soane's sketches were used in consultations between Soane and Dance concerning the roofing of St. Luke's Hospital (see my chap. 3).

25. Robert Adam's praise of Sammicheli, as reported to James Adam by Torelli, is noted by Fleming, *Adam Circle,* p. 274.

26. The James Adam quotations come from his "Journal of a Tour in Italy," published in *Library of the Fine Arts* 2 (1831):169. Robert Adam's "operations" are tantalizingly alluded to in a letter of 17 November 1757 (SRO, G 18/4844).

27. BCV, L. Trezza MS 1,010, foreword.

28. Torelli's rough draft of his letter of 19 March 1771 to the Bishop is BCV, MS B. 75, Item 16. A published version is in Torelli's *Opere varie in verso e in prosa di Giuseppe Torelli Veronese,* ed. Alessandro Torri (2 vols.; Pisa, 1833–34), 2:233–34. Subsequent Torelli correspondence with John Strange refers to later visits by the Bishop; BM, Add. MS 23,737, fols. 296, 297; 23,730, fols. 7, 258, 262, 296. The Bishop's first visit to Verona in 1766 is mentioned in William Shakespeare Childe-Pemberton, *The Earl Bishop,* 1:81. Marco Menato, assistant to the director, Franco Riva, helped me with Torelli and Trezza-related material in the BCV.

29. See my "Eighteenth-Century English Sources for a History of Swiss Wooden Bridges."

30. BCV, L. Trezza MS 1,010, p. 110.

31. BM, Egerton MS 2,002, fol. 28, letter of 16 August 1779; and SM, AL, Sir John Soane's Case, Shelf A, "Notes Italy and Italian Language," p. 318, respectively.

32. SM, "Notes Italy," p. 317, lists the expense "Drawgs £2.2.0," which may refer to a payment to Trezza.

33. Ibid., p. 315, entry for 8 May 1780.

34. See Paolo Carpeggiani, "Un Documento dell'architettura di Giulio Romano la Villa Zani di Villimpenta," *Corti e dimore del Contado Mantovano* (Florence, 1969), pp. 49–63. Carpeggiani accepts the attribution to Giulio.

35. John Soane, *Memoirs of the Professional Life of an Architect,* p. 16.

36. SM, CC 1, Division 3, B(2), Item 1, letter of 4 April 1780; and Arthur T. Bolton, *The Portrait of Sir John Soane,* pp. 27–28. Burdon's advance of £40 to

Soane against expenses "at Verona in measuring the Works of Michele San Michele," is noted in Ledger A, p. 159. Journal 1781–1797, p. 15, speaks of "Expenses at Verona."

37. SM, CC 1, Division 4, P(2), Item 32, letter of 6 May 1789.

38. BCV, L. Trezza MS 6.a. 40, is an engraved portrait of Temanza inscribed by Trezza "Luigi Trezza si pregia d' essere stato in continuo corrispondenza studioso ed amichevole col il Temanza."

39. Tommaso Temanza, *Vite dei più celebri architetti e scultori Veneziani,* p. 328, note quoting Algarotti's letter of 1759. This text is also referred to by Ottavio Bertotti-Scamozzi, *Le Fabbriche e i disegni di Andrea Palladio* (2 vols.; Vicenza, 1778), 2:6.

40. The Soane collection of fascimiles (SM, Drawer 45, Set 4, Items 1–3, 5–9) includes two drawings dated 29 September 1779 (Items 2–3). For a fuller discussion, see my *John Soane's Architectural Education,* pp. 260–62. A recent discussion of the original S. Petronio drawings in Rudolf Wittkower's *Gothic versus Classic: Architectural Projects in Seventeenth Century Italy* (New York, 1974), pp. 72–78.

41. A curious Soane drawing is the ground plan of a finished version of Michelangelo's Palazzo Capitolino, Rome (SM, Drawer 45, Set 4, Item 11).

42. Giovanni Stern, *Piante, elevazioni, profili, e spaccati degli edifici della villa suburbana di Giulio III* (Rome, 1784), pls. xxvii–xxix, shows views of S. Andrea very close to the Soane cross section of the church dated 30 November 1779 (SM, Drawer 45, Set 2, Item 22; see my *John Soane's Architectural Education,* pl. 239). But the resemblance is not so close as to suggest a collaboration between the two contemporaries without further evidence being forthcoming.

43. My strong suspicion is that what goes for eighteenth-century students also applies much earlier. Wolfgang Lotz has raised the specter of copied drawings with the graphic output of the young Palladio. See Lotz, "Osservazioni intorno ai disegni Palladiani," *Bolletino del Centro Internazionale di Studi di Architettura "Andrea Palladio"* 4 (1962):61–68. See also idem, "Zu Michelangelos Kopien nach dem Codex Coner," *Stil und Überlieferung in der Kunst des Abendlandes: Akten der 21. Internationalen Kongresses für Kunstgeschichte in Bonn 1964* (3 vols.; Berlin, 1967), 2:12–19.

CHAPTER NINE

1. RA, Council Minutes, vol. 1, p. 139, entry for 3 July 1772.

2. John Soane quoting Brettingham in *Memoirs of the Professional Life of an Architect,* p. 14. The critique was supposedly sent to Rome in a letter to Robert Furze Brettingham, Soane's traveling companion.

3. On Adam, see John Fleming, "James Adam and the Houses of Parliament," *Architectural Review* 119 (1956), pt. 1, pp. 327–29. Mylne's superb submission for the Concorso Clementino of 1758 has been discussed by John Harris, "Robert Mylne at the Academy of St. Luke," *Architectural Review* 130 (1961), pt. 2, pp. 341–42. Dorothy Stroud, *George Dance,* pl. 14, illustrates Dance's *magnifica gal-*

leria (also see my fig. 2.3). Finally, J. Mordaunt Crook, "The Architecture of Thomas Harrison 3," *Country Life* 149 (1971):1088–91, discusses and illustrates Harrison's Roman designs for the Piazza del Popolo.

4. Thomas Leverton Donaldson, *A Review of the Professional Life of Sir John Soane,* p. 10, first observed a resemblance between the *piazza* of St. Peter's and the British senate house. Soane attended Easter ceremonies at St. Peter's in 1779 (see chap. 7).

5. On the chronology of Peyre's Roman designs, see the Académie de France à Rome exhibition catalogue *Piranèse et les français, 1740–1790,* p. 267.

6. Soane's exact address in Rome has never been confirmed. My own lengthy search among the Stato delle Anime records of the Archivio Vicariato, S. Giovanni in Laterano was fruitless. In 1779, however, the Grand Tourist Lord George Herbert reported Robert Furze Brettingham to be living at the "Quartiere" of the Avignonese papal guards (near SS. Trinità). Soane was his companion. Soane's name appears immediately ahead of Brettingham's on Herbert's list, suggesting they lived in the same place. See Sidney Charles Herbert, ed., *Henry, Elizabeth, and George (1734–80),* pp. 273–74.

7. William Shakespeare Childe-Pemberton, *The Earl Bishop,* 1:202.

8. Rupert Gunnis, *Dictionary of British Sculptors, 1660–1851,* p. 39, quotes from a sale catalogue that noted that before returning from Rome in 1779, the British sculptor Thomas Banks had prepared an "original model for a monument to Lord Chatham, a great composition of five figures . . . . This model arrived in England too late for the decision of the Judges."

9. For a discussion of the topic, see Damie Stillman, "Death Defied and Honor Upheld: The Mausoleum in Neo-Classical England." A useful appendix lists the numerous mausolea exhibited from 1768–93.

10. RA, Council Minutes, vol. 1, p. 303, entry for 13 April 1781.

11. *Royal Academy Exhibition Catalogue* (London, 1781), pp. 18 (for Paine), 20 (for Park); and ibid. (London, 1779), p. 12 (for Harrison). Harrison's reference to Parliament seems to relate to the *Proceedings of the House of Commons,* where on 11 May 1778, Mr. Rigby, M.P., opened an inconclusive debate about a proper "monument" to be erected for the deceased Earl of Chatham. (See also the implication in n. 8 supra of some sort of competition.)

12. The Stockholm drawing is mentioned by Peter Howell in his notes to the Grosvenor Museum's exhibition catalogue, *The Modest Genius: An Exhibition of Drawings and Works of Thomas Harrison* (Chester, 1977), pp. 8, 24. I am most grateful to Mr. Howell for drawing my attention to the catalogue, for discussing Harrison with me, and for showing me an illustration of the Stockholm drawing. Howell's entries on Harrison should be consulted in the *Catalogue of the Drawings Collection of the Royal Institute of British Architects,* vol. G–K (Farnborough, 1973).

13. SM, Dance Cabinet, Slider 4, Set 11, Item 1 verso, letter of 7 June 1763 to his father. Damie Stillman deals with the whole question of competitions in "British Architects and Italian Architectural Competitions, 1758–1780."

14. See my chap. 2.

15. BM, Egerton MS 2,002, fol. 28, letter of Rowland Burdon to John Strange,

16 August 1779, written from Bologna, expressed the intention of arriving at Milan in a week's time. The normal route would be through Parma.

16. SM, AL, Sir John Soane's Case, Shelf C, OSMAS, Item 182. The section written in Italian closely follows the program as set out in IPT, Atti della Reale Accademia Pittura Scultura Architettura Instituita in Parma, vol. 1, pp. 130–31. For the full text of the letter, see Arthur T. Bolton, *The Portrait of Sir John Soane*, pp. 22–23, or the more carefully transcribed version in my *John Soane's Architectural Education, 1753–80*, pp. 243–45.

17. RIBA, Library, Sandby Lecture 2, p. 38, exhorted his pupils to "contribute something . . . towards the completion of an Art, which may not yet [have] arrived to its utmost perfection." And see the passage of William Chambers's letter to Edward Stevens quoted in my chap. 7.

18. The second set of sketches is inserted as SM, OSMAS, Item 183 recto and verso. Soane's letter (Item 182) has become separated from the sketches, but a close inspection demonstrates that they originally formed one piece of paper. The fold marks of letter and sketches match exactly, as does the line of the tear. Finally, the watermark of the paper was severed in two at the time of the separation, and part of it appears on the one sheet, part on the other. For some reason Soane carefully erased the name of his recipient at a later date. The missing two words can now be confidently supplied as "Mr. Pitt."

19. Ibid.

20. See my article "'Je N'Oublieraj Jamais': John Soane and Downhill," p. 19 and n. 8 for a discussion of the doghouse design, and pl. 3 for an illustration of the earliest surviving drawing of it.

21. Soane's letter, which bore the dateline "Milan, Aug[u]st The [day left blank] 1779," must have been sent near the end of that month. Hence there is no chance that it reached its destination of Naples while Pitt was still there. According to Lord George Herbert (*Henry, Elizabeth, and George*, p. 233), Pitt was well enough to leave Naples on 28 August. Whether there was subsequent contact or correspondence between Pitt and Soane is open to speculation. Some further documentation does, however, narrow down the range of possibilities. After Pitt's departure from Naples he proceeded to Pisa, from where, on 12 September, he wrote the British resident in Venice, John Strange, of his intention of traveling to that city on his homeward journey in about a week's time (BM, Egerton MS 1,970, fol. 27). Soane meanwhile had arrived in Venice himself on or around 19 September (Archivio di Stato, Venice, Inquisitori di Stato, Busta 760, Note dei Forestieri 1773–1789, see under Ordi 2 Ottobre 1779). Soane, in order to. pick up mail from Pitt in Florence "by the latter end of September," would have had to head south from Venice shortly before. Both Pitt and Soane traveled the same road from opposite directions at about the same period. A meeting en route cannot, therefore, be excluded. Soane returned to his home base at Rome sometime in the month of October. Some drawings done in Rome are dated in the early days of November (e.g., SM, Drawer 45, Set 1, Item 15), and are close in style to the final schemes for Parma.

22. The inspiration for these fountains could come from the very similar ones

in Dance's *magnifica galleria* design (fig. 2.3). Soane would appear to have worked on the canny principle that, what had succeeded so well at Parma in 1763, might serve to please again. Alternatively Soane mentioned his familiarity with the celebrated Villa Albani fountain in his *Lectures on Architecture,* p. 45. Soane's plans of the Villa Albani are SM, Drawer 45, Set 1, Item 7, and Drawer 45, Set 3, Item 18. See also fig. 11.15.

23. The statue is erroneously identified by an inscription amid the stairs as "Jacobus Infanta di Parma" (see fig. 9.14 *bottom*). No Duke of Parma by such a name reigned in Soane's day.

24. SM, Drawer 48, Set 6, Item 2, is a signed Carlo Labruzzi drawing of St. Peter's Basilica. Two notes were addressed to Soane while in Rome by a correspondent named Labruzzi. One of these is SM, CC 1, Division 2, S(30), Item 1 verso; the other is bound in with the copy in SM, GL, 15E of Charles Brand's *Tables of Interest, Discount, Annuities, etc.* (London, 1780). The signatures complicate matters because another Labruzzi, Carlo's elder brother Pietro, was also living in Rome at this time. But two samples of Pietro's handwriting eliminate him, I think, as a possibility (see IPT, Letter Box 1761–1763). On the Labruzzis in general, see Brinsley Ford, et al., *Il Settecento à Roma* (Rome, 1959).

25. IPT, Atti, pp. 143, 136, respectively, lists the winners and the five runners-up who were: Francesco Poncet, Antonio Bicchieri, and Domenico Artusi (all of Parma Academy), and Luigi Gibelli and Francesco Santini, both Bolognese (Gibelli was studying in Rome with Antonio Bonetti). Artusi and Bicchieri got honorable mentions, not a shared third prize; cf. Stillman, "British Architects and Italian Architectural Competitions," p. 63, on this point.

26. The extract given from the IPT, Atti, p. 133, makes certain Soane's non-attendance at the 1780 *concorso.* But cf. Stillman, "British Architects and Italian Architectural Competitions," p. 63.

27. Why Soane abandoned the *concorso* of 1780 is difficult to ascertain; certainly his drawings were pretty far advanced. The explanation may lie in the fact that in December 1779, Soane's protector, the Bishop of Derry, succeeded to the title and estates of his brother the Earl of Bristol. Soane, in his *Memoirs,* p. 15, recalled that the Bishop immediately wrote him, summoning him back to England with promises of employment. Perhaps Soane's desire for rapid success, coupled with the uncertainty of the outcome at Parma, outweighed in the architect's mind the lure of carrying off the laurels at the *concorso.*

28. SM, CC 2, Division 14, A, Item 4, is the diploma dated on 13 March 1781. SM, AL, Sir John Soane's Case, Shelf A, Downhill Notebook, p. 88, lists letters in conjunction with the *morceau de réception* written to Count Carlo Gastone della Torre di Rezzonico, perpetual secretary of Parma Academy, and to Jean-François Ravenet, a professor of engraving there. Ravenet, son of the London-based French engraver Simon-François, may have been recommended to Soane by English acquaintants. According to Soane's *Memoirs,* p. 76, the architect received the further distinction of being elected by Parma Academy a "Consigliere Corrispondente con voto" in 1836.

29. Anatole de Montaiglon and Jules Guiffrey, eds., *Correspondance des di-*

recteurs de l'académie de France à Rome, 13:373, 389–90. The latter passage also gives Saint-Hubert's letter of 25 November 1778, according to which he had prepared sketches for the 1779 *concorso,* to which, however, he never submitted an entry. IPT, Atti, pp. 97, 101, describe Saint-Hubert as a 1778 contestant, and as second prize winner, respectively. For Saint-Hubert's subsequent career as an architect during the French Revolution (when he wisely dropped the "Saint" from his name), see Stillman, "British Architects and Italian Architectural Competitions," p. 61, nn. 54–56; to which bibliography may be added the brief account of Saint-Hubert's work for his brother-in-law, Jacques-Louis David, contained in David L. Dowd, "Pageant-Master of the Republic: Jacques-Louis David and the Revolution," *University of Nebraska Studies,* n.s. 5 (1948):133. Also, mention should not be omitted of Giuseppina Allegri-Tassoni's exhibition catalogue, *Mostra dell'Accademia Parmense, 1752–1952* (Parma, 1952), pl. 18, which reproduced for the first time part of Saint-Hubert's elevation for the *castello d'acqua.* Allegri-Tassoni's next plate illustrates a public fountain in the form of a mountain, covered with warring statues, and set in a piazza. She ascribes no name or date to this project, but it might very well represent the design of one of the runners-up in 1780. I did not find this drawing during my researches in the disorganized but rich collection of architectural projects preserved at Parma.

30. IPT, Atti, pp. 97, 127, respectively. Ulrich Thieme and Felix Becker, *Allgemeines Lexikon der Bildenden Künstler* (37 vols.; Leipzig, 1907–50), 27:232, mention a painter and an architect named Poma who were probably relations of Vincenzo's.

31. On the long tradition of successful French participation in Parmesan *concorsi,* see Louis Hautecoeur, "L'Académie de Parme et ses concours à la fin du XVIIIe siècle," *Gazette des beaux-arts,* 4th ser., 4 (1910):147–65.

32. Stillman, "British Architects and Italian Architectural Competitions," p. 61, points out the close resemblance between the Saint-Hubert *castello d'acqua* design and his design for a *lazaret,* which won him the Prix de Rome in 1784. It should be noted that a 1787 *château d'eau,* by Réverchon, complete with quadriga and cascade, bespeaks a direct knowledge of Saint-Hubert's *castello d'acqua* (see Emil Kaufmann, *Architecture in the Age of Reason,* p. 204, pl. 185). Saint-Hubert, having copied de Seine, was in turn plagiarized by Réverchon!

33. IPT, Atti, pp. 143–44. These minutes note the receipt from Saint-Hubert of an apologetic note drawing attention to his error in delineating the hypotrachelion, which he attributed to haste in meeting the deadline. Unfortunately, Saint-Hubert's original letter has not been preserved.

34. Henry Lemonnier, ed., *Procès verbaux de l'académie royale d'architecture,* 8:299–300, 313, discusses the *château d'eau* program and the winner. The friendship of the two students is further pointed to by the fact that in 1786 Saint-Hubert petitioned to be able to complete the studies of the Pantheon left unfinished by de Seine at his untimely death (de Montaiglon and Guiffrey, eds., *Correspondance des directeurs,* 15:67, 73).

35. IPT, Atti, pp. 161–70, 198, 211–21, 229, 252, record that Poma unsuccessfully attempted to win first prize in the *concorsi* of 1781, 1783, 1784, 1785, and

1786, respectively. Obviously Poma was persistent. Already in 1783 he had moved away and was submitting from "Ardena sullo stato di Milano." Apparently this town was situated near Turin, but I have been unable to identify the locality, or to shed any further light on Poma's subsequent career.

36. IPT, Atti, pp. 144–45. Stillman, "British Architects and Italian Architectural Competitions," p. 63, states that the academicians saw in Poma's design "il genio de'Giovani." But the phrase should read, "d'esercitare il genio de'Giovani"; that is, "to exercise the genius of the youths." It refers to the reason for asking that the waterworks be sited in a city and does not apply to Poma's scheme.

37. The debate, with special emphasis on Piranesi's crucial role in it, is nicely summarized by Rudolf Wittkower, "Piranesi's 'Parere su l'Architettura,'" *Journal of the Warburg Institute,* 2 (1938–39):147–58. Wittkower wrote: "Peculiar as it may seem . . . the discussion about the originality and merit of the Tuscan order was of central importance in the battle of the 'Grecians' and 'Romans'" (p. 151).

38. See my n. 17 of chap. 7 concerning Soane in Paestum. Soane's negative comments about Paestum Doric would seem to be at variance with the favorable interpretation imputed to him by Dorothy Stroud, "Soane's Designs for a Triumphal Bridge," p. 262, and by Michael J. McCarthy, "Documents on the Greek Revival in Architecture," *Burlington Magazine* 114 (1972):760–69. Nikolaus Pevsner and S. Lang, "Apollo or Baboon," discuss the controversy in England regarding the baselessness of the Doric.

39. See my chap. 12 concerning Laugier's primitivism.

40. That primitive connotations were associated with the Doric in Soane's mind cannot be doubted. Many decades later he published a version of the waterworks in which the columns were shown sheathed in bark, a direct reference to the primordial nature of the order. See John Soane, *Designs for Public and Private Buildings,* 1832, pl. xxxiv*.

41. See the second edition of Edmund Burke's *A Philosophical Enquiry into the Origin of Our Ideas of the Sublime and Beautiful,* pp. 58–59, and 151. Both Dora Wiebenson, "'L'Architecture Terrible' and the 'Jardin Anglo-Chinois,'" *Journal of the Society of Architectural Historians* 27 (1968):136–39, and Helen Rosenau, *Social Purpose in Architecture,* p. 13, comment on the influence of Burke's philosophy on the Continent.

42. Stillman, "British Architects and Italian Architectural Competitions," p. 65.

CHAPTER TEN

1. Soane's annotated copy of Louis Dutens's *Itinéraire des routes les plus fréquentées,* p. 110 (SM, AL, 34B), lists the architect's arrival at Brussels on 18 or 19 June 1780, en route for embarcation at a Channel port.

2. Rumors about the loss of all Soane's material gathered abroad were innocently started by individuals like James Irvine, who had sent belongings back

to England in Soane's care (BM, Add. MS 36,493, vol. 3, fol. 68, letter of 16 December 1780). Later, Joseph Farington manipulated these stories with malicious intent to discredit the architect (FD, entry for 4 March 1810; see my n. 5 of chap. 8 for this quotation). Soane's biographer, Thomas Leverton Donaldson, felt obliged to refute the rumors, so widespread had they become (*A Review of the Professional Life of Sir John Soane*, p. 11). Soane listed the lost contents of his trunk in an undated letter to a Swiss official, SM, CC 2, Division 14, B(1), Item 6; and Arthur T. Bolton, *The Portrait of Sir John Soane*, pp. 31–32; but cf. my *John Soane's Architectural Education, 1753–80*, pp. 334–35, for a more faithful transcription.

3. Derek L. Howard, *John Howard: Prison Reformer*.

4. Cesare Beccaria, *Crimes and Punishments*, trans. James Anson Farrer (London, 1880), p. 119. The first English translation appeared in 1768.

5. James Baldwin Brown, *Memoirs of the Public and Private Life of John Howard, the Philanthropist; Compiled from His Own Diary* (2d ed.; London, 1823), pp. 232, 234–35, 308. Baldwin states that the actual authors of the bill were Justice Sir William Blackstone and Mr. Eden, later, Lord Auckland. Howard's fellow members of the board were Dr. John Fothergill and George Whately.

6. Ibid., p. 309, and see also Howard, *John Howard*, p. 87, for the full text of the letter to George Whately. Malcolm Ramsey, "John Howard and the Discovery of the Prison," p. 9 writes: "Like other reformers, Howard . . . was perhaps more concerned to sell . . . than to provide an 'after sales' service."

7. A copy of the Privy Council decree from the *Court Gazette* is preserved in HMST, vol. 94, 3d series, fol. 47. See BM, Egerton MS 2,002, fol. 72 verso for Bowdler's letter to John Strange in Venice (letter of 20 January 1781). Gilbert Elliot, *Life and Letters of Sir Gilbert Elliot, First Earl of Minto* (3 vols.; London, 1874), 1:56–73, tells of Elliot's departure from England for Russia in July 1781 and his return that September. This absence slowed down activities. For Bowdler's election as F.R.S., see Journal Book of the Royal Society, vol. 30, p. 198 (minutes of 8 February 1781), in the possession of the Royal Society, London.

8. HMST, vol. 94, 3d series, fol. 51 recto and verso, and fol. 52 recto (letter of 1 July 1781). Fol. 52 recto ends with the salutation: "I can hardly expect that Lord Loughborough will be at the trouble of reading so much of my nonsense." This positively identifies the recipient of the letter as Loughborough.

9. John Soane, *Memoirs of the Professional Life of an Architect*, p. 16.

10. Bowdler's letter made clear that, on the recommendation of Sir Gilbert Elliot, Leverton had been allowed to perform certain surveying jobs for the supervisors (HMST, vol. 94, 3d series, fol. 51 verso).

11. Ibid., fol. 49 recto. This is Bowdler's important memorandum recording the various actions of the supervisors. Fol. 57 recto is a clipping from the *Public Advertiser*.

12. HMST, vol. 94, 3d series, fol. 58, broadsheet dated 25 August 1781, and entitled: "To the Gentlemen who Intend Composing Designs for the Penitentiary Houses."

13. SM, Soane Notebooks, 1, p. 21. Ibid., p. 51, is a reference to one or more letters to Bowdler.

14. See John Howard, *State of the Prisons* (Warrington, 1780), pp. 129–30, 132–35. On the various editions of Howard's books the best source is Leona Baumgartner's exemplary bibliographic study, *John Howard (1726–1790), Hospital and Prison Reformer: A Bibliography* (Baltimore, 1939). Soane's library preserves an unannotated copy of the second edition (SM, AL, 41B). The identification of the second edition as that used by Soane can be substantiated on the basis of small textual variations, and differences in the engraving copied by Soane in my fig. 10.3.

15. Allan Braham, *The Architecture of the French Enlightenment* (London, 1980), pl. 264, reproduces Jacques-Pierre Gisors's prison design for the 1778 grand prix of the Paris academy. The rival design of Louis Combes, which also uses some radial symmetry, is discussed by Georges-François Pariset, "L'Architecture néo-classique de Bordeaux: l'architecte Combes," *Stil und Überlieferung in der Kunst des Abendlandes: Akten der 21. Internationalen Kongresses für Kunstgeschichte in Bonn 1964* (3 vols.; Berlin, 1967), 1:175–84. Neither student won a prize because the contest was called off at the last moment (Henry Lemonnier, ed., *Procès verbaux de l'académie royale d' architecture*, 8:350–51, 359–60). A radial prison plan is engraved in Jean-François de Neufforge, *Recueil élémentaire d' architecture*, supplementary volume, cahier 49, pl. 5. This appeared in Paris in 1779, which makes it roughly contemporary with the Ghent prison, called by Thomas A. Markus, "The Pattern of the Law," pp. 251–52, "the first radial prison." Nikolaus Pevsner, *A History of Building Types,* p. 161, refers to the Maison de Force as begun in 1772 to the design of the Vicomte J. P. Villain, Malfaison and S. J. Kluchman. It was not completed until the 1830s. Helen Rosenau, *Social Purpose in Architecture,* pp. 79–80, includes the Ghent prison in her general discussion of prison architecture.

16. SM, AL, Sir John Soane's Case, Shelf A, "Notes Italy and Italian Language," p. 317 (entry for 7 May 1780). Pevsner, *A History of Building Types,* p. 164, notes the Milan Hospital as a source for the House of Correction built in the same city in ca. 1775. Dutens's *Itinéraire,* contains no annotated references to Soane having visited Ghent or its prison. See n. 1 on Dutens.

17. 19 George III, cap. 74, p. 1409, gives the maximum internal cell width as 8 feet.

18. Ibid., pp. 1413, 1417, and see Howard on Vilforde prison, *State of the Prisons,* pp. 129–30.

19. 19 George III, cap. 74, pp. 1397, 1399, and 1414, respectively. On the necessity of a chaplain, see Howard, *State of the Prisons,* pp. 25–50, and pp. 5–15 (on the idea of "reformation").

20. 19 George III, cap. 74, pp. 1399, 1397, 1416–23, respectively. On the need for resident governors in Bridewells, see Howard, *State of the Prisons,* pp. 25–50.

21. Howard's various pronouncements on prison infirmaries are principally to be found in *State of the Prisons,* pp. 24–50. 19 George III, cap. 74, pp. 1397, 1399, 1415, enacted the construction of an infirmary, appointment of an apothecary, and confinement of those who were ill to the sick ward, respectively.

22. For this practice, see Howard, *State of the Prisons,* pp. 130–33. The Act of

Parliament makes similar elaborate provisions (19 George III, cap. 74, p. 1412).

23. 19 George III, cap. 74, p. 1409, and Howard, *State of the Prisons,* pp. 5–15.

24. Leslie Fairweather, in *United Nations Social Defence Research Institute: Prison Architecture* (London, 1975), p. 18, dismisses Soane's scheme on account of "administrative difficulties." But Mr. Fairweather told me in conversation that he had not examined Soane's original drawings with their detailed inscriptions.

25. Howard, *State of the Prisons,* pp. 24–50 and 19 George III, cap. 74, p. 1391, which described the proposed penitentiaries as "plain, strong and substantial." These same adjectives are repeated in the broadsheet for competitors (HMST, fol. 94, 3d series, fol. 58).

26. See Harold D. Kalman, "Newgate Prison," pp. 53, 55; Dorothy Stroud, *George Dance,* pp. 98–99; and Howard, *State of the Prisons,* pp. 16–23.

27. Burke went on to add "length strikes least; a hundred yards of even ground will never work such an effect as a tower a hundred yards high" (*A Philosophical Enquiry into the Origin of Our Ideas of the Sublime and Beautiful,* p. 127). Kalman, "Newgate Prison," p. 55, would have had a stronger argument had he emphasized the Burkean concept of "difficulty" rather than that of "vastness." See also J. Mordaunt Crook's note on Newgate in the Council of Europe's exhibition catalogue *The Age of Neo-Classicism,* p. 521.

28. Markus, "Pattern of the Law," p. 255, and Rosenau, *Social Purpose in Architecture,* pp. 80–82 and 89–91. See also Nils G. Wollin, *Gravures originales de Desprez* (Malmö, 1933), p. 129, and pl. 184.

29. For a discussion, see Kerry Downes, *Vanbrugh* (London, 1977), p. 48. Stroud, *Dance,* p. 99, when referring to the fenestration of the keeper's house at Newgate Prison, notes the Vanbrughian air of the details. Soane, in his *Lectures on Architecture,* p. 145, expressed particular admiration for Vanbrugh's chimneys.

30. Warren Hunting Smith, *Architecture in English Fiction* (New Haven, 1934), p. 11, cites a fictional character's remark from Frances Burney's *Cecilia, or the Memoirs of an Heiress* (London, 1782), bk. 6, chap. 9, to the effect that, with the addition of a few iron bars, medieval Delville Castle could easily be transformed into a "gaol for the county." See also my n. 43 infra on Burney's observations about jails.

31. Pevsner, *A History of Building Types,* p. 164, describes Soane's women's penitentiary as "on the Panopticon principle," referring to Jeremy Bentham's 1791 book on this subject. But Soane's scheme lacks the single vantage point at the core of Bentham's design.

32. Rosenau, *Social Purpose in Architecture,* p. 84. But see also my review of her book in *RACAR* 1 (1974):63–65.

33. I make reference here to the drawings in SM, Drawer 13, Set 1, Items 12 and 13, which show this feature of a rooftop terrace. By contrast, the designs make no provision for the dungeons as found in the men's penitentiary. This may be an oversight on Soane's part or a result of his belief in the greater intractability of men compared with women.

34. Jacques-François Blondel, *Cours d'Architecture,* 1:410–12, 419–21, com-

pared masculine and feminine characteristics of buildings to their rectangularity or curvilinearity.

Notes to Pages 215–17   371

35. See the newspaper clipping dated 23 August and the broadsheet of 25 August 1781 (HMST, vol. 94, 3d series, fol. 57 recto, and fol. 58, respectively). Ibid., fol. 49 verso is Bowdler's memorandum of the supervisors' actions. It is not clear whether Bowdler meant 60 drawings or 60 competitors. But the Dublin Exchange competition of 1769 attracted no less than 64 entrants (see Thomas J. Mulvany, *The Life of James Gandon,* p. 30).

36. SM, Soane Notebooks, 1, pp. 2–4, 9, and Ledger A, p. 158, and Journal 1781–1797, p. 7, all give details of Soane's involvement with Newgate in 1781.

37. SM, Soane Notebooks, 2, p. 11, and see HMST, vol. 94, 3d series, fol. 54 (Plan of Lands in the Parish of Battersea), which may relate to Soane's survey though it is not in his hand.

38. John Soane, *Designs for Public and Private Buildings* (1832), p. 44, and cf. the slightly different version in his *Memoirs,* p. 17.

39. Soane, *Memoirs,* p. 17, dryly commented that Hardwick "was not so successful" when it came to the actual building of the women's penitentiary. The primary evidence of the competition's outcome is the newspaper clipping datable to between 23 March and 1 April 1782 in HMST, vol. 94, 3d series, fol. 56 recto. It announces Hardwick and George Richardson as first and second prize winners of the women's penitentiary, and Bowdler's memorandum (ibid., fol. 49 verso), gives Blackburn first prize in the men's penitentiaries. Leverton displayed drawings at the Royal Academy in 1783 for "which a premium was received" so he must be the second prize winner. The *Royal Academy Exhibition Catalogues* list the following exhibitors who may also have shown competition drawings: T. Field (1785), John Harvey (1785), Samuel Robinson (1785), William Tyler (1785), and James Paine the Younger (1783). It should be noted, however, that the RA gold medal subject for 1784 had been a "national prison" along Howardian lines (RA, Council Minutes, vol. 1, p. 352, entry for 17 January 1784). The only contestant and eventual winner was George Hadfield (RA, General Assembly Minutes, vol. 1, p. 184, entry for 10 December 1784).

40. Soane, *Designs for Public and Private Buildings* (1832), p. 67, quoted also in Frank Jenkins, *Architect and Patron,* p. 152.

41. SM, CC 1, Division 3, D(5), Item 1; and see Bolton, *Portrait,* pp. 44–45. The extent of Dance's knowledge of Soane's designs is important to note in the likelihood that they exchanged ideas on prison design. Another of Soane's friends, John Stuart, wrote on 25 December 1781: "What has become of the penitentiary Houses? is Dr. Bowdler Dead? Write me for Heaven sake what has befallen you" (SM, CC 1, Division 4, S(3), Item 64). This letter indicates the degree of Soane's involvement with the penitentiary designs.

42. J. Mordaunt Crook and Michael H. Port, *The History of the Kings Works,* 6 (London, 1973):1–10, indicate the effects of the economical reforms of Burke and Gilbert on building in the early 1780s. Dr. Kippis, the biographer of William Blackburn, one of the successful competitors, wrote of the penitentiaries: "the circumstances of the times . . . diverted the attention of public men from this

important object"; see John Hutchins, *The History and Antiquities of the County of Dorset* (2d ed.; 4 vols.; London, 1796–1814), 2:25.

43. A drawing of St. Stephen's Walbrook by Baldwin is inscribed as a gift to Soane (SM, AL, folio 1, Item 7A and B). The date of the drawing cannot be determined despite my effort to match the address given with one of Baldwin's numerous changes of abode. On Baldwin's relations with Dance and Peacock, see n. 24 of my chap. 2, and Stroud, *Dance,* pp. 89–90. Markus, "Pattern of the Law," fig. 9, reproduces the same Baldwin plan or one similar to that illustrated here (fig. 10.14), but assigns it a date of ca. 1792. I do not know the grounds for that dating. Whereas the provisions of the plan in the Soane Museum far exceed the 600 male prisoners specified in the competition regulations, many other aspects relate closely to Soane's designs of 1782.

44. Alexander Wedderburn (Lord Loughborough), *Observations on the State of English Prisons and the Means of Improving Them* (London, 1793), p. 12.

45. For Fanny Burney's comments, also quoted in part at the beginning of this chapter, see *Diary and Letters of Madame d'Arblay* (4 vols.; London, 1876), 2:576. Pevsner, *A History of Building Types,* discusses the early Howardian jails in England. The one at Dorchester is the subject of Miss M. B. Weinstock's "Dorchester Model Prison, 1791–1816," *Proceedings of the Dorset Natural History and Archaeological Society* 78 (1956):94 ff.

CHAPTER ELEVEN

1. SM, AL, Sir John Soane's Case, Shelf A, Downhill Notebook, pp. 92–94.

2. See the *Daily Advertiser,* no. 17,195 (3 March 1783) for the house on Powis Place off Great Ormond Street. The valuation on the Cheapside properties of Adams is SM, CC 1, Division 8, G, Item 17 (signed by George Wyatt and dated 4 October 1784). See also, SM, Ledger A, p. 2, and Account Book 1781–86, p. 100.

3. Details concerning Francis Adams are contained in old editions of *Burke's Landed Gentry.* Bills paid to Soane by the Bristol Bank and Soane's mention of Mrs. Adams's maternal grandfather, the Reverend Mr. F. C. Fowell (SM, Soane Notebooks, 12, p. 1) confirm Francis Adams as the patron in question. Shute Adams's will is PRO, PROB. 6/142. He is described as "of Bristol." Francis Adams's will is PRO 660, fo. 639 (1807). I owe this last piece of information indirectly to Miss Dorothy Stroud. In Stroud's "The Early Work of Soane," p. 121, and in her *Architecture of Sir John Soane,* p. 157, she describes Adams Place as "the tidying up" of an existing complex.

4. SM, Soane Notebooks, 1, p. 17 (memo of 4 July valuing "Mr. Adams half" at £260). My hope to find property deeds among the papers of the Adams family solicitors, Bolton and Lowe of the Temple, proved forlorn.

5. SM, Soane Notebooks, 3, p. 24; 4, pp. 36, 45; 5, pp. 4, 16; 6, pp. 7–8; Journal 1781–1797, pp. 52 left and also the St. George's Southwark Parish Poor Rate Book for 1783 in the Newington District Library, Walworth Road, London.

6. SM, Soane Notebooks, 6, p. 35 and Journal 1781–1797, p. 52 right; a copy

of Soane's correspondence with Adams is in Precedents in Architecture 1784, fols. 17 recto–18 recto (letters dated 25 February and 30 March 1784). Soane's final breakdown of costs is in Abstract of Bills 1782, pp. 52–54.

7. The best source on Southwark is William Rendle and Philip Norman, *Inns of Old Southwark and Their Associations.* On p. 245 they mention a manuscript account (19 September 1789) according to which the Falcon Inn and the Half Moon across the street were destroyed by fire. I have been unable to corroborate this information and assume the date of 1789 is incorrect.

8. Although documentary evidence is somewhat scanty, it would seem that the back-to-back row house was a more recent development than the tenement. For a discussion, see M. W. Beresford, "The Back to Back House in Leeds, 1787–1937," in Stanley D. Chapman, ed., *The History of Working-Class Housing: A Symposium,* pp. 95 ff.

9. Ibid.

10. See Donald J. Olsen, *Town Planning in London,* pp. 20–21, 128, 209, 211 and especially his review of C. W. Chalklin, *The Provincial Towns of Georgian England: A Study of the Building Process, 1740–1820,* in *Journal of the Society of Architectural Historians* 35 (1976):76–77. Olsen writes: "London houses intended from the outset for working class occupation were virtually non-existent until the nineteenth century."

11. SM, AL, 3B. The copy is not annotated and is the second edition published in London in 1776, not the first edition of 1775.

12. See n. 8 supra.

13. On Dance's activity as a designer of commercial premises, see Harold D. Kalman, "The Architecture of Mercantilism: Commercial Buildings by George Dance the Younger," in Paul Fritz and David Williams, eds., *The Triumph of Culture: Eighteenth-Century Perspectives* (Toronto, 1972), pp. 69–95. A popular pattern book on shop fronts has been dated as early as 1792 by David Dean, *English Shop Fronts from Contemporary Source Books, 1792–1840* (London, 1970).

14. 14 George III, cap. 78, pp. 483–542. The provisions of the act are well summarized by John Summerson, *Georgian London,* pp. 125–30.

15. SM, Account Book 1781–86, p. 2, Abstract of Bills 1782, p. 54, and Journal 1781–1797, p. 13, respectively.

16. 14 George III, cap. 78, pp. 514–15 speaks of the materials permitted under the act as including "artificial stone."

17. See the *Descriptive Catalogue of Coade's Artificial Stone Manufactory* (London, 1784), p. 8, item 186. Summerson, *Georgian London,* pp. 130–32, gives a succinct history of Coade stone. Other discussions include K. A. Esdaile, "Coade Stone," *Architect and Building News* 161 (1940):94–96, 112–14; S. B. Hamilton, "Coade Stone," *Architectural Review* 116 (1954):295–301; and Alison Kelly, "Mrs. Coade's Stone," *Connoisseur* 197 (1978):14–25; idem; "Coade Stone at National Trust Houses," *National Trust Studies* (London, 1980), pp. 95–111. The chief visual record of Coade's output remains the set of etchings and engravings she produced from 1777 onwards, a copy of which is in the BM, Library (1802.b.24). My fig. 11.8 is reproduced from it.

18. In the Guildhall Library, London, Photographic Collection, Box BS2/ BOR, is a photo dated ca. 1930, showing the entrance arch into Eve's Place. The GLC street indexes preserved the name until 1955. Today a modern curtain-wall type office building occupies the site, and there is no trace of Eve's or Adam's Place, that I could discover.

19. No plan of the upper storeys of the public house exists, nor any elevation, but it is unlikely that it exceeded the 21 foot height restriction for a "third rate" building.

20. For the payments to Meymoth, see SM, Journal 1781–1797, pp. 13–14, 52 right and Soane Notebooks, 3, p. 7; 5, p. 10; 9, p. 16. The Surrey Record Office does not preserve the deputy surveyor's records for Southwark at this period. I have been able to determine that the certificates were printed and pro forma (examples are in CLRO, Judicial Records, 220E. Sessions).

21. SM, Abstract of Bills 1782, p. 56. The GLC Record Office, Surrey and Kent sewer commission, Court Minutes, no. 55 (1776–85), records a meeting of 21 August 1783, in which Adams's petition was passed upon.

22. SM, Abstract of Bills 1782, pp. 55–57.

23. For provincial cost averages, see Christopher W. Chalklin, *The Provincial Towns of Georgian England,* p. 204.

24. GBB, passim, and SM, Abstract of Bills 1782, pp. 52, 54; Account Book 1781–86, p. 1 (for rents collected). Soane charged a small rent-collector's commission.

25. SM, Soane Notebooks, 1, pp. 10–17. SM, Journal 1781–1797, p. 38, gives the total rents before construction as £113. This is confirmed by Account Book 1781–86, p. 1.

26. St. George's Southwark Parish Poor Rate Books, vol. 1776–84 west division, passim. These tenants of Adams Place in no case overlap with those listed by Soane as renting the original, older premises (see previous note). No occupations are given, but the complete change of clientele suggests a more affluent group had moved in.

27. SM, Abstract of Bills 1782, pp. 52–53; Account Book 1781–86, p. 1; and Journal 1781–97, p. 52 left.

28. Chalklin, *Provincial Towns,* pp. 270–71, 274. For Soane's commission, see SM, Ledger A, p. 3.

29. John Soane, *Memoirs of the Professional Life of an Architect,* p. 17. See also Stroud, "Early Work of Soane," p. 121, *Architecture of Sir John Soane,* p. 31, and "Soane's Designs for a Triumphal Bridge," p. 262.

30. Margot Gayle, "Iron Bridge 200 and Still Going Strong," *Historic Preservation* 31, no. 4 (October 1979):40–42, claims the official opening occurred 1 January 1781, and she gives the history of Coalbrookdale Bridge. Ted Ruddock, *Arch Bridges and Their Builders, 1735–1835* (Cambridge, 1979), p. 135, notes that an engraving of the bridge existed in 1782 and this would have increased its influence.

31. Nikolaus Pevsner, *Buildings of England: North-East Norfolk and Norwich* (Harmondsworth, 1962), p. 266 (Coslany Bridge). This same James Frost even-

tually got his revenge on Soane. In the minutes of the Tonnage Committee for 23 May 1785 (NNRO, Case 19, Shelf C), Frost was selected in preference to Soane for the construction of the Hellesdon Bridge near Norwich. Soane's original drawing for the Hellesdon Bridge, dated February 1785, is in NNRO, Norwich Maps and Plans, Item 71.

32. SM, Soane Notebooks, 6, pp. 43, 45–46; Journal 1781–97, p. 57 left; and minutes of the Tonnage Committee for 12 March 1783 (NNRO, Case 19, Shelf C).

33. NNRO, Assembly Minute Book 1776–1790, entries for 17 March and 7 April 1783 (NNRO, Case 16, Shelf 10), and relevant minutes in the Tonnage Committee Book. A Soane estimate for £1,282.19.6, dated March 1783, is in SM, CC 2, Division 14, K, Item 1.

34. John Stacy, *A Topographical and Historical Account of the City of Norwich* (Norwich, 1819), p. 105 ("the strength of its construction [is] remarkable"). Stacy's detailed description follows closely that given by Soane in his *Plans, Elevations, and Sections of Buildings.*

35. See n. 70 of my chap. 4. SM, AL, 38B is a copy of Perronet's *Description des projets et de la construction des ponts* (3 vols.; Paris, 1782–89). I could find no mention of iron being used for reinforcement except in the piers of the bridge at Neuilly.

36. Compare Soane's drawings SM, Drawer 57, Set 8, Item 17 recto (Reichenau Bridge), and Portfolio 3, Item 13 verso (Wettingen Bridge). For a full discussion, see my "Eighteenth-Century English Sources for a History of Swiss Wooden Bridges," pp. 56–57.

37. SM, Ledger A, p. 72, and Soane, *Memoirs,* p. 17.

38. SM, Soane Notebooks, 12, p. 4, notes Soane's personal reception by the Mayor of Norwich and the Speaker of the Assembly, on 2 July 1784.

39. On the Society of Dilettanti's history and membership, see Lionel Cust and Sydney Colvin, *History of the Society of Dilettanti.* The early expeditions sponsored by the Society have been dealt with in detail by Dora Wiebenson, *Sources of the Greek Revival in Architecture,* and J. Mordaunt Crook, *The Greek Revival.* But no mention is made of Soane's design in any of the literature on his work.

40. Cust and Colvin, *History of the Society of Dilettanti,* p. 59, record the resolution for a new clubhouse moved 1 March 1761. Vardy's design is listed in Algernon Graves's *Society of Artists of Great Britain,* p. 266. The entry itself dates Vardy's design to 1751. Unless this is an instance of Graves's incorrect transcription, the clubhouse designs of Vardy would appear to go back ten years further. I am tempted to connect with these clubhouse schemes a recently published James Stuart drawing for a sculpture gallery. But there seems no compelling internal evidence for the link other than Stuart's close ties with the Society. See pl. 25b in John Harris's "Newly Acquired Designs by James Stuart in the British Architectural Library, Drawings Collection," *Architectural History* 22 (1979):72–77.

41. Cust and Colvin, *History of the Society of Dilettanti,* p. 60; Wiebenson, *Sources of the Greek Revival,* p. 62; and *Catalogue of the Drawings Collection of the Royal*

Institute of British Architects, vol. L–N (Farnborough, 1973), pp. 128, 136–37, lists Newton's 17 drawings.

42. The *Survey of London*, vol. 39, "The Grosvenor Estate" (London, 1977), pp. 119–20, gives the details of Crunden's speculation in Hereford Street. Some accounts of Crunden's from 1777 relating to Pitt's properties are preserved in SM, Copies of Bills 1782, pp. 129–31. For Crunden's affiliation with Holland, see Dorothy Stroud, *Henry Holland, His Life and Architecture*, p. 26.

43. *Daily Advertiser*, nos. 17,357, 17,358, and 17,591 (8–9 September 1783 and 7 June 1784), respectively. SM, Soane Notebooks, 11, pp. 41, 56, record Soane's attendance at Christie's salesrooms on 23 June 1784.

44. SM, CC 1, Division 4, P(2), Item 1, copy of a letter to Banks of 7 February 1785, referring to an earlier conversation. The original is in SDSA, MSS vol. 1 (1736–1800), fols. 310–11.

45. In these years the Dilettanti possessed two fragments of the north frieze of the Parthenon, though neither one showed oxen. The provenance of these pieces, now in the British Museum, is traced in Arthur H. Smith, *A Guide to the Sculptures of the Parthenon* (London, 1908), pp. 94, 97.

46. Anna Riggs Miller, *Letters from Italy*, 2:165–69. John Soane, *Lectures on Architecture*, p. 45.

47. Mural types of museological arrangement are mentioned by Helmut Seling, "The Genesis of the Museum," *Architectural Review* 141 (1967):104, 112; Nikolaus Pevsner, *A History of Building Types*, p. 116; and Germain Bazin, *The Museum Age* (New York, 1967), p. 160. The topic of evolving display techniques needs greater study.

48. See John Fleming, *Robert Adam and His Circle*, p. 251 and fig. 13.

49. The dating of Towneley's interior arrangements at Park Street can be narrowed down to the decade 1772–82. See Mary Webster, "Zoffany's Painting of Charles Towneley's Library in Park Street," *Burlington Magazine* 106 (1964):316–23. More recently a compendium of contemporary views of the various rooms at Park Street has appeared in Brian Cook's, "The Towneley Marbles in Westminster and Bloomsbury," *British Museum Yearbook* 2 (1977):34–78.

50. SM, CC 1, Division 4, P(2), Item 1, and SDSA, MSS vol. 1 (1736–1800), fol. 310–11. The Soane Museum retains the copy of the letter and Pitt's original manuscript proposal. The Society has the letter in Pitt's hand and a neat Soane copy of the proposal. The various copies and originals are virtually identical.

51. SDSA, Minute Book of the Society of Dilettanti, vol. 4 (1778–1798), meeting of 13 February 1785; and Cust and Colvin, *History of the Society of Dilettanti*, p. 63.

52. Colvin and Cust, *History of the Society of Dilettanti*, pp. 105–6. See also J. Mordaunt Crook, *The British Museum* (New York, 1972), for a discussion of that museum and its predecessors in England and abroad.

53. *Royal Academy Exhibition Catalogue* (London, 1784) listed two museum designs alongside that by Soane. One was exhibited by George Meredith (p. 17) and another by Soane's friend, Robert Furze Brettingham (p. 17).

1. The most thorough discussion of Soane's primitivism to date remains John Summerson's *Sir John Soane*. But, see also my "John Soane, Philip Yorke, and Their Quest for Primitive Architecture."

2. Charles James Fèret, *Fulham Old and New: Being an Exhaustive History of the Parish of Fulham* (London and New York, 1900), pp. 90–93, gives the history of the cottage and some illustrations. Other views are in the Fulham Collection of the Hammersmith Public Library, 598 Fulham Road, London. It is also worth remarking that Soane may have known the cottage built for the Hon. Robert Drummond at Cadland, Hampshire, about 1772. On Cadland, see also my n. 35 infra. I owe this information to the generosity of John C. Riely.

3. SM, Ledger A, p. 157, "Making a fair drawing of the Cottage at Fulham." The designer of Craven Cottage has never been established. Henry Holland's name has been plausibly suggested by Dorothy Stroud, *Henry Holland, His Life and Architecture*, p. 84.

4. Elizabeth Craven, *Memoirs of the Margravine of Ansbach*, 1:5, 12.

5. Nathaniel Kent, *Hints to Gentlemen of Landed Property*, p. 248.

6. V&A, 93 E. 18, No. 3306.160. For an illustration, see the color plate in my "John Soane, Philip Yorke, and Their Quest for Primitive Architecture."

7. Wolfgang Herrmann, *Laugier and Eighteenth-Century French Theory*, p. 45.

8. Herrmann discusses Laugier's theories, and (ibid., pp. 180–82) Soane's reliance on them, first noted by Summerson, *Soane*, p. 21.

9. Summerson, *Soane*, p. 17; Dorothy Stroud, *The Architecture of Sir John Soane*, p. 31, both accept the later Hammels dairy as the first manifestation of Soane's primitivism.

10. William Chambers, *Treatise on Civil Architecture*, pl. opposite p. 25; William Wrighte, *Grotesque Architecture*, pl. 1; for a discussion of the vogue for houses made from roots, see Morrison Heckscher, "Eighteenth-Century Rustic Furniture Designs," *Furniture History* 11 (1975):59–65.

11. *English Art, 1714–80* (Oxford, 1976), p. 378.

12. For an illustration and discussion of the surreal root bower at Marino, see Desmond Guinness and William Ryan, *Irish Houses and Castles* (2d ed.; New York, 1974), p. 9. The drawing in question (B1977.14.294 K) is now in the Yale Center for British Art, New Haven, Connecticut. On the authorship of this drawing, see Michael Wynne, "The Charlemont Album," *Bulletin of the Irish Georgian Society* 21 (1978):1–3. For Chambers's drawing of a primitive hut in the Royal collection at Windsor (Misc. Chambers no. 63), see John Harris, *Sir William Chambers*, pl. 196. Ironically the literature on cottage books is almost disproportionately vast. Some recent contributions are: Michael McMordie, "Picturesque Pattern Books and Pre-Victorian Designers," *Architectural History* 18 (1975):43–59; Georges Teyssot, "Cottages et Pittoresque," *Architecture Mouvement Continuité* 34 (1974):26–37; Cynthia Wolk Nachmani, "The Early English Cottage Book," *Marsyas* 14 (1968):67–76.

13. SM, Adam Drawings, vol. 42, Item 91, is a drawing of Chamier's Surrey property, Fenmells Park, dated 1765 on the verso. Item 101 is a finished version of my fig. 12.3. For William Chambers's Gothic-style dairy of about the same date at the Hoo, Hertfordshire, see *Catalogue of the Drawings Collection of the Royal Institute of British Architects,* vol. C–F (Farnborough, 1962), p. 16.

14. Lady Craven claimed credit for subsequently having an influence on French and German dairying (see her *Memoirs,* 1:75–77). French dairy designing in general had been dealt with by Johannes Langner, "Architecture pastorale sous Louis XVI," *Art de France* 3 (1963):171–86. For specific French experiments in the mode, see Paul Guth, "La Laiterie du Rambouillet," *Connaissance des Arts* 75 (1958):74–81; Raoul de Broglie, "Le Hameau et la laiterie de Chantilly," *Gazette des beaux-arts* 37 (1950):308–24; and Pierre de Nolhac, *Le Trianon de Marie Antoinette* (Paris, 1914), pp. 150–55 in particular. Dora Wiebenson, *The Picturesque Garden in France* (Princeton, 1978), mentions dairies within the general context of garden *fabriques.*

15. The Soane references to the assistance of Dance and Webber are SM, Soane Notebooks, 6, pp. 17, 20, respectively. I have compared the style of my pl. 6 with John Webber's two scenes for Sterne's *Sentimental Journey* hanging in the Soane Museum.

16. David Watkin, *Thomas Hope,* p. 87, draws attention to what he calls the "primitivist" Doric of Hammels. He implies a possible connection with Brogniart's cottage of ca. 1780 at Maupertuis near Coulommiers. The rustic cottage is illustrated in Alexandre-Louis-Joseph de Laborde, *Description des nouveaux jardins de la France et de ses anciens châteaux* (Paris, 1808), pl. 94. While some similarity to the Hammels dairy exists, the order at Maupertuis is distinguished by having a wooden plinth under the tree trunk–column, in the manner preferred by Chambers (see n. 10 supra), but not adhered to by Soane.

17. SM, Soane Notebooks, 6, p. 43, records that Yorke "ordered" work to begin 10 March 1783. The relevant accounts are in SM, Abstract of Bills 1782, pp. 4–5; Journal 1781–1797, pp. 12, 66, and Journal 1, p. 162 left. The drawing exhibited by Soane at the Royal Academy in April–June of that year is SM, Drawer 59, Set 10, Item 4, which has been so heavily coated with a layer of varnish as to become virtually invisible. Summerson, *Soane,* p. 33, and Stroud, *Architecture of Sir John Soane,* p. 31, discuss the Hammels dairy. In an amusing instance of mistranslation, Joachim Gaus describes it as a *Hammelstall* (*Hammel,* "ram"). See his "Die Urhütte: über ein Modell in der Baukunst und ein Motiv in der bildenden Kunst," *Wallraf-Richartz Jahrbuch* 33 (1971):31. I am grateful to Joseph Burke for bringing this article to my attention.

18. SM, Journal 1, p. 162 left, and Soane Notebooks, 1, p. 41, respectively. John Martin Robinson, "Model Farm Buildings of the Age of Improvement," p. 29, refers to the dairy for Lady Harrowby at Sandon, Staffordshire, executed in 1784 to the designs of Samuel Wyatt. The present Lord Harrowby showed me the HMST, vol. 437, Estate Notes 1758–1802, Doc. 67, p. 2 and Doc. 72, p. 19, which are relevant to the dairy (first conceived in 1977), but no references

could be found to Soane, nor any drawing by him at Sandon. In any event, the Hammels dairy exerted no detectable influence on the much plainer Sandon one. But Robinson informs me that the Soane Museum possesses a ground plan of the Sandon dairy complex. Perhaps, Robinson suggests, a swap of information took place between Soane and Samuel Wyatt.

19. Soane's copies of Hill Park accounts are preserved in SM, AL, Sir John Soane's Case, Shelf A, Soane's Price Book, p. 86. On the Hill Park commission, see Dorothy Stroud, *Capability Brown,* p. 229, and idem, *Henry Holland,* p. 25. The dairy was actually constructed, according to the authoritative John Preston Neale, *Views of the Seats of Noblemen and Gentlemen* (6 vols.; London, 1818–23), 2 (1819). But Neale is wrong to state the dairy derived from the much later one for Queen Charlotte, built at Frogmore, Great Windsor Park. John Carter's *Builder's Magazine,* pl. 140, is a cross section through a pyramidal dairy design (see fig. 5.7), and it too shows milk jugs on ledges.

20. For the Gothic-style ornamental dairy at Sherborne Castle, see the RCHM volume for *Dorset West* (London, 1952), p. 69.

21. SM, Soane Notebooks, 10, p. 29, and 13, p. 10, refer to Soane's purchase for Lady Elizabeth Yorke of Goethe's *Sorrows of Young Werther,* and one of Fanny Burney's fashionable sentimental novels.

22. SM, Soane Notebooks, 7, p. 19. In a letter to Soane from Thomas Pitt, dated 20 September 1788, Pitt wrote of the Boconnoc dairy: "the outside of the walls may be gravel'd as cottages sometimes are with very good effect." See SM, CC 1, Division 4, P(2), Item 23.

23. See J. Anderson, "On the Management of the Dairy, particularly with respect to the making and curing of Butter," *Letters and Papers . . . Addressed to the Society Instituted at Bath,* 5 (1790):67–122, especially, p. 94.

24. Relevant material on the building history of the Hammels lodges is contained in SM, Soane Notebooks, 1, pp. 36, 55, 58, 70, 80; 2, pp. 17, 26; 3, pp. 4, 13; 4, p. 50; 5, pp. 16, 52; 7, p. 9; 11, p. 42; and SM, Abstract of Bills 1782, pp. 8, 13; Journal 1781–1797, p. 11; Journal 1, p. 162 left. See Stroud, *Architecture of Sir John Soane,* p. 31, and idem, "The Early Work of Soane," p. 121.

25. The Brown lodge designs for Blenheim are illustrated by Stroud, *Capability Brown,* pl. 30C. The Trentham ones are dated to 1775–76 and attributed to Pickford by John Cornforth, "Trentham, Staffordshire 1," *Country Life* 143 (1968):180, and ibid., letter to the editor, p. 240, which shows the two Pickford lodge designs now in the Staffordshire Record Office (D 593/H/13/58 A and B). Mr. F. B. Stitt, the County Archivist, kindly sent me particulars relating to these drawings.

26. Chambers's higher lodges at Milton Abbey are discussed by Nikolaus Pevsner and John Newman, *Buildings of England: Dorset* (Harmondsworth, 1972), p. 293, and also the RCHM volume for *Dorset Central,* pt. 2 (London, 1970), p. 197.

27. On dentilation as a common builder's technique, see Ronald Brunskill and Alec Clifton-Taylor, *English Brickwork* (2d ed.; London, 1977), p. 79.

28. Summerson, *Soane,* p. 34.

29. The documents relevant to the Doric lodges at Langley are SM, Soane Notebooks, 12, pp. 38, 45, 47; 13, pp. 34, 50; Account Book 1781–86, p. 39; Journal 1781–1797, p. 85; Ledger A, pp. 44–45, 98–99.

30. An interesting discussion of the theories about the Doric and the primitive hut is contained in Joseph Rykwert, *On Adam's House in Paradise: The Idea of the Primitive Hut in Architectural History* (New York, 1972). Laugier, *Essai,* pp. 63, 65, called the Doric "le premier," and "le seul . . . sans base," respectively.

31. SM, Precedents in Architecture 1784, fol. 53 recto, gives Soane's profile drawing for the Langley Doric order. It was simplified in execution. Other drawings related to Langley lodges in this volume are: fols. 29 recto and verso; 52 recto and verso; 53 verso; Drawer 62, Set 8, Item 55 recto and verso.

32. John Soane, *Plans, Elevation, and Sections,* pl. 22, and see chap. 14.

33. Robert Morris, *The Art of Architecture in Imitation of Horace's Art of Poetry* (London, 1742), as quoted in his *Second Letter to the Rt. Hon. the Earl of* ——————— *Concerning the Qualities and Duties of a Surveyor* (London, 1752), p. 32. For the attribution of these anonymously published works to Morris, see Howard M. Colvin, *Biographical Dictionary of British Architects, 1600–1840,* p. 558.

34. The accounts relevant to the Burn Hall cow barn are: Account Book 1781–86, p. 29; Journal 1781–1797, p. 67 left; Ledger A, pp. 10–11; and Ledger 1, p. 100. See also, Soane Notebooks, 8, pp. 6–10, 12, 19, 27, 29, 56; 10, p. 10; 11, pp. 28–29.

35. Maldrin Drummond of Cadland kindly writes me that a home farm was built there, but that it was demolished in the 1950s.

36. A very complete review of this pattern book literature is provided by Eileen Spiegel, "The English Farm House: A Study of Architectural Theory and Design" (Ph.D. diss., Columbia University, 1960).

37. Carter, *Builder's Magazine,* pls. 27 (cottage or pub), 42 (hunting pavilion), 52 (lodges), and so forth.

38. The documents relating to Yorke Place are SM, Soane Notebooks, 13, pp. 11, 38, and Account Book 1781–86, pp. 15–16.

39. The early history of the model village in England was first provided by Gillian Darley, "In Keeping with the Mansion: The Making of a Model Village," *Country Life* 153 (1975):1080–82. In my opinion this study remains a better treatment of the subject than the same author's book *Villages of Vision.* The work of John Howard at Cardington is discussed by Nicholas Cooper, "The Myth of Cottage Life," *Country Life* 141 (1967):1290–93.

40. See Arthur Oswald, "Market Town into Model Village," *Country Life* 140 (1966):762–66. Harris, *Chambers,* p. 238, and Darley, *Villages of Vision,* p. 12, both credit Chambers with the layout, whereas Stroud, *Capability Brown,* p. 119, claims the entire design for Brown on the basis of a payment made to him. Oswald says the houses are brick, the RCHM volume says cob (see n. 26 supra).

41. SM, CC 1, Division 4, S(3), Item 2 (letter of 5 September 1780 from Stuart to Soane). Stuart wrote: "The great Brown you know is not come at able." Item 67 (ibid.), mentions a "public building," which would be battlemented. Item 69 (letter of 20 August 1782; ibid.) Stuart facetiously signed as "John Castle." See

Allanbank model village. Although Stuart may have fancied himself a "castle" builder, as his nom de plume indicates, all evidence points to Soane as the one who translated his notions into concrete schemes.

42. Kent, *Hints to Gentlemen*, p. 243. Some of Kent's illustrations are included in John Woodforde's strange little book *Georgian Houses for All* (London, 1978).

CHAPTER THIRTEEN

1. John Summerson, "The Idea of the Villa: The Classical Country House in Eighteenth-Century England," p. 585.

2. Sandra Blutman, "English Country Houses: 1780–1815." See also idem, "Books of Designs for Country Houses, 1780–1815," *Architectural History* 11 (1968):25–33.

3. Summerson, "Idea of the Villa," p. 582. But, on p. 570, Summerson did warn: "in the eighteenth century the word was never used with any *architectural* precision at all and in identifying a certain type of early eighteenth-century house as a villa I am going a little beyond the warrant of contemporary usage." See also Blutman, "English Country Houses," p. 141.

4. A discussion of many of the reconstructions after Pliny is contained in Helen Tanzer, *The Villas of Pliny the Younger* (New York, 1924). See also my joint article with Clara Bargellini, "Sources for a Reconstruction of the Villa Medici, Fiesole," *Burlington Magazine* 111 (1969):597–605; and David R. Coffin's recent *The Villa in the Life of Renaissance Rome* (Princeton, 1979). Stevens's reconstruction, shown at the RA exhibition in 1771, must have impressed the young Soane, who later purchased it (SM, Drawer 22, Set 6). Thomas Wright's "*villula*" near Durham was a literary as much as an architectural imitation of Pliny. See "Mr. Wright's Description of His Villa at Byer's Green," *Gentleman's Magazine* 63 (1793), pt. 1, pp. 213–16.

5. Alexander Pope, "Epistle to Burlington" (1731) in *Epistles to Several Persons (Moral Essays)* (London and New Haven, 1961), p. 146. See also Frances Burney, *Cecilia, or Memoirs of an Heiress* (3 vols.; London, 1893), 2:235.

6. Coventry's satirical essay appeared in the *World* on 12 April 1753 and is reprinted in full by Alexander Chalmers, ed., *The British Essayists*, 22 (Boston, 1856):152–58. The passages cited by me are on pp. 156 and 158, respectively. I owe this reference to Mr. Robert Metcalfe.

7. Books published between 1715 and 1788 which were likely to mention the word "villa" were

C. Campbell, *Vitruvius Britannicus* 3 (1725)	1 reference(s)
W. Adam, *Vitruvius Scoticus* (1720–40)	0
W. Kent, *Designs Inigo Jones* (1727)	0
J. Gibbs, *Book of Architecture* (1728)	2
R. Morris, *Select Architecture* (1755)	3
C. Over, *Ornamental Architecture* (1758)	0

J. Wood, *Description of Bath* (1765)   1 reference(s)
T. Overton, *Original Designs* (1766)   6
J. Gandon, *Vitruvius Britannicus* 4 (1767) 2
J. Paine, *Plans and Elevations* (1767) 0
W. Wrighte, *Grotesque Architecture* (1767) 0
T. Rawlins, *Familiar Architecture* (1768) 2
W. Chambers, *Treatise* (1768)   0
J. Crunden, *Convenient Architecture* (1768) 7
S. Riou, *Grecian Orders* (1768)   2
J. Gandon, *Vitruvius Britannicus* 5 (1771) 0
J. Carter, *Builder's Magazine* (1774–86) 8
R. and J. Adam, *Works* I (1778)   1
J. Soane, *Designs in Architecture* (1778) 0
J. Lewis, *Original Designs* (1780–97) 9
W. Thomas, *Original Designs* (1783) 1
J. Peacock, *Oikidia* (1785)   1
W. Pain, *British Palladio* (1786)   1
J. Miller, *Country Gentleman's Architect* (1787) 6
J. Soane, *Plans, Elevations, and Sections* (1788) 2

This information has been collected with the help of Mr. B. Weinreb and of Johannes Dobai's *Die Kunstlerliteratur des Klassizismus und der Romantik in England.*

8. Between 1770 and 1785 every Royal Academy exhibition catalogue contained mention of a "villa" design.

Year	Total Designs	"Villas"
1769	7	0
1770	13	2 (15%)
1771	16	3 (19%)
1772	23	3 (13%)
1773	21	4 (19%)
1774	12	3 (25%)
1775	23	3 (13%)
1776	14	3 (22%)
1777	17	3 (18%)
1778	17	5 (29%)
1779	14	2 (14%)
1780	47	6 (13%)
1781	41	4 (10%)
1782	38	6 (16%)
1783	31	1 (3%)
1784	38	5 (13%)
1785	44	4 (9%)

An interesting by-product of this analysis is that it shows the considerable jump in numbers of architectural exhibits between 1779 and 1780. Surely it is no coincidence that the catalogues themselves change from alphabetical to non-alphabetical. Some switch in Academy policy is implied, but I have never seen any reference to what the change might have been.

9. George Tappen, *Professional Observations on the Architecture of the Principal Ancient and Modern Buildings in France and Italy,* p. 98. Tappen's 1802 eyewitness description of Soane's drawing clarifies greatly the conflicting information from the records of the Florentine Academy itself. Archivio Accademia di belle arti, Florence, "Inventario Generale" for 1785, lists on p. 27 among the framed architectural drawings "Uno . . . disegnatovi da Gio. Soan Inglese una pianta, ed una facciata di chiesa con vetro, ed ornamento d'Ebano." By the time of the 1807 inventory, however, Soane's subject was described as a "caffehaus." My two visits to the Accademia di belle arti failed to locate Soane's drawing. I now suspect that if it still exists it was transferred not so long ago to the separate quarters of the Accademia del disegno, to which I could not gain access. Wyatt Papworth's monumental but unfootnoted *Dictionary of Architecture,* vol. R–S (London, 1887), p. 97, put me on the track of the drawing, and ultimately I was able to identify Tappen's *Professional Observations* as the source of Papworth's information.

10. V&A, Q.2.C., nos. 3417–16. See also Algernon Graves, *The Society of Artists of Great Britain,* p. 56. Graves's entries, spanning the years 1760–91, list 34 villa designs exhibited at various times.

11. Le Butard is discussed by Christopher Tadgell, *Ange-Jacques Gabriel,* pp. 43–44, 163. John Harris, *Sir William Chambers,* p. 21, gives the architect's dates in Paris.

12. The question of the bombé facade in France has been dealt with in a valuable footnote by Louis Hautecoeur, *Histoire de l'architecture classique en France* (7 vols.; Paris, 1943–57), 4:372. Since the plan type was favored by such prominent architects as de Wailly, Rousseau, Louis, Belanger, and lesser lights like Combes, the whole matter deserves a detailed study. In passing it may be mentioned that the plan type appears at least nine times in the volumes of Jean-François de Neufforge's *Recueil élémentaire d'architecture.*

13. Robert and James Adam, *The Works in Architecture of Robert and James Adam,* introduction to vol. 1 (London, 1773). See also Alistair Rowan, "After the Adelphi: Forgotten Years in the Adam Brothers' Practice—Ideal Villas as Projected and Built," *Journal of the Royal Society of Arts* 122 (1974):695–710. Executed plans with bowed fronts by Adam are discussed by Nicholas Thompson, "Moccas Court, Herefordshire," *Country Life* 140 (1976):1474–77, 1554–57, and Christopher Hussey, *English Country Houses: Mid Georgian* (2d ed.; London, 1967), pp. 98–104 (Mersham le Hatch, Kent).

14. Summerson, "Idea of the Villa," p. 577, n. 26. He mentions a dated plan of 1726 among the Talman drawings in the Ashmolean Museum, Oxford. I have not seen the plan in question.

15. Marcus Binney, "The Villas of Sir Robert Taylor," *Country Life* 142 (1967):17–21, 78–82. I have also been fortunate to have been given a copy of Binney's 1970 lecture on the villas by the Thames, delivered to the Society of Architectural Historians (GB).

16. Arthur Oswald, *Country Houses of Dorset* (2d ed.; London, 1959), pp. 169–70, discusses the house and illustrates it. The Dorset Record Office, Dorchester made available to me the account book and diaries of the patron, John Bragge (no. 8871A, and 83/6–83/9, respectively). Commander and Mrs. W. J. Eyre welcomed me to Sadborow.

17. Dorothy Stroud, in her otherwise fairly complete catalogue in *The Architecture of Sir John Soane,* omits mention of Mottram. SM, Journal 1, pp. 160 left and right, make reference to "designs for the villa," in May 1788 and March of the following year.

18. John Soane, *Designs for Public and Private Buildings* (1832), pl. xxxiv**.

19. SM, Drawer 45, Set 1, Item 15 (see my *John Soane's Architectural Education,* pl. 234), relates to the design mentioned in the previous note and to its text attributing a hand in the design to Henry Bankes, squire of Kingston Lacy, Dorset. Bankes's presence in Rome during the winter of 1779/80 is recorded by Sidney Charles Herbert, ed., *Henry, Elizabeth, and George (1734–80),* p. 263. A further "casino" type scheme is on the back of one of Soane's Veronese drawings after Trezza, which tends to prove that Soane was developing his ideas along these lines while in Italy (see SM, Drawer 45, Set 2, Item 7 verso).

20. A casino, attached to the Earl Bishop's episcopal palace in Londonderry, is mentioned in the diaries of Dr. Daniel Augustus Beaufort, now in the Trinity College, Dublin, Archives, no. K.6.57 (4027), 3, pp. 25–26, entry for 16 November 1787. For a discussion, see Edward Malins and Desmond FitzGerald, the Knight of Glin, *Lost Demesnes: Irish Landscape Gardening 1660–1845* (London, 1976), p. 150.

21. Documents relating to the Spencers Wood commission are in SM, Soane Notebooks, 2, p. 35; 8, pp. 10, 13, 16; Journal 1781–1797, p. 17; and Ledger A, p. 154. Stroud, *Architecture of Sir John Soane,* p. 157, interprets all these references as being connected with a library addition to an existing building. She bases her inference on a 1783 account book entry, which I take to refer instead to a townhouse of Sotheby's that Soane altered internally. Certainly, Soane's *Sketches in Architecture,* p. 3, makes clear that the Berkshire "villa" was never built.

22. Cf. SM, Drawer 4, Set 3, Item 7 and Soane, *Sketches in Architecture,* pls. 32–33.

23. I could discover no documents confirming Sotheby's ownership of property at Spencers Wood, either in the Berkshire or Wiltshire Record Offices. But I have found indirect confirmation that Soane's patron was the William Sotheby, author and translator, mentioned in the *DNB.* Miss M. V. Stokes, archivist of Coutts and Company, kindly communicated to me the information that the Sotheby who paid Soane £21 from a Coutts account was a member of the well-known Essex family by that name.

24. The documents relevant to this commission are SM, Account Book 1781–86, p. 33, and Ledger A, p. 19. Soane's notebooks are singularly silent on the matter. A further clue may be the inscription on the drawing (fig. 13.12) referring to Ralph Winter, whom Soane knew in Rome and for whom he eventually designed a house. (See Soane's *Plans, Elevations, and Sections of Buildings,*

pl. 37; Stroud, *Architecture of Sir John Soane,* p. 158; and my *John Soane's Architectural Education,* p. 289, nn. 86–89.) But it is hard to imagine what connection Winter's name might have; perhaps it is an idle memo, totally unrelated.

25. See n. 41 of chap. 7. Although Soane's bills only mention "M." Pepper, the name Michael can be deduced on the basis of the informative tomb plaque commemorating his son, John, placed on the nave wall of St. Mary the Virgin, the parish church of Great Dunnow, Essex.

26. Dorothy Stroud, *Henry Holland, His Life and Architecture,* fig. 2 and pp. 53, 55.

27. See SM, Soane Notebooks, 8, pp. 19, 25, 29; Account Book 1781–86, p. 29; Journal 1781–1797, p. 67 left. See also Stroud, *Architecture of Sir John Soane,* p. 157. Little is known about the exact identity of Smith, and with a name such as his, research is the more difficult. A variant elevation of Burn Hall is SM, Drawer 5, Set 2, Item 10.

28. Soane, *Plans, Elevations, and Sections,* p. opposite pl. 33. SM, CC 1, Division 7, L, Item 23, is an announcement of the sale of Burn Hall in 1793.

29. See n. 25 of chap. 1.

30. Soane's meeting with Dillingham and first visit to Letton are documented in SM, Soane Notebooks, 7, p. 41; 8, p. 19. The *Journals of the House of Lords,* vol. 37 (1783–87), (London, 1808), p. 645, gives a summary of Theophilus Dillingham's bequest.

31. SM, Precedents in Architecture 1784 has a copy of the stable design for Letton, dated November 1783 (fol. 35 verso) and a copy of the letter (fol. 16 verso). The bulk of the Letton drawings are in Drawer 28, Set 7.

32. SM, Soane Notebooks, 11, pp. 9–10.

33. On the date of ground breaking, see SM, Soane Notebooks, 12, p. 4. This is in agreement with Account Book 1781–86, p. 20, which also provides details of Philip Barnes's contract. For Letton, see Dorothy Stroud, "The Country Houses of Sir John Soane," p. 783; and idem, *Architecture of Sir John Soane,* p. 31.

34. SM, Drawer 28, Set 7, Item 2, is the undated but early drawing of four plans and two alternate elevations for the west, or entrance, front.

35. Plans dated 1919 by A. W. Gordon, of the firm of Hampton and Sons of London, were in the possession of the former owners, the Eglingtons, who welcomed me to Letton.

36. SM, Ledger B, p. 44, gives the final breakdown of costs and fees at Letton. Other accounts relating to Letton are contained in Bill Book 1, pp. 58, 83–108; Bill Book 4, pp. 36–37; Journal 1, pp. 9 right to 15 left, 92 left to 136 right; Journal 1781–1797, p. 55 left.

37. SM, Abstract of Bills 1782, pp. 58, 80, conveniently lists the craftsmen who worked on Saxlingham Rectory. The original MS for this is CC 1, Division 1, G(14), Item 5. A comparable list for Letton can be compiled from Abstract of Bills 1782, pp. 78–79, and Copies of Bills 1785, pp. 4–5, 119–23.

38. Details on the family of John Gooch are given by Charles Linnel, *Some East Anglian Clergy* (London, 1961), p. 146; Philip Brown, *History of Norwich* (Norwich, 1814), p. 279, *Alumni Oxoniensis, 1715–1866,* 2d ser. (4 vols.; Oxford, 1888),

2:536; and, of course, the entries in the *DNB* and *Burke's Peerage*. Sir Thomas Gooch requested lodge designs from Soane in 1785 (SM, Journal 1, p. 60 right). Intended for Benacre Hall, Suffolk, these were never executed according to Stroud, *Architecture of Sir John Soane*, p. 157. Stroud, ibid., p. 31, gives a brief account of Saxlingham, and again in "Country Houses of Sir John Soane," p. 782.

39. SM, Soane Notebooks, 10, p. 45, gives the first reference to Gooch; Account Book 1781–86, p. 47, documents the start of work.

40. SM, Ledger A, p. 34. Other accounts relating to Saxlingham are contained in Account Book 1781–86, pp. 47–48, 133; Bill Book 1, pp. 44–58; Copies of Bills 1785, pp. 6–7, 124–27; Journal 1, pp. 6 right to 8 left; Journal 1787–1796, p. 25.

41. Mostyn J. Armstrong, *The History and Antiquities of the County of Norfolk* (10 vols.; Norwich, 1781), 7:59.

42. SM, Soane Notebooks, 11, pp. 7–8. The Dean of Norwich at this period was Philip Lloyd, D.D. (d. 1790).

43. I owe this reference to Gilbert's Act to B. Anthony Bax, *The English Parsonage* (London, 1964).

44. After several appeals, Soane received the outstanding balance in 1798 (SM, Ledger A, p. 34).

45. Soane, *Plans, Elevations, and Sections*, pl. 42, which is based on SM, Drawer 28, Set 1, Item 6, a 1784 redrawing of the original.

46. The only candidates for inclusion in the Royal Academy exhibition are Letton and Saxlingham. The first drawings for Shotesham, also in Norfolk, were only sent to the patron in April 1785 (SM, Account Book 1781–86, p. 5) and hence were too late to be exhibited that same spring.

47. SM, Soane Notebooks, 12, p. 48.

48. SM, Account Book 1781–86, p. 133.

49. SM, contains a variety of documents relating to the service courts, e.g., Soane Notebooks, 13, p. 48; Account Book 1781–86, pp. 47–48, 133; Journal 1781–1797, p. 25; Precedents in Architecture 1784, fol. 50 recto (stable plan dated April 1785). The Carvers gave me several opportunities of enjoying the comforts of the old rectory at Saxlingham, which they have admirably modernized. The architects for the restoration, Fielden and Mawson, put at my disposition their photographs and drawings.

CHAPTER FOURTEEN

1. There is considerable disagreement about the actual date of Tendring's demolition. Dorothy Stroud, "The Early Work of Soane," p. 121, reports the year 1956. But John Summerson, *Architecture in Britain, 1530–1830*, p. 469, opts for a date four years earlier. Peter Reid in his contribution to *The Destruction of the Country House* (London, 1974), p. 190, erroneously states 1960. Howard M. Colvin, *A Biographical Dictionary of British Architects, 1600–1840*, p. 768, is nearest to Stroud, with the date 1955. There seems to be little concrete information on Tendring in the modern literature.

2. John Bernard Burke, *A Visitation of the Seats and Arms of the Noblemen and Gentlemen of Great Britain*, 2d ser. (2 vols.; London, 1853), 1:101.

3. Avery Colebrook tells me that he was commissioned by Sir Joshua Rowley to take photos of Tendring. Now in retirement, Mr. Colebrook generously gave me all the prints and negatives he could locate from the series. The subsequent history of the original set is mysterious. Sir Joshua writes me that he intended them for the National Monuments Record, but it has none of the Colebrook photos. The only complete set appears to be in the possession of Miss Dorothy Stroud.

4. Copies of the estimate are in SM, Drawer 28, Set 3, and V&A, Box A173, D1434A-'98.

5. SM, Soane Notebooks, 11, p. 20. For Rowley, see the *DNB* and *Burke's Peerage*.

6. SM, Soane Notebooks, 11, pp. 25–27, gives Soane's reactions to the site on his first visit. The plan of the existing house, dated 1783, is Drawer 28, Set 2, Item 1. *The Private Acts*, 24 George III, cap. 22, pp. 8–9, describes the age and ruinous condition of the previous house. As with Letton, the sale of reusable materials from the old building would help defray the costs of the new.

7. SM, Soane Notebooks, 11, p. 38. For George Wyatt's involvement with Tendring, see Journal 1, p. 172 left.

8. Soane's attendance at the House of Lords is recorded in SM, Soane Notebooks, 11, p. 46; 12, p. 16. In V&A, Box A 173, D1441-'98 is a ground plan of Tendring signed by Joshua Rowley in which reference is made to a previous set shown at the House of Lords on 7 July 1784.

9. *The Private Acts*, 24 George III, cap. 22, pp. 1–13, "Act to enable the trustees . . . of the late Sir William Rowley to apply part of the trust monies in rebuilding the mansion house called Tendring Hall." *Journals of the House of Lords*, vol. 37 (1783–89), pp. 93, 96, 120, gives the first and second readings of the bill and the report. More details of the passage of the bill are revealed in SM, CC 1, Division 1, R(14), Item 1 (legal opinion of Counsel John Scott of Lincoln's Inn dated 19 February 1785).

10. SM, Soane Notebooks, 13, pp. 14, 45, for the ground breaking and foundation laying, respectively. The full set of contract drawings for Tendring is V&A, Box A173, D1435-'98, D1441-'98–D1447-'98.

11. Dorothy Stroud, *The Architecture of Sir John Soane*, p. 31, implies that the columns are an original substitution of order by the architect.

12. Letter of Avery Colebrook to the author (13 July 1975). Sandra Blutman, "English Country Houses: 1780–1815," p. 146, writes of Tendring: "Spatially this must have been among Soane's most exciting works."

13. See n. 9 supra.

14. References to insuring the house and to materials used are in SM, Journal 1781–1797, pp. 46, 48, 72 left. The dated working drawing is Drawer 28, Set 2, Item 19. The other drawings of the house and adjacent offices are grouped together in Drawer 28, Set 2, Items 2–21, and Set 3, Items 1–2.

15. Summerson, *Architecture in Britain*, p. 457. On stairhalls, see Mark Girouard, *Life in the English Country House*, pp. 198–99.

16. Nikolaus Pevsner and David Lloyd, *Buildings of England: Hampshire and the Isle of Wight* (Harmondsworth, 1967), p. 184.

17. SM, Soane Notebooks, 1, pp. 1, 3, 18 (June 1781) document Soane's direct connection with Cranbury through the supply of a chimneypiece made by John Vidler. On Cranbury, see Dorothy Stroud, *George Dance,* pp. 92–96.

18. Georges Teyssot, *Città e utopia,* p. 161, surmises correctly, I think, that Soane visited Cranbury when in Hampshire. Stroud, *Dance,* p. 95, does the same. But she does not make the logical connection between Lymington and Cranbury, though it is to her (p. 93) that I owe the information that Thomas Dummer was the M.P. for Lymington.

19. Dance wrote Soane in 1802: "let me look at your plan of Mr Praed's house [Tyringham], I want to steal from it" (Arthur T. Bolton, *Portrait of Sir John Soane,* pp. 94–95).

20. John Soane, *Plans, Elevations, and Sections of Buildings,* pl. 19.

21. SM, Journal 1781–1797, p. 72 right.

22. For the Adams' use of the Spalatro order, see Damie Stillman, *The Decorative Work of Robert Adam,* pls. 65–66, and also his section on Adam ceiling designs.

23. Anonymous poem "The Modern Goth" (1796), quoted by Bolton, *Portrait,* p. 62.

24. For Lee, see the first mention of him in SM, Journal 1, p. 70 left, 13 January 1787; and two subsequent payments, p. 70 right and p. 75 left, on "setting out to Tendring Hall," 20 February 1787 and 22 March 1789. Holloway is referred to in ibid., p. 71 right, 28 May 1787.

25. Stillman, *Decorative Work of Robert Adam,* pp. 24–25.

26. Sketches for alterations to Mrs. Pery's townhouse are in SM, Miscellaneous Sketches 1780–82, pp. 15–23, and Soane Notebooks, 3, p. 44; 4, p. 54; and 5, pp. 8–9, 52. Accounts are in Journal 1781–1797, p. 43.

27. SM, Precedents in Architecture 1784, fol. 7 recto.

28. SM, Portfolio II, Item 70, drawing for Earsham dated December 1784. Despite the lack of physical evidence at Earsham, the statuary, John Deval the Younger, was paid £38.14.0 for a chimneypiece, presumably the one for which the drawing still exists (Account Book 1781–86, p. 45, entry for 25 November 1785). See also Rupert Gunnis, *Dictionary of British Sculptors,* p. 129.

29. The Letton chimneypiece drawing is dated 29 November 1786 (SM, Portfolio II, Item 38). I discovered the chimneypiece itself, executed almost exactly to the specifications of the drawing, removed to the cellars of the house from its position upstairs in the breakfast room. Another similar chimneypiece of comparable date was in the now-lost dining room at Taverham (Precedents in Architecture 1784, fol. 45 verso).

30. SM, Journal 1, p. 71 right, entry for 7 June 1787; p. 71 left, entry for 6 April 1787, respectively. For a Samuel Davies (*fl.* 1759), see Gunnis, *Dictionary of British Sculptors,* p. 122.

31. The reference I obtained from the SM, library catalogue to Soane's copy of the Keir and Co. sales catalogue (PC.K) could not be traced.

32. For Bramah's separate account with Soane, see SM, Journal 1, p. 92 left.

His career has been discussed by Lawrence Wright, *Clean and Decent: The Fascinating History of the Bathroom and the Water-Closet* (London, 1967), and more recently by Girouard, *Life in the English Country House,* p. 265.

33. V&A, Box A173, D1441-'98.

34. SM, Journal 1, p. 72 right, 10 December 1787, and p. 76 left, 12 September 1789.

35. Ibid., p. 68 right and Journal 1781–1797, p. 48 (entry for 16 July 1786: "Sir Josh: agreed to £15 for lower[in]g the windows").

36. SM, Journal 1, p. 76 left. The sum is broken down into 9 separate payments over a period of 5 years. Ibid., pp. 76 right, 95 left, 97 left, 98 left, give details of Soane's litigation.

37. See SM, CC 1, Division 4, P(2), Item 3.

38. John Summerson, *John Nash, Architect to King George III* (2d ed.; London, 1949), recounts Nash's bankruptcy on account of speculative building ventures.

39. Arthur T. Bolton, *Architectural Education a Century Ago,* pp. 12–13, tabulates the entries of Soane's pupils and assistants into his employment. Their articles are to be found in SM, CC 2, Division 15, C.

40. For Soane's visit of 6 July 1787, see SM, Journal 1, p. 72 left. Ibid., p. 73 left, states that a design for the stables was sent as late as 15 March 1788. Drawings for the stables, lodges, garden wall, and hothouses are in SM, Precedents in Architecture 1784, fols. 26 verso, 27 recto, 59 verso, 70 recto; Drawer 28, Set 3, Items 3–4; Drawer 8, Set 3, Items 11, 28; Drawer 64, Set 3, Items 101–2.

41. The late Raymond Erith showed me his handsome Royal Academy drawing for the Tendring alterations, and his partner, Quinlan Terry, sent me a copy of it, for which I am most grateful.

Bibliography

Académie de France à Rome. *Piranèse et les Français.* Rome, 1976.

Adam, Robert and James. *The Works in Architecture of Robert and James Adam.* 3 vols. London, 1773–78, 1779, 1822.

Anonymous. [James Northcote?]. "Memoir of John Soane, Esq., F.A.S., Architect to the Bank of England, and Member of the Royal Academies of London, Parma, and Florence." *European Magazine* 63 (1813):3–7.

Battie, William. *A Treatise on Madness.* London, 1758.

Blondel, Jacques-François. *Cour d'architecture, ou traité de la décoration, distribution et construction des bâtiments; contenant les leçons données en 1750, et les années suivantes.* 9 vols. Paris, 1771–77.

Blutman, Sandra. "English Country Houses: 1780–1815." Master's thesis, London University, 1968.

Bolton, Arthur T. *Architectural Education a Century Ago: Being an Account of the Office of Sir John Soane, R.A., Architect of the Bank of England, with Special Reference to the Career of George Basevi, His Pupil, Architect of the Fitzwilliam Museum at Cambridge.* London, n.d.

————. *The Portrait of Sir John Soane, R.A. (1753–1837) Set Forth in Letters from His Friends (1775–1837).* London, 1927.

————. "St. Luke's Hospital, Old Street: George Dance, R.A., and His Pupil, John Soane, 1781–2." *Britannia Quarterly* 4 (1924):197–201.

————. *The Works of Sir John Soane, F.R.S., F.S.A., R.A. (1753–1837).* London, 1924.

Britton, John. "Sir John Soane, R.A., F.R.S., F.S.A., Professor of Architecture in the English Royal Academy." In *National Portrait Gallery of Illustrations and Eminent Personages of the Nineteenth Century, with Memoirs.* Edited by William Jerdan. 5 vols. London, 1830–34. Vol. 5, pp. 1–12.

Brydone, Patrick. *A Tour through Sicily and Malta in a Series of Letters to William Beckford Esq. of Somerly in Suffolk.* 4th ed. 2 vols. London, 1776.

Burke, Edmund. *A Philosophical Enquiry into the Origin of Our Ideas of the Sublime and Beautiful.* 2d ed. London, 1759.

Carter, John. *The Builder's Magazine: Or Monthly Companion for Architects, Carpenters, Masons, Bricklayers, etc. Consisting of Designs in Architecture in Every Style and Taste; with Plans and Sections. (Alphabetical Description of the Terms of Art, which are Used in Building.) By a Society of Architects.* London, 1774–86.

Chalklin, Christopher W. *The Provincial Towns of Georgian England: A Study of the Building Process, 1740–1820.* Montreal, 1974.

Chambers, William. *Plans, Elevations, Sections, and Perspective Views of the Gardens and Buildings at Kew in Surrey, the Seat of Her Royal Highness the Princess Dowager of Wales.* London, 1763.

———. *A Treatise on Civil Architecture.* London, 1759.

Chapman, Stanley D., ed. *The History of Working-Class Housing: A Symposium.* Totowa, N.J., 1971.

Chide-Pemberton, William Shakespeare. *The Earl Bishop: The Life of Frederick Harvey, the Bishop of Derry, Earl of Bristol.* 2 vols. London, 1925.

Colvin, Howard M. *A Biographical Dictionary of British Architects, 1600–1840.* London, 1978.

Council of Europe. *The Age of Neo-Classicism.* London, 1972.

Coxe, William. *Travels in Switzerland in a Series of Letters to William Melmoth.* 3 vols. London, 1789.

Craven, Elizabeth. *Memoirs of the Margravine of Ansbach, Formerly Lady Craven.* 2 vols. London, 1826.

Crook, J. Mordaunt. *The Greek Revival: Neo-Classical Attitudes in British Architecture, 1760–1870.* London, 1972.

Cust, Lionel, and Colvin, Sydney. *History of the Society of Dilettanti.* London, 1898.

Darley, Gillian. *Villages of Vision.* London, 1975.

Dobai, Johannes. *Die Kunstlerliteratur des Klassizismus und der Romantik in England.* 3 vols. Bern, 1974–77.

Donaldson, Thomas Leverton. *A Review of the Professional Life of Sir John Soane, Architect, R.A., M.I.B.A., F.R.S., and Member of Various Foreign Academies Deceased 20th January, 1837. With Some Remarks on His Genius and Productions. Read at the First Subsequent Ordinary Meeting of the Institute of British Architects, Held Monday, 6th February, 1837.* London, 1837.

Du Prey, Pierre de la Ruffinière. "Eighteenth-Century English Sources for a History of Swiss Wooden Bridges." *Zeitschrift für schweizerische Archäologie und Kunstgeschichte* 36 (1979):51–63.

———. "'Je N'Oublieraj Jamais': John Soane and Downhill." *Bulletin of the Irish Georgian Society* 21 (1978):17–40.

————. *John Soane's Architectural Education, 1753–80.* New York, 1977.

————. "John Soane, Philip Yorke, and Their Quest for Primitive Architecture." *National Trust Studies.* London, 1979. Pp. 28–38.

————. "Soane and Hardwick in Rome: A Neo-Classical Partnership." *Architectural History* 15 (1972):51–67.

Dutens, Louis. *Itinéraire des routes les plus fréquentées, ou journal d'un voyage aux villes principales de l'Europe en 1768, 1769, 1777, et 177* . London, 1777.

Farington, Joseph. *The Diary of Joseph Farington.* Edited by Kenneth Garlick and Angus Macintyre. 6 vols. New Haven and London, 1978–79.

Feinberg, Susan Gail. "Sir John Soane's 'Museum': An Analysis of the Architect's House-Museum in Lincoln's Inn Fields, London." Ph.D. dissertation, University of Michigan, Ann Arbor, 1979.

Fleming, John. *Robert Adam and His Circle in Edinburgh and Rome.* London, 1962.

Fothergill, Arthur Brian. *The Mitred Earl: An Eighteenth-Century Eccentric.* London, 1974.

Foucault, Michel. *Histoire de la folie à l'age classique.* Paris, 1961.

French, Charles Newenham. *The Story of St. Luke's Hospital.* London, 1951.

Girouard, Mark. *Life in the English Country House: A Social and Architectural History.* New Haven and London, 1978.

Graves, Algernon. *The Society of Artists of Great Britain, 1760–1791; The Free Society of Artists, 1761–1783: A Complete Dictionary of Contributors and Their Works from the Foundation of the Societies to 1791.* London, 1907.

Gunnis, Rupert. *Dictionary of British Sculptors, 1660–1851.* 2d ed. London, 1968.

Gwynn, John. *London and Westminster Improved, Illustrated by Plans, To which is Prefixed, a Discourse on Public Magnificence, with Observations on the State of Arts and Artists in this Kingdom, wherein the Study of the Polite Arts is Recommended as Necessary to a Liberal Education: Concluded by Some Proposals Relative to Places not Laid down in the Plans.* London, 1766.

Harris, John. *Sir William Chambers.* London, 1970.

Herbert, Sidney Charles, ed. *Henry, Elizabeth, and George (1734–80): Letters and Diaries of Henry Tenth Earl of Pembroke and His Circle.* London, 1939.

Herrmann, Wolfgang. *Laugier and Eighteenth-Century French Theory.* London, 1962.

Howard, Derek Lionel. *John Howard: Prison Reformer.* London, 1958.

Howard, John. *The State of the Prisons in England and Wales with Preliminary Observations and an Account of Some Foreign Prisons and Hospitals.* 2d ed. Warrington, 1780.

Hunter, Richard, and MacAlpine, Ida, eds. *Three Hundred Years of Psychiatry, 1535–1860.* London, 1963.

Hutchison, Sidney C. "The Royal Academy Schools, 1768–1830." *Walpole Society* 38 (1960–62):132–91.

Jenkins, Frank. *Architect and Patron: A Survey of Professional Relations and Practice in England from the Sixteenth Century to the Present Day.* London, 1961.

Kalman, Harold David. "The Architecture of George Dance the Younger." Ph.D. dissertation, Princeton University, 1971.

———. "Newgate Prison." *Architectural History* 12 (1969):50–61.

Kaufmann, Emil. *Architecture in the Age of Reason: Baroque and Post-Baroque in England, Italy, and France.* Cambridge, Mass., 1955.

Kaye, Barrington. *The Development of the Architectural Profession in Britain.* London, 1960.

Kent, Nathaniel. *Hints to Gentlemen of Landed Property.* London, 1775.

Laugier, Marc-Antoine. *Essai sur l'architecture.* 2d ed. Paris, 1755.

Le Français de Lalande, Joseph-Jérôme. *Voyage d'un Français en Italie fait dans les anneés 1765 et 1766.* 8 vols. Venice, 1769.

Lemonnier, Henry, ed. *Procès verbaux de l'académie royale d'architecture, 1671–1793.* 10 vols. Paris, 1911–29.

Markus, Thomas A. "The Pattern of the Law." *Architectural Review* 116 (1954):251–56.

Miller, Anna Riggs. *Letters from Italy Describing the Manners, Customs, Antiquities, Paintings, etc. of that Country, in the Years 1770 to 1771: To a Friend Residing in France. By an English Woman.* 2d ed. 2 vols. London, 1777.

Money, Walter. *Stray Notes on the Parish of Basildon.* Newbury, 1889.

Montaiglon, Anatole Courde de, and Guiffrey, Jules, eds. *Correspondance des directeurs de l'académie de France à Rome.* 18 vols. Paris, 1887–1912.

Morris, Robert. *Lectures on Architecture: Consisting of Rules Founded upon Harmonic and Arithmetic Proportions in Building, Designed as an Agreeable Entertainment for Gentlemen; and more Particularly Useful to All who Make Architecture, or the Polite Arts, Their Study.* London, 1734.

Mulvany, Thomas J. *The Life of James Gandon, Esq.; With Original Notices of Contemporary Artists, and Fragments of Essays, from Material Collected and Arranged by His Son, James Gandon.* 2d ed. London, 1969.

Neufforge, Jean-François de. *Recueil élémentaire d'architecture.* 10 vols. Paris, 1757–80.

O'Donoghue, Edward Geoffrey. *The Story of Bethlehem Hospital from Its Foundation in 1247.* London, 1914.

Oppé, A. Paul, ed. "Memoirs of Thomas Jones." *Walpole Society* 32 (1946–48).

Olsen, Donald J. *Town Planning in London: The Eighteenth and Nineteenth Centuries.* New Haven and London, 1964.

[Peacock, James.] *An Essay on the Qualifications and Duties of an Architect, etc., with Some Useful Hints for the Young Architect or Surveyor.* London, 1773.

————. *Subordinates in Architecture: Consisting of 1) Solutions of Interesting Problems; 2) A New and Simple Model of Forming the Diminution of Columns; 3) Mensuration of Distances from a Single Station; 4) The Value of Building Ground in London; 5) A Hint to Lessors and Lessees; 6) Memorandums and Monitions upon the Three Capital Operations in Architecture: Composition, Speculation, and Elimination; 7) Clauses for Contracts etc.* London, 1814.

Peacock, James (alias José MacPacke). *Oikidia; or, Nutshells: Being Ichnographic Distributions for Small Villas; Chiefly upon Economical Principles; in Seven Classes; with Occasional Remarks.* London, 1785.

Pevsner, Nikolaus. *A History of Building Types.* Princeton, 1976.

Pevsner, Nikolaus, and Lang, S. "Apollo or Baboon." *Architectural Review* 104 (1948):271–79.

Peyre, Marie-Joseph. *Oeuvres d'architecture.* Paris, 1765.

Ramsay, Malcolm. "John Howard and the Discovery of the Prison." *Howard Journal of Penology and Crime Prevention* 16 (1977):1–16.

Rendle, William, and Norman, Philip. *Inns of Old Southwark and Their Associations.* London, 1888.

Robinson, John Martin. "Model Farm Buildings of the Age of Improvement." *Architectural History* 19 (1976):17–31.

Rosenau, Helen. *Social Purpose in Architecture: Paris and London Compared, 1760–1800.* London, 1970.

Soane, John. *An Appeal to the Public: Occasioned by the Suspension of the Architectural Lectures in the Royal Academy. To which is Subjoined an Account of a Critical Work, Published a Few Years Ago, Entitled, "The Exhibition; or, a Second Anticipation:" With Observations on Modern Anglo-Grecian Architecture; and Remarks on the Mischevious Tendency of the Present Speculative System of Building, etc. In Letters to a Friend.* London, 1812.

————. *Description of the House and Museum on the North Side of Lincoln's Inn Fields.* London, 1830.

————. *Description of the House and Museum on the North Side of Lincoln's*

Inn Fields, the Residence of Sir John Soane. 2d ed. London, 1835.

————. *Designs in Architecture: Consisting of Plans, Elevations, and Sections for Temples, Baths, Cassines, Pavilions, Garden Seats, Obelisks, and Other Buildings; for Decorating Pleasure Grounds, Parks, Forests, etc.* London, 1778.

————. *Designs for Public and Private Buildings.* 2d ed., with additional illustrations. London, 1832.

————. *Lectures on Architecture: Delivered to the Students of the Royal Academy from 1809 to 1836 in Two Courses of Six Lectures Each.* Edited by Arthur T. Bolton. London, 1929.

————. *Memoirs of the Professional Life of an Architect between the Years 1768 and 1835.* London, 1835.

————. *Plans, Elevations, and Perspective Views of Pitzhanger Manor House, and of the Ruins of an Edifice of Roman Architecture, Situated on the Border of Ealing Green, with a Description of the Ancient and Present State of the Manor House, in a Letter to a Friend, 1802.* London [1833?].

————. *Plans, Elevations, and Sections of Buildings Erected in the Counties of Norfolk, Suffolk, Yorkshire, Staffordshire, Warwickshire, Hertfordshire, etc.* London, 1788.

————. *Sketches in Architecture: Containing Plans and Elevations of Cottages, Villas, and Other Useful Buildings, with Characteristic Scenery.* London, 1793.

————. *A Statement of Facts Respecting the Designs of a New House of Lords, as Ordered by the Lords Committees, and Humbly Submitted to the Consideration of Their Lordships by John Soane.* London, 1799.

Stillman, Damie. "British Architects and Italian Architectural Competitions, 1758–1780." *Journal of the Society of Architectural Historians* 32 (1973):43–66.

————. "Death Defied and Honour Upheld: The Mausoleum in Neo-Classical England." *Art Quarterly* 1 n.s. (1978):172–213.

————. *The Decorative Work of Robert Adam.* London, 1966.

Stroud, Dorothy. *The Architecture of Sir John Soane.* London, 1961.

————. *Capability Brown.* 3d ed. London, 1975.

————. "The Country Houses of Sir John Soane." *Country Life* 114 (1953):782–85.

————. "The Early Work of Soane." *Architectural Review* 121 (1957):121–22.

————. *George Dance, Architect, 1741–1825.* London, 1971.

————. *Henry Holland, His Life and Architecture.* London, 1966.

————. "Soane Barn." *Architectural Review* 108 (1956):336–37.

————. "Soane's Designs for a Triumphal Bridge." *Architectural Review* 121 (1957):260–62.

Summerson, John. *Architecture in Britain, 1530 to 1830*. 6th ed. Harmondsworth, 1977.

———. *Georgian London*. 2d ed. Harmondsworth, 1962.

———. "The Idea of the Villa: The Classical Country House in Eighteenth-Century England." *Journal of the Royal Society of Arts* 107 (1959):539–87.

———. *A New Description of Sir John Soane's Museum*. 4th ed. London, 1977.

———. *Sir John Soane*. London, 1952.

———. "Sir John Soane and the Furniture of Death." *Architectural Review* 163 (1978):147–55.

———. "Soane: The Case-History of a Personal Style." *Journal of the Royal Institute of British Architects* 58 (1950–51):83–91.

Swinburne, Henry. *Travels in the Two Sicilies in the Years 1777, 1778, 1779, and 1780*. 2 vols. London, 1785.

Tadgell, Christopher. *Ange-Jacques Gabriel*. London, 1978.

Tappen, George. *Professional Observations on the Architecture of the Principal Ancient and Modern Buildings in France and Italy: With Remarks on the Painting and Sculpture, and a Concise Local Description of those Countries, Written from Sketches and Memoranda Made during a Visit in the Years 1802 and 1803*. London, 1806.

Temanza, Tommaso. *Vite dei più celebri architetti e scultori Veneziani che fiorirono nel secolo decimosesto*. 2d ed. Venice, 1778.

Teyssot, Georges. *Città e utopia nell' illuminismo inglese: George Dance il giovane*. Rome, 1974.

Thompson, John D., and Goldin, Grace. *The Hospital: A Social and Architectural History*. New Haven, 1975.

Watkin, David. *Thomas Hope, 1769–1831, and the Neo-Classical Idea*. London, 1968.

Wiebenson, Dora. *Sources of the Greek Revival in Architecture*. London, 1969.

Wightwick, George. "The Life of an Architect—My Sojourn at Bath—The Late Sir John Soane." *Bentley's Miscellany* 34 (1853):108–14, 402–9.

Wrighte, William. *Grotesque Architecture; or, Rural Amusement: Consisting of Plans, Elevations, and Sections for Huts, Retreats, Summer and Winter Hermitages, Terminaries, Chinese, Gothic, and Natural Grottos, Cascades, Baths, Mosques, Moresque Pavilions, Grotesque and Rustic Seats, Green Houses, etc. Many of which May Be Executed with Flints, Irregular Stones, Rude Branches, and Roots of Trees*. London, 1767.

Index